# TRANSLATING CANADA

Charting the Institutions and Influences of Cultural Transfer:
Canadian Writing in German/y

**Perspectives on Translation**

This series consists of works that analyze translation from a theoretical or practical point of view. In addition to history, methodology, and theory, the series covers lexicology, terminology and interpretation. Textbooks for students as well as for professional translators and interpreters can be found in the Didactics of Translation series. Both series welcome manuscripts in French or English.

---

The University of Ottawa Press gratefully acknowledges the support extended to its publishing programme by the Canada Council for the Arts and the University of Ottawa.

We also acknowledge with gratitude the support of the Government of Canada through its Book Publishing Industry Development Program for our publishing activities.

We would also like to thank Regina Seib for permitting us to reproduce a detail of her painting *Crossroads* as our cover illustration.

© University of Ottawa Press, 2007
524 King Edward Avenue, Ottawa, Ontario, K1N 6N5, Canada
press@uottawa.ca / www.uopress.uottawa.ca

# TRANSLATING CANADA

Edited by

Luise von Flotow

and

Reingard M. Nischik

# TABLE OF CONTENTS

Introduction     1
    *Luise von Flotow and Reingard M. Nischik*

1   Telling Canada's "Story" in German:     9
    Using Cultural Diplomacy to Achieve Soft Power
    *Luise von Flotow*

2   "Two Solitudes"? Anglo-Canadian Literature     27
    in Translation in the Two Germanies
    *Barbara Korte*

3   Translating the Canadian Short Story into German     53
    *Klaus Peter Müller*

4   The "Other Women": Canadian Women Writers     79
    Blazing a Trail into Germany
    *Brita Oeding and Luise von Flotow*

5   Margaret Atwood in German/y: A Case Study     93
    *Stefan Ferguson*

6   The "AlterNative" Frontier:     111
    Native Canadian Writing in German/y
    *Eva Gruber*

7   From *Beautiful Losers* to *No Logo!*     143
    German Readings of Jewish Canadian Writing
    *Fabienne Quennet*

| 8 | Contemporary (English) Canadian Plays in German/y Equivalence in Difference?<br>*Albert-Reiner Glaap* | 165 |
| 9 | Translated or Traduced? Canadian Literary and Political Theory in a German Context: Northrop Frye, Michael Ignatieff, and Charles Taylor<br>*Georgiana Banita* | 187 |
| 10 | Selecting Canadiana for the Young: The German Translation of English Canadian Children's Literature<br>*Martina Seifert* | 219 |
| 11 | French, Female, and Foreign: French Canadian Children's Literature in German Translation<br>*Nikola von Merveldt* | 243 |
| 12 | Northern Lights in German Theatres: How Quebec Plays Come to Germany<br>*Andreas Jandl* | 257 |
| 13 | Low Motility: Transferring Montreal Playwright Stephen Orlov's *Sperm Count* to Germany<br>*Brita Oeding* | 269 |
| 14 | Antonine Maillet in German: A Case Study<br>*Klaus-Dieter Ertler* | 283 |

| Contributors | 293 |
| Name and Title Index | 299 |
| Subject Index | 333 |

# INTRODUCTION

*Luise von Flotow and Reingard M. Nischik*
*University of Ottawa and University of Constance*

This book starts from the premise that translation is one of the most important vehicles of cultural transfer and at the same time one of the least studied. Considered and treated as an "invisible" activity for many years, and even praised for being "invisible," translation is at the centre of this study of German versions of Canadian writing, which examines its various manifestations and effects. Narratives about Canadian life and society have appeared in Germany for decades, shaping views and perceptions of Canada for generations, and translation has been the necessary vehicle for this exchange. Translation has, indeed, been the vital connector—underlying and predating most other forms of cultural transfer, such as rewriting, adapting, anthologizing, staging, and even filmmaking.[1]

The contributors to this volume examine the motivations, processes, "translation effects," and responses that have touched Canadian source materials in their move into Germany. They explore the reasons for translating certain materials at certain times, the interventions of those involved in producing the transfer, and the outcomes of these processes in German-speaking countries. This work has involved close comparative readings, on the one hand, and analyses of broader issues, such as political environments, Canadian public diplomacy, and German cultural needs, on the other. The studies look at adult and children's fiction, non-fiction and essays, drama, and some poetry—all originally written in either English or French. Canadian film, which has travelled into German-speaking cultures through subtitling and dubbing and has played a role in cultural transfer, has been left for future research since its analysis requires other tools.

---

1. It is worth noting here that the "exchange" has been quite lopsided, with Germany importing Canadian literature yet never seeing its own materials translated in Canada.

The time span 1967–2000 was chosen because the year 1967 marked Canada's centenary with nationalist celebrations, a focus on Canadian identity, and a strong impulse for the continued construction and support of Canadian culture. The year 2000 closed off the millennium. Since such limits are never absolute, in this case too certain chapters overshoot them.

An international, interdisciplinary, and multicultural effort, this project has brought together work from English and French Canada, Germany, and Austria, and it adds to our understanding of how translation has worked to fashion and configure images and perceptions of Canada abroad. It has benefited enormously from the cooperation of German-speaking academics, whose interest in and publications on Canada over the past thirty years of *Kanada-Studien* have served to keep Canada in the cultural news and to present differentiated views of a very diverse country. The volume thus explores and reveals the important role that translation plays between two specific partners, and it examines the many connected activities, such as selection, funding, editing, publishing, marketing, and reviewing. With its focus on translation, it flies in the face of conventional, usually unstated, approaches to work on cultural transfer that tend to ignore the multiple aspects of this interlinguistic and intercultural activity as well as their implications in affecting transfer (Susam-Sarajeva 2006, 1–17).

Translation is a deliberate activity and is therefore neither innocent nor accidental. On the contrary, as much recent work in the domain of Translation Studies has shown,[2] translating means processing a text through the mind, emotions, and personal and public history of another intelligence, which is never neutral and always also subject to the vagaries of ideology, political pressure, funding problems, time constraints, and even indifference and neglect. Not only are translators active and often highly creative interventionists, but they also work within a web of other power brokers. These include entrepreneurial source culture agents—in this case, Canadian culture workers, diplomats, publishers, literary agents, and associations all seeking to "sell" or at least move certain texts abroad. They also include German/Austrian publishing houses, looking to buy saleable goods and keen on producing another bestseller. In Germany, where publishing tends not to be subsidized, the marketable aspect of translations is vital. Other players in the system are the local reviewers and academics, who develop and provide opinions on the incoming materials. In German-speaking countries, where, unlike Canada, most daily newspapers have culture pages and an extensive weekend feuilleton ("cultural section") featuring book reviews of

---

2. See Bachleitner et al. (2004); Berman (1985, 1995); Lefevere (1992); Simon and St. Pierre (2000); Venuti (2000); and von Flotow (1997).

translations, among many other types of cultural journalism, an interested and often well-read readership is kept up to date on the latest trends and writers. Interestingly, these feuilleton articles often discuss translations in terms of how they address or respond to the "needs" of contemporary German-speaking society, setting aside the Canadian source culture that the translations represent (von Flotow 2004). Indeed, since Canadian books are often marked as "translated from American English" rather than British English, their source can be quite ambiguous—an interesting problem that must irritate the national funding agencies, such as the Canada Council for the Arts, that subsidize translation. All in all, the diverse interests and players involved in the cultural transfer that is subsumed under one simple term—"translation"—make the analysis, evaluation, and discussion of the phenomenon very complex. This book demonstrates that complexity.

In an attempt to orient or rein in the many possible directions this work could have taken, we asked four basic questions.

1. What kinds of materials are selected and "exported" by Canada?
2. Which materials are selected by German publishers?
3. How are these materials translated?
4. How are they received?

These questions raised many others, of course, some of which the chapters here explore.

The book opens with a Canadian contribution on "cultural" or "public diplomacy," a concept familiar to Europeans from various cultural institutes, such as the British Council, the Alliance française, and the Goethe-Institute, which have been active for years. In Canada, however, where the construction of Canadian culture became paramount only in the second half of the twentieth century, the notion of strategically exporting this culture is comparatively recent. The idea of implementing culture as part of foreign policy in Canada can be traced to the mid-1990s and a foreign affairs review that made "the projection of Canadian values and culture" one of the three pillars of the new policy. Whether culture can be deliberately selected for export, and whether it arrives and is understood abroad in the way it was "at home," are questions that come up throughout the book.

At the height of the first vogue of Canadian fiction in German-speaking countries, in the mid- to late 1980s, there were still two Germanies, with different publishing and production policies. These policies affected imported literatures—not only in the kinds of materials that were imported and the prices paid for them, but also in their treatment by translators. Barbara Korte (Freiburg) studies the fate of certain English Canadian authors and texts in this double environment, examining the importance of target culture mechanisms and manoeuvrings in regard to economic and ideological environments. Her focus is on the German target culture frameworks and the limitations or possibilities they present.

Similarly, Klaus Peter Müller's (Mainz) work on the English Canadian short story in German starts from the conditions the translating culture seems to set, establishing six main reasons why a Canadian text may be translated and published; these reasons range from exoticism to literary quality. Müller's analysis of the situation confirms the metaphor used in a recent study by Michael Cronin (2000), who writes that one of the dangers of translation is its tendency to restrict the "other culture" to the equivalent of a lovely postcard, in this case a clichéd view of mountains, meadows, fresh streams, and wildlife (excluding black flies and mosquitoes) and humans ably confronting the difficulties of nature.

The next two contributions deal with Canadian women writers, whose popularity in Germany reached a zenith in the late 1980s. Brita Oeding and Luise von Flotow (Ottawa) study German reviews for their perception of Canadian women writers of the 1980s and 1990s as "other women" whose work differs in many important ways from what German women writers were producing yet participates in the wider feminist/womanist currents of the period. Margaret Atwood, Alice Munro, and Carol Shields are the most successful in terms of numbers of translations and reviews, and the reasons are all located within the translating culture. Yet their success is not exclusive; it opens the doors to others. Stefan Ferguson (Constance) zeroes in on Atwood and traces the history of the double German translation(s) of *Surfacing*—a translation produced by the same translator yet featuring marked differences for the East and West German editions respectively. He details the effects of the East-West gap and the influence of the editors, as shown in the translation of passages expressing anti-American sentiments. The Western version attenuates while the Eastern exaggerates. Again, in both chapters, the target culture imposes itself as the measure of translation, adapting the foreign author to its own interests and issues.

Eva Gruber's (Constance) contribution to the book is focused on the translation of Native writers, and Gruber contextualizes this translation within the huge interest in books *about* Indians that developed in Germany in the late nineteenth century. This "Indianthusiasm" (Lutz 2003) persisted over the course of the twentieth century, seriously affecting the German perspective on and perception of Canadian Natives at the expense of translations of texts written by actual First Nations writers. Gruber traces the slow development of translations of work by Native writers, discusses their rarity, seeks to understand why certain texts move while others do not, and finally tackles the enormous translation problems that emerge as translators face fragments of Cree or Ojibway language in the texts, vernacular and slang diction, and huge cultural differences that they often smooth over for the German reading public. The target culture reading public becomes a silent force for which texts are produced and which remains ambiguous and undefined.

Fabienne Quennet (Marburg) explores the possibility of studying Jewish Canadian writers as a specific phenomenon in German translation and examines their reception by German reviewers. She traces the history of their appearance in translation, starting with Mordecai Richler in 1955, and notes that, with the exception of Richler and Anne Michaels, their religious/ethnic affiliations have generally passed unnoticed or been ignored. In German translation, they are not perceived as a distinct group.

Children's writing has had an enormous effect on the perceptions of Canada in Germany, as Martina Seifert (Belfast) shows. The "great white North," with its backwoods, bears, and men surviving against all odds, has been the staple of English Canadian children's literature in German, a situation that is only gradually beginning to incorporate the occasional girl protagonist or urban setting. Indeed, such recent changes are Nikola von Merveldt's (Montreal) focus on the developing German interest in francophone children's writing, where the wilderness is conspicuously absent and girls abound. Oddly, though, the work usually comes to German through its English translations and is thus twice refracted, with its French Canadian source completely obscured. Such are the vagaries of distribution, international book sales, contracts, and marketing.

The two contributions on Canadian theatre texts on German stages by Albert-Reiner Glaap (Düsseldorf) and Andreas Jandl (Berlin) discuss a recent phenomenon and provide detailed lists of the plays that have been translated and performed since the late 1960s. The recent interest in French Canadian drama is noteworthy, with theatres in centres such as Berlin, Cologne, and Düsseldorf regularly staging authors such as Daniel Danis, Michel Bouchard, and Marie Laberge. Jandl traces the roundabout journey of Canadian plays via particular theatre festivals and stages in France on their way to Germany. Glaap's focus is on the translation problems that arise when English vernacular and Canadian expressions need to travel into German: the recent plays *Shape of a Girl* and *Cherry Docs* receive special attention.

Brita Oeding (Ottawa) and Klaus-Dieter Ertler (Graz) are also concerned with the details of translation in their studies of Steven Orlov's play *Sperm Count* and Antonine Maillet's novel *Pélagie-la-Charrette* respectively. How can the Jewish immigrant accent and biting sarcasm of the angry old father in Orlov's play be transferred onto a German stage? And what forms of German can render the Acadian French of Maillet's earthy characters? Both authors are also concerned with the selection and publication processes and politics that drive German-language publishing houses. As in the chapter by Jandl, the translator is shown to play the role of cultural entrepreneur who comes face to face with budgets, perceived audience expectations, and publishers' biases.

Georgiana Banita (Constance) is the only contributor to engage with Canadian non-fiction in German. Her focus is on literary and political theory by Northrop Frye, Michael Ignatieff, and Charles Taylor and their confrontation with German traditions in the same domains. In this case, Banita shows that, while translation may seek to transfer foreign ideas and theories, they will always be read critically and in counterpoint to existing materials and traditions in the target culture. Indeed, in the case of Frye, the influx of contemporary French theories into German literary criticism prior to the translation proved to be a major factor in the lack of success of Frye's *Anatomy of Criticism* in Germany.

It is clear from the overview of the chapters in this volume that as we unravel the many operations concealed in one word—"translation"—we discover a multifaceted and very complex field of study. As we have seen in this specific case of Canadian work translated into German, these operations can involve the source culture, which might like to and sometimes does steer and support the translation of certain types of materials in the interests of foreign policy and perception. Yet it seems that translation is much more a factor of the *translating* culture, whose publishers, academics, dramaturges, and sometimes translators make the decisions about which materials to present to the reading public. These decisions are affected if not determined by social "needs" (as in the selection of multicultural or women writers at certain times), by fashions such as the ongoing "Indianthusiasm" and its revision through postcolonial and Aboriginal studies, and by marketing strategies. Beyond these choices and overarching strategies, however, individual translators play important roles as they find ways not only to render the details of the foreign texts but also to make them accessible and meaningful to a public that has little or no direct experience of the source culture: how else can we explain someone agonizing over *Cherry Docs* and the cultural and political nuances carried by such a term?

It is the hope of the editors and contributors that this book will mobilize more interest in the phenomenon and effect of translation, not only as cultural transfer and bridge building (a relatively tired cliché), but also as a complex and therefore rewarding field of investigation and research.

**SINE QUIBUS NON**

The editors thank Julia Breitbach, Florian Freitag, Christine Schneider, Emily Petermann, and Barbara Giehmann (Constance) for their reliable, prompt, and excellent help in the preparation of the manuscript. In Canada, Brita Oeding and Ryan Fraser deserve special thanks for their contributions and enthusiasm. The impetus and support for much of the work done in this project were provided by a seed grant from the University of Ottawa, a PIRL grant from the International Council for Canadian Studies, and a subsequent research grant from the Social Sciences and Humanities Research Council of Canada. The University of Ottawa Faculty of Arts also provided a publication grant.

**REFERENCES**

Bachleitner, Wolf, et al. *Internationales Archiv für Sozialgeschichte der deutschen Literatur* 29.2, Themenheft: Soziologie der literarischen Übersetzung. Tübingen: Niemeyer, 2004.

Berman, Antoine. *L'épreuve de l'étranger*. Paris: Gallimard, 1984.

———. *Pour une critique des traductions : John Donne*. Paris: Gallimard, 1995.

Cronin, Michael. *Across the Lines: Travel, Language, Translation*. Cork: Cork University Press, 2000.

Lefevere, André. *Literary Translation, Rewriting, and the Manipulation of Literary Fame*. London: Routledge, 1992.

Lutz, Hartmut. "'Okay, I'll Be Their Annual Indian for the Next Year': Thoughts on the Marketing of a Canadian Indian Icon in Germany." In *Imaginary Relocations: Tradition, Modernity, and the Market in Contemporary Native American Literature and Culture*, ed. Helmbrecht Breinig. Tübingen: Stauffenburg, 2003. 217-45.

Simon, Sherry, and Paul St. Pierre. *Changing the Terms: Translating in the Postcolonial Era*. Ottawa: University of Ottawa Press, 2000.

Susam-Sarajeva, Sebnem. *Theories on the Move: Translation's Role in the Travels of Literary Theories*. Amsterdam: Rodopi, 2006.

Venuti, Lawrence. *The Translation Studies Reader*. London/New York, 2000.

von Flotow, Luise. *Gender and Translation: Translating in the "Era of Feminism."* Manchester and Ottawa: St. Jerome Publishing and University of Ottawa Press, 1997.

———. "Internationale Bastarde ... irgendwo im weiten Kanada: Canadian Writing Tempered by Austrian Reception." In *canadiana oenipontana* 6 (2004): 269-84.

# Telling Canada's "Story" in German: Using Cultural Diplomacy to Achieve Soft Power

*Luise von Flotow*
*University of Ottawa*

The focus of this chapter, and of this book, is the translation of Canadian writing into German. Three distinct elements are involved, of which the most important is "storytelling." Stories travel through translation; they are the raw material of the translation process. However, we are not concerned here with producing literary criticism of Canadian writing, so our interest in the "source texts" will be limited. We are dealing instead with translation and reception: we want to understand why certain texts are selected for translation and why others are left aside. Which aesthetic, economic, or ideological considerations enter into the selection process? In what condition do Canadian stories arrive in the target language, German? And how are they read once they have been translated into the new cultural environment? Our third focus—with which we will start our overview—is on the use of stories by national governments and agencies in the service of cultural or public diplomacy: that is, as an instrument in gaining "soft power."

In October 2001, Adrienne Clarkson, then the Governor General of Canada, and her writer husband John Ralston Saul led an official delegation on a state visit to Germany. In the delegation of about forty people, there were twenty "culture workers": writers, poets, visual artists, actors, about half of whom were francophone: for instance, two writer-translators (Émile Martel and Daniel Poliquin), a dramatist (Michel Marc Bouchard), a literary critic (Pierre Cayouette), and a poet (Pierre Morency). The film director Atom Egoyan and two actors who are often associated with him, Don McKellar and Arsinée Khanjian, as well as academics and even wine growers were also part of the group. The focus was clearly on cultural exchange, an apparent attempt to further reinforce interest in Canada in a country that has had Canadian books on its bestseller lists and an extensive network of academics involved in Canadian Studies for more than twenty years. The strong francophone participation that marked this venture may have been related to a previously published anthology of Canadian writing translated into German, *Anders schreibendes Amerika: Literatur aus Quebec 1945–2000* (Baier and Filion 2000), a collection of short fiction from Quebec, as well as recent stagings of contemporary drama from Quebec in Berlin and Cologne (see Jandl in this volume).

Since the early 1980s, Canada has become a cultural success in Germany and Austria,[1] with Germany outranking every other country in terms of its great interest in Canadian fiction in translation.[2] While this fascination is undoubtedly related to the strong Canadian Studies initiatives at German universities, there are many other factors in such a success story. They include Canadian government initiatives, which have made available extensive and repeated travel and translation grants for authors such as Margaret Atwood, Barbara Gowdy, Michael Ondaatje, Anne Michaels, and many others. But many of the reasons for the success also seem to lie with the German-speaking audience for whom Canada became a popular tourist destination throughout the 1980s and 1990s. Among the decisive factors were the emergence of green politics, a romantic notion of pristine Canadian nature, a broad, middle-class reading culture that is very interested in other (especially anglophone) cultures, the idea of Canada as an attractive North American alternative to the United States, and narrative topics in Canadian writing that are not plagued with the weighty themes and post–World War II soul searching of much contemporary German literature. In other words, when German-speaking readers read Canadian stories, they gain access to the engaging aspects of North American storytelling, set in an environment that they conceptualize as being closer to nature, and they find a pleasant alternative to both contemporary German prose and the increasingly difficult political flavour of the United States.

In the following section, I examine a number of aspects of cultural policy as initiated by the government. Such policy is used by many countries, including Canada, to create interest in their products in a highly competitive global market. I also explore nation branding as a more recent facet of this promotional form of diplomacy.

---

1. In 2000, the Austrian weekly magazine *Profil* announced a "goldenes Zeitalter der kanadischen Literatur" ("a golden age of Canadian literature").
2. The funds allotted to foreign publishers by the Canada Council for the Arts over the past decade have largely gone to German publishing houses. Germany is followed by the Scandinavian countries and Holland and most recently by Korea, Japan, and China; see the website of the AECB (www.aecb.org) and Statistics Canada, which publish statistics covering the past twenty years and note recent increases in foreign rights sales to Asian countries.

**CULTURAL OR PUBLIC POLICY**

When Canadian "culture workers" such as Émile Martel or Arsinée Khanjian travel abroad in official delegations, they represent the cultural establishment of Canada and are usually funded by the Department of Foreign Affairs and International Trade (DFAIT). In the words of Chris Barlow, one of the government officials responsible, they help to promote a "positive image of Canada as *culturally diverse, creative, innovative and modern*" (emphasis added) in countries designated as priorities by DFAIT.[3] Barlow's words give some indication of what is at stake in this activity: the promotion of Canada through the dissemination of its culture, the creation of images of Canada, and the globalization of Canada by making the country more visible in the context of increasing global competition. Such promotion may include the establishment of a chair in Canadian Studies (Mexico, 2002), or the launching of an anthology of Canadian poetry in translation (*Nieve Immaculada*, Guanajuato, Mexico, 2002), or a grand tour with the governor general (Russia and circumpolar tour, 2003), or funding for the dissemination and translation of Canadian plays in Germany (CEAD, Playwrights' Union, International Translation Program). While these may seem to be mainly academic or cultural activities, foreign affairs and even more importantly trade initiatives are increasingly establishing business connections in the context of cultural events rather than reverting to traditional diplomacy or trade deals. Thus, the founding of a chair in Canadian Studies and the launching of anthologies of Canadian literature in translation can indeed be seen as foreign affairs and trade ventures.

As the so-called middle powers of the world compete for visibility and influence in an increasingly deregulated world, as far as information exchange and the media are concerned, they are turning to culture as a trademark or brand. Hence the official excursions to Germany (2001), Mexico (2002), and Russia (2003) and the founding of the 2002 "Trade Routes" initiative by the Canadian Ministry of Heritage, a "$500 million investment in Canadian arts and culture," which clearly seeks to fuse culture and trade. The official government publication states that

> Trade Routes supports the Government of Canada's trade agenda to enhance prosperity and job growth in the knowledge-based sectors of the new economy. Through Trade Routes the Department of Canadian Heritage ensures that Canada's arts and cultural entrepreneurs and organizations have access to the full range of the Team Canada Inc. network of government trade programs

---

3. Cited in www.dfait-maeci.gc.ca/canada-magazine/wv_17/cervant-en.asp [consulted 15 January 2003].

and services in order to expand export capacity and market development opportunities.[4]

It is hard to tell from this excerpt, and from much of the rest of the text, whether this program is supposed to support cultural production at home, use Canadian cultural products to enhance trade abroad, or simply aid Canadian culture workers in exporting their work. In any case, the point is that trade and culture are being explicitly linked in government documents and strategies. Indeed, the Government of Canada foreign policy document *Canada in the World* (1995) lists three "key objectives" for the "international actions of Canada in the years to come":

- the promotion of prosperity and employment;
- the protection of our security, within a stable global framework;
- the projection of Canadian values and culture. (10)[5]

Prosperity, employment, and security appear to be assigned the same importance as the export of Canadian "values and culture." The culture initiative is further explained as follows: "Canadian foreign policy should celebrate and promote Canadian culture and learning as an important way of advancing our interests in international affairs" (11). The approach is clearly that of *public* or *cultural diplomacy* that foreign affairs strategists in many countries were developing and pursuing over the course of the 1990s, a practice described by Evan Potter (2002):

> Public diplomacy is the effort by the government of one nation to influence public or elite opinion of another nation for the purpose of turning the policy of the target nation to advantage [see www.publicdiplomacy.org[6] for a variety of related definitions]. National goals and interests are communicated to foreign publics through a variety of means, including international broadcasting, cultivation of foreign journalists and academics, cultural activities, exchanges, programmed visits, speakers, conferences, and publications. (179)

Canada's activities in Germany in 2001 were in line with this definition: a foreign public was approached through its journalists and academics, with cultural activities, programmed visits, speakers, and publications of Canadian works in

---

4. www.pch.gc.ca/progs/ac-ca/progs/rc-tr/index_e.cfm [consulted 11 November 2005].
5. Funding for the projection of Canadian values and culture has been considerably reduced by the recently elected minority government of the Conservatives.
6. [Consulted 11 November 2005].

translation. Whether trade agreements or simply sales will follow is another question, but a certain visibility was presumably achieved: that is, a step toward *branding* (a buzzword and concern of the 1990s and the beginning of the twenty-first century).

International affairs and communications specialists have traditionally called the larger scheme of intergovernmental contact "diplomacy." But what we are discussing here is not diplomacy in the traditional sense of the term that Eyton Gilboa (2002, 83) describes. This type of diplomacy was once the realm of officials; it was "highly personal, formal, slow and usually protected by secrecy" (84). The version of diplomacy that Canada has recently been deploying in Russia, Germany, and Mexico has consisted of short trips with deliberately public events: readings, discussions, performances, and book sales. Professional diplomats were involved, but many other players appeared as well and in even more influential roles.

This is the kind of response that governments are developing to the decline in traditional diplomacy and to the growth in mass participation in political processes, a development that has transformed the power bases of many societies in recent years (Potter 2002). Analysts describe cultural/public diplomacy as a revolution in international relations. They ascribe it to a more open media access to information and a wider distribution of this information to the public. Public diplomacy results in *soft power*, which is defined as "the ability to achieve desired outcomes in international affairs *through attraction rather than coercion*" (Gilboa 2002, 84; emphasis added) and may gradually be replacing military and economic power. Attraction requires the effective use of global communication to persuade people around the world to support one's causes and, presumably, buy one's products.[7] In other words, increasing globalization, often seen as increasing homogenization, has led to individual countries seeking to differentiate themselves through soft power, mobilizing culture to make the difference.

Image making at this level is based upon cultural nationalism and attempts at protectionism. Indeed, these have been driving and controlling forces in various cultural bodies in Canada ever since the 1950s, when ideas about Canadian culture and the need to create and protect it began to coalesce.[8] Now in the early twenty-first century, after this extended period of cultural nationalism, there are,

---

7. At the twenty-fifth anniversary celebrations of the Canadian Studies program, held at the Department of Foreign Affairs and Trade in Ottawa in the spring of 2001, Saul made explicit the connection between the export of attractive cultural products and trade.
8. The process began with the findings of the Massey Commission that Canada lacked a "national" literature.

however, increasingly critical voices that insist on the need to widen the scope, if only because of technological changes. Proliferating new technologies now give consumers of culture a much greater say in what they can read, listen to, and watch. Consumers, Christopher Maule (2002) notes, have "an enlarged range of choice resulting from the ability to access material anywhere in the world" (2), and they cannot be constrained by protectionist walls of domestic policies. This freedom, in turn, affects cultural policies as well as content. In the Canadian context, analysts claim that Canadians can no longer just tell Canadian stories to other Canadians. They now have to "cooperate with others to tell stories of widespread interest to Canadians *and others,*" as Maule argues (7; emphasis added). And in the end, the more cooperative and international process of projecting Canadian values and culture in the world will make the materials less parochial and thus more "attractive."

Maule, who writes from a hands-on foreign affairs position, seems to be echoing a recent cultural studies approach to the same issue. In *Modernity at Large: Cultural Dimensions of Globalization* (1996), Arjun Appadurai also takes up the mediazation of culture when he discusses "the mediascapes produced by private or state interests that are image-centred, narrative-based accounts of strips of reality" (35). He, too, asserts that increasing human mobility and the vast power of media-driven image making have thrown the nation-state into a crisis that may render it obsolete and cause other forms of allegiance and identity to develop, forms that are "largely divorced from territorial states" (169).

Nevertheless, Canada, and other nations, continue to seize upon national culture as an instrument of national foreign policy, ignoring the apparent paradox caused by technological and media developments that seriously impinge upon governments' ability to control culture and cultural content in any nationalistic or protectionist way.

The recent Canadian government initiatives in public or cultural diplomacy (e.g., Trade Routes and the cultural venture to Germany described above)[9] seem to have been inspired by Saul's report on "Culture and Foreign Policy," commissioned for the 1994 parliamentary review of Canadian foreign policy,[10] and to some extent may predate the massive influence of new technologies. Saul clearly associates culture with foreign policy and in his conclusion expressly states that "culture is the image of Canada abroad. It is therefore central to foreign

---

9. The million-dollar excursion by the Canadian National Arts Centre Orchestra to the United States and Mexico in October 2003 has also been billed as a foreign affairs and trade venture; see *National Post,* 17 November 2003.

10. See www.media-awareness.ca/english/resources/articles/sovereignty_identity/culture_policy. cfm.

policy. Both political and trade initiatives are dependent on that image." He calls for a "healthy home market for culture" and advocates policies on culture that do not shape or control it but simply deliver it. For him, this means improved production at home with increased culture budgets, better distribution methods abroad, with the possible establishment of a cultural agency akin to the British Council or the German Goethe-Institute, and changes in the profiles of diplomats to make them culturally informed salespeople.

Saul's discourse on culture within Canada and its use abroad fluctuates between a focus on the old question of identity, on Canadians' sense of themselves, and a mercantile focus on making Canada look interesting abroad. Recently, marketing strategists such as Simon Anholt (2002) have echoed this approach, apparently contradicting the globalizing effects of the technological revolution. Anholt, too, talks of this double purpose: "If a nation observes that its civic and cultural achievements are recognized abroad, this will help to create a more productive cultural environment [at home]" (4). In the world of foreign policy and trade (and in marketing), culture is thus still being assigned both an internal and an external purpose—its successes create feelings of national pride and creative energy at home while serving to sell products and push influence abroad. But the situation is rife with problems: one is funding; another is the perception within organizations such as DFAIT, which largely control the purse strings, that the culture "desk," the culture portfolio, is a career dead end;[11] still another is the reception of the translated cultural product in the new target culture environment.

**NATION BRANDING**

The job of branding Canada seems to have been enthusiastically embraced by the Department of Canadian Heritage. One of the goals of its Trade Routes program is "to brand Canada through arts and cultural exports."[12] Branding, which once referred to the ownership mark burned onto the flank of grazing cattle, is now a buzzword in marketing; according to one somewhat ironic definition, it has been "co-opted by the MBA crowd and now seems to refer to any activity that supports a company's desire to clearly define its products and/or services."[13] Although critical, this definition gives the gist of the term, which has, in the era of soft diplomacy, shifted from products such as Coca-Cola, or services such as

---

11. Conversation with Robin Higham, Centre for Governance, University of Ottawa, February 2003.
12. www.pch.gc.ca/progs/ac-ca/prop/rc-tr/progs/perc-trap/index-e.cfm [consulted 9 February 2007].
13. From Lake Superior State University, 2003, "List of Banished Words," www.lssu.edu/bnished/current/default.html [consulted 19 January 2003].

those offered by McDonald's, to the cultural exports of individual countries. In branding *products,* the focus is on three main points:

(1) the unique selling point (USP) of a product or service;
(2) its status and the forums of visibility that will make it an international symbol of excellence;
(3) the experience of belonging that it promotes by reaching out to the most personal areas of the human imagination with such confidence and familiarity that it feels like a kindred spirit. (Macrae 1991, 31–40)

It may be difficult for those of us working in literary and cultural fields to imagine that the marketers of Coca-Cola or McDonald's could aspire to create an "experience of belonging" or reach out to "the most personal areas of the human imagination" with their products. It is a fact, however, that these companies try to do so by *telling stories:* that is, by engaging their clients through narratives closely related to literature and culture. New marketing strategies developed in the mid-1990s have moved away from producing the same glossy images of products for dissemination throughout the world. Instead, they have turned to narrative, to finely tuned storytelling, carefully adapted to individual cultures. Story lines are developed for specific audiences, with specific cultural backgrounds and beliefs, and may relate to the product only tangentially—what counts is the *story.* A key factor, as John Heilemann (1997) indicates, is the need to constantly provide updates of the old stories, to refocus the narratives toward new, often younger, or specialized audiences/consumers. This applies to marketing techniques for alcohol, for instance, where marketers seek to dislodge ingrained perceptions: Heilemann notes that "Gin is young and trendy and exciting, except in the U.K. where it's a stuffy old drink that majors and bishops and retired members of the Tory party drink" (17).

The principle applies to marketing techniques for nations as well. Anholt writes about the need for countries seeking to "brand" themselves to "continually present and re-present their past cultural achievements alongside their modern equivalents in ways that are fresh, relevant and appealing to younger audiences" (2002, 6). This approach will not only encourage the continual renewal of culture (which enhances the sale of products) but also force the country to resist the temptation to rest on its laurels and live in the past (i.e., become as stuffy as gin in the United Kingdom). This may be one possible explanation for the more recent Canadian foreign affairs discourse on Canada as *modern, innovative, creative,* and *diverse* that is replacing the older notion of Canada as influenced by "the great North, the oceans, and its Aboriginal roots" (Government of Canada 1995, 37).

## TRANSLATING THE STORIES

While the nation branders and producers of cultural policy do not yet concoct stories about their particular countries the way that advertisers do about their products, they do resort to mobilizing literary works, especially those that tell mainstream stories, to "softly powerful" effect. And translation is a vital factor in this increasingly international activity. How else would Canada or any other place get its stories out? The anthologies of Canadian texts produced in Germany or feted in Mexico, and the rash of Quebec playwrights recently staged in Germany,[14] *must* appear in translation to find an audience and render Canada attractive or interesting to that audience. The films of Jean-Paul Lauzon, Denys Arcand, and Patricia Rozema, the novels of Margaret Laurence and Carol Shields, must be translated if they are to further the cause of Canada's cultural diplomacy in any country where neither French nor English is a major language. Yet the fact of translation is seldom acknowledged. This seems to be the case in much of the discourse around branding as well. The British marketers of various alcoholic beverages who were interviewed by Heilemann refer briefly to the "nightmare of translation" in their trade (1997, 176) and then resort to telling their stories almost exclusively through images, carefully adapting them to the targeted consumers. Anholt, who very much supports the use of culture as a strategic communicator of national image, avoids the issue completely by addressing himself exclusively to marketers working in English; he writes that "some countries are luckier than others—the English-speaking nations are blessed with the advantage of being able to purvey the most sought-after language on the planet at this time" (2002, 7). While Anholt acknowledges that the attractive cultural aspects of another country can serve to offset more unpleasant features, he never addresses the fact that this desirable knowledge is acquired through translation, or some other form of "rewriting" (Lefevere 1992), which must move it out of its source context to face (and in some ways seduce) the international consumer. In Canada, too, there has largely been silence on this topic.

Saul's 1994 paper alone identifies and discusses translation of literature as the primary vehicle of export for Canadian culture and briefly reviews the two funding programs that exist; both are managed by the Canada Council for the Arts, and both are subject to sudden budget cuts, which Saul views as "strangling the success which people have worked hard to produce." No other government department involved in devising or implementing cultural policy addresses this fundamental question.

---

14. Since 2000, they include Normand Chaurette, Larry Tremblay, Daniel Danis, Michel Marc Bouchard, and Carole Frechette.

The general silence on translation, on the linguistic and cultural transfer without which cultural policy can hardly exist as a form of strategic communication, has been one of the key motivations in our research. What role has translation played in the contact between Canada and Germany? Which texts has Canada subsidized for translation and why? Which stories have the German-speaking publishing houses selected and why? How are these stories translated? And how are they read once they arrive in a foreign public space? What effects do they in fact have? And what images of Canada do they transport? These were some of the questions that we set out to investigate. In the following, I discuss some of the participants and processes involved in this particular cultural transfer.

### MAKING CULTURAL CONTACT: CANADIAN STUDIES IN GERMAN

In the Canada-Germany connection, cultural translation has taken place on several different levels in the public domain—in publishing houses, universities, newspapers, theatres—all engaging in different types of transfer. Academic German interest in Canada has had far-reaching effects on the translation of Canada to German-speaking parts of the world. When, in the late 1960s, Canadian Studies was first initiated as a rather mild attempt to address the lack of academic interest in and materials on Canada, it occurred at a national level and was directed toward Canadian academics.[15] However, in 1975 the Department of Foreign Affairs took up the cause, in the then new name of "cultural diplomacy," and produced policy on the question. By the 1980s, international Canadian Studies was in full swing, and at the present moment there are members and associations in over thirty countries. A fledgling idea that sought at first to boost Canadian and foreign interest in Canada by providing funding to academics who would study Canada, it has become an international event and an important participant in cultural policy. Literary studies—studies of "stories"—have played an important role in all the Canadian Studies associations, and the German Canadian Studies Association (Gesellschaft für Kanada-Studien),[16] founded in 1980 as one of the first of the international Canadian Studies associations, has consistently pursued

---

15. Canadian Studies can be seen as a development that is parallel to the establishment of the Canada Council for the Arts, though it came about ten years later. Both initiatives have sought to promote national Canadian identity as well as writing and research on this phenomenon or its lack. For a pioneering survey of the early development of Canadian (literature) Studies in the German-speaking countries (and Europe at large), see Kroetsch and Nischik (1985).
16. The website of the Canadian Embassy in Germany describes the development of the *Gesellschaft für Kanada-Studien* in some detail; see www.dfait-maeci.gc.ca/canadaeuropa/germany/academicrelations-de.asp. The cooperation of the Department of Foreign Affairs and Trade and the Canadian Embassy in this development is noteworthy.

important studies of Canadian literature, with the Anglo-Canadian literature section of the association having been the most productive.

The most spectacular sign of this organization's interest in Canadian writing is indeed the publication history of its members, including many doctoral dissertations and several *Habilitationsschriften*[17] on Canadian writing so far, anthologies of translated contemporary literature with scholarly introductions (e.g., *Literatur in Quebec: Eine Anthologie 1960–2000*, edited by Hans-Jürgen Greif and François Ouellette in 2000), critical introductions to a specific Canadian genre or type of writing (e.g., *Kleine Geschichte des franko-kanadischen Romans*, 2000, by Klaus Dieter Ertler or *Quebec und Kino: Die Entwicklung eines Abenteuers*, 2002, edited by Michel Larouche and Jürgen E. Müller). In addition, there are countless articles, published in the association's journal (*Zeitschrift für Kanada-Studien*), in special thematically linked collections, in conference proceedings, or in other international publications,[18] such as the recent collection *The Canadian Short Story: Interpretations*, in which twenty-seven German-language scholars, mainly from Germany, provide, with twenty-nine original articles written in English, a far-reaching introduction to the Anglo-Canadian short story, published by an American publisher (see Nischik 2007). In 2005, a substantial literary history of Canada appeared in Germany, *Kanadische Literaturgeschichte,* edited by Konrad Groß, Wolfgang Klooß, and Reingard M. Nischik, which surveys both English Canadian and French Canadian literature. And the international critical survey publication on Margaret Atwood, published on the occasion of her sixtieth birthday, both in the United States and later in paperback in Canada, was edited by German Atwood scholar Nischik (2000, 2002).

But these German academics have not restricted themselves to academic writing; they have also produced and published translations, taught numerous university courses in CanLit, and, just as importantly, have written popularizing overview articles as well as book reviews that appear in the weekly feuilleton/culture sections of national newspapers such as the *Frankfurter Allgemeine Zeitung, Süddeutsche Zeitung,* or *Die Zeit*—thus creating ever wider audiences. A brief look at a few of these popularizing newspaper articles reveals the wide range of the German academics fostering CanLit.

Relatively early on, Walter Pache, a professor of English at the University of Augsburg, published a landmark text in *Süddeutsche Zeitung* on 17 and 18 July 1976 that announces "Es gibt eine kanadische Literatur" ("There Is Such a Thing as

---

17. A major study that is written after the doctoral dissertation and has traditionally been required by German universities for a tenured university appointment as professor.
18. A bibliography of this work appeared in 2001; see Grünsteudel. The bibliography was funded by the GKS, the Canadian Embassy in Germany, and the University Library in Augsburg.

Canadian Literature"). Ostensibly a review of two short-story anthologies published in West and East Germany respectively, his text was the first to announce to the general public in Germany that Canadian literature exists, even though this may still have been news—even to Canadians at that point. Some years later, in 1984, the Austrian scholar Waldemar Zacharasiewicz, a professor of English and American literature at the University of Vienna, published a long text in the local *Presse* (26 and 27 May 1984) that presents a history of contemporary English Canadian literature, discussing its development, main themes and preoccupations, as well as the works of individual authors. Zacharasiewicz writes about the marginalization of Canadian writing by the American publishing and film industries, describes Canadian anti-Americanism in the wake of the Vietnam War and increased American media presence in Canada, draws a clear picture of Canadian writers' interests in overcoming colonial (both British and French) attitudes as well as the clichés of settler survival themes, and discusses developing approaches to Canadian identity. In a very opportune manner, this four-page account preceded an international symposium on English Canadian literature held a few days later in Vienna—with Robertson Davies, Jack Hodgins, and Margaret Atwood, among others. Similarly, in 1994, in the wake of many successful translations of novels by Atwood and others, and by then numerous visits by Canadian writers to Germany, Susanne Bach, a university lecturer, published a long overview article dealing once again with the heterogeneous nature of Canadian literary efforts since the findings of the Massey Commission, the clichés of survival that it was (still) in the process of overcoming, and its participation in postmodernism (*Stuttgarter Zeitung*, 19 March 1994). Finally, and only in the mid-1990s, articles appeared presenting Quebec literature as a new, exciting artistic development. Peter Klaus, a lecturer at the Free University Berlin, published a long piece in the *Berliner Tagesspiegel* (14 November 1995) that celebrates the four Canadian female writers who have been honoured by the French Prix Médici or Prix Goncourt (Gabrielle Roy, Marie-Claire Blais, Antonine Maillet, and Anne Hébert) and then moves on to discuss language politics in Quebec, Quebec immigrant writers from Italy, the Caribbean, Chile, Brazil, and China, developments in theatre, and the powerful institutionalization and subsidization of literature in the province that is the motor for so much creative activity.

Over the past twenty to thirty years, then, well-read German-speaking academics have provided the German public with a steady public/academic discourse on Canadian writing and have systematically participated in the public diplomacy efforts of the Canadian government. Theirs has been an invaluable contribution.

**GERMAN PUBLISHERS AND REVIEWERS**

Unlike Canadian publishers, German book publishers do not receive government subsidies and are focused on expected sales. In locating and translating materials for a broad audience, they shop according to this marketing need, and in the case of translated literature they often seek "a good story," usually in novels and short-story collections thought to appeal to the targeted mainstream readers. Experimental or innovative writing such as that of Nicole Brossard, who has had one book published in German by a small feminist press (*Le désert mauve/Die malvenfarbene Wüste,* Munich: Frauenoffensive, 1985/1989), is the exception. On the other hand, special series within publishing houses are often set up to respond to a momentary reading fashion; in the 1980s, for example, with the vogue of women's writing, larger publishers created "women's" series (see Oeding and von Flotow in this volume). They provided fertile ground for certain Canadian writers, but by the 1990s another fashion interest had taken hold, and readers' interests (were) turned in other directions. Yet even with the framework of a series in place, big houses rarely undergo the risk of publishing lesser-known writers.

As we know from large-scale studies of translations, translators and publishers often construct "a domestic representation of a foreign text and culture, and simultaneously construct a domestic subject ... shaped by the codes and canons, interests and agendas of certain domestic social groups" (Venuti 1998, 10). In other words, publishers and translators work *for* the home culture—creating interest there and then supplying it with reading materials that shape its readers. In such processes of selection and construction carried out by the target language publishing industries, Canadian federal programs that may want to shape and steer the image making of Canada are likely to have little influence beyond providing the money for translation. The importing social groups, here certain publishing houses, will make the major decisions.

Reviewers, the professional target culture readers who tell their audiences what to think of a new book in the daily or weekly feuilletons of newspapers, are another unknown quantity when it comes to spreading Canadian stories abroad. Reviews often seem less concerned with Canada than with those aspects of the book that might apply to or be "useful" for the home culture. Political, social, or historical facts of Canada are largely absent from these reviews.[19] To return to the case of women's writing of the 1980s, Atwood, Munro, and many other Canadian women writers seem to have been more important for

---

19. For a more detailed discussion of professional readers' work on Canadian literature, see von Flotow (2004).

providing alternatives to German feminist literature, which German reviewers had grown tired of, than for Canadian image making. And when the tide turned toward a new interest in "international writers" in the 1990s, as Germany faced pronounced xenophobia, reviewers were focused on multiculture and its international aspects, not necessarily on Canada. This is no great surprise since some of the Canadian writers translated then, such as Rohinton Mistry, Michael Ondaatje, or Joy Kogawa, may write about Canada as a country of immigration, but they are just as interested in issues of identity and place, or the loss of homes elsewhere, and some of them, such as Mistry in *A Fine Balance,* do not mention Canada in their work at all. Again, the reviewers—possibly moved by Germany's own difficulties with immigrants, exiles, political asylum seekers, and the social challenges connected with the upheavals of German unification—focus on the social issues around displacement, separation, and loss of home in their reviews. They largely ignore the Canadian aspect, even when it is present in the source texts.

Foreign, in this case German, publishers and reviewers can thus be relatively unpredictable, precarious elements in the international communication strategies pursued through cultural policy or diplomacy. Their first concern is not promotion of the foreign country and its culture; they are focused on the home market.

## CANADIAN CONUNDRUMS IN CULTURAL DIPLOMACY

Funding is always a problem. Exact information about how Canadian materials are selected for export and funded is also impossible to trace and indeed may not exist in any systematic way since funding is hardly static but subject to sudden changes in response to budget adjustments. Some aspects, such as discretionary funding by embassies, are considered confidential,[20] while others are so fragmented that the paper trail is very faint. Suffice it to say that various government departments are involved to varying and overlapping degrees.

Government agencies with a mandate to support the translation and export of Canadian writing are few. Their budgets fluctuate, and statistics are difficult to come by. Information on questions such as the funding of certain authors over others, payments made for travel and book-fair participation, or decisions on the books supported for translation grants is fragmentary. In general, though, the Canada Council for the Arts has the mandate regarding translation, and it maintains lists of works that have received translation grants. Its 2003 budget for

---

20. Discussion with Astrid Holzamer, cultural employee at the Canadian Embassy in Berlin, August 2001.

translation was around $380,000, of which approximately $65,000 was provided by DFAIT. This was the entire budget for translation, both within Canada—that is, between the official languages—and for the export of Canadian books into all other languages. DFAIT's International Cultural Relations Program also plays a role in this framework, supplying discretionary funds for travel, book fairs, and exhibitions and supplementing the culture budgets of both the Canada Council for the Arts and Heritage Canada. Together with Heritage Canada it supports another organization, the Association for the Export of Canadian Books (AECB). Established as a non-profit organization in 1972, "with a mandate to help Canadian publishers develop foreign markets and promote export sales of their books,"[21] the AECB advertises award-winning and other selected books for rights availability and sale, relates "success stories" of foreign rights sales and prizes, and promotes book exhibitions in cooperation with Canadian embassies and international book fairs. Some of the AECB's funding also comes from revenue received from those Canadian publishers who have paid to participate in book fairs—publishers who are funded by other Canadian cultural monies. The situation is complex and difficult to describe clearly, and it appears to be wholly government subsidized. It subscribes, however, to the general principles of "cultural policy," as the statement of the minister of Canadian heritage on the occasion of a recent influx of funding shows:

> Books represent 21 percent of all cultural property that Canada exports. We are delighted with the success that our authors and publishers achieve internationally. I congratulate members of the AECB on the work they do. They provide professionals in our book industry with substantial assistance so they can represent us abroad and better promote Canada's creativity and rich cultural diversity.[22]

The minister's statement obviously participates in the hope that Canadian creativity and especially diversity will travel well and have effect. The minister does not address the issue of translation, though, or the conundrum posed by the label "Canadian."

It is indeed a conundrum. Given that the export of culture is almost exclusively government funded, largely for the purposes of projecting "Canadian values and culture abroad," and of introducing foreign audiences to Canada, the Canadian

---

21. www.aecb.org [consulted November 2005].
22. In late October 2005, the Ministry of Canadian Heritage announced $4.8 million more funding for the AECB; www.canadianheritage.qc.ca/newsroom/news_e.cfm [consulted 18 November 2005].

nature of a book—the Canadian aspect of the "story"—must be of some importance. How is this established? Through the citizenship of the author? The place of publication? The subject matter? The author's residence? Is Malcolm Lowry, for example, to be listed as a Canadian author, as he sometimes is? While he spent some years living in a squatter's shack on the coast of British Columbia, does this make a British writer whose most famous book, *Under the Volcano,* is set in Mexico a Canadian writer? Is Elizabeth Bishop, an American, whose short stories are set in Nova Scotia and who spent a few childhood years there, to be considered Canadian? And, just as intriguingly, what are we to make of the "international writers" who immigrated to Canada from elsewhere and often, if not exclusively, write about that other place—authors such as Ying Chen, Marlene Nourbese Phillip, Dany Laferrière, Alberto Manguel, and Gérard Etienne come to mind here. Their presence and success both in Canada and in German translation can only further destabilize the "idea of a clear homogeneous literary Canadian voice," which critic W. H. New describes as "a wishful ideological construction" in any case (1990, xxxii) and which has emerged in counterpoint to the efforts at cultural nationalism triggered in the late 1950s and pursued throughout the 1960s and 1970s. Yet these authors add enormously to the notion of diversity and multiculture, part of the current brand for Canada. To some extent, Canadianness seems to be relative, and this relativity is reflected in the funding made available; recent Canada Council for the Arts policies, for instance, make translation funding more readily available for books that win prizes—such as the Governor General's Literary Award, the Giller Prize, the Goncourt, the Booker, or the Medici—than for so-called emerging authors or otherwise less successful Canadian writers.[23]

While we can assume that Canada is no longer "the snow-white spot on the literary map of German readers" (my translation), as Pache stated in 1976, and that translation along with vigorous Canadian Studies programs has helped to remedy this situation, the question is whether the insights and images that German readers have constructed through their access to Canadian "stories" do indeed contribute to a more conscious knowledge and understanding of Canada and to friendlier trade relations. Critic Tom Henighan has charged that what is sold as Canadian culture today "is becoming amorphous worldwide culture" (2002, 100), and this may be true in the German scenario. It may have more to do, however, with German publishers' and buyers' needs and tastes than with any government strategies in Canada. Indeed, the amount of control over image making that government agencies can ever hope to exert in such a variegated environment—where the interests of authors, translators,

---

23. Personal conversation with Suzanne Bruneau, Canada Council for the Arts, June 2001.

publishers, and readers crisscross—seems to be questionable. At a time when nationalism seems to be increasingly unimportant in a globalized world, and when "stories" sell largely as good narrative material that may, for a moment, fulfill some purpose in the local environment, the *cultural diplomatic* effect must also be questionable. Yet the translation of Canadian writing and its success abroad undoubtedly motivates writers at home. Whether this work will serve to brand Canada in any permanent way remains an open question, however. And while translation is the most effective way to carry stories across cultures, the outcome of the process can never truly be controlled. Once a translation is dispatched into the new culture, it takes on a life of its own; it has been set free, to some extent, from its national and other source affiliations and has become a hybrid, a world traveller, more cosmopolitan than the home-grown artifact that was the original text. The capacity to provide such new life to a literary work may be the greatest achievement of translation. When this new life in turn aids cross-cultural understanding (and perhaps even the sales of Canadian softwood lumber), then much has been done.

## REFERENCES

Anholt, Simon. "Foreword" to *Journal of Brand Management* 10.8 (Sept. 2002): 1–8.

Appadurai, Arjun. *Modernity at Large: Cultural Dimensions of Globalization*. Minneapolis: University of Minnesota Press, 1996.

Baier, Lothar, and Pierre Filion, eds. *Anders schreibendes Amerika: Literatur aus Quebec 1945–2000*. Heidelberg: Wunderhorn, 2000.

Gilboa, Eyton. "Real-Time Diplomacy: Myth and Reality." In Potter, 2002, 83–109.

Government of Canada. *Canada in the World*, 1995.

Grünsteudel, Günther, ed. *Canadiana Bibliographie 1900–2000*. Hagen: ISL-Verlag, 2001.

Heilemann, John. "All Europeans Are Not Alike." *The New Yorker*, 28 April and 5 May 1997, 174–81.

Henighan, Tom. "Canadian Culture: New Challenges and Opportunities in the Global Context." In *Canadian Identity Through Literature*, ed. Mary Koutsoudaki. Athens: Savalas, 2002. 89–105.

Kroetsch, Robert, and Reingard M. Nischik, eds. *Gaining Ground: European Critics on Canadian Literature*. Edmonton, Alberta: NeWest, 1985.

Lefevere, Andre. *Translation, Rewriting and the Manipulation of Literary Fame*. London: Routledge, 1992.

Macrae, Chris. *World Class Brands*. Addison-Wesley, Wokingham, U.K. and Reading, Mass: MacRae, 1991.

Maule, Christopher. "Overview of Trade and Culture." *Canadian Foreign Policy* 9.2 (2002): 1–14.

New, W. H. *Literary History of Canada: Canadian Literature in English*. Vol. 4, 2$^{nd}$ ed. Toronto: University of Toronto Press, 1990.

Nischik, Reingard M., ed. *Margaret Atwood: Works and Impact.* Rochester, N.Y.: Camden House, 2000.

———. *Margaret Atwood: Works and Impact.* Toronto: Anansi, 2002.

———. *The Canadian Short Story: Interpretations.* Rochester, N.Y.: Camden House, 2007.

Potter, Evan, ed. *Cyber-Diplomacy: Managing Foreign Policy in the $21^{st}$ Century.* Kingston/Montreal: McGill-Queen's University Press, 2002.

Venuti, Lawrence. "Translation and the Formation of Cultural Identities." In *Cultural Functions of Translation*, ed. Christina Schäffner and Helen Kelly-Holmes. Clevedon: Multilingual Matters, 1998. 9–25.

von Flotow, Luise. "Internationale Bastarde ... irgendwo im weiten Kanada: Canadian Writing Tempered by Austrian Reception." In *canadiana oenipontana* 6 (2004): 269–84.

# "Two Solitudes"? Anglo-Canadian Literature in Translation in the Two Germanies

*Barbara Korte*
*University of Freiburg*

### CANADIAN LITERATURE IN TWO LITERARY SYSTEMS, 1949–1990

The two Germanies that were reunited in 1990 had different ideological outlooks on English literatures and their dissemination. Research into the reception of English literatures in the German Democratic Republic (GDR) is still nascent—with the exception of Anna-Christina Giovanopoulos's substantial study (2000) of the reception of American literature in the GDR.[1] Regrettably, this research has been conducted so far without significant participation of scholars (formerly) active in the GDR who might have more to say on the issue than academics like me originating from West Germany.[2] The following look at the reception of Anglo-Canadian literature in the two postwar Germanies is an

---

1. Giovanopoulos also concentrates on literature translated into German and the textual system—readers' reports and afterwords—into which these translations were habitually embedded. The first part of her study provides a very helpful introduction to the GDR's institutionalization of literature. The study is her PhD dissertation submitted to Dresden University and was written under the supervision of teachers with a West German background. With a few exceptions, academic work on the reception of Canadian literature in Germany has been restricted to the former Federal Republic of Germany. Walter Riedel's overview (1980) includes only a few comments on GDR anthologies of Canadian short stories, and even a fairly recent collection of essays (Kuester and Wolff 2000) pays little attention to the situation in the GDR. The notable exception in this volume is Hanspeter Plocher's comparison of translations of French Canadian literature in the two Germanies, again with a strong focus on anthologies.
2. All the more valuable are the personal comments that I received from Professor Eva Manske (a former lecturer in American literature at Leipzig University and now the director of the German-American Institute in Freiburg), Dr. Reinhild Böhnke (a translator of English literature based in Leipzig), and Gabriele Bock, MA, MBA (a former editor at Reclam Leipzig and now at the German Embassy in London). My thanks also go to my research assistant, Christina Spittel, for sifting through documents in the German Federal Archives, the Bundesarchiv (BArch) in Berlin, and many helpful suggestions.

outsider's view as far as the GDR is concerned and should be taken as preliminary. The survey is restricted to Anglo-Canadian literature in translation, and since translations of drama and poetry are comparatively rare it focuses on fiction (with the exception of children's literature,[3] which was published in both Germanies, and detective and crime fiction, which was published in greater numbers in West Germany only).

While in the old Federal Republic of Germany (FRG) Canadian literature was accessible in the original to anyone who wished to read it (and there were even a number of editions specifically designed for teaching in schools and universities), the GDR was programmatically restrictive in the access that it granted to foreign literatures, especially those of the capitalist West.[4] If available in the original at all, such books were kept in special library sections, and even academics in English and American Studies required special permission to read them. The general reader's access to Western literatures depended on the availability of translations, and this availability was determined not only by ideology. Acquiring translation rights raised the issue of foreign exchange (i.e., Western currency), a notorious problem for the GDR and other countries in the former East Bloc. The GDR's official print-licence form required that not only the amount of paper needed for a book (paper being subject to strict allocation) but also the hard currency be specified. The form for the translation of Margaret Laurence's *The Stone Angel* (*Der steinerne Engel*), for example, gives the following data: number of copies (20,000); amount of paper required (3,525 tons), retail price (ca. 2,50 East German marks), hard currency (1,800 West German marks).[5] Both ideology and economy, then, limited the transfer of works from English-speaking countries, and it is hardly surprising that the total number of titles of Canadian fiction published in the GDR is lower than the figures found for the FRG.

At the same time, though, limited availability lent a special weight to the literature that was translated and reached a general readership. In the GDR, foreign literature in translation enjoyed the status of rare cultural capital that was hard to get, despite a relatively high number of copies printed. In a country that imposed severe restrictions on its citizens' freedom to travel, literature in translation served as a window onto the world. As a matter of fact, the phrase

---

3. See the article on English-language children's literature in German translation by Martina Seifert in this volume.
4. Seven Seas was a publisher through which the GDR made selected titles available in the original for overseas distribution. In terms of Canadian literature, I have only been able to trace a title by Farley Mowat here, *People of the Deer* (Berlin: Seven Seas, 1962).
5. The form is part of the files from the GDR's Ministry of Culture, now in the Bundesarchiv: BArch, DR1/2221, f.225.

*Fenster zur Welt* ("Window to the World") served as the title of a publication (Barck and Lokatis 2003) that accompanied a recent exhibition on the aptly named Volk und Welt, the GDR's prime publisher for (twentieth-century) foreign literature. The very existence of a publisher with this name and function indicates that the GDR was well aware of what its citizens lacked and had to be compensated for— if only by an opportunity to see the world through books. Siegfried Lokatis points out that (at least some) editors at Volk und Welt enjoyed comparatively liberal access to foreign books and reference material and had less difficulty in getting travel permits, precisely because they provided an urgently needed substitute for real mobility (Barck and Lokatis 2003, 22). One of the most popular publications of Volk und Welt was *Erkundungen* ("Explorations"), a series comprising over fifty anthologies, each designed to introduce a country through its literature (the volume dedicated to Canada is discussed below).

There was a significant contrast in reception climate between the two German states, then, and the organization of their respective literary systems made for further differences.[6] In the FRG, translations of Canadian literature were produced for a book market that was (and still is) determined by the mechanisms of supply and demand. Agents of cultural transfer such as the cultural section of the Canadian Embassy or Canadianists in academia may have been able, in certain cases, to rouse an editor's interest, but usually the presence of Canadian literature on West Germany's free market depended on a book's potential to compete with others and its appeal to audience tastes. As Walter Riedel concludes from his survey of Canadian literature translated before 1980 for German-speaking markets in the West,

> the decisive criteria for a text to be translated are not its literary quality, modernity, or representativity, but rather market factors based on readers' expectations. If, with a few exceptions, the prevailing image of Canada is determined by the topics of landscape and man's encounter with nature (that is, the motif of survival), this basically corresponds to the expectations, prejudices, and romantic preconceptions of the German-speaking audience. (1980, 104–5; my translation)

The GDR's literary system, in contrast, was programmatically governed by political objectives and not by market demands.[7] As in other countries under

---

6. For background on the GDR's literary system, see Giovanopoulos (2000); Köhler (1990); Köhler-Hausmann (1984); Scharfschwerdt (1982); and, specifically on the exchange of licences between the two German states, Lehmstedt and Lokatis (1997).
7. For writers who were able to come to terms with the GDR's ideological framework, this non-commercial system meant that they enjoyed, on average, greater financial security than most

a communist regime, art was deemed an important factor in the development of society and the socialist human being (*"sozialistische Persönlichkeit"* in GDR officialese) and thus had to be integrated into the processes of political planning. The Bitterfeld Conference of 1959 formulated influential ideas about the socially educative and public role of literature in a communist society. These ideas pertained, above all, to writers in the GDR itself, but they also had repercussions on what kinds of literature were sanctioned for translation. Resulting restrictions were addressed by Eberhard Brüning (then at Leipzig University) in open and positive terms when he reviewed the early reception of Australian literature in the GDR in 1978:

> The survey ... leaves no doubt that there were certain emphases and areas of concentration. Apart from occasional problems in licence acquisition, this reflects, of course, basic assumptions concerning the role of literature in a socialist society and the relationship between literature and society in general.
>
> In 1973, a Munich publisher brought out an interesting study about North American literature in the German-speaking countries since 1945. ... One can only agree with ... Horst Frenz, who writes at the beginning of his remarks on North American literature in the GDR: "One has to say in advance that a GDR publisher's decision to publish a book from the capitalist West is made on the basis of very different criteria than in a non-socialist country." In other words, the policy of socialist publishing is not determined by market conditions, best-seller hysteria, manipulation of taste, and profit-seeking, but by the pursuit of creating socialist men and women who are universally educated and shaped by the ideals of real humanism. (101–2; my translation)[8]

In the four decades of the GDR's existence, its ideological framework was subject to political winds of change whose extremes were marked, first, by Cold War rhetoric and, eventually, by *glasnost* and *perestroika*. Broadly speaking, the GDR increasingly aimed to present itself as a more liberal country, especially in the wake of the Helsinki CSCE of 1975 and in particular throughout the 1980s. Nevertheless, basic premises about the relationship between socialist society and literature prevailed, and so did the need to control the literature made available to

---

of their colleagues in the West. This fact is often stressed in GDR scholarship, for example in the introduction to an anthology of Canadian short stories that claims that "only few Canadian writers are able to make a living with their pen. ... Like other Canadian artists, writers are confronted with the fact that art and culture in Canada are commercialised and that it is less costly and easier to import art work from abroad" (El-Hassan and Militz 1986, 325; my translation).

8. Here the reference is to Frenz and Hess (1973). As might be presumed, the quoted statement, in its original context, is slightly more critical of GDR practice than Brüning's interpretation suggests.

the people. Until the *Wende* of 1989, all agents for the production and distribution of literature (writers, translators, publishing houses and their editorial staffs, booksellers, libraries, reviewers, academic journals,[9] schools, and universities) remained under state and party (i.e., the Sozialistische Einheitspartei Deutschlands [SED]) supervision. The prime agency of this control was the Ministry of Culture, more specifically one of its departments, the Hauptverwaltung Verlage und Buchhandel (HV), the main administration for the book trade. It was founded in March 1963, replacing other administrative units with a comparable function. The HV issued the print licences obligatory for all publications in the GDR, and it directed and coordinated the publishing houses' output. The main purpose of this coordination was to pool know-how and resources and to eliminate competition. Publishers (of which the major ones were nationally owned or tied in with political organizations) were assigned specializations or profiles within which they had to operate; they had to submit an annual thematic catalogue into which their output of individual titles for that year had to fit. As mentioned above, Volk und Welt was profiled for twentieth-century world literature; other major publishing houses permitted to publish translations of *belles lettres* were Reclam Leipzig and Aufbau-Verlag, one of the biggest publishing houses for fiction in the German-speaking countries.

Proposals for the publication of a translation came from within the publishing houses, usually from the foreign-language editors, who might take up suggestions from outside, for example, from academics or even contacts abroad. These editors knew perfectly well that a project would only succeed if a translation licence was affordable and, first and foremost, if the book could be made to pass ideological screening. It is typical of the GDR's system of censorship[10] that much of this screening was delegated to the publishing houses themselves. The process involved a certain amount of self-censorship but also left room for skilful manoeuvring, through which a book could be made to appear desirable for

---

9. The main scholarly journal in GDR English and American Studies was *Zeitschrift für Anglistik und Amerikanistik (ZAA)*. In its review section, ZAA published reviews not only of scholarly work but also of original and translated fiction from the English-speaking countries to ensure the "proper" reception of that kind of literature in academic circles. On the occasion of the GDR's twentieth anniversary, Karl-Heinz Wirzberger confirmed the journal's commitment to the central aims of socialism, including the formation of true socialists "with an all-round education" and "a variety of cultural interests" (1969, 343; my translation).

10. Officially, censorship did not exist in the GDR, but in practice, of course, it did. For more detailed information on GDR mechanisms of censorship and self-censorship, see Barck, Langermann, and Lokatis (1997), especially chapters 1 and 5 on the role of the HV; see also Zipser (1995). The former authors point out that the GDR system of censorship was highly complex, in fact a "discursive and bureaucratic jungle" (15; my translation).

publication even when it was ideologically "flawed." Publishers had to submit their applications to the HV with at least two reports on the respective book, one of which had to be by an external expert. For translations of English literature, these experts were usually members of one of the GDR's departments of English and American Studies. Their commitment to a project had an important influence on its eventual success; Giovanopoulos even speaks of academia's "power of consecration" (2000, 380; "Konsekrationsmacht").

Judging from some (though definitely not all) of the scholarship published in the GDR, there must have been a significant number of doctrinal reports. However, the majority of reports relating to translations of Canadian literature accessible in the Bundesarchiv[11] are comparatively low key in this respect (most of them date from the mid-1970s onward) and mainly emphasize the artistic quality of the texts in question. Nevertheless, a certain amount of reference to a book's ideological suitability was not to be avoided and might, in fact, actively help a book to pass censorship. Thus, a report on *Strömung,* the translation of Atwood's *Surfacing,* is seasoned with convenient references to the novel's anti-Americanism (BArch, DR1/2212, f.40)—references that one also finds in much Canadian and other Western criticism of the novel.[12] The dominant impression is that the experts had a genuine interest in getting good and interesting books published rather than suppressing them. And, I should note, once a work was selected for translation, the translation was usually "faithful" to the original (it usually had to be under the respective licence rights). It was at the stage of selection for publication that the GDR mechanisms of censorship took hold, not in the process of translating or editing a translation.

Table 2.1 below reveals a significant overlap of the Canadian writers and works offered to readers west and east of the inner-German border. In the majority of cases, the two German audiences even read the same (or at least almost the same[13]) translation; where a West German (or Austrian or Swiss) translation

---

11. Files on translations are located in the Bundesarchiv and include Margaret Atwood, *Strömung (Surfacing),* DR1/2212; Fred Bodsworth, *Der Fremde von Barra (The Strange One of Barra),* DR1/3949, and *Lauft, Füße, lauft (The Sparrow's Fall),* DR1/2102; Margaret Laurence, *Der steinerne Engel (The Stone Angel),* DR1/2221; Stephen Leacock, *Abenteuer der armen Reichen (Arcadian Adventures with the Idle Rich),* DR1/5025; Malcolm Lowry, *Unter dem Vulkan (Under the Volcano),* DR1/2367a; Farley Mowat, *Chronik der Verzweifelten (The Desperate People),* DR1/5182; anthologies of short stories: *Die weite Reise,* DR1/2356; *Erkundungen,* DR1/2387a; *Gute Wanderschaft, mein Bruder,* DR1/2493a.
12. Anti-Americanism was a point not usually missed in the para- and metatext for *Strömung;* see the afterword of *Strömung* (198) and its review by Marianne Müller (1981, 382). See also Stefan Ferguson's article in this volume.
13. Occasional stylistic differences between East and West German editions of the same translation result from the fact that they underwent two editing processes. For examples, see the two versions

already existed, GDR publishers were legally obliged to adopt this version rather than to commission a new translation.[14] Less frequently, publishers in the West used work by East German translators, such as Reinhild Böhnke's *Strömung* (*Surfacing*), a novel originally discovered by Gabriele Bock at Reclam Leipzig; in West Germany, it appeared under the title *Der lange Traum*. But even in the case of duplicate editions, there was one essential difference: all GDR editions embedded the translation in paratextual material, which again involved GDR Anglicists and Americanists in almost every publication.

Gérard Genette elaborated his notion of "paratext" in *Seuils* (1987), using the term to refer to all textual and non-textual elements that surround the literary text proper and thus form "a threshold, or ... a 'vestibule' that offers the world at large the possibility of either stepping in or turning back" (Genette 1997, 1–2). Genette's notion comprises "peritextual" elements such as titles, prefaces, or blurbs as well as "epitextual" elements such as an author's comments on her or his work in the media or in private correspondence. Forewords or more frequently afterwords are the only paratextual elements to be considered here, and strictly speaking they form a borderline case in Genette's system since they are not written by the author and thus verge on the metatextual critical essay or review.

It was fairly uncommon for West German translations to appear with accompanying text (except blurbs, of course, with their obvious marketing function). The GDR editions, however, had to have paratext, and—just like the reports discussed above—this paratext had to be ideological at least to a certain degree. So, with few exceptions, Anglo-Canadian literature reached GDR readers only with background information about the author and his or her culture as well as instructions for the book's ideologically profitable consumption. In an article in *ZAA* (*Zeitschrift für Anglistik und Amerikanistik*), Günther Klotz (1969, 409) explicitly welcomed this type of afterword as a "form of comment ... which facilitates access to literature for many new readers"—especially those readers

---

of Atwood's *Surfacing* (discussed by Stefan Ferguson in this volume) and of Bodsworth's *The Sparrow's Fall* (published as *Lauft, Füße, lauft* with both the West German and the East German publishing house). On mechanisms of literary transfer between the two German states, see Lehmstedt and Lokatis (1997).

14. Thus, for the anthology *Gute Wanderschaft, mein Bruder* (1986), a new translation of Alice Munro's "The Moons of Jupiter" had to be replaced by an already existing and licensed West German one (see DR1/2493a, f.524). Klotz (1969, 406) regretted explicitly that GDR publishers were often forced to use West German or Austrian translations even when they were considered deficient. Klotz attributes this lack of quality to poor remuneration of translators in the West, that is, mechanisms of capitalist exploitation. In contrast, he emphasizes the quality of GDR translations, a quality confirmed, in his view, by the fact that several of these translations were adopted by publishers in the West (418).

who were particularly dear to the ideologues: "working men and women with a desire to read, relax while improving their minds, broaden their horizons and range of experience, develop their personalities" (my translation). Depending on the individual author, afterwords varied in dogmatic conformity (especially in the later 1970s and the 1980s), but a book could not have appeared if its afterword had contained any remark offensive to the HV. On the other hand, like a reader's report, an afterword might help a book pass censorship if it highlighted suitable elements of anti-Americanism or humanism and optimism. According to Hans Petersen, Volk und Welt's long-term editor for the English literatures, William Faulkner could not have been brought out in the 1960s without a comment emphasizing his conformity with at least some tenets of socialist society. Incidentally, Petersen believed that the usual "reading aids" were widely ignored by the GDR reading public and that they were written primarily for the more specialized readership in the HV and the party's Central Committee. (His suggestion that the respective pages be perforated so that they could be more conveniently removed by the general reader was not received favourably; see Petersen in Barck and Lokatis 2003, 175–78.) A work by another modernist writer,[15] *Under the Volcano* by Malcolm Lowry, required careful paratextual support even in the late 1970s. The publisher's report submitted to the HV had made a great effort to point out that this "work of art of the first rank" was beyond any suspicion of suggesting antisocialist values such as "resignation," "pessimism," or "nihilism" (BArch, DR1/2367a, f.421 and 424), and finally *Unter dem Vulkan* appeared in the GDR in 1979, using Susanna Rademacher's translation for the West German publishing house of Rowohlt from 1963. The afterword emphasizes the novel's criticism of a society haunted by fascism on the eve of the Second World War, claiming that only a few other writers in Western postwar literature had revealed "the essence and the mechanics of a person's moral decay in bourgeois society" with comparable completeness (462; my translation). Lowry's main character, the consul, exemplifies this decay, but his half-brother Hugh is presented in a positive light as a character who "does not stand for feeble bourgeois individualism but that elementary, anarchic and in many respects petit-bourgeois spirit which can, under certain circumstances, be turned into class-conscious, revolutionary thinking," so that Hugh will eventually join the fight against fascism (469; my translation).[16]

Despite the (presumably) limited reception of afterwords, the consequences

---

15. On the GDR's generally negative attitude toward modernist art, see Erbe (1993).
16. This interpretation deviates considerably from the afterword of the 1963 West German edition, written by Rudolf Haas, which emphasizes the existential crisis of *all* of Lowry's main characters, including Hugh (399).

that they might have had for a book assigned a considerable responsibility to their authors. Officially, academics were assigned seminal roles in the early reconstruction of English Studies in the GDR:

> Rightly do they consider it their duty to familiarize wide circles of our people with the revolutionary traditions and the present endeavours of the English and American nations—as reflected in their literatures—to thus arouse understanding for the great cultural achievements of these people but also their social and political struggles. (Hofmann 1960, 183; my translation)[17]

But when writing paratexts and other reports, many academics had another responsibility in mind—helping to get a good piece of literature published. The citations given from paratexts in the subsequent sections should be read in this light. Of course, until the final days of the GDR, literary scholarship at GDR universities was contained in the channels of Marxist-Leninist interpretation[18] but with increasing space to think in different categories. Reviews in *ZAA* document to what extent the work of critics from the West (including Canada and West Germany) was noted by GDR scholars, at least by that group of GDR academics permitted to conduct research and attend conferences in the West. The GDR's most active disseminators of Anglo-Canadian literature in the years before the *Wende* were Karla El-Hassan (University of Jena) and Marianne Müller (Humboldt University, Berlin), both of whom lost their positions in the aftermath of the restructuring of East German universities after 1990. El-Hassan and Müller wrote a considerable number of afterwords and reviews for GDR editions of Canadian literature, and El-Hassan edited anthologies of Canadian literature.[19]

**THE WORK OF INDIVIDUAL CANADIAN AUTHORS IN THE FRG AND GDR**

As has already been mentioned, the number of Canadian titles in translation on the West German book market outnumbered the GDR production. However,

---

17. See also Klotz, who praises the "fruitful cooperation" between academics and publishers (1969, 411). For a general assessment of the development of English Studies in the GDR, see also Wicht (1991).
18. As late as 1988, a history of English literature, *Englische Literatur im Überblick*, edited by Georg Seehase, was explicitly praised by a reviewer for its Marxist orientation and consistent attention to the literature of the working class (see Magister 1988).
19. In her scholarly work, El-Hassan demonstrates great familiarity with Canadian literature and its criticism. She did pioneering work on the Canadian short-story ensemble, which after the *Wende* found an academic publisher in the West. At the same time, most of the articles that El-Hassan published in the GDR are well seasoned with the desired formulas of Marxist-Leninist literary criticism. See, for example, El-Hassan (1980, 1984, especially 55–57).

prior to the late 1970s, West German awareness of Canadian literature was also limited.[20] Translated authors included a handful of writers who had already come to international attention and been translated into German before World War II (Charles G. D. Roberts, Ernest Thompson Seton, "Grey Owl," and the prolific and popular Mazo de la Roche) as well as some writers who enjoyed success or at least acclaim on the American and/or British markets, such as the best-selling Arthur Hailey (a "doubtful" Canadian), "middle-brow" writers with more obviously Canadian concerns such as Fred Bodsworth, and more "high-brow" writers such as Ethel Wilson, Robertson Davies (most of whose novels, however, did not appear in German before the 1980s), Mordecai Richler, Margaret Laurence (*The Stone Angel* was translated in 1965), Hugh MacLennan, and Norman Levine. Brian Moore also began to be translated before the 1970s; the German version of Timothy Findley's *The Wars* came out in 1978 and that of Atwood's *Surfacing* in 1979, and Leonard Cohen's status as a cult star of the 1970s explains the translations of his writing, brought out by the publishing house Zweitausendeins.

Although this list spans quite a variety of writing, Walter Riedel (1980, 102) concludes that the translations into German that had appeared in the West by the late 1970s promoted an image of Canada as a northern wilderness that appealed to a German readership traditionally fascinated by Native North Americans and increasingly intrigued by countercultural spaces as an alternative to modern civilization. This image began to change—or was expanded upon—when, in the course of the 1980s, Canadian women writers were translated in greater numbers, acknowledging the role that these writers played in the boom of Canadian literature during that decade: Laurence and Atwood, of course, but also Aritha van Herk, Joan Barfoot, Marian Engel, Mavis Gallant, and Alice Munro.

In the GDR, as Marianne Müller (1983) notes, publishers did not show any notable interest in Canadian literature until the late 1970s. The few earlier examples that one finds confirm the GDR's initial policy of concentrating on foreign titles that could either be considered classics, and thus part of a universal humanist heritage (with the additional advantage of being out of copyright), or titles that qualified as socially progressive: that is, left-wing and working-class literature. Stephen Leacock's *Arcadian Adventures with the Idle Rich* had already been translated in 1925 as *Die Abenteuer der armen Reichen;* in 1955, this translation was used for a new GDR edition issued by Eulenspiegel, a publisher profiled

---

20. The following survey is based on the list of "Canadian Authors in German Translation" ("Kanadische Autoren in deutscher Übersetzung") compiled by Astrid H. Holzamer and published by the Canadian Embassy in Germany in November 2001 (www.kanada-info.de/Canada/Culture/xccubibs.htm [consulted 4 July 2002]) and the appendix in Riedel (1980).

for humorous and satirical writing. The print permit for the book notes that it "might practically have been written for us" (BArch, DR1/5025 f.1, verso; my translation).[21] Translations of Seton's animal stories were republished for young readers, though not to the extent that Seton was available in the West. As for pronounced left-wing writing, Canada had less to offer than Australia, whose literary reception in the GDR during the 1950s and 1960s was dominated by the work of Katharine Prichard and Frank Hardy. However, the Canadian Dyson Carter (who is not listed in companions to Canadian literature or literary histories of Canada such as *The Oxford Companion to Canadian Literature*) is mentioned alongside favoured Australian writers in the standard GDR history of English literature, Helmut Findeisen and Georg Seehase's *Englische Literatur* (1965, 31–34), where Carter is identified as the "most prominent representative of progressive contemporary literature." His novels, they claim, depict "the rise of the labour movement and of the movement for peace and [international] understanding" (34; my translation). Carter was never published in translation in the West, but for GDR readers at the peak of Cold War tensions *Spionagefall Alan Baird* (1951), the translation of *To-Morrow Is with Us,* confirmed an openly anti-West, particularly anti-"Yankee," and pro-communist world picture. A few years after World War II, a young Canadian engineer quits his job in the aircraft industry when asked to work on a secret project that he believes will be used in another imminent war. This means, however, that he will also have to give up work on a private humanitarian project dear to him: the development of medical equipment that might save many lives. When the engineer reads about a Russian clinic that might benefit from the equipment, he tries to make contact with the Russians and is thus drawn into Canadian communist circles and the witch hunts conducted against them.

From the communist point of view, Canadian literature presented itself predominantly as a product of the late-bourgeois system—a circumstance that ceased to pose a fundamental obstacle for publication in the course of the 1970s. It became increasingly possible to offer work of bourgeois realism as a reflection of a capitalist world in decay, as afterwords (as well as reviews and criticism) make abundantly clear. Opening up to this kind of literature, however, meant that the GDR's supply of Canadian literature in translation began to overlap with the West German market. In fact, one area of overlap can be identified even before the 1970s.

Readers in the FRG and GDR shared a traditional interest in Canada's

---

21. In the West, apart from his inclusion in short-story anthologies, Leacock was not published in translation again until the 1980s, despite his status as a (minor) classic.

indigenous population[22] that, in East Germany, could easily be exploited to criticize the suppression of indigenous minorities in imperialist societies. A range of Farley Mowat's books was published in the FRG, including many of his novels specially adapted for young readers, but also a translation of his first publication, *People of the Deer* (1952), which came out as *Gefährten der Rentiere* in 1954. With his criticism of missionary and government treatment of the Inuit population, Mowat was a controversial figure in his own country, but the GDR hailed him as a "progressive" writer (see the enthusiastic reports in the HV files, BArch, DR1/5182). *People of the Deer* was chosen for dissemination by Seven Seas, the GDR's English-language publisher, in 1962. It was in the GDR, not the FRG, that *The Desperate People* was translated (*Chronik der Verzweifelten: Der Untergang der Karibu-Eskimos*, 1962), another book that expressed harsh criticism of Canada's treatment of its indigenous population. There were also straightforward doubles, however. For example, Fred Bodsworth's *The Strange One* came out in a West German translation under the title *Kanina* in 1962; this translation was taken over by Aufbau-Verlag and entitled *Der Fremde von Barra* in 1965, its author's attitude having been diagnosed in an expert's report as "critically bourgeois [bürgerlich-kritisch]" though not fully "anticapitalist" (BArch, DR1/3949, f.400). *Lauft, Füße, lauft*, the translation of Bodsworth's *The Sparrow's Fall*, first appeared in the West in 1968 (and one year later in the Bertelsmann book club) and in 1973 in the East. The novel portrays the plight of an Ojibwa couple that almost starves to death because a missionary has told them that hunting animals is murder.

In some cases, one wonders why certain writers were not published in the GDR. Hugh MacLennan, for instance, received academic attention in the GDR as early as 1960, when an article in ZAA (Boeschenstein 1960) praised him as a realist writer familiar with the working class, critical of Canadian society, and committed to optimism and humanism. Nevertheless, a GDR edition did not materialize, possibly for financial reasons. *The Watch that Ends the Night* came out in a West German translation in 1961 (*Die Nacht der Versöhnung*), so one may surmise that the German-language rights for MacLennan had already been acquired by the West German publisher when GDR academics drew attention to this writer and that, in the early 1960s, the GDR could not afford hard currency for a licence. Other ideologically suitable writers were not published in the GDR until several years after their first appearance on the West German market. A

---

22. On German readers' long-standing fascination with Native North Americans, see Lutz (2000). Riedel (1980, Chapter 1) also discusses that subject area in Canadian literature and its special popularity with German readers. Chapter 2 is devoted to Farley Mowat and Allen Roy Evans as two of the most popular translated writers up to the time of Riedel's survey. See also Eva Gruber's much more up-to-date and extensive survey in this volume.

selection of Norman Levine's stories, for instance, translated by Annemarie and Heinrich Böll and Reinhard Wagner, had come out in the FRG in 1971 under the title *Ein kleines Stückchen Blau*. Of these, a GDR edition, *Der Mann mit dem Notizbuch*, presented nine stories—on the grounds of artistic quality, criticism of society, and thematic variation (see BArch, DR1/2208, f.159). The collection appeared in 1975 in a fairly large edition of 30,000 printed copies (the average for translations of Canadian literature was then 15,000 to 20,000) and was expanded in 1979. The external reader's report in the HV file identified Levine as a writer working "within the limits of critical bourgeois realism" but lending memorable expression to the "symptoms of decline in capitalist society" (BArch, DR1/2208 f.167; my translation). This view is echoed in Karla El-Hassan's afterword to the collection; El-Hassan emphasizes Levine's underprivileged background in a poor Jewish immigrant family and the fact that, during his studies in London, Levine wrote a thesis about the decay of absolute values in modern society. According to El-Hassan, Levine's work is appreciated for its critical analysis of life under the late-bourgeois system, which is marked by angst and "individual helplessness in the face of the seemingly uncontrollable power of the state-monopolist system" (in Levine 1975, 110; my translation).

An interesting ideological difference emerges in the paratexts written for Canadian women's novels published in the GDR. In the West, Canadian women writers became part of a general, feminist-inspired vogue of women's writing that originated in the 1970s. But in the GDR, feminist relevance was not a recommendation per se. Women's emancipation was taken for granted under socialism, and Western feminism was generally regarded with skepticism.[23] The afterword to the GDR edition of Atwood's *Surfacing*, for example, emphasizes that the novel is not "aggressively" feminist (in Atwood 1979a, 198). Significantly, the only other major novel by a Canadian woman writer to come out during the existence of the GDR was Margaret Laurence's *The Stone Angel* (*Der steinerne Engel*), which did not appear until 1988, using Herbert Schlüter's translation for a West German publisher in 1965. Karla El-Hassan's afterword (dated January 1987) also explicitly mentions that, during the 1960s, Laurence "sympathized" with the women's movement "but without officially declaring her support for it" (in Laurence 1988, 299; my translation). In 1990, Reclam Leipzig published the translation of Atwood's *The Handmaid's Tale* (*Der Report der Magd*); the edition was prepared when the GDR was still in existence but came out after the *Wende*. Marianne Müller's afterword (dated January 1990) addresses Atwood's treatment of women's rights in this novel but stresses that Atwood did not consider

---

23. See, for instance, Nagelschmidt (1995) and Secci (1988), who show that prominent women writers in the GDR, such as Christa Wolf, also distanced themselves from Western feminism.

herself a "propagandist of the feminist movement" (in Atwood 1990, 341; my translation). Incidentally, the afterword manages to discuss Atwood's indictment of totalitarianism with explicit reference to the United States but without a single reference to the totalitarian systems just being deconstructed everywhere in the former East Bloc.

In general, and apart from a few ideological selections during the GDR's early years, most titles made available for East German readers had matches on the West German market, which offered a greater number of titles but, all in all, also a selection that could hardly be considered representative of the Canadian literary scene. This is somewhat different in another area of publication, the anthology. Anthologies of short fiction provide an opportunity to present a wider range of writers and their work, and, as the subsequent section shows, it was in this sector that GDR publishers were able to compete with the Western book market.

## ANTHOLOGIES OF SHORT STORIES IN THE FRG AND GDR

Walter Riedel, a German Canadian, not only commented on German Canadian literary transfer but also contributed to it by editing anthologies for publishers both in the West and in the East. For Riedel, "anthologies provide the most complete impression of Canada's narrative literature. ... These samples of Canadian short fiction can be regarded as a cultural reflection of the country and its people; they form a cross-section of Canadian literature generally" (1980, 56; my translation). As representative mirrors, many anthologies published in the two Germanies include work of both English and French Canadian writers (the latter contingent has to be neglected here) and reveal a tendency to select stories that are characteristic of the Canadian geographical and cultural context. We have seen that translations of foreign literature in the GDR opened windows onto a world not otherwise accessible, and anthologies of fiction were exemplary in fulfilling this function. The titles of some of the anthologies of Canadian short fiction are telling in this respect: the *Erkundungen* volume, of course, but also *Die weite Reise* and *Gute Wanderschaft, mein Bruder,* all from the GDR—as opposed to more neutral titles of West German anthologies such as *Kanadische Erzähler der Gegenwart* or *Kanada erzählt*. Nevertheless, the intention of introducing the country through its literature marks the Western anthologies as well.

The first anthology of Canadian short stories in German, edited by Armin Arnold and Walter Riedel, was published by the Swiss Manesse-Verlag in 1967. The first GDR anthology, edited by Ernst Bartsch and published by Volk und Welt, was entitled *Die weite Reise: Kanadische Erzählungen und Kurzgeschichten* (1974). Riedel's Canadian volume in the series *Moderne Erzähler der Welt* was issued in the West in 1976. The GDR's *Erkundungen: 26 kanadische Erzähler,* edited by Karla El-Hassan and Helga Militz, followed in 1986. In the same year, a church-owned publisher in the GDR, St. Benno-Verlag (profiled for a Catholic readership), brought out *Gute Wanderschaft, mein Bruder: Eine kanadische Anthologie*, a volume co-edited by Gottfried Friedrich and Walter Riedel and illustrated with photographs of Canada's various regions to provide a visual impression of the country that is "so remote and unfamiliar to us" (blurb; my translation). One story originally intended for this compilation had to be exchanged after an external report pointed out that the respective story—a satire involving Heinrich Heine—"had absolutely nothing to do with Canada" and was thus incapable of providing insight into the Canadian way of life and mentality (BArch, DR1/2493a, f.526; my translation). Two anthologies, whose planning was begun when the two Germanies were still in existence, did not appear until after unification: Stefana Sabin's *Kanada erzählt: 17 Erzählungen* (West) and Karla El-Hassan's *Kolumbus und die Riesendame: Kurzgeschichten aus Kanada* (East), both published in 1992. As late as that year, anthologies were still being designed to reflect Canadian realities. Sabin's anthology, for instance, identifies "nature's grand wilderness and the ethnic plurality of urban life" as leading themes of Canadian literature (blurb; my translation). Thus, both East and West anthologies feature stories dealing with familiar Canadian themes such as an overpowering natural environment, survival and existential hardship, the living conditions of Canada's indigenous people, the ethnic diversity of an immigrant country, the cultural divide between English and French Canada, Canada's dilemma over identity, and latent anti-Americanism.

As Table 2.1 illustrates, there is a striking overlap in the writers[24] included in anthologies published East and West—and, incidentally, a further overlap of these anthologies with Canadian ones (several of which were examined for the table's last column), since Canadian anthologies were a major inspiration and/or an acknowledged source for the editors of German-language selections.[25]

---

24. Only three stories are doubled, however, possibly to avoid licence fees. Eric Cameron's "The Turning Point" in Arnold and Riedel (1967) as well as Bartsch (1974); Hugh Garner's "One-Two-Three Little Indians," with three different translations in Arnold and Riedel (1967), Bartsch (1974), and Uthe-Spencker (1969); and Mordecai Richler's "Some Grist for Mervyn's Mill" in Bartsch (1974) and Sabin (1992).
25. Canadian anthologies are explicitly named as sources in Uthe-Spencker (1969; all stories are taken from Robert Weaver's *Canadian Short Stories*, 1960) and in Arnold and Riedel (1967; apart from Weaver's collection, they name Raymond Knister's *Canadian Short Stories*, 1928; Desmond Pacey's *A Book of Canadian Stories*, 1962; and Giose Rimanelli and Roberto Ruberto's *Modern Canadian Stories*, 1966). In addition to the anthologies mentioned, the following were consulted for the table: Clark Blaise and John Metcalf's *Here and Now* (1977), Wayne Grady's *Penguin Book of Canadian Short Stories* (1980), John Metcalf's *Making It New* (1982), Margaret Atwood and Robert Weaver's *The Oxford Book of Canadian Short Stories in English* (1986), as well as several volumes of the annual *Canadian Short Stories* series.

**TABLE 2.1**

*Overlap of Writers in Anthologies East and West*

| AUTHORS | \multicolumn{9}{c}{SHORT STORY ANTHOLOGIES} |
|---|---|---|---|---|---|---|---|---|---|
|  | I | II | III | IV | V | VI | VII | VIII | IX |
| Alford, Edna |  | x |  | x |  |  |  |  | x |
| Atwood, Margaret |  | x |  |  |  |  |  |  | x |
| Bailey, Don |  |  |  |  |  |  | x |  | x |
| Bishop, Elizabeth |  |  |  |  |  |  |  | x |  |
| Blaise, Clark |  |  |  | x |  |  |  |  | x |
| Bowering, George |  | x |  | x |  |  |  |  | x |
| Bowie, Douglas |  | x |  |  |  |  |  |  |  |
| Callaghan, Morley | x |  | x |  |  | x | x | x | x |
| Cameron, Eric | x |  |  |  | x |  |  |  |  |
| Carr, Emily |  |  | x |  |  |  |  |  |  |
| Clutesi, George |  |  | x |  |  |  | x |  |  |
| Cohen, Matt |  | x |  | x |  |  |  |  | x |
| Copeland, Ann |  |  | x |  |  |  |  |  |  |
| Davies, Robertson |  |  |  |  |  |  |  | x |  |
| Dickenson, Don |  | x |  |  |  |  |  |  |  |
| Drew, Wayland |  | x |  |  |  |  |  |  | x |
| Engel, Howard |  | x |  |  |  |  |  |  |  |
| Findley, Timothy |  |  |  | x |  |  |  |  | x |
| Gallant, Mavis | x |  |  |  |  |  |  | x | x |
| Garner, Hugh | x |  |  | x | x | x | x |  | x |
| Godfrey, Dave |  |  |  |  |  |  | x |  | x |
| Grove, F. P. | x |  |  |  | x |  | x |  | x |
| Haliburton, T. C. |  |  |  |  | x |  |  |  | x |

| AUTHORS | \multicolumn{9}{c|}{SHORT STORY ANTHOLOGIES} |
|---|---|---|---|---|---|---|---|---|---|
| | I | II | III | IV | V | VI | VII | VIII | IX |
| Helwig, David | x | | | | | | | | x |
| Hodgins, Jack | | x | x | | | | | | x |
| Hood, Hugh | x | | x | | | | | | x |
| Kaey, Arden | | | | | | | x | | |
| Kennedy, Leo | | x | | | | | | | x |
| Kinsella, W. P. | | x | | x | | | | | x |
| Kreisel, Henry | | x | | x | | x | | x | |
| Laurence, Margaret | x | | x | x | | | x | | x |
| Layton, Irving | | | | | | | x | | x |
| Leacock, Stephen | | | | | x | x | | | x |
| Levine, Norman | x | | | | | | | x | x |
| Lowry, Malcolm | | | | | | | | x | x |
| Ludwig, Jack | | | | | | | x | | x |
| Marriott, Ann | x | | | | | | | | |
| McCourt, Edward | | | | | | | x | | |
| MacEwan, Grant | | | x | | | | | | |
| MacEwen, Gwendolyn | | | | x | | | | | |
| MacLeod, Alistair | | | | x | | | | | x |
| McNamara, Eugene | x | | | | | | | | |
| Metcalf, John | x | | | x | | | x | | x |
| Mitchell, W. O. | | | | | x | | | | x |
| Mowat, Farley | | | x | | | | x | | |
| Munro, Alice | x | | x | | | | | | x |
| Nowlan, Alden | | x | | | | | x | | x |
| O'Hagan, Howard | | | x | | | | x | | |

44 Barbara Korte

| AUTHORS | \multicolumn{9}{c|}{SHORT STORY ANTHOLOGIES} |
|---|---|---|---|---|---|---|---|---|---|
|  | I | II | III | IV | V | VI | VII | VIII | IX |
| Page, P. K. |  |  |  |  |  | x |  |  | x |
| Raddall, Thomas H. |  |  |  |  | x |  |  |  | x |
| Richler, Mordecai | x |  |  |  |  |  | x | x | x |
| Roberts, Charles G. D. |  |  |  | x |  | x |  |  | x |
| Ross, Sinclair | x |  | x |  | x |  | x | x | x |
| Scott, D. C. |  |  |  |  |  | x |  |  | x |
| Simpson, Leo |  | x |  |  |  |  |  |  | x |
| Smith, Ray |  |  |  |  | x |  |  |  | x |
| Spettigue, Douglas | x |  |  |  |  | x |  |  | x |
| Stein, David L. | x |  |  |  |  |  |  |  |  |
| Thomas, Audrey |  |  |  |  | x |  |  |  | x |
| Valgardson, W. D. |  | x | x | x |  |  | x |  | x |
| Vanderhaeghe, Guy |  |  |  |  | x |  |  |  | x |
| Waddington, Miriam |  |  |  |  | x |  |  |  |  |
| Waltner-Toews, David |  |  |  | x |  |  |  |  | x |
| Wiebe, Rudy |  |  |  | x |  |  |  |  | x |

**LEGEND**

I *Die weite Reise,* GDR, 1974
II *Erkundungen,* GDR, 1986
III *Gute Wanderschaft,* GDR, 1986
IV *Kolumbus und die Riesendame,* GDR, 1992
V *Kanadische Erzähler der Gegenwart,* Zurich, 1967
VI *Stories from Canada / Erzählungen aus Kanada* (bilingual), FRG, 1969
VII *Moderne Erzähler der Welt: Kanada,* FRG, 1976
VIII *Kanada erzählt,* FRG, 1992
IX Included in Canadian anthologies and/or annual collections

In the GDR, the demand that anthologies be representative of Canada and its culture placed a particular weight on the ideological suitability of their selections. Nevertheless, one finds only a few stories in GDR anthologies that appear to have been included mainly for ideological reasons rather than artistic quality and/or representativeness in terms of region and culture. For *Die weite Reise,* for instance, Bartsch included Eric Cameron's "Der Wendepunkt" ("The Turning Point"), a story set in an Indian reserve that is presented in highly critical terms. The story practically invites a reading as a critique of imperialism, as confirmed by the publisher's report in the HV files (BArch, DR1/2356, f.357). On the other hand, the same story was included earlier in the anthology that Arnold and Riedel had compiled for Manesse. Bartsch also selected the clearly anti-American Atwood story "When It Happens" ("Wenn es passiert"). In fact, one report in the HV file for *Die weite Reise* explicitly regrets that Bartsch's selection was not ideological enough, that the editor had not "grasp[ed] the nettle" ("heiße Eisen wurden nicht angefaßt") and avoided topics such as workers in industry, life in the centres of southern and eastern Canada, American draft dodgers seeking refuge in Canada, and others (BArch, DR1/2356, f.340; my translation).

Since one hardly finds a Canadian writer in a GDR anthology who is not also represented in a Western anthology, it is once again in the paratexts that major differences between West and East emerge. But here, in contrast to editions of novels and author collections, the anthologies published in the West also include prefaces and afterwords that explain their principles of selection. These are, in general, not as openly ideological as Michael Rehs's short prefatory remark to Riedel's *Moderne Erzähler der Welt,* which suggests that West German readers should get acquainted with Canadian literature—and thus with Canada—if only for the reason that "Canadian military units are stationed in Germany as part of the Western defence alliance" (my translation).[26] This rather curious and casual remark may be explained by the fact that Rehs was affiliated with the Stuttgart Institut für Auslandsbeziehungen (Institute for Foreign Relations), which had commissioned the anthology.

---

26. Walter Pache reviewed the *Moderne Erzähler der Welt* volume alongside *Die weite Reise* in *Süddeutsche Zeitung* (17 July 1976), noting the ideological paratext of each anthology and emphasizing that neither represented the full spectrum of Canada and Canadian literature. The review is quoted in excerpts in Riedel (1980, 64). When El-Hassan reviewed the *Moderne Erzähler der Welt* anthology (1979, 187), she was quite justified in noting the omission of several important writers, such as Hugh Hood, Alice Munro, Clark Blaise, Norman Levine, and Ray Smith.

In the GDR, the paratext of an anthology bore a much heavier burden of legitimizing its publication, especially when the stories included were unable to carry that burden on their own. Thus, Bartsch's afterword to *Die weite Reise* emphasizes that the stories selected present a reality marked by the "complex problems of capitalist society on the one hand and specifically Canadian phenomena on the other" (1974, 398), including the disorientation and "aimless" protest of Canada's young generation, exemplified by "hippies," whose presence is diagnosed as a typical consequence of the capitalist social order (400; my translations). Canada's infiltration by the United States in "political, military, economic, and cultural" terms is perceived as particularly harmful (394), not least with respect to Canadian literature: "Pursuit of the dollar has become the sole measure of value. Porn magazines, comic strips, and horror stories swamp the market. Good literature is fairly expensive even in paperback. Recent statistics prove that books are kept in alarmingly few Canadian households" (401; my translations).

A decade later the *Erkundungen* volume offered an almost identical paratext, claiming that French Canadian resistance against English assimilation "was at the same time resistance against capitalist expansion" (El-Hassan and Militz 1986, 316), that the quest for a Canadian cultural and literary identity was intensified "under the massive pressure of U.S. infiltration," and that the "danger" posed by this domination, in conjunction with resistance against the American war in Vietnam, had led to a new political nationalism and cultural revival in the early 1960s (318; my translations).

Notwithstanding these paratexts and the overlap between East and West anthologies, readers in the GDR were given, all in all, a more up-to-date impression of the Canadian short story than readers in the West. A list of the writers found only in GDR anthologies on the one hand and only in anthologies from the FRG and Switzerland on the other, yields — arranged according to date of birth — the result that East German compilations (in particular the later ones) include a greater number of more recent writers. Anthologies in the West tended to prefer a more traditional selection, writers such as Thomas Chandler Haliburton, Duncan Campbell Scott, or Stephen Leacock (see Table 2.2).

**TABLE 2.2**

*Recent and Older Writers in Anthologies East and West*

| EAST | WEST |
|---|---|
|  | Thomas Chandler Haliburton (1796) |
|  | Duncan Campbell Scott (1862) |
| Emily Carr (1871) | Stephen Leacock (1869) |
| John Walter Grant MacEwan (1902) | Thomas H. Raddall (1903) |
|  | Arden Fortner Keay (1904) |
| Leo Kennedy (1907) | Edward McCourt (1907) |
| Malcolm Lowry (1909) |  |
| Elizabeth Bishop (1911) |  |
|  | Irving Layton (1912) |
| Anne Marriott (1913) | Robertson Davies (1913) |
|  | W. O. Mitchell (1914) |
| Miriam Waddington (1917) | P. K. Page (1916) |
|  | Jack Ludwig (1922) |
| Hugh Hood (1928) |  |
| Timothy Findley (1930) |  |
| Eugene McNamara (1930) |  |
| Howard Engel (1931) |  |
| Alice Munro (1931) |  |
| Ann Copeland (1932) |  |
| Wayland Drew (1932) |  |
| Leo Simpson (1934) |  |
| George Bowering (1935) |  |
| W. P. Kinsella (1935) |  |
| Audrey Thomas (1935) |  |
| Alistair MacLeod (1936) |  |
| David Helwig (1938) | Dave Godfrey (1938) |
| Jack Hodgins (1938) |  |
| David L. Stein (1938) |  |
| Margaret Atwood (1939) |  |
| Clark Blaise (1940) |  |
| Ray Smith (1941) |  |
| Matt Cohen (1942) | Don Bailey (1942) |
| Edna Alford (1947) |  |
| Don Dickenson (1947) |  |
| David Waltner-Toews (1948) |  |
| Guy Vanderhaeghe (1951) |  |

Thus, while the novels considered in the previous section convey the impression that the GDR presented an even narrower segment of Canadian literature than the West German market, the image gained for short fiction is quite the opposite. El-Hassan's 1992 *Kolumbus und die Riesendame* is more comprehensive and fresh than what was presented in the West German equivalent for the same year, Sabin's *Kanada erzählt*. Through her extensive research in the area of the Canadian short story, El-Hassan was simply better equipped to make a more up-to-date selection. In general, however, the impressions that readers were able to derive from the anthologies published in the two Germanies were relatively similar. And from this chapter's presentation, we may draw the same conclusion: the GDR and FRG may have been "two solitudes" as far as their political systems were concerned, but the images that they conveyed of Canadian literature were noticeably alike.

**REFERENCES**

Arnold, Armin, and Walter Riedel, eds. *Kanadische Erzähler der Gegenwart*. Zurich: Manesse, 1967.

Atwood, Margaret. *Der lange Traum* [*Surfacing*], transl. Reinhild Böhnke. Düsseldorf: Claassen, 1979b.

———. *Der Report der Magd* [*The Handmaid's Tale*], transl. Helga Pfetsch, afterword Marianne Müller. Leipzig: Reclam, 1990.

———. *Strömung* [*Surfacing*], transl. Reinhild Böhnke, afterword Gabriele Bock. Leipzig: Reclam, 1979a.

Barck, Simone, and Siegfried Lokatis, eds. *Fenster zur Welt: Eine Geschichte des DDR-Verlages Volk und Welt*. Berlin: Ch. Links Verlag, 2003.

Barck, Simone, Martina Langermann, and Siegfried Lokatis. *'Jedes Buch ein Abenteuer': Zensur-System und literarische Öffentlichkeit in der DDR bis Ende der sechziger Jahre*. Berlin: Akademie Verlag, 1997.

Bartsch, Ernst, ed. *Die weite Reise: Kanadische Erzählungen und Kurzgeschichten*. Berlin: Volk und Welt, 1974.

Bodsworth, Fred. *Der Fremde von Barra* [*The Strange One*], transl. Herbert Roch. Berlin: Aufbau, 1965.

———. *Kanina* [*The Strange One*], transl. Herbert Roch. Berlin: Universitas, 1962.

———. *Lauft, Füße, lauft* [*The Sparrow's Fall*], transl. Ernst Larsen. Berlin: Universitas, 1968.

———. *Lauft, Füße, lauft* [*The Sparrow's Fall*], transl. Ernst Larsen. Berlin: Aufbau, 1973.

———. *The Strange One*. New York: Dodd, Mead, 1959.

Boeschenstein, Hermann. "Hugh MacLennan, ein kanadischer Romancier." *ZAA* 8 (1960): 113–35.

Brüning, Eberhard. "Australische Literatur in der DDR." *ZAA* 26 (1978): 97–114.

Carter, Dyson. *Spionagefall Alan Baird* [*To-morrow Is with Us*], transl. Herbert Bräuning and Walter Czollek. Berlin: Volk und Welt, 1951.

El-Hassan, Karla, ed. *Kolumbus und die Riesendame: Kurzgeschichten aus Kanada.* Berlin: Aufbau, 1992.

———. "Die Kurzgeschichten Norman Levines: Ein Beitrag zum Problem des literarischen Zyklus." *ZAA* 29 (1981): 154–66.

———. "Review of *Moderne Erzähler der Welt.*" *ZAA* 27 (1979): 187–88.

———. "Voraussetzungen und Ursachen für die Entstehung von Kurzgeschichtenensembles in der anglokanadischen Literatur." *ZAA* 32 (1984): 49–58.

———. "Zum Problem des Nationalen und des Internationalen in der zeitgenössischen bürgerlichen Literaturkritik Anglokanadas." *ZAA* 28 (1980): 139–47.

El-Hassan, Karla, and Helga Militz, eds. *Erkundungen: 26 kanadische Erzähler.* Berlin: Volk und Welt, 1986.

Erbe, Günter. *Die verfemte Moderne: Die Auseinandersetzung mit dem 'Modernismus' in Kulturpolitik, Literaturwissenschaft und Literatur in der DDR.* Opladen: Westdeutscher Verlag, 1993.

Findeisen, Helmut, and Georg Seehase. *Englische Literatur.* Leipzig: VEB Bibliographisches Institut, 1965.

Frenz, Horst, and John Hess. "Die nordamerikanische Literatur in der deutschen Demokratischen Republik." In *Nordamerikanische Literatur im deutschen Sprachraum seit 1945: Beiträge zu ihrer Rezeption*, ed. Horst Frenz and Hans-Joachim Lang. Munich: Winkler, 1973. 171–99.

Friedrich, Gottfried, and Walter E. Riedel, eds. *Gute Wanderschaft, mein Bruder: Eine kanadische Anthologie.* Leipzig: St. Benno-Verlag, 1986.

Genette, Gérard. *Seuils.* Paris: Seuil, 1987.

———. *Paratexts: Thresholds of Interpretation.* Cambridge: Cambridge University Press, 1997.

Giovanopoulos, Anna-Christina. *Die amerikanische Literatur in der DDR: Die Institutionalisierung von Sinn zwischen Affirmation und Subversion.* Essen: Die Blaue Eule, 2000.

Hofmann, Christa. "Die Anglistik-Amerikanistik in der Deutschen Demokratischen Republik." *ZAA* 8 (1960): 171–85.

Klotz, Günther. "Zwei Jahrzehnte englische und amerikanische Belletristik im Aufbau-Verlag und im Verlag Rütten & Loening." *ZAA* 17 (1969): 406–420.

Köhler, Ursula E. E. (1990). *Lesekultur in beiden deutschen Staaten: 40 Jahre—ein Vergleich. Archiv für Soziologie und Wirtschaftsfragen des Buchhandels,* 64 and 65.

Köhler-Hausmann, Reinhild. *Literaturbetrieb in der DDR: Schriftsteller und Literaturinstanzen.* Stuttgart: Metzler, 1984.

Kuester, Martin, and Andrea Wolff, eds. *Reflections of Canada: The Reception of Canadian Literature in Germany.* Marburg: Universitätsbibliothek Marburg, 2000.

Laurence, Margaret. *Der steinerne Engel* [*The Stone Angel*], transl. Herbert Schlüter, afterword Karla El-Hassan. Leipzig: Reclam, 1988.

Leacock, Stephen. *Die Abenteuer der armen Reichen* [*Arcadian Adventures of the Idle Rich*], transl. E. L. Schifter-Williams. Berlin: Eulenspiegel, 1955.

Lehmstedt, Mark, and Siegfried Lokatis, eds. *Das Loch in der Mauer: Der innerdeutsche Literaturaustausch*. Wiesbaden: Harrassowitz, 1997.

Levine, Norman. *Ein kleines Stückchen Blau*, transl. Annemarie and Heinrich Böll and Reinhard Wagner. Düsseldorf: Claassen, 1971.

———. *Der Mann mit dem Notizbuch*, transl. Annemarie and Heinrich Böll, Reinhard Wagner, afterword Karla El-Hassan. Leipzig: Reclam, 1975.

Lowry, Malcolm. *Unter dem Vulkan* [*Under the Volcano*], transl. Susanna Rademacher, afterword Rudolf Haas. Reinbek: Rowohlt Taschenbuch Verlag, 1974 [1963].

———. *Unter dem Vulkan* [*Under the Volcano*], transl. Susanna Rademacher, afterword Wladimir Skodorenko. Berlin: Volk und Welt, 1979.

Lutz, Hartmut. "Receptions of Indigenous Canadian Literature in Germany." In Kuester and Wolff 2000, 36–63.

MacLennan, Hugh. *Die Nacht der Versöhnung* [*The Watch that Ends the Night*], transl. Maria Wolff. Stuttgart: Goverts, 1961.

———. *The Watch that Ends the Night*. Toronto: Macmillan of Canada, 1958.

Magister, Karl-Heinz. "Review of *Englische Literatur im Überblick*." ZAA 36 (1988): 154–56.

Mowat, Farley. *Chronik der Verzweifelten: Der Untergang der Karibu-Eskimos* [*The Desperate People*], transl. Anneliese Dangel. Leipzig: Brockhaus, 1962.

———. *Gefährten der Rentiere* [*People of the Deer*], transl. Heinz Geck. Stuttgart: Deutsche Verlags-Anstalt, 1954.

Müller, Marianne. "Review of *Erkundungen*." ZAA 37 (1989): 284–85.

———. "Review of Margaret Atwood, *Strömung*." ZAA 29 (1981): 381–82.

———. "Review of Norman Levine, *Der Mann mit dem Notizbuch*." ZAA 31 (1983): 91.

Nagelschmidt, Ilse. "Vom Aufbruch der Frauen in der Literatur der sechziger Jahre (Brigitte Reimann, Christa Wolf)." In *'Es genügt nicht die einfache Wahrheit': DDR-Literatur der sechziger Jahre in der Diskussion*, ed. Michael Hametner and Kerstin Schilling. Leipzig: Friedrich-Ebert-Stiftung, Büro Leipzig, 1995. 126–37.

Plocher, Hannspeter. "Mehr Zufall als Beifall: Frankokanadische Prosa in deutscher Übersetzung—Versuch einer Standortbestimmung." In Kuester and Wolff 2000, 64–79.

Riedel, Walter. *Das literarische Kanadabild: Eine Studie zur Rezeption kanadischer Literatur in deutscher Übersetzung*. Bonn: Bouvier, 1980.

———, ed. *Moderne Erzähler der Welt*. Tübingen: Erdmann, 1976.

Sabin, Stefana, ed. *Kanada erzählt: 17 Erzählungen*. Frankfurt: Fischer Taschenbuch Verlag, 1992.

Scharfschwerdt, Jürgen. *Literatur und Literaturwissenschaft in der DDR: Eine historisch-kritische Einführung*. Stuttgart: Kohlhammer, 1982.

Secci, Lia. "Von der realen zur romantischen Utopie: Zeitgenössische Entwicklungen in der Erzählprosa der DDR." In *Deutsche Literatur von Frauen. Zweiter Band, 19. und 20. Jahrhundert*, ed. Gisela Brinker-Gabler. Munich: Beck, 1988, 417–32.

Seehase, Georg, ed. *Englische Literatur im Überblick*. Leipzig: Reclam, 1986.
Uthe-Spencker, Angela, ed. and transl. *Stories from Canada / Erzählungen aus Kanada*. Ebenhausen: Langewiesche-Brandt, 1969.
Wicht, Wolfgang. "Entwicklung und Stand der anglistischen Literaturwissenschaft in der DDR." In *Dialog ohne Grenzen: Beiträge zum Bielefelder Kolloquium zur Lage von Linguistik und Literaturwissenschaft in der ehemaligen DDR*, ed. Jörg Drews and Christian Lehmann. Bielefeld: Aisthesis 1991, 90–105.
Wirzberger, Karl-Heinz. "20 Jahre Deutsche Demokratische Republik—17 Jahre *Zeitschrift für Anglistik und Amerikanistik*." ZAA 17 (1969): 341–43.
Zipser, Richard, ed. *Fragebogen Zensur: Die Literatur vor und nach dem Ende der DDR*. Leipzig: Reclam, 1995.

# Translating the Canadian Short Story into German

*Klaus Peter Müller*
*University of Mainz*

## INTRODUCTORY REMARKS

The translation and reception of Canadian literature in the German-speaking countries in the second half of the twentieth century demanded much tenacity and enthusiasm from all involved. As late as 1980, Walter Riedel stated that Canada was not yet regarded as an autonomous literary entity by German-speaking Europeans, and he still saw great lacunae in what had been translated into German by that time (14, 102, 104)—namely, hardly anything by writers such as Robertson Davies, E. J. Pratt, and Margaret Atwood. Riedel asserted that Canadian short stories offered the most comprehensive insight into Canadian narrative literature, an excellent mirror reflecting the nation's multiculturalism. German anthologies of short fiction by Canadians provided their readers with an image of Canada that he found fairly realistic and adequate (103). Twenty years later Astrid Holzamer (2000) at the Canadian Embassy in Berlin observed that Canadian writing was booming on bestseller lists in German-speaking countries and related this boom to both the literary quality of the texts and the enthusiasm of individual publishers. What is on offer in German translations today is still very selective, however, dependent on the publishers' specific interests, on the international popularity of the writers, and on what is considered marketable.

Marketing has become so important in the past forty years that the decision on a book's title, for example, is made not by its translator but by the publisher's marketing department. All of the many German translators whom I have spoken to simply take this approach for granted. Marketing is thus an important factor in deciding which Canadian short stories by which authors are selected for translation. I therefore take into account here not only the traditional sources used for an analysis of the reception and translation of literary texts—namely, scholarly books and articles as well as comments by translators and readers—but also statements by publishers and booksellers expressing their reasons for the publication of a book containing Canadian short stories. These statements and (implicit) marketing strategies are most easily accessible either directly in the books' blurbs or on the websites of publishers and booksellers. While paying attention to economic and marketing strategies in connection with literary and cultural factors for the translation of Canadian short stories into German, I base this chapter on six main reasons for translation that are most often put forward in regard to the selection of texts. These reasons reflect contemporary concerns and interests that are widely considered in Western cultures, especially in literary and cultural studies, but also in economics and marketing strategies. Marketing is concerned not only with selling a tangible object but also with "selling the invisible" (see Beckwith 1997), especially a sense of *identity* and *meaning*, which is always connected with a certain *style* and, in the postmodern consumer age, with the *packaging of pleasure*.[1] The six reasons for translation of certain texts provide the structure for this overview of Canadian short stories in German translation, explaining why certain Canadian short stories have made it into German and which authors and stories have most often been connected with which motivations for translation. Authors and stories not yet translated are also accounted for within this framework. Briefly listed, the main reasons for translations are (1) the exotic otherness of Canada, (2) ethnicity, (3) regionalism, (4) Canada as a contemporary (post)modern nation, (5) the authors' renown and popularity, and (6) the texts' literary qualities.

## 1. THE EXOTIC OTHERNESS OF CANADA

A traditional reason for many publishers' as well as readers' interest in Canadian texts is the supposedly exotic otherness of Canada, most typically the immense size of the country, its landscapes, its wildlife, its Aboriginal peoples, the North, et cetera. This is how W. H. New explains American interest in Canadian literature, and it holds true for German-speaking countries due to their "taste for romantic tale and provincial stereotype" (1987, 43). The stereotype of Canada as a wild, unsettled land of animals, adventurers, trappers, and Natives has attracted Europeans to Canada at least since the nineteenth century. This attraction becomes evident in almost all short-story collections in German, especially in Bartsch (1974) and Mowat (1977/1997) but also in Sabin (1992) and Herrmann (1993).[2]

---

1. The italicized words are from Alan Tomlinson's *Consumption, Identity, and Style: Marketing, Meanings, and the Packaging of Pleasure* (1997). Other useful sources revealing the links between marketing and cultural concerns are Baverstock (2000) and Greco (1997).
2. See Riedel (1980, 19–25) on the representation of Natives in translations, the realistic but also idealized portrayal of wildlife and the North, and the importance of the motif of survival in the "Canadian Experience" (103) for European readers.

This idea(l) of exotic otherness materializes whenever Canadian landscape and wildlife are portrayed, even in books that feature photographs with apparently descriptive texts, such as Patterson's *Kanada: Photo-Impressionen aus der letzten Wildnis* (1991). Exotic otherness can, of course, also be expressed in fictional narratives. In the twentieth century, German-speaking readers found it in the stories of Ernest Thompson Seton—in *Die schönsten Tiergeschichten* (1960), *Der Wolf von Winnipeg und andere Tiergeschichten* (1963, a selection from *Animal Heroes* [1905], which by 1914 was already into its fourteenth edition in German), and *Zottelohr und andere Geschichten* (1972). More than twenty books by Seton were available in translation between 1921 and 1985, all of them adventure stories about animals, the lives of hunters, Natives, or the harshness of nature.[3]

Charles G. D. Roberts was almost as successful as Seton in the same subgenre; he had eight story collections translated in the 1920s and again between 1950 and 1973. *Augen im Busch*, his best-known collection of animal stories, taken from *The House in the Water: A Book of Animal Stories* (1908), *Hoof and Claw* (1913), and *The Secret Trail* (1916), was first published in 1923 and re-edited in 1965.[4] Two of his stories appeared in story collections: "Das letzte Hindernis" ("The Last Barrier," 1958, in Arnold and Riedel 1967) and "Mütter des Nordens" ("Mothers of the North," 1911, in Friedrich and Riedel 1986).

Such stories continue to fascinate young readers in particular, and Ludmilla Zeman's *Die Rache der Ischtar* (2004; *The Revenge of Ishtar*, 1993) is a recent case in point. Exotic otherness is still extremely relevant in the promotion of Canada as a tourist destination and in texts on Canadian geography and natural scenery. And, happily, the endeavour to *understand* otherness, rather than simply being emotionally *affected* by it, has increased in recent years. The fact that there have been no new publications of work by Roberts and Seton since the 1970s thus becomes explicable: (1) the need for such stories has been satisfied, (2) otherness is now increasingly presented in media such as (documentary) film, and (3) the very concept of "otherness" has been deconstructed and reframed in terms of different ethnicities.

## 2. ETHNICITY

Readers of German translations of Canadian texts have always been strongly interested in the various ethnic groups living in Canada, intrigued by both Canada's

---

3. Riedel (1980, 136–38) gives a survey of these translations.
4. The other books with stories by Roberts in translation are *Jäger und Gejagte*, 1921 (*The Feet of the Furtive*, 1912); *Gestalten der Wildnis*, 1921 (*Babes of the Wild*, 1912); *Tiermütter*, 1926 (*The Kindred of the Wild*, 1902); *Die Burg im Grase*, 1927 (*Wisdom of the Wilderness*, 1922); *Elen, Wolf und Bär*, 1929 (*The Feet of the Furtive*, 1912); *Der gefleckte Fremdling*, 1965 (same sources as *Augen im Busch* and *Gestalten der Wildnis*); and *Der rote Fuchs*, 1973 (*Red Fox*, 1905).

multiculturalism and long history of immigration. They have wanted to find out how people from their own countries have fared in Canada. Kloss's *Ahornblätter* (1961), Hermann Böschenstein's *Unter Schweizern in Kanada: Kurzgeschichten* ("Among the Swiss in Canada: Short Stories," 1974), and Schaffer's *Der Turm* (1978) are books belonging to this context. A somewhat different example is the collection that Böschenstein edited in Toronto in 1980 for the German-Canadian Historical Association, *Heiteres und Satirisches aus der deutschkanadischen Literatur: John Adam Rittinger, Walter Roome, Ernst Loeb, Rolf Max Kully* ("Light Satiric Pieces from German Canadian Literature: John Adam Rittinger, Walter Roome, Ernst Loeb, Rolf Max Kully"). With introductions by the editor in German and English, the book was clearly intended for the Canadian market and readers, not for Europe. Georg Epp and Heinrich Wiebe edited a similar collection in 1977, locating it in the context of Canadian ethnic literature, where Canadianness is defined by ethnicity and ethnicity by the acceptance of one's country of origin.[5] Ethnicity has been highlighted for the past forty years, but it has been an issue much longer, as the story collections by Klassen (1939) and Friesen (1949) reveal, which are earlier examples of German texts published in Canada.[6] Hartmut Fröschle's collection *Nachrichten aus Ontario: Deutschsprachige Literatur in Kanada* ("News from Ontario: German-Language Literature in Canada," 1981), on the other hand, is a German publication with poetry, short fiction, and essays by writers living in Canada.

This diversity in the kinds of books published about ethnic groups speaking German is indicative of the many aspects of this topic. Two authors, one with a German, the other with an Austrian background, also belong to this context: Frederick Philip Grove and Henry Kreisel. Grove grew up in Hamburg as Felix Paul Greve and—after faking suicide and changing his name—applied for Canadian citizenship in 1920 while living in Manitoba. His work provides early examples of prairie realism, with short stories first published in a series in the Winnipeg *Tribune* in 1926–1927 and then selected in *Tales from the Margin* in 1971. Only two stories have been translated into German: "Wasser" ("Water," in Riedel 1976, from Grove's 1971 collection) and "Schnee" ("Snow," in Arnold and Riedel 1967 and in Bartsch 1974, first published in *Queen's Quarterly* in 1932). Both stories relate the harshness of life in Canada, the hostility of nature toward humans, and the latter's yielding to fate—ethnicity is only of secondary importance.

Henry Kreisel, born in Vienna, left Austria in 1938 after the *Anschluss* and eventually settled in Alberta. His influential essay "The Prairie: A State of Mind"

---

5. See Epp and Wiebe (1977, ix); for many other texts of German-speaking Canadians, see www.clcwebjournal.lib.purdue.edu/library/germancanadianliterature(bibliographie).html.
6. See also Riedel (1984) for this group.

(1968) claimed that writing is shaped by the physical aspects of a writer's milieu much more than by the country's literary tradition. Three of his stories were published in German: "Zwei Schwestern in Genf" ("Two Sisters in Geneva," in Arnold and Riedel 1967), "Der verbeulte Globus" ("The Broken Globe," 1965, in Riedel 1976), and "Chassidische Weise" ("Chassidic Song," 1978, in Friedrich and Riedel 1986). The texts reveal that the ethnic aspect, most evident in the "Chassidic Song," is of less interest than questions of exile, humanity, morality, human integrity, understanding, and love.

Canada's Indian ethnic group is exemplified by Rohinton Mistry, published in Germany as an Indian writer or a writer now living in Canada but still writing about India. Mistry's *Tales from Firozsha Baag* (1987) was translated as *Das Kaleidoskop des Lebens* (1999), well after the success of his novels.[7] The changed title indicates the German perspective: the tales provide a kaleidoscopic view of human existence. There are some elements with a specifically Indian aspect, such as being Parsi, but ethnicity is again only one part of a cluster of reasons essential for the marketing of the collection: the stories are meant to be interesting because they are (1) about life in general, (2) about life in India, and (3) about funny, peculiar incidents. Canada is not a relevant topic in this book.

Of the relatively large group of Canadian writers who immigrated from the Caribbean, almost none have been translated into German. Dionne Brand's story "Kein klarblauer Himmel, kein Zaun aus roten Blumen" ("No Rinsed Blue Sky, No Red Flower Fences," in Herrmann 1993, from Brand's collection *Sans Souci and Other Stories*, 1988) is the only translation of short fiction that I have found. Nothing from the short-story collections of Neil Bissoondath, *Digging Up the Mountains* (1985) and *On the Eve of Uncertain Tomorrows* (1990), has been translated. The same is true of Canadian short-story writers from other ethnic groups.[8]

The most important ethnic group in connection with the German-speaking book market is undoubtedly that of Canada's Aboriginal peoples. A strong demand for translations of works dealing with this group already existed in the

---

7. *Such a Long Journey* (1991), published as *So eine lange Reise: Ein Indien-Roman* (1994), and *A Fine Balance* (1995), *Das Gleichgewicht der Welt* (1998), show that novels are usually translated more quickly than short-story collections.

8. Moyez G. Vassanji, for instance, wrote *Uhuru Street* (1991), a collection of linked stories set in the Asian community of Dar es Salaam, depicting the changes in Uhuru Street from the sheltered innocence of colonial rule in the 1950s to the shattered world of the 1980s. Ven Begamudré, born in India, published two collections of short stories, *A Planet of Eccentrics* (1990) and *Laterna Magika: Stories* (1997), which also have not yet been translated. Kristjana Gunnars, a long-established writer with an Icelandic background, has had none of her collections translated in spite of the fact that *The Axe's Edge* (1983), for instance, is regarded as a pioneering work of short fiction.

nineteenth century and continued throughout the twentieth century. The history of these translations reveals that our contemporary awareness of ethnic identities is indeed fairly recent. It is illuminating, for example, that there were seven translations of Archibald Stansfeld Belaney, alias Grey Owl, available in German between 1937 and 1990 (six of them as books for children and adolescents), and four of his books are still in print: *Kleiner Bruder: Grau-Eule erzählt von Indianern, Bibern und Kanufahrern*, 2000 (*Pilgrims of the Wild*, 1934, first translated in 1935 and Belaney's best-known book); *Sajo und ihre Biber*, 1973 (*The Adventures of Sajo and Her Beaver People*, 1935, first translated in 1936); *Im Land der Nordwinde: Wäschakwonnesin erzählt*, 1990 (first edition), 2000 (fifth edition) (*The Book of Grey Owl: Selected Wildlife Stories*, 1938); and *Ihre Mokassins hinterließen keine Spuren: Grau-Eule erzählt, aufgeschrieben im Jahre 1930*, 1992 (first edition), 2002 (fifth edition) (*Tales of an Empty Cabin*, 1936). Belaney's interest in the lives of North America's Native peoples, his descriptions of animal behaviour and the wilderness, and his ecological concerns and appeals have evidently been shared and enjoyed by many German-speaking readers.

The publication of translations of genuine Native literature has increased since the 1980s, when Maria Campbell's *Halfbreed* (1973), with its focus on the lives of Native women, was published as *Cheechum's Enkelin: Autobiographie einer kanadischen Halbindianerin* (1983). These perspectives were also important in the translation of Minnie Aodla Freeman's *Life among the Qallunaat* (1978), published as *Tochter der Inuit* in 1980. Three books of Ojibway stories by Basil H. Johnston were published in the 1980s, and they were so successful that the first one achieved its fifth edition in 1994: *Und Manitu erschuf die Welt: Mythen und Visionen der Ojibwa*, 1979 (*Ojibway Heritage*, 1976); *Nanabusch und Großer Geist: Geschichten der Odschibwä-Indianer*, 1985 (*Tales the Elders Told*, 1981); and *Großer Weißer Falke: Der Lebenskreis eines Ojibwa*, 1987 (*Ojibway Ceremonies*, 1982). Johnston, called the "best Native short-story writer" of the 1960s and 1970s by Penny Petrone (1997, 11), thus received quite a bit of attention in German translation in the 1980s as well as a first complete translation in 1979, just three years after the original version had come out. His most popular book in Canada, *Moose Meat and Wild Rice* (1978), has not, however, been translated. Whether this is because it is a collection of twenty-two stories or because it chooses to portray reserve life and Native-white relations humorously is hard to tell. Perhaps publishers have found the difficulties of translating the jokes and oral speech patterns too challenging.

Currently, there are four other books by Canadian Natives in print in German, two of them short-story collections by women: Anne Cameron's *Töchter der Kupferfrau: Mythen der Nootka-Indianerinnen und andere Frauengeschichten*, 1993 (*Daughters of Copper Woman*, 1981), and Eden Robinson's *Fallen Stellen*, 2002

(*Traplines*, 1997), plus the novels by Thomas King, *Wenn Coyote Tanzt*, 2003 (*Green Grass, Running Water*, 1993), and Richard Wagamese, *Hüter der Trommel*, 1997 (*Keeper 'n Me*, 1994). Interestingly, all of these texts are advertised with emphasis on their Native content, although King's texts are as much imbued with postmodern paradigms that transcend cultural boundaries and identities. The marketing of the German versions of Robinson's stories is much more typical: they "represent the rougher, wilder Canada far away from its urban centres and at the same time reveal the problems of young people growing up and having to come to terms with the dark sides of life."[9] The advertisement thus combines exotic otherness with universal human experiences in the contemporary modern world and culturally specific, ethnic experiences with common human interests. Several of the criteria for publishing translations come together here, where otherness, ethnicity, and contemporaneity are linked. The literary quality of the texts by Aboriginal writers is still somewhat underrated, too little investigated, and accordingly not sufficiently advertised.

German short-story anthologies have often presented Indian and Inuit lives in stories written by non-Native writers: by Eric Cameron, "Der Wendepunkt" ("The Turning Point," 1966, in Arnold and Riedel 1967 and Bartsch 1974); Hugh Garner, "Ein, zwei, drei kleine Indianer" ("One, Two, Three Little Indians," 1952, in Arnold and Riedel 1967, Uthe-Spencker 1969, and Bartsch 1974); William Patrick Kinsella, "Von Geburt Indianer" (in El-Hassan 1992); and Emily Carr, "Sophie: Mutter der Gräber" ("Sophie," 1941, in Friedrich and Riedel 1986), and "Kitwancool" ("Kitwancool," 1941, in Herrmann 1993). But Walter Riedel's 1976 collection already included a story by Markoosie, "Die beiden Schwestern," and one by George Clutesi, "Ko-ishin-Mit und die Schattenwesen," in the category "Eskimo- und Indianer-Erzählungen" ("Eskimo and Indian Stories"). In 1986, Clutesi's "Ko-ishin-Mit und der Adler" was published by Friedrich and Riedel ("Ko-ishin-mit and Son of Eagle," from Clutesi's collection *Son of Raven, Son of Deer*, 1967). All translated Clutesi stories are from this book. Herrmann's book of texts by Canadian women (1993) continued this tradition and published Beth Brant's "Ein Todesfall in der Familie" (from Brant's collection *Food and Spirits*, 1991) and Lee Maracle's "Wer ist hier eigentlich politisch?" (from Maracle's collection *Sojourner's Truth and Other Stories*, 1990). While it took fifty-two years for the translation of Carr's story, fifteen years for the Garner story, twelve years for the Anne Cameron collection mentioned above, ten years for Eric Cameron's story, and nine and nineteen years for the Clutesi stories, it took only two and three years respectively for Brant's and Maracle's texts. Apparently, there is now

---

9. See www.amazon.de/exec/obidos/ASIN/3499232065/qld%3D1107766877/sr%3D1-2/ref%3Dsr%5F1%5F8%5F2/302-3861523-4497647 [consulted 22 February 2006].

a much greater awareness of the need to translate genuine Aboriginal voices, but there are still no translations of entire story collections by King, Maracle, or Brant, or of King's *All My Relations: An Anthology of Contemporary Native Writing* (1990), or of the significant secondary literature by Native critics/scholars, such as Jeannette Armstrong's *Looking at the Words of Our People: First Nations Analysis of Literature* (1993). We can only assume that the awareness of fundamental differences between Aboriginal and non-Aboriginal views on life that is widespread in academia is not necessarily shared with the general reading public in German-speaking countries.

General interest in the Inuit was slow to develop both in Canada and in Europe. German-speaking readers' fascination with the North was satisfied to a great extent by Farley Mowat, whose *Snow Walker* (1975) was quickly translated as *Inuit: Vom Mut der Eskimo* (1977) and has often been reprinted. Since the 1997 edition, the title has been *Der Schneewanderer,* and the term "Eskimo" has been replaced by "Inuit." Nevertheless, the word *Eskimo* is still often seen to be necessary to evoke German expectations of the North. Mowat's collections are advertised as giving voice to the Inuit directly or as passing on stories that they have related to Mowat.

Translations of "genuine" Inuit stories have also been published since the 1970s but in small numbers. Germaine Arnaktauyok Markoosie's "Die beiden Schwestern" ("Two Sisters," in Riedel 1976) came out only five years after the English text. Ashoona Pitseolak's biographical narrative, edited in English by Dorothy Harley Eber in 1971 as *Pitseolak: Pictures out of My Life,* was not available in German until 1993, when Herrmann translated at least some excerpts as "Das alte Leben" for their portrayal of the old traditions remembered by Pitseolak. While a number of representative story collections exist in English—Zebedee Nungak and Eugene Arima, *Eskimo Stories from Povungnituk, Québec* (1969), republished as *Inuit Stories: Povungnituk* (1988); Maurice Metayer's edition of *Tales from the Igloo* (1972); Anthony Apakark Thrasher's *Thrasher: Skid Row Eskimo* (1976); or any later collections of Inuit stories, such as Howard Norman's *Northern Tales: Traditional Stories of Eskimo and Indian Peoples* (1990)—only Metayer has been translated as *Geschichten der Eskimos* (1982). Nor has the establishment of Nunavut in 1999 had any significant effect on the number of Inuit texts translated into German. Publishers apparently assume that German-speaking readers are interested in traditional, idealized, idyllic representations of Aboriginal lives rather than in contemporary, realistic, critical, or humorous ones. Exotic otherness thus appears to be more important than ethnic or contemporary (post)modern aspects of the literary texts.[10]

---

10. This conclusion is corroborated not only by the translated short stories but also by the few novels available in German. Markoosie's *Die Harpune des Eskimos,* 1974 (*Harpoon of the Hunter,* 1970), is a typical example since it depicts an Inuit way of life that had already disappeared.

## 3. REGIONALISM

Regional aspects of Canadian texts are basic to the historical European interest in this aspect of literature, which has further increased since globalization. Margaret Laurence's work is as clearly related to a particular region as is Alistair MacLeod's, Alice Munro's, or even Margaret Atwood's. I will discuss these authors, however, in the section emphasizing Canadian writers of renown and popularity, and I have presented in the section above Aboriginal writers in whose work regional aspects are also of great importance. The section here shows that, while regionalism is an important topic in Canadian writing, and might spur valuable discussions in a European context, it has so far been rather neglected in German translation.

Regional identity has been a widely discussed topic in Canada in debates about the relationships between language, literature, and people's understanding of reality and themselves. Eli Mandel's *Another Time* (1977), stating that the environment is a literary construct of the mind, is as much about this subject as the often quoted book by Benedict Anderson, *Imagined Communities* (1983; see also Allen 1973). The discussions about regionalism in Canada are particularly interesting and relevant for German-speaking countries against the backdrop of an expanding European Union as well as that of globalization. A comparison of Canadian and European treatments of regionalism reveals intriguing similarities and incentives for the exchange of opinions and experiences.[11]

Two writers who deal with the importance of region are Sandra Birdsell and Bernice Morgan. Yet not one of Birdsell's story collections or novels has been translated into German so far. What is apparently missing here is what helped Morgan's *Topography of Love* (2000), in contrast, to get published as *Topographie der Liebe* in 2002: namely, that Morgan was already known as a writer of novels (*Am Ende des Meeres*, 1998 [*Waiting for Time*, 1994]) and that her stories could be promoted to present topics of common interest, such as love, family life, et cetera. Newfoundland is an additional asset for Morgan, being a strange, foreign, unknown region by the sea (and thus playing into the notion of exotic otherness). The book hardly reveals that it is a collection of stories. The advertisements on the cover and the blurbs remind possible buyers that they already know the author, who deals with topics of general human interest, and that Newfoundland provides a significant backdrop. Canada as such is of no significance in the advertisements or the stories.

There have been no translations of the numerous regional short-story anthologies, such as George Peabody's edition of *Best Maritime Short Stories* (1988);

---

11. Important Canadian authors in this context are Foley (1976); Melynk (1981); Tomblin (2004); and Young and Archer (2002). A European perspective is provided by Haseler (1996); Morley and Robins (2001); and Shields (1991).

Aritha van Herk's *Alberta Rebound: Thirty More Stories by Alberta Writers* (1990); Leah Flater, Aritha van Herk, and Rudy Wiebe's *West of Fiction* (1983); Carole Gerson's *Vancouver Short Stories* (1985); and Muriel Whitaker's *Stories from the Canadian North* (1980). Regionalism is clearly not the most important factor in the translation market, though it is often mentioned in connection with other criteria.

## 4. CANADA AS A CONTEMPORARY (POST)MODERN NATION

Canadian literature is often promoted as originating from a modern or postmodern nation significantly more similar to Europe than the United States, sharing European values of community, social security, and mutual responsibility. Numerous important questions are related to this aspect, such as whether Canada has been able to provide an alternative to Europe or the United States on political, social, and spiritual issues. Canada is frequently perceived as providing a balance between the extremes of Europe and the United States.

One key problem in the modern and postmodern context is how to define identity, whether personal, local, communal, or national. Canada's repeated questioning of such (fixed) identities makes Canadian texts particularly intriguing for European readers today. Germany, which had to redefine its identity after World War II, has more or less consciously become involved in this process again since unification in 1989, but like countries such as Austria it is also doing so in the context of an expanding European Union in which it is necessary for all member countries to redefine their positions in relation to their European neighbours and world markets. In this regard, Canada is very advanced in at least thinking about relevant questions if not in giving significant answers. For Europeans, it is urgent to ask "Where is here?" and "Who do you think you are?" For Canadians, these are familiar questions, representatively raised by Northrop Frye (1965) and Alice Munro (1978), with very different answers provided by Canadian writers.

Stories about gender roles and gender relations, life in families, in cities, in peer groups, et cetera, fit into this (post)modern context. Typical recent examples are the stories by Evelyn Lau, whose Chinese background is not important for the marketing of *Fetisch und andere Stories,* 1996 (*Fresh Girls and Other Stories,* 1993); what *is* important is the fact that the stories portray contemporary city life, sexuality, the violent world of prostitution, and the problems of outsiders with various addictions. Shaena Lambert's *Die fallende Frau: Kurzgeschichten,* 2003 (*The Falling Woman,* 2002), has also been promoted as a book about existential problems in life, such as love, the loss of friends, memories, and beginning one's life all over again. Martha Brooks's *Weiter ins Licht und andere Geschichten,* 2000 (*Travelling on into the Light and Other Stories,* 1994), is advertised as a collection of stories about the need to preserve good memories and to open oneself up to new experiences and new people.[12] These are all recent collections addressing a general public with an interest in typical contemporary situations and problems (earlier examples are the collections by renowned authors that I discuss in the next section). Birgit Herrmann's anthology *Frauen in Canada: Erzählungen und Gedichte* (1993) also explicitly aims to present the views, opinions, and experiences of Canadian women to the German-speaking public.

Another example of the (post)modern appeal is Yann Martel's *Aller Irrsinn dieses Seins: Vier Erzählungen* (*The Facts behind the Helsinki Roccamatios*, 1993), published by Verlag and Welt, Berlin, in 1994 and dealing with contemporary problems such as AIDS as well as the universal difficulty of coping with death, pain, and suffering. The Frankfurt publisher Fischer brought out another translation of Martel's collection in 2005, both in print and on CD, *Die Hintergründe zu den Helsinki Roccamatios*. The two translations thus have significantly different titles, the first one apparently expressing the folly of human existence, and the second promising information on a specific problem about which readers know nothing. The information is then provided in the title story on AIDS. Both titles make perfect sense in relation to the title story, but the older title is more comprehensive and includes a reference to the other stories too. It thus has more immediate appeal to readers, which advertisements for the later publication attempt to create with references to AIDS and related topics.

An example of a thematic German anthology of Canadian short stories is Gottfried Friedrich and Walter Riedel's *Gute Wanderschaft, mein Bruder*, published in 1986 by St. Benno, a Christian publisher in Leipzig, that is in the former GDR. The book focuses on the religious contexts of Canadian short stories and takes its title from Farley Mowat's story "Walk Well, My Brother" (from *The Snow Walker*, 1975). Morley Callaghan, "the father of the modern Anglo-Canadian short story" (Bartsch 1974, 397), who has had five stories published in five different German anthologies, is included here with "Der junge Priester," 1986 ("The Young Priest"), from *Morley Callaghan's Stories* (1959), which provides the religious backdrop required in this collection.[13] Friedrich and Riedel's anthology is typical of a phenomenon evident in other collections: the stories selected for anthologies in German are usually different from those found in Canadian

---

12. A typical example of such presentations and descriptions of translated short stories can be found at www.amazon.de/exec/obidos/ASIN/378769708X/qid=1110791591/sr=1-2/ref=sr_1_10_2/302-3861523-4497647 [consulted 24 January 2005].

13. The other stories by Morley Callaghan published in German are "Im letzten Frühling kamen sie herüber" ("Last Spring They Came Over," 1929), in Uthe-Spencker (1969); "Ein Krankenbesuch" ("A Sick Call," 1959), in Bartsch (1974); and "Zwei Männer Angeln" ("The Two Fishermen," 1959), in Sabin (1992), also translated as "Die beiden Angler," in Riedel (1976).

collections. This variance is due to the often rather specific purposes of such collections in translation and to the great number of stories from which editors can choose. Friedrich and Riedel selected Callaghan specifically for the Christian humanism that offers answers to the problems of human beings in the modern world.

Sinclair Ross is another writer of stories about modern life that are included in Friedrich and Riedel (1986) and in four other collections: "Die Lampe am Mittag," 1968 ("The Lamp at Noon," 1938), in Arnold and Riedel (1967) and in Bartsch (1974); "Die frisch gestrichene Tür," 1968 ("The Painted Door," 1939), in Riedel (1976) and Sabin (1992); and "Ein Kornett in der Nacht" ("Cornet at Night," 1968), in Friedrich and Riedel (1986). Ross is one of the first modernists in Canadian fiction, but this is not the main reason why he has been translated into German. Instead, his appeal probably stems from his realistic depiction of people's struggle for survival and a decent life in oppressive rural and urban areas, in particular in the Prairies during the Depression. His characters show an endurance grounded in hope and faith, which is why "Ein Kornett in der Nacht" fits well into Friedrich and Riedel's religiously motivated anthology.

Rudy Wiebe is included in the same collection as a writer with a strong moral vision deriving from his Mennonite background. He describes the loss of community, the alienation of the individual in a world of disintegrating and conflicting cultures, and the dire need for (Christian) values such as charity, mutual respect, and freedom. Only two stories by Wiebe have been translated: "Die rätselhafte Stimme" ("Where Is the Voice Coming From?" 1974), in Riedel (1976), and "Der Engel des Teersandes" ("The Angel of the Tar Sands," 1979), in Friedrich and Riedel (1986).[14] One reason for this reluctance undoubtedly lies in the fact that his fiction is experimental in style and form. Another may be that the various forms of Christian action and commitment, of people struggling for a moral and spiritual life in his works, may be regarded as obsolete and not appropriate for a postmodern society. Certainly, there are a host of other excellent stories and novels by Wiebe waiting to be translated.

Of the many other Canadian writers translated into German who could be mentioned here for their depiction of contemporary life, I have chosen five to represent the diversity and the great time span that they cover. Isabella Valancy Crawford has had just one of her stories translated, "Ausgeliefert" ("Extradited," *The Globe*, 1886), in Herrmann (1993). She was selected to convey the voice of a female writer from the end of the nineteenth century, and for that purpose

---

14. Only fairly recently have two of Wiebe's novels been translated, *Land jenseits der Stimmen*, 2001 (*A Discovery of Strangers*, 1994), and *Wie Pappeln im Wind*, 2004 (*The Blue Mountains of China*, 1970).

Herrmann picked Crawford's best-known and most often anthologized story from Rosemary Sullivan's *Stories by Canadian Women* (1984).

Stephen Leacock has had two stories translated into German, "Das fürchterliche Schicksal des Melpomenus Jones" ("The Awful Fate of Melpomenus Jones," 1910), in Arnold and Riedel (1967), and "Die Wasserfahrt der Pythia-Ritter" ("The Marine Excursion of the Knights of Pythias," 1912), in Uthe-Spencker (1969). His complete *Literary Lapses: A Book of Sketches* (1910) and *Sunshine Sketches of a Little Town* (1912), from which these stories are taken, still await translation. Four of Leacock's story collections have been published in German, though: *Die Abenteuer der armen Reichen*, 1925 and 1955 (*Arcadian Adventures with the Idle Rich*, 1914); *Der Asbestmann und andere Nonsens-Novellen*, 1982 (*Nonsense Novels*, 1911); *Die liebreizende Winnie: Neue Nonsens-Novellen*, 1988 (*Winsome Winnie and Other New Nonsense Novels*, 1920); and *Die Hohenzollern in Amerika und andere Satiren*, 1989 (*The Hohenzollerns in America: With the Bolsheviks in Berlin and Other Impossibilities*, 1919). All of these books contain funny stories, anecdotes, humorous reflections, and essays on a wide variety of topics. Not only are they entertaining texts, but they also present a view of an agricultural, partly idyllic community slowly being transformed into a modern, indifferent, or hostile world. The texts parody, ridicule, and criticize this development. Apart from their humorous tone, Leacock's stories are intriguing for European readers since they portray Canada and the United States in the process of being encroached upon by modernity at the end of the nineteenth century and the beginning of the twentieth century.

Currently, however, none of these books is in print in German. Publishers evidently do not expect their readers to be intrigued by early modern Canada. That is why there are no translations available of stories by either Thomas Chandler Haliburton or Duncan Campbell Scott. Haliburton's *Sam Slicks Reden und Thun* was published in 1841 (*The Clockmaker: Or, The Sayings and Doings of Samuel Slick, of Slickville*, 1837) but never since, and "Jim Munroes Werbung" (in Arnold and Riedel 1967) is the only story by Haliburton that has been translated. Scott's *In the Village of Viger* (1896), a collection of interrelated tales of life in a quiet village near Montreal, has never been translated, only the story "Labries Frau" ("Labrie's Wife," 1923), in Arnold and Riedel (1967). Arnold and Riedel's interest in earlier Canadian short stories has been out of fashion for so long that a reversal is long overdue, but marketing has clearly emphasized contemporary perspectives over historical ones.

William Dempsey Valgardson has an Icelandic background, and his stories are concerned with people's endless struggles with an unrelenting, overwhelming environment or a hostile society. They have presumably been translated and read mainly for this perspective on contemporary modern life. His characters usually find themselves in a situation where their mental and moral integrity is tested. Human failure is the result when people do not recognize their proper place in the community, when they are either too selfish or too conformist. Four of his stories have been translated: "Schnee," in Riedel (1976); "Gleichgewicht" ("A Matter of Balance," 1982), in El-Hassan and Militz (1986); "Gott ist kein Fischereiinspektor" ("God Is Not a Fish Inspector," 1975), in Friedrich and Riedel (1986); and "Gelegenheitskauf im Dezember," in El-Hassan (1992), from his collection *Red Dust* (1978). The inclusion of "Gott ist kein Fischereiinspektor" in Friedrich and Riedel's anthology was probably motivated by the story's depiction of people playing God in order to gain power over others. Above all, the story advocates a belief in oneself and thus demonstrates the typically modern need for human beings to give meaning to their own lives rather than to expect it from others or from God. Valgardson's collection of short stories, *What Can't Be Changed Shouldn't Be Mourned* (1990), continues in the same vein; it has not yet been translated into German, nor has any of his earlier collections or his novels.

## 5. THE RENOWN AND POPULARITY OF AUTHORS

The fifth and most evident explanation for translations is the renown and popularity of an author. With regard to Riedel's complaint in 1980 that there were hardly any books available in translation by Robertson Davies, E. J. Pratt, and Margaret Atwood, let alone less-well-known writers, there have been considerable changes indeed. All of Atwood's novels have been translated,[15] as have most of her short stories and even some of her poetry. Atwood was actually the first Canadian writer to have a contract with a German publisher, offered to her by Arnulf Conradi for Claassen in 1978–1979. Alice Munro followed in 1981, when Klett-Cotta in Stuttgart published *Das Bettlermädchen* (*The Beggar Maid*, 1980) (*Who Do You Think You Are?* 1978).

Even Atwood became profitable for her publisher only in the late 1980s and early 1990s (Holzamer 2000, 18). Currently, twelve Atwood novels plus six collections of stories are in print. But it was only after the successful publication of the earlier novels that Atwood's short stories appeared: *Die Giftmischer: Horror-Trips und Happy-Ends*, 1985 (*Murder in the Dark*, 1983), and *Unter Glas: Erzählungen*, first published by Claassen in 1986, then in a paperback edition by Fischer in 1988 (*Dancing Girls and Other Stories*, 1977). Both of these collections were republished by Berlin Verlag in 2000 and 2001 and are still in print. The third short-story collection translated was *Tips für die Wildnis*, first published by Fischer in the same year as the English version *Wilderness Tips* (1991) and republished by Berlin Verlag

---

15. See the article by Stefan Ferguson in this volume.

in 2003. *Der Salzgarten,* published by Fischer in 1994 (*Bluebeard's Egg,* 1983), was republished by Berlin Verlag in 2001 and is also still in print. *Gute Knochen* (1995) is the fifth collection of short stories by Atwood, published three years after the English version, *Good Bones.* This edition has been out of print in recent years, but it is due to be reprinted in 2007. The sixth collection is *Das Zelt,* published by Berlin Verlag in 2006, the year of the English publication, *The Tent.* The gaps between original and translated publications thus decreased considerably in the 1990s, but to have a short-story collection published in translation in the same year as the original text remains very unlikely in contrast to translation policies regarding successful novels. If there is an exception to this rule, it is usually Atwood, and the translation of her most recent story collection, *Moral Disorder* (2006), can be expected before long.

The number of books by Atwood published in German is rather unique for any writer, and this is particularly true with regard to her short-story collections. Since so many of them have been translated, single stories by Atwood have been published only three times in the collections investigated here: "Wenn es passiert" ("When It Happens," from *Dancing Girls,* 1977), in El-Hassan and Militz (1986); "Unter Glas" ("Under Glass," from *Dancing Girls,* 1977), in Sabin (1992); and "Happy-Ends" ("Happy-Ends," from *Murder in the Dark,* 1983), in Herrmann (1993). A few statements must suffice to show how her stories have been presented to the German-speaking public. Atwood is usually described by reviewers and critics as one of the best contemporary writers, she deals with topics of general interest, and her success as a novelist is regularly mentioned. *Unter Glas,* for example, is said to be a collection of stories dealing with the lives of women, revealing how thin the layer of normality is and how easily life is threatened by unexpected catastrophes. *Der Salzgarten* is presented as full of strange characters and situations that are portrayed with much wit, irony, and creative originality in stories about first love and fragile relationships. With regard to *Gute Knochen,* critics point out the irony and subversive rewritings of Hamlet's mother or Bram Stoker's Dracula. The metafictional quality of this collection of short fiction and prose poems is probably the main reason why it has been out of print. Atwood is generally marketed as a writer dealing with contemporary issues, especially life in (post)modern cities, gender roles, and relationships. These elements of her stories are usually highlighted, linked with her popularity and the literary qualities of her writing.

Of the big names in Canadian short-story writing, Margaret Laurence was one of the first to have a complete collection translated into German, *Die Stimmen von Adamo: 10 Erzählungen,* 1969 (*The Tomorrow-Tamer,* 1963), an anthology of her African short stories published in Canadian journals between 1957 and 1962, dealing with people in Ghana and the relationship between Europe and Africa and Canada. Laurence's reputation in Germany was so great that Herrmann in 1993 still called Laurence "Canada's most popular and most renowned writer". It had nevertheless taken twenty-two years before her short-story cycle, *A Bird in the House* (1970), was translated as *Ein Vogel im Haus: Eine Kindheit in der kanadischen Prärie* (1992), a (sub)title that emphasizes the Canadian context. Only four other stories have been translated, namely "Die Seetaucher" ("The Loons," 1970), in Bartsch (1974); "Ein Vogel im Haus" ("A Bird in the House," 1970), in Riedel (1976); "Der Weltentrommler" ("The Drummer of All the World," 1963), in Friedrich and Riedel (1986); and "Pferde der Nacht" (from *A Bird in the House*, 1970), in El-Hassan (1992). "Die Stätte des Unrats," in Herrmann (1993), is not a story but an excerpt from the second chapter, "The Nuisance Grounds," of her novel *The Diviners* (1974), which, although it won the Governor General's Literary Award, has not yet been completely translated into German.

Other writers with a strong reputation for short stories have received similar treatment. Norman Levine, for instance, has had three of his collections translated, *Ein kleines Stückchen Blau: Erzählungen*, 1971 (selections from *One Way Ticket: I Don't Want to Know Anyone Well*, 1961); *Der Mann mit dem Notizbuch: Erzählungen*, first edition in 1975, a second, enlarged edition in 1979 (*I Don't Know Anyone Too Well, and Other Stories*, 1971); and *Django, Karfunkelstein & Rosen: Erzählungen*, 1987 (*Django, Karfunkelstein, and Roses,* 1971); plus two stories, "Ein kleines Stückchen Blau" ("A Small Piece of Blue," from *One Way Ticket*, 1961), in Bartsch (1974), and "Eine kanadische Jugend" (from *Canada Made Me*, 1958), in Sabin (1992); as well as his autobiographical *Canada Made Me*, which was literally translated as *Kanada hat mich gemacht* in 1967. The fact that Annemarie and Heinrich Böll, the 1972 winner of the Nobel Prize for Literature, translated Levine's stories in the 1960s and 1970s certainly helped Levine on the German-speaking market.

William Patrick Kinsella has had only two of his many stories published in translation, "Spaßvogel" ("Jokemaker," 1986), in El-Hassan and Militz (1986), and "Von Geburt Indianer" ("Born Indian," 1981), in El-Hassan (1992). Of his several short-story collections, none has been translated. The same applies to Jack Hodgins, Leon Rooke, William Dempsey Valgardson, and Rudy Wiebe, who have had only a few individual stories translated. Timothy Findley is another well-known author without a collection of short stories translated into German. He has had, however, four novels translated, as well as the title story of his collection *Dinner along the Amazon* (1984), "Dinner entlang des Amazonas" (in El-Hassan 1992). The situation is similar for Hugh Hood, who has had one story ("Flying a Red Kite," 1962) translated twice by two different translators, first as "Der rote Drachen" (in Bartsch 1974) and again as "Einen roten Drachen steigen lassen" (in El-Hassan 1992)—that is, twelve and thirty years respectively after it appeared in English. Writers who have fared much the same are Michael Ondaatje with "Tanten" (in Sabin 1992), which is not really a story but a section from his autobiographical book *Running in the Family* (1982); Mordecai Richler with "Wasser auf Mervyns Mühle" ("Some Grist for Mervyn's Mill," 1962), in Bartsch (1974) and Sabin (1992) and "Bambinger" ("Bambinger" from his autobiographical sketches *The Street*, 1969), in Riedel (1976); and Guy Vanderhaeghe's story "Schlagzeuger" ("Drummer"), in El-Hassan (1992), from his collection *Man Descending* (1982), which won a Governor General's Literary Award. These writers thus have not been able to make an impression on the German market unless they have also had some novels translated. Richler, for example, is rather well known to German-speaking readers, as seven of his novels have been published in German.[16] It is a safe assumption that Richler was included in the three story collections in German because of his status as a well-known novelist.

Mavis Gallant is a writer with a unique position in Canadian writing since she left Canada to live in Europe in 1950 and began publishing in *The New Yorker* in 1951. Of her two novels and twelve collections of short fiction, one novel has been translated, *Grünes Wasser, grüner Himmel*, 1997 (*Green Water, Green Sky*, 1959), and three story collections have been published in German: *Späte Heimkehr: Eine Novelle und acht Erzählungen*, 1989 (*From the Fifteenth District*, 1979); *Blockstelle Pegnitz*, 1991 (*The Pegnitz Junction*, 1978); and *Die Lage der Dinge*, 1996 (*Across the Bridge*, 1993). It thus took thirty-eight, ten, thirteen, and three years respectively for these translations to appear, making Gallant a rare case in which short-story collections were translated before any novel. In 1998, Hans Magnus Enzensberger edited *Transitgäste: Erzählungen* as his personal tribute to Gallant, spurred by the publication of her *Collected Stories* (1996), which have not yet been translated into German.

Gallant's texts have clearly been translated for their connections with German and European history; they could thus also be discussed in sections two and four of this chapter. The collections are advertised as presenting a whole range of human lives in the twentieth century, centring on the experience of exile, and delivering chronicles of European existence from the 1930s to the present, which reveal the psychological aspects of European catastrophes: Mussolini's Italy, the

---

16. The novels are *Die Akrobaten*, 1955 (*The Acrobats*, 1954); *Der Boden trägt mich nicht mehr*, 1958 (*A Choice of Enemies*, 1957); *Sohn eines kleineren Helden*, 1963 (*Son of a Smaller Hero*, 1955); *Joshua damals und jetzt*, 1981 (*Joshua Then and Now*, 1980); *Der Traum des Jakob Hersch*, 1981 (*St. Urbain's Horseman*, 1971); *Solomon Gursky war hier*, 1992 (*Solomon Gursky Was Here*, 1989); and *Wie Barney es sieht*, 2000 (*Barney's Version*, 1998).

German occupation, Spain under Franco, the Cold War and its consequences. The stories are read as offering a "picture of postwar Germany," where "the individual is on trial" and where "multiple voices evoke various cultural issues ... so that the perspectives from which German society and history are considered are diversified." Others inform readers that Gallant explicitly wants to understand "why and how German fascism started ..., for 'there was hardly a culture or civilization [that she] would have placed as high as the German'" (Schaub 1994, 435). Gallant's stories deal not with big events but with their (devastating) consequences, whose symptoms are often hardly noticeable and know no remedy. Canada does not play a significant role in any of these collections. It is thus quite appropriate that the cover of *Transitgäste* shows Frankfurt's central station in 1959. Gallant has been translated as a Canadian living in Paris and writing about human problems in the modern world, especially in war-ridden Europe. This is repeatedly stated as the most important reason for the translations of her stories and for her readers' strong responses to them.

Significantly, Gallant's collection of purely Canadian stories, *Home Truths* (1981), has not been translated into German, even though it won a Governor General's Literary Award, and her stories in German collections are, for the same reason, usually not the ones found in Canadian anthologies. Herrmann (1993), however, consciously selected a story from *Home Truths* for her edition featuring stories on and by women in Canada, "Der Waisenkinder Reise" ("Orphans' Progress"), first published in *The New Yorker* in 1965. There are only two other stories by Gallant in German collections: "Bernadette," in Bartsch (1974), and "Aus dem fünfzehnten Bezirk" ("From the Fifteenth District," 1979), in Sabin (1992). This shortage is due to the fact that her stories—like Atwood's—are already published and well known and are too expensive for other publishers because of their author's renown and popularity.

Alice Munro's fate in the German-language book market is again different from that of Gallant or Atwood. Apart from the generalizations that can be and have been made, every author with translations into German needs to be seen individually. International renown, for example, is in itself not always sufficient, although one can repeatedly see that short stories are also translated once an author has published one or more successful novels. Other aspects, however, are often equally important, as is clearly the case with Munro. Her first collection of short stories in Canada, *Dance of the Happy Shades* (1968), won the Governor General's Literary Award but was not a commercial success. This changed in 1971 with *Lives of Girls and Women*. *Dance* has never been translated into German; *Lives,* however, came out in 1983 as *Kleine Aussichten: Ein Roman von Mädchen und Frauen* and in 1988 as a paperback. The subtitle is clearly meant to address female readers, though the back cover points out that the book is also worth reading by boys and men. Yet this is a novel (or a short-story cycle) about a girl growing up and the difficulties of becoming a woman. The Canadian setting is of no great importance; the main reason for the book's translation is again related to the fact that this is a text about contemporary problems of vital interest to many readers. The writer's popularity and the literary qualities of Munro's works are additional reasons for the publisher's and readers' fascination.

Munro's first book translated into German was the short-story collection *Das Bettlermädchen*, 1981 (*Who Do You Think You Are?*, 1978). The British edition, *The Beggar Maid*, was nominated for the Booker Prize in 1980, and the Canadian edition received the Governor General's Literary Award. The latter fact is mentioned on the cover of the German edition, which advertises the stories as being about everyday life and common situations as well as universal experiences (thus addressing the same aspects as in the later translation). The advertisement also points out the wit, excellent style, and narrative faculties of the author. The German blurb mentions that Munro is a Canadian writer living in and writing about Ontario, but in contrast to the English and Canadian editions it does not state that the setting is rural Ontario. The book was republished as a paperback in 2003 by Berlin Verlag as *Das Bettlermädchen: Geschichten von Flo und Rose*, emphasizing its focus on women's experiences.

Since that first edition in 1981, there has been a steady flow of Munro translations, all of them published in hardcover and paperback editions by Klett-Cotta and Fischer: *Die Jupitermonde*, 1986, republished in 1999 and 2002 (*The Moons of Jupiter*, 1982), and *Der Mond über der Eisbahn: Liebesgeschichten*, 1989 (*The Progress of Love*, 1985). The latter book is advertised as dealing with the universal topic of love, which, as the blurb puts it, is presented in this collection with much sensitivity and narrative artistry. The fact that the collection received the Governor General's Literary Award is mentioned too; there is also a reference to the Canadian landscape, which is said to provide the backdrop to all of Munro's stories.

*Friend of My Youth* (1990) was published as *Glaubst Du, es war Liebe?* in 1991 (republished in 2005), *Open Secrets* (1994) as *Offene Geheimnisse* (1996). *The Love of a Good Woman* (1998) was published in two separate editions, each containing four of the original eight stories: *Die Liebe einer Frau: Drei Erzählungen und ein kurzer Roman* (2000, paperback edition 2004) and *Der Traum meiner Mutter: Erzählungen* (2002, paperback edition 2005). *Hateship, Friendship, Courtship, Loveship, Marriage* (2001) was translated as *Himmel und Hölle* in 2004. In 2006, Munro equalled Atwood in having her collection *Runaway* translated in the same year as *Tricks: Acht Erzählungen* by Fischer. The stories that she has developed out of her Scottish family history, *The View from Castle Rock,* published in the same year, will surely also be translated soon into German. The titles of these translations reiterate what has been said before and what is prominent in the marketing of Munro's collections: the topics and contents of the books are highlighted, predominantly love, human relationships, and women's lives in contemporary times, where human beings aspire to reach heaven but often create hell. This is what the title *Himmel und Hölle* suggests, where the long Canadian title has been changed into three words connoting everyday experiences in extreme forms. *Tricks* serves the same function and suggests stories about how human beings can survive the difficulties of everyday life.

Munro's *Selected Stories* (1996) has not been translated into German. Instead, Berlin Verlag published an *Alice Munro Lesebox* ("Alice Munro Reading Box") in 2005, which contains three volumes already published in the 1980s, namely *Das Bettlermädchen: Geschichten von Flo und Rose* (1981, reprinted 2003), *Die Jupitermonde* (1986, reprinted 2002), and *Der Mond über der Eisbahn: Liebesgeschichten* (1989, reprinted 2001). Since Munro is so successful with her short-story collections in German, hardly any single stories have been published in anthologies or elsewhere. "Jungen und Mädchen" ("Boys and Girls" from *Dance of the Happy Shades,* 1968), in Bartsch (1974), "Was glaubst du, wer du bist?" ("Who Do You Think You Are?," 1978), in Sabin (1992), and "Wilde Schwäne" ("Wild Swans" from *Who Do You Think You Are?*, 1978), in Herrmann (1993) are the exceptions.

Alistair MacLeod belongs to that large group of Canadian writers whose short stories are translated only after the authors have become known as novelists. His novel *No Great Mischief* (1999) was published in German as *Land der Bäume* by Fischer in 2002. A year later the same publisher brought out *Die Insel: Erzählungen,* the translation of *Island: Collected Stories* (2000). The German collection contains the same sixteen stories as the Canadian book and preserves its chronological order but does not mention that these stories were first published in *The Lost Salt Gift of Blood* (1976) and *As Birds Bring Forth the Sun* (1986). The blurb speaks of these texts as stories about life on Canada's Atlantic coast, about people struggling with rough weather, their own feelings, memories of the past, loneliness, and hopeless love. Advertisements and reviews emphasize the roughness of the landscape and the Celtic past of immigrants from Scotland and Ireland, a past that lives on in the people of this region. MacLeod's collection is an excellent example of the diversity of explanations put forward for translations of Canadian stories: his texts are meant to satisfy readers' interest in unknown regions of Canada, in foreign cultures, but it is equally claimed that they portray typical human experiences, deal with essential questions and problems of human life, such as the redefinition of one's identity after emigration, after the loss of one's work, or simply after leaving home. The ethnic element is mentioned in connection with the Celtic past in the stories, but much more important is the regional aspect of the stories, their setting in Cape Breton. The German edition compares MacLeod with Hemingway and quotes Michael Ondaatje, who puts MacLeod on a par with Faulkner and Chekhov.

Before the publication of *Die Insel: Erzählungen,* only "Das Boot" ("The Boat," from *The Lost Salt Gift of Blood,* 1976), had appeared in German, in El-Hassan (1992). The first German publisher to print one of MacLeod's stories, "The Return," also from *The Lost Salt Gift of Blood,* was Reclam in 1990; however, the story appeared in English as part of the anthology *Contemporary Canadian Short Stories* (see Müller 1990). The market for German translations of Canadian short stories is still very volatile—any author can potentially be a success or a failure, and even a highly reputed writer does not guarantee sufficient sales, as the market is evidently not strongly influenced by aesthetic concerns.

## 6. LITERARY QUALITIES

This motivation for translation is connected with established and well-known writers and is usually put forward to support the other reasons mentioned so far. In fact, it does not seem to be possible to advertise a book merely for its literary qualities. Of the short-story anthologies published in German, only El-Hassan's 1992 collection emphasizes the literary achievements in Canadian short stories as their main asset. The blurb rightly denies that short stories are a minor genre demanding fewer skills than a novel. The text was probably written by the editor, an expert, and the publication was a clear indication that the Canadian short story had firmly established itself as a remarkable literary genre. But the book was not very successful, and it must be assumed that the expert assessment of the quality of Canadian short stories has not yet been acknowledged by the book-buying public. Individual writers and their literary abilities have been accepted, of course, but their appeal still derives from novels rather than short stories and much more from the topics dealt with than from aesthetic qualities.

Two Canadian writers, whose work has been translated into German since the 1990s, provide typical examples of how the literary quality of narrative (short) fiction is advertised: Barbara Gowdy and Diane Schoemperlen. Gowdy is published in German by Kunstmann, Munich. It started with a novel in 1992, *Fallende Engel* (*Falling Angels,* 1989), from which Margaret Atwood selected one chapter, the story "Disneyland," for the *Best American Short Stories 1989.* That story has not yet been published in an anthology in German. But in 1993, Kunstmann brought out *Seltsam wie die Liebe* (*We So Seldom Look on Love: Stories,* 1992), translated with the support of the Canada Council for the Arts and promoted as a book of stories about a fascinating world of obsessions and monstrosities, intriguingly and humorously presented by a witty and entertaining narrator. The collection was successful enough to require a second edition only a year later. The promotion of Gowdy's novel *Der weiße Knochen*, 2002 (*The White Bone*, 1998), is very similar: it tells potential buyers that if they enjoy fantasy and marvellously narrated stories they should buy this book.[17] The literary qualities of the short-story collection as well as of the novel are thus always connected with the subject matter and the kinds of narrative that the books offer. These are the elements that count; Canada is of no importance at all, and literary values are reduced to stories that are "marvellously narrated."

Diane Schoemperlen's *Formen der Zuneigung: Geschichten und Bilder*, 1999 (*Forms of Devotion: Stories and Pictures*, 1998) is one of the rare cases in which a short-story collection appears as the first book in German by a Canadian writer. It is explicitly advertised as a book for bibliophiles, with precious and curious old wood and copper engravings and witty, playful texts about love and other human concerns. The fact that this collection won the Governor General's Literary Award is also mentioned, and Schoemperlen is presented as one of the most intriguing new Canadian writers. If there is anything exotic in these stories, it is connected with the strangeness and marvels of human life, not with a particular region, ethnic group, or nation. This collection, like Gowdy's, is thus linked with the fourth motivation for producing translations: it is a book about contemporary life. Schoemperlen's collected stories, *Red Plaid Shirt* (2002), have not yet appeared in German, however, and only one novel, *In der Sprache der Liebe*, 2000 (*In the Language of Love*, 1996), has been translated. The translations of these books by Gowdy and Schoemperlen have thus clearly been spurred by their marketable aspects, especially their dealing with love, and their literary quality. Single stories in German translation have not yet been published by either of the two writers.

## CONCLUDING REMARKS

It has become evident that there are usually several reasons involved when a Canadian story is translated into German, and literary quality is only a minor incentive in this context. This is not really surprising since aesthetic and literary perspectives have always been thought to interest primarily specialists, whereas publishing houses need more arguments to sell a book to the public. Of the six motivations for translation presented here, the most important one is clearly the focus on contemporary life, which caters to the experiences, questions, problems,

---

17. See www.amazon.de/exec/obidos/ASIN/3898308642/qid=1110573671/sr=1-1/ref=sr_1_10_1/302-3861523-4497647 [consulted 22 February 2005].

and interests of the readers. Canada and its present-day authors are regarded as dealing with relevant and intriguing topics in the modern, postmodern, and postindustrial world and perhaps as offering alternatives to European and American experiences and models. This strong concern with contemporary issues is also responsible for the lack of interest in nineteenth-century and early-twentieth-century stories. The recent collections by Gowdy and Schoemperlen reveal another aspect of this context: namely, that Canada as such is no longer an important issue. This is clearly a result of both postmodernism and globalization, where national aspects are less significant than the problem of defining one's identity in either international or local and communal terms.

Interest in Canadian First Nations is the second most important stimulant, affecting both publishers' and readers' selections of Canadian texts from the wide range of books available. It is the oldest reason and still valid in many cases, especially due to the Canadian landscape, its wildlife, and its Aboriginal peoples. The shortage of stories by Aboriginal writers in translation—especially of those portraying critical views of their lives rather than idyllic, heroic, and tragic notions of the cultural outsider—is regrettable.

Another gap is connected with ethnicity and the lack of translations of stories by immigrants to Canada. This perspective could provide Europeans with views on ethnic groups that offer foils for contrasts and comparisons with similar phenomena in Europe. The shortage of translations of "regional" works might diminish when this perspective is more widely acknowledged in Europe and not linked only with Canadian exoticism.

Authors' celebrity has always been and will remain one of the most important assets for translations. But international renown is clearly not sufficient on its own, which again shows how various interconnected motivations are necessary for translating a Canadian book into German.

A further surprising gap is the fact that there have been no translations into German of the best short-story anthologies, such as Atwood and Weaver's *Oxford Book of Canadian Short Stories* (1986), their *New Oxford Book of Canadian Short Stories* (1995), or Ondaatje's edition of *The Faber Book of Contemporary Canadian Short Stories* (1990). Three reasons have evidently prevented publishers from offering such translations: (1) money—it is probably less expensive to publish one's own collection of short stories, (2) the market—it is useful to assemble texts for a specific purpose/public, and (3) the genre—short stories generally do not sell as well as novels; the generic question is thus intimately linked with the first two reasons.

Canadian short-story translations are still not generally connected with notions of the avant-garde, of strong experimentalism, aesthetic innovation, et cetera. This is clearly the main reason why such short-story writing has hardly been translated. There is no German version of Brian Fawcett's *Capital Tales* (1984) or *The Secret Journal of Alexander Mackenzie* (1985), with their violent and grotesque postmodern stories. Nor have the surreal stories of Monty Reid, *Dog Sleeps: Irritated Texts* (1993), of Geoffrey Ursell, *Way out West!* (1990), or of Ernest Hekkanen, *Medieval Hour in the Author's Mind* (1987) met with any interest from European publishers. Richard Truhlar's *Figures in Paper Time* (1989) evidently owes too much to French literary theory to be attractive for a translation into German. Greg Hollingshead's *The Roaring Girl* (1995) won the Governor General's Literary Award and was a bestseller for twenty weeks in Canada, but it was a big surprise to see the book translated into German, thanks to Berlin Verlag, in 1998 as *Ratte mit Mandarine*. Even a writer such as Leon Rooke, who has been widely acknowledged for his inventiveness, has had none of his collections, or even a single story, translated. The lack of response among German publishers to *Painting the Dog: The Best Stories of Leon Rooke* (2001) shows that the situation has not changed. Publishers evidently think that, if there is a German market for such texts at all, readers will not expect to find them in Canadian short stories.

The second half of the twentieth century saw considerable developments in the number of Canadian authors and the range of texts translated into German. Many gaps notwithstanding, Canada and Canadian short stories made a remarkable showing on the German book market. Even though Canada is probably still not regarded as an autonomous literary entity by the general German-speaking public, but as part of the (exotic) American north or of the (post)modern contemporary Western world, its renown as the origin of excellent writers has definitely increased. The short stories that have been translated offer considerable insight into Canada's various cultures and have clearly enhanced intercultural understanding. But tenacity, enthusiasm, and high quality will continue to be required if one wants to preserve or even further improve the high status that Canadian short stories have obtained in their translations into German.

**REFERENCES**

Allen, Richard, ed. *A Region of the Mind: Interpreting the Western Canadian Plains*. Regina: University of Saskatchewan, 1973.

Anderson, Benedict. *Imagined Communities: Reflections on the Origin and Spread of Nationalism*. London: Verso, 1983.

Arnold, Armin, and Walter Riedel, eds. *Kanadische Erzähler der Gegenwart*. Zurich: Manesse, 1967.

Bartsch, Ernst, ed. *Die weite Reise: Kanadische Erzählungen und Kurzgeschichten*. Berlin: Volk und Welt, 1974 [2nd ed. 1976].

Baverstock, Alison. *How to Market Books: The Must Read Introductory Guide to Book Marketing.* 3rd ed. London: Kogan Page, 2000.
Beckwith, Harry. *Selling the Invisible: A Field Guide to Modern Marketing.* New York: Warner Books, 1997.
El-Hassan, Karla, ed. *Kolumbus und die Riesendame: Kurzgeschichten aus Kanada.* Berlin: Aufbau, 1992.
El-Hassan, Karla, and Helga Militz, eds. *Erkundungen: 26 kanadische Erzähler.* Berlin: Volk und Welt, 1986.
Epp, Georg K., and Heinrich Wiebe, eds. *Anthology of German-Mennonite Writing in Canada.* Winnipeg: The Mennonite German Society of Canada 1977. 290–92.
Foley, James. *The Search for Identity.* Toronto: Macmillan, 1976.
Friedrich, Gottfried, and Walter E. Riedel, eds. *Gute Wanderschaft, mein Bruder: Eine kanadische Anthologie.* Leipzig: St. Benno-Verlag, 1986.
Friesen, Abram Johann. *Prost Mahlzeit.* Grünthal, Manitoba: Private publ., 1949.
Fröschle, Hartmut, ed. *Nachrichten aus Ontario: Deutschsprachige Literatur in Kanada.* Hildesheim: Olms, 1981.
Frye, Northrop. "Conclusion." In *Literary History of Canada: Canadian Literature in English*, ed. Carl F. Klinck. Toronto: University of Toronto Press, 1965. 821–49.
Greco, Albert N. *The Book Publishing Industry.* Boston: Allyn & Bacon, 1997.
Haseler, Stephen. *The English Tribe: Identity, Nation and Europe.* London: Macmillan, 1996.
Herrmann, Birgit, ed. *Frauen in Kanada: Erzählungen und Gedichte.* München: dtv, 1993.
Holzamer, Astrid H. "Zur Rezeption kanadischer Literatur in Deutschland: Vom garstigen Haarbüschel zum süßen Zimtschäler." In *Reflections of Canada: The Reception of Canadian Literature in Germany*, ed. Martin Kuester and Andrea Wolff. Marburg: Universitätsbibliothek Marburg, 2000. 10–26.
Klassen, Peter J. *Grossmutters Schatz.* Superb, Sask.: Private publ., 1939.
Kloss, Heinz, ed. *Ahornblätter.* Würzburg: Holzner, 1961.
Kreisel, Henry. "The Prairie: A State of Mind." In *Transactions of the Royal Society of Canada.* 4th ser., vol. 6, sec. 2. Toronto: University of Toronto Press, 1968. 171–80.
Mandel, Eli. *Another Time.* Erin, Ont.: Porcépic, 1977.
Melynk, George. *Radical Regionalism.* Edmonton: NeWest, 1981.
Morley, David, and Kevin Robins, eds. *British Cultural Studies: Geography, Nationality, and Identity.* Oxford: Oxford University Press, 2001.
Mowat, Farley. Inuit: *Vom Mut der Eskimo.* Zurich: Albert Müller, 1977, publ. as *Der Schneewanderer.* Zurich: Unionsverlag, 1997.
Müller, Klaus Peter, ed. *Contemporary Canadian Short Stories.* 2nd ed. Stuttgart: Reclam, 2002.
Munro, Alice. *Who Do You Think You Are?* Toronto: Macmillan, 1978.
New, W. H. *Dreams of Speech and Violence: The Art of the Short Story in Canada and New Zealand.* Toronto: University of Toronto Press, 1987.
Petrone, Penny. "Aboriginal Literature." In *The Oxford Companion to Canadian Literature*,

ed. Eugene Benson and Villain Toye. 2nd ed. Don Mills, Ont.: Oxford University Press, 1997. 6–15.

Riedel, Walter E., ed. *Moderne Erzähler der Welt.* Tübingen: Erdmann, 1976.

———. *Das literarische Kanadabild: Eine Studie zur Rezeption kanadischer Literatur in deutscher Übersetzung.* Bonn: Bouvier, 1980.

———. ed. *The Old World and the New: Literary Perspectives of German-speaking Canadians.* Toronto: University of Toronto Press, 1984.

Sabin, Stefana, ed. *Kanada erzählt: 17 Erzählungen.* Frankfurt: Fischer, 1992.

Schaffer, Ulrich. *Der Turm.* Wuppertal: Oncken, 1978.

Schaub, Danielle. "Slices of Life as Historiographic Discourse: Mavis Gallant's *The Pegnitz Junction.*" In *Historiographic Metafiction in Modern American and Canadian Literature,* ed. Bernd Engler and Kurt Müller. Paderborn: Schöningh, 1994. 435–45.

Shields, Rob. *Places on the Margin: Alternative Geographies of Modernity.* London: Routledge, 1991.

Tomblin, Stephen G., ed. *Regionalism in a Global Society: Persistence and Change in Atlantic Canada and New England.* Peterborough: Broadview Press, 2004.

Tomlinson, Alan, ed. *Consumption, Identity, and Style: Marketing, Meanings, and the Packaging of Pleasure.* New York: Warner Books, 1997.

Young, Lisa, and Keith Archer, eds. *Regionalism and Party Politics in Canada.* Toronto: Oxford University Press, 2002.

# The "Other Women": Canadian Women Writers Blazing a Trail into Germany

*Brita Oeding and Luise von Flotow*
*University of Ottawa*

One of the stereotypical German associations with Canada and its history is that of pioneers, explorers, and conquerors of the wilderness. Some of them must have been women, "roughing it in the bush," as Susanna Moodie, the Canadian "Ur-pioneer," has described it. However, while this particular stereotype usually excludes women, they played an important role as *literary* pioneers in contemporary Germany, blazing the trail for later Canadian writers. From the late 1970s onward, German translations of Canadian adult fiction were dominated by books written by women.

In this chapter, we focus mainly on English Canadian writers for the reason that our interest lies in the German mainstream response to Canadian writing in translation: far more English Canadian than French Canadian writers were translated into German during the time frame discussed here. The reviews printed in the 1980s and 1990s predominantly focused on English Canadian authors and only on the best-selling ones. This focus reflects a general tendency both in Canada and in the majority of international Canadian Studies.

This chapter is concerned, then, with German responses to the wave of translations of English Canadian women writers,[1] a response that, in its enthusiasm, undoubtedly had a strong effect on the international success of the works. Most of the reviews that we use to trace this response come from the

---

1. There have been recent attempts to stimulate Germany's interest in French Canadian writing and to overcome the tendency to ignore the existence of French cultures on the North American continent. The anthology *Anders schreibendes Amerika: Literatur aus Quebec 1945–2000* was published in 2000, and in October 2001 then Canadian Governor General Adrienne Clarkson visited Germany with a delegation of about forty "cultural workers," half of them French Canadian. Among them were dramatist Michel Marc Bouchard, poet Pierre Morency, and the writer-translator pair Émile Martel and Daniel Poliquin.

archive of newspapers and journals in Innsbruck, Austria, and appeared between 1980 and 1999 in major German-language publications, mainly in *Die Zeit, Süddeutsche Zeitung, Frankfurter Allgemeine Zeitung (FAZ), Der Spiegel, Frankfurter Rundschau, Die Welt,* and *Neue Zürcher Zeitung.*

## PIONEERS IN WOMEN'S WRITING

In the late 1980s and 1990s, a reader living in Germany could easily have got the impression that virtually all Canadian writers were women. New books by Canadian women appeared regularly in bookstores and were reviewed in the arts and culture sections of all the major newspapers. Photographs of the authors were everywhere: Margaret Atwood looked out of bookstore windows and many newspaper and magazine pages, Barbara Gowdy beguiled readers (of reviews at least) with charming photographs, and many travelled widely to readings and book signings, to book fairs and academic events, as well as to the Canadian Embassy. Indeed, people might have been led to think that Canada was women writers' heaven on Earth, a secret paradise that especially encouraged and nurtured creative writing by women.

While Canadian fiction had been appearing in translation since before World War II, German readers had hitherto been offered a rather spotty selection: six books by Mazo de la Roche were translated in the forty years from 1936 to 1975;[2] Arthur Hailey and Malcolm Lowry were translated as Canadian authors in the 1970s, although their status as "Canadian" writers is rather dubious.[3] Some of Leonard Cohen's work was translated in the wake of his success as a singer-songwriter in the early 1970s (but hardly reviewed);[4] a novel by Margaret Laurence, one by Morley Callaghan, as well as two books by Mordecai Richler had been translated by the late 1970s. A number of books by women writers from French Canada had arrived in Germany at various unrelated moments: three novels by Gabrielle Roy were translated between 1956 and 1970, Anne Hébert's *Kamouraska* (1970) appeared in 1972, even one year earlier than the English translation (two other works were published in the 1990s), Marie Claire Blais's Médici Prize-winning *Une saison dans la vie d'Emmanuel* (1965) was published in German as *Schwarzer Winter* in 1967. Until the late 1970s, however, there was no more than a fragmented transfer of Canadian fiction writing into German, with Canadian

---

2. De la Roche (1879–1961) is best known for the "Jalna" series, a family history set in fictitious Whiteoaks, Ontario.
3. Hailey immigrated to Canada from England after World War II and spent many years living in the Bahamas. Lowry, too, came from Britain, spent several years in Canada and Mexico, and returned to the United Kingdom.
4. See the chapter by Fabienne Quennet in this volume.

works being selected either because of prizes that they had been awarded or just at random. Furthermore, translated works were rarely, if ever, reviewed as texts coming from or relating to Canada, and the work was often marked as translated "aus dem amerikanischen Englisch" ("from American English").

Anthologies were the most coherent representations of Canadian writing at this time, and by 1976 four of them had appeared (Arnold and Riedel 1967; Weaver 1969; Bartsch 1974; Riedel 1976). Two (Bartsch 1974 and Riedel 1976) were reviewed in a groundbreaking text by Walter Pache, a German academic versed in Canadian writing, whose title announced "Es gibt eine kanadische Literatur" ("There Is Such a Thing as Canadian Literature")[5] (*Süddeutsche Zeitung*, 17 and 18 July 1976) and encouraged German readers to fill in that blank spot on their literary world map. By reading these two anthologies (one published in West Germany, the other in East Germany), readers could become acquainted with stories by well over thirty Canadian writers. Paradoxically, given the huge success of women writers just a few years later, only five stories by women writers (less than sixteen percent of the work) were included, with four of them in the East German publication (by Mavis Gallant, Alice Munro, Ann Marriott, and Margaret Laurence).

The relative "explosion"[6] of Canadian women's writing in German had to wait a few more years. It began in 1979 with Margaret Atwood's *Surfacing*, translated as *Der lange Traum* in West Germany and as *Strömung* in East Germany,[7] and continued with the enormous subsequent production, translation, and enthusiastic reception of her works. Given the fact that *Surfacing* was Atwood's first German translation, it is surprising but also telling that all of the major newspapers—*Die Zeit, Frankfurter Allgemeine Zeitung, Die Welt, Neue Zürcher Zeitung,* and *Süddeutsche Zeitung*—published uncharacteristically long, detailed reviews of the book, each one noting her success at home and her participation in the nationalist, identity-seeking aspects of contemporary Canadian writing, some commenting on the

---

5. This and all further translations into English are, if not otherwise noted, by the authors of this chapter.
6. We take this term from an enthusiastic article in 2000 by Julia Kospach in the Austrian weekly magazine *Profil*. Entitled "Wie eine Explosion," it discusses numerous Canadian writers, claims that Atwood and Ondaatje are outdoing and outselling American writers, and announces "the Golden Age" of Canadian writing, an era in which women's work predominates. However, the term must be seen in relation to actual book imports. In 1990, for example, of the over 9,000 works of literature published in Germany, almost fifty percent were translations. The eight Canadian works among them (the average per year in the 1990s) would hardly warrant the term "explosion."
7. See Stefan Ferguson and Barbara Korte in this volume on the phenomenon of this double (East/West German) translation.

anti-American elements of the book as well as the more general effort to create a Canadian culture. Many of the reviews of her subsequent books referred back to *Surfacing*, always commenting on the noteworthy success of this first work of hers to appear in German. By the mid-1980s, Atwood had conquered the hearts of reviewers, media personalities, and presumably readers to such an extent that all her work was translated—and new books appeared almost simultaneously with the English versions.[8] A further measure of her success in Germany may be the fact that *The Handmaid's Tale*, 1987 (*Der Report der Magd*, 1987)—note the simultaneous translation—was made into the film *Die Geschichte der Dienerin* (1989) by German film director Volker Schlöndorff.

An important aspect of her success was that Atwood was systematically identified as a Canadian writer who wrote about Canada; this identification undoubtedly ushered in changes in reception and selection for translation that influenced the success of many other writers. Indeed, during the 1980s, a total of thirty-eight books of adult fiction by Canadian authors were translated and published in German, and in the 1990s the overall figures rose further still, bringing seventy-seven books of adult Canadian fiction onto the German-language market. The number of women writers in each decade easily outmatched the number of male writers, with twenty-six books by women and twelve by men in the 1980s and fifty-one books by women versus twenty-six by men in the 1990s—a situation that was hardly foreshadowed by the earlier anthologies or reflected in later ones.[9] Success came as the translations were teamed with enthusiastic reviews and public appearances that responded to readers' needs and interests while reflecting shifts in the literary landscapes in both countries. Canadian women's writing had found a niche in Germany.

There is no easy explanation for this phenomenon, but there can be no doubt that the so-called second-wave feminism played an important role. Canadian women writers were garnering a lot of attention at home in this period, focusing as they did on women's issues, lives, voices, and histories, and German-speaking countries, though more conservative on questions of gender difference, were also strongly affected by the women's movement. But there seems to have been a

---

8. After *Surfacing*, the following Atwood books appeared: *Die Unmöglichkeit der Nähe*, 1980 (*Life before Man*, 1979); *Lady Orakel*, 1984 (*Lady Oracle*, 1976); *Wahre Geschichten*, 1984 (*True Stories*, 1981); *Verletzungen*, 1984 (*Bodily Harm*, 1981); *Die essbare Frau*, 1984 (*The Edible Woman*, 1969); *Die Giftmischer*, 1985 (*Murder in the Dark*, 1983); and *Unter Glas*, 1986 (*Dancing Girls and Other Stories*, 1977).

9. Gottfried and Riedel (1986) has four women writers out of a total of seventeen, El-Hassan (1992) includes five women out of a total of eighteen, and even Sabin (1992) includes a total of two women writers in seventeen stories. This situation may be due in part to the sources of the German anthologies, which were often existing Canadian anthologies.

dearth of accessible literary or narrative texts written in German with a feminist / womanist approach, a fact that may go some way toward explaining why so much Canadian fiction by women was translated. We know from polysystem models (Even-Zohar 1990, 1997) that literatures work as systems, the way that biotopes might, and just like biotopes they might lack necessary elements at certain times. This lack is often filled by translations.

A brief look at the literary scene in Germany preceding the Canadian "boom" may help us to contextualize the situation. After World War II, German writing focused heavily on difficult themes such as *Vaterland* ("homeland" / "fatherland") and on German "identity" after the twelve years of Nazi dictatorship. And even though there was a new international focus in the publishing and book industry by the 1970s and 1980s that brought fresh perspectives to the German literary landscape, German writing largely continued with this "heavy" focus.[10] Women's writing was no exception. As in much Canadian feminist writing, oppression, social structures, and gender roles were the predominant topics addressed in the often semi-autobiographical works published by women in the 1960s, 1970s, and 1980s (Elfriede Jelinek, Verena Stefan, Karin Struck, etc.). Yet these works tended to be aggressively provocative and to demand "women's liberation" rather than produce a good story line, use interesting narrative techniques, focus on writing style and quality, let alone employ humour. Furthermore, some of the higher-profile writers, such as Stefan and (later Nobel Prize–winner [2005]) Jelinek, saw language as the main problem that feminists should address and thus set out to find or create a "new" language. Stefan, for instance, writes that "Language fails me as soon as I try to speak of new experiences. Supposedly new experiences that are cast in the same old language cannot really be new" (1984, 53).

Writing that experiments with language generally does not attract mainstream readers or sell. Such writing is not "gehobene Unterhaltungsliteratur" ("higher-class writing for entertainment"),[11] the epithet often used for Atwood and other

---

10. The issue is discussed at length in a longer article in *Der Spiegel*, 16 March 1992, entitled "Gedankenschwere Nabelschau" ("Heavy Thoughts while Navel Gazing"). The anonymous author argues that reasons for the postwar German literary disaster (especially abroad) include, among other things, its "reflective writing style, the way language circulates around itself," and "its introversion and egotism." Moreover, it is absolutely outdone by "Anglo-Saxon writing" in terms of "storytelling."
11. This is perhaps best illustrated by reference to the reviews of Canadian writing, which always compare German and Canadian trends. Here is an example: "Da gehobene Unterhaltungsliteratur nicht gerade eine Stärke der jungen oder nicht mehr jungen deutschsprachigen Autorinnen ist, empfiehlt sich Margaret Atwood nachdrücklichst als Produzentin gescheiter Bücher dieser Sorte" ("Since high-class literary writing for entertainment is hardly a strength that our young and not so young women writers exhibit, Margaret Atwood can be recommended as the producer of intelligent books of this sort"], review of *Lady Orakel, Die Welt*, 22 and 23 September 1984.

English Canadians in German reviews. Nonetheless, despite the difficult German reading materials, the new engagement of German women in literary life fostered discussions about gendered writing, women's role models, and perspectives, and as the 1980s progressed there was more fictionalization and more distance to personal experience in writing (Bammer 1991). Yet the focus still remained on the political situation of contemporary Germany and on women's emancipation as a controversial political issue, and many perceived German writing in this vein as wooden.

## THE PROFESSIONAL RECEPTION OF THE "OTHER WOMEN"

The reviews published in daily or weekly papers, in the feuilleton/culture sections of big national newspapers or in glossy magazines give some idea of the impact that books by Canadian women writers were assigned. While quantity alone may not count for much, it is remarkable that the reviews of books by female authors far outnumber those of male authors; the set of reviews from the Innsbruck clipping service has three times as many reviews of Canadian books by women as by men for the period 1980–2000.

The literary review is a discursive form that carries considerable weight, especially in middle-class German culture, where the feuilleton pages of the daily newspapers keep thousands of interested readers informed about recent publications by the latest authors. Indeed, for many readers, the review *is* the book. The reviews written about Canadian women writers in the course of the 1980s are interesting examples of this literary form and its impact.

First and foremost, the literary review is a form that is firmly rooted "at home," narcissistically relating and comparing the incoming materials to literary and other conditions at home (see von Flotow 2004). Atwood and other Canadian mainstream writers, for instance, are always compared favourably to German versions of "women's writing," which are largely seen as boring and too introspective, on the one hand, or crude, shrill, aggressive, programmatic, and far too politicized ("Kampfliteratur" or "battle writing"),[12] on the other hand. Atwood's, and the "quieter" novels of writers such as Margaret Laurence, Bonnie Burnard, or Jane Urquhart, are considered works that "even men might read"[13]—works that address women's interests but refrain from polemics and, most importantly, tell good stories. Atwood gets special praise for writing about issues that most modern women face—career and family, emancipation and

---

12. See the review of Atwood's *Der Report der Magd* (*The Handmaid's Tale*) by Susanne Mayer, who compares her favourably to the German feminist/women writers; "Schöne freie Welt," *Die Zeit*, 11 November 1987.
13. Günther Schloz, for example, writes that there is nothing in them that would interest *only* women: "weder Weiberkram noch Frauensache" ("neither women's nonsense nor women's stuff"); "Schön kühl gehaltene Frauen," *Frankfurter Allgemeine Zeitung*, 9 October 1985.

(in)dependence—and for doing so "mit Witz und Tiefe und weniger Ernst als deutsche Schriftstellerinnen"[14] ("with wit and depth and less gravity than German female authors"). In other words, she does not exaggerate the political import of these topics and creates protagonists who contrast with the suffering or angry heroines of the vituperative German women's writing of the period.[15]

Second, the literary review is a genre that works with stereotypes, easing readers into foreign materials by providing shortcuts and succinctly setting this material into commonly known facts about the culture from which the book originates. Many reviews of Canadian writing evoke Canada's climate or topography in the title of the review, discuss it at some length, and often draw parallels between these clichés and the content of the work. A review of Hébert's *Kamouraska*, for example, is entitled "Eiskalt in Quebec" ("Freezing Cold in Quebec"), and the reviewer links this neatly to the plot: "The story is set in a harsh landscape with winter storms and ice floes—in a hellish outdoors that mirrors the inner hell of these characters."[16] Similarly, the comprehensive review of Atwood's work, published in *Buchkultur* 27 (1994), and entitled "Guerilla in der Wildnis" ("Guerrilla in the Wilderness"), opens with a list of Canadian scenes as we all know them: "Wiesen, Wälder, Seen und Stille; schneebedeckte Gipfel vor strahlend blauem Horizont ..." ("meadows, forests, lakes, silence; snow-covered summits and bright blue horizon").[17] There's not a mosquito or blackfly in sight and no vicious, subzero temperatures either.

Third, literary reviews are seldom original pieces of work; they are derivative and repetitive—often based on the press package that the publisher provides— and reviewers seem to operate in packs, unobtrusively citing each other or the press package. They develop a fascination for a certain type of writing or a particular author and then remain faithful to this predilection. Canadian women writers such as Atwood[18] have drawn considerable benefit from this tendency, not only because many of their reviewers were also women in an "era" of women's writing, but also because their German reviewers stayed with them and developed a readership for them.

Fourth and finally, literary reviews can often be didactic, explaining the

---

14. Kyra Stromberg, "Gefährliche Seiten," *Süddeutsche Zeitung*, 9 October 1985.
15. Jutta Duhm-Heitzmann and Margaret Atwood, "Zeit der Zauberbräute," *Cosmopolitan* 2 (1994).
16. "Die Handlung fand vor einer harten Landschaft mit Winterstürmen und Eistreiben [statt]—in einer äußeren Hölle, die der inneren Hölle dieser Menschen in nichts nachstand"; Armin Arnold, "Preisgekrönte kanadische Autorin: Eiskalt in Quebec," *Die Welt*, 16 March 1972.
17. Patrizia Zauneck, "Guerilla in der Wildnis," *Buchkultur* 27 (1994): 46–47.
18. Kyra Stromberg and Margarete von Schwarzkopf are regular Atwood reviewers—positive, intelligent, and dedicated.

usefulness or the possible function of the reviewed book or its main idea in the new environment. This aspect comes out strongly in the reviews of women's writing—particularly in the contrasts established between German feminists and Canadian women writers—but also, in the 1990s, in the reviews of so-called multicultural or international authors. Ondaatje is a good example: *The English Patient* is described as "evidence of a search for a new equilibrium to be won by crossing cultural boundaries,"[19] a direct reference to the multicultural problems plaguing German society at the time.

## HOW GERMAN REVIEWERS READ ATWOOD, MUNRO, AND SHIELDS

When the German women's magazine *Cosmopolitan*[20] described Atwood as "a female writer from whom we might take advice" in its review of *The Robber Bride*, it was referring to the new type of woman whom Atwood ostensibly conjures up: a woman who is unscrupulous, egotistical, demonic, and beautiful. Indeed, Atwood is depicted as a writer who does not believe in women's solidarity; she is quoted as saying that there is no reason why a woman should love and trust other women since there is no such thing as "sisterly solidarity." And, the review informs us, her writing should not be mistaken for that of a "feminist" because "she does not approve of ideology in any form." Although *Cosmopolitan* differs somewhat in style and coverage from the daily or weekly papers, we quote it here for this representative response to Atwood, which also sets the tone for the reception of other Canadian women writers. It is a very local response that includes at least two of the themes in German women's writing that reviewers had grown tired of: women's solidarity and feminist politics.

In the early 1980s, Atwood was being celebrated as innovative and humorous, as a Canadian woman who wants to entertain rather than weigh down her readers with heavy feminist topics. Her writing and her persona were praised in all the major newspapers, and reviewers appreciated that her stories were truly relevant because modern. Kyra Stromberg, one of Atwood's most loyal reviewers, regularly emphasizes the specific woman's perspective in Atwood's writing as a "rebellion against a form of life that assassinates all that is genuine, natural. This rebellion is specifically female; it is strongest where destruction is experienced at closest range."[21]

While most of Atwood's reviewers are women, a couple of men also make themselves heard. Günter Schloz claims in the *FAZ* that Atwood lets her female

---

19. Paul Jandl, *Der Standard*, 8 October 1993.
20. Jutta Duhm-Heitzmann, "Zeit der Zauberbräute," *Cosmopolitan* 2 (1994).
21. Kyra Stromberg, "Es ist alles da unter der Oberfläche," *Süddeutsche Zeitung*, 10 November 1982.

protagonists try out models that break stereotypes while adding humour to that struggle ("Schön kühl gehaltene Frauen," 9 October 1985). Matthias Wegner writes about *The Handmaid's Tale (Der Report der Magd)* that, even though "the novel does not hide its feminist roots and the author traces a woman's psyche, the book can be recommended to many male readers as well."[22] Similarly, Kyra Stromberg assures readers in her review of *Cat's Eye (Katzenauge)* that "this novel is not a woman's book, even though the experiences are specifically those of a woman."[23] While all these reviews discuss Atwood's works at length, they also make clear statements about the mainstream perspective on women's and/or feminist writing in Germany. The relief at Atwood's lack of dogmatism is widespread, and there is new excitement and pleasant anticipation in the air.

In the 1990s, reviewers continue to acclaim Atwood and develop a new element of praise, mostly of *Cat's Eye (Katzenauge)* and *The Robber Bride (Die Räuberbraut)*. They describe Atwood's protagonists as the new femmes fatales and as devilish. Atwood is admired for showing the "dark" side of women and their relationships and for destroying stereotypes, such as that of the good woman who can handle every challenge and does not have a single skeleton in her closet.[24] According to the reviewers, Atwood shows the "mephistophelian" type of woman—the witch, the madwoman, and the ugly hag—who proves to be far more interesting than the virtuous one. One of the few male reviewers, Frank Rumpf, remarks that Grace in *Alias Grace,* the "murderer with the beautiful angel face," is far smarter and more appealing than the male doctor who treats her,[25] and Tanya Lieske in her review of the same book asserts pointblank that no woman should henceforth be allowed to present herself as a victim.[26] In short, Atwood's writing is seen as having a liberating effect by presenting women who are evil, destructive, smart, egotistical, and beautiful.

The mass of reviews in a variety of newspapers, journals, and magazines usually mention Canada and sometimes discuss it extensively, and they always refer to Atwood as a *Canadian* writer, a woman successful in her art and in her

---

22. Matthias Wegner, "Kasernierte Frauen," *Frankfurter Allgemeine Zeitung,* 18 May 1985.
23. Kyra Stromberg, "Die schrecklichen Mädchen," *Süddeutsche Zeitung,* 4 April 1990.
24. See Hella Boschmann, "Dem weiblichen Dämon eine Chance geben," *Die Welt,* 11 January 1994; Annette Dittert, "Wettstreit—Eifersucht—Zerstörung: Beziehungen zwischen Frauen," *Tagesspiegel,* 8 May 1994; Erdmute Klein, "Klassische Femme Fatale," *FAZ,* 3 April 1994; Heiner Boehnke, "Schattengefechte—Eine Männerfresserei," *Frankfurter Rundschau,* 26 March 1994; Thomas Steinfeld, "Der Teufel in Toronto," *FAZ,* 15 March 1994; and Hilke Veth, "Hexe und Venus," *Deutsches Allgemeines Sonntagsblatt,* 25 March 1994.
25. Frank Rumpf, "Keine Erinnerung an den Mordtag," *Kölner Stadt-Anzeiger,* 10 January 1997.
26. Tanya Lieske, "Nicht ich war's, Mary ... Können schöne Frauen morden?," *Die Welt,* 7 September 1996.

life. Her work is assigned a pioneering role. Its reception and success can be said to be a guide for the further import of Canadian writing and the interest that German publishers and readers have subsequently developed for other Canadian writers.

Alice Munro and Carol Shields have been two of the most frequently translated Canadian women writers since the success of Atwood's first novels. In 1981, Klett-Cotta published Munro's short-story collection *Who Do You Think You Are?*, which had appeared ten years earlier in Canada. Its publication as *Das Bettlermädchen*, adopted from the American title *The Beggar Maid* (1982), was directly related to Atwood's success, and longer reviews and articles about Munro appeared in all the major papers. While a long review by Gerhard Kirchner in the *FAZ* expresses surprise at the fact that Munro does not write from the "freedom and adventure point of view," which is apparently what he expects from a Canadian writer, it also offers less stereotyped criticism. Kirchner laments Munro's lack of irony and distanced description and is not convinced by the female protagonist, although he finds the depiction of the atmosphere of small-town Canada before World War II convincing. He wonders, however, why Munro received the Governor General's Literary Award in 1979 and assumes that the jury did not read the second half of the book.[27]

Female reviewers react very differently to Munro's work. In her positive review in *Die Zeit*, Manuela Reichart focuses on one of the two main female protagonists and her desperate love life and on woman's search for self in Munro's stories. Reichart appreciates that Munro discusses the difficult relationship between love and dependency and women's enduring struggle with it.[28] Elisabeth Kaiser points out in the *FAZ* that Munro's stories were written in 1971 and that it may seem strange to the German reader in 1983 that Munro is considered a feminist in Canada. This, she suggests, is due to the temporal gap between the publications of the original and the translation but also to the differences between Canadian and German feminism. Kaiser recommends the book for its effective description of how girls grow up, no matter whether they live in a small town in Ontario or in a big city anywhere in the world, and she points out that Munro accomplishes this description without getting into the "popular mother-daughter analysis" pervasive in Germany.[29] In regard to Munro's *The Moons of Jupiter* (1983) (*Die Jupitermonde*, 1986), the same reviewer writes in 1986 that Munro fills a "literary gap for the German reader" who is weary of the radical feminist models provided by writers such as Kate Millet and Germaine Greer and their German

---

27. Gerhard Kirchner, "Jagdszenen aus Kanada," *Frankfurter Allgemeine Zeitung*, 4 May 1981.
28. Manuela Reichart, "Auf der Suche," *Die Zeit*, 4 July 1981.
29. Elisabeth Kaiser, "Wachstumsschmerzen," *Frankfurter Allgemeine Zeitung*, 22 March 1983.

imitators. Munro, in her view, narrates "women's life how it really is" in authentic descriptions of their daily struggles for independence and individuality. Munro's women, she claims, are internally strong, while her men hide a helpless, lost soul within strong bodies. Kaiser concludes that Munro enriches the continuously evolving North American women's contribution to fiction (in German translation) and that these works should be seen as requiring a distinct form of criticism.[30] Margarete von Schwarzkopf compares Atwood's and Munro's stories in *Die Welt,* alleging that the main differences between the two lie in Atwood's "aggressive, egotistical prose" and the acceptance of human weaknesses and feelings in Munro. Yet she finds parallels in the fact that both Atwood and Munro give their female characters the strength to distance themselves from the pressing everyday emotional burdens that women bear.[31] Renate Schostak also praises Munro in her extensive review of *The Progress of Love* (1986) (*Der Mond über der Eisbahn,* 1986) published in the *FAZ,* where she points out that Munro was unjustly cast into the shade of Atwood's "aggressive and sensational storytelling."[32] Munro describes lives without palliation, with ups and downs, abysses and climaxes, and she recognizes the frailty of human lives and relationships. And even though Munro often "shows the positive, she is neither boring nor naive, nor does she display a sour resignation or a sanctimonious fake freshness." Munro describes women's labours of love and ingeniously uses her talents as an extraordinary writer, "discreet and skilled, tireless, friendly, but never hiding any of the terrors of life." While both faithful reviewers, Schostak and Reichart seem to be somewhat disappointed about Munro's surfacing pessimism regarding love in her *Friend of My Youth* (1990) (*Glaubst du es war Liebe?,* they do not abandon their support of her as a writer—somehow they have "grown up with her" and now see love and marriage with clear, disillusioned eyes. Fascinated, both critics agree that Munro has taught them that "there is no institution of happiness."[33] Her critical support seems to come from reviewers who have time for and appreciate the detailed, quiet, and profound look that she takes at the "lives of girls and women."

Finally, there is Carol Shields, whose works were reviewed in the mid- and late 1990s. Shields is always reviewed as a Canadian writer, although she was born and raised in the United States. Yet she lived in Canada for much of her adult life, and

---

30. Elisabeth Kaiser, "Leben, Liebe und Tod," *Frankfurter Allgemeine Zeitung,* 11 November 1986.
31. Margarete von Schwarzkopf, "Der Tod, die andere Seite des Mondes: Kanada auf der Suche nach sich selbst," *Die Welt,* 7 March 1987.
32. Renate Schostak, "Fortwährende geschickte Führung," *Frankfurter Allgemeine Zeitung,* 12 December 1989.
33. Renate Schostak, "Wozu das stolze Blut?," *Frankfurter Allgemeine Zeitung,* 8 February 1992; Manuela Reichart, "Vergebliche Lieben, wahre Empfindungen," *Die Zeit,* 25 September 1992.

Canada claims her as a national voice. Shields garnered attention in the German media when her work was short-listed for the prestigious British Booker Prize in 1993 and when she won the American Pulitzer Prize in 1995 for *The Stone Diaries* (1993). Some time earlier her book *Swann: A Mystery* (1987) had been published in Germany as *Mary Swann* (1993) and received some disappointed but nevertheless long reviews in larger newspapers. In 1995, *The Stone Diaries* appeared in German as *Das Tagebuch der Daisy Goodwill*. Each review mentions the "typical women's topics" and the extent to which Shields explores them in her writing. She is described as a storyteller who knows about women's daily toils. Her protagonists do not have much in common with Atwood's female eccentrics; Shields's women have "both feet on the ground." One of her reviewers, Maria Frisé, expresses both her own and Shields's hope that, if men read her books, "they will learn something about women's psyche and develop more understanding for them."[34] Katharina Rutschky sees Shields's work as a parody of feminist complaints about women's limited possibilities, their being undervalued, and their incarceration in family life. Shields manages to describe the ordinary life of a not very emancipated woman who lives a dignified and peaceful life. She provides a model for the "non-feminist existence," for a "normal but rich and fulfilling life" that still leaves room for individual development and some eccentricity. Shields is seen as a woman writer who is able to describe love between man and woman without bitterness and sarcasm, even if there is some regret and disappointment.[35] Similarly, Eva-Elisabeth Fischer writes, "A writer who can describe a simple stonemason's love for an emotionally impoverished woman with such impressive and skilful sentences undoubtedly deserves a prize." In this reviewer's opinion, Shields's description of women (and men) shows empathic interest and understanding.[36]

In 1998, Shields received the British Orange Prize for fiction for *Larry's Party* (1997), which was then promptly translated into German as *Alles über Larry* (1997). The only available review of *Alles über Larry* was written by a male reviewer in *Die Welt*. Interestingly enough, Elmar Krekeler speaks about Larry, a man who "needs two marriages, one broken relationship, twenty-two days of coma, and five decades to feel relatively content," as "an archetypal new man in new fiction ... who was born in the post-macho, post-war nirvana," and he attests that seldom has a writer managed to create a more detailed and apt portrait of modern man. Much like his fellow critics of Canadian women's writing, and in line with a long tradition in literary criticism and reception, Krekeler pits the protagonist against

---

34. Maria Friesé, "Ratschläge für die Blumenzucht," *Frankfurter Allgemeine Zeitung*, 3 November 1995.
35. Katharina Rutschky, "Respekt vor dem Gänseblümchen," *Der Tagesspiegel*, 2 December 1995.
36. Eva-Elisabeth Fischer, "Sich täglich neu erfinden," *Süddeutsche Zeitung*, 13 December 1995.

"real" life. Fiction and life are blurred and interfere with each other, and Larry, the gardener from Winnipeg, evolves into the "new man," much like, before him, the "new" woman had emerged from the pages of Atwood.[37]

Shields's "new" women, however, are different from Atwood's and Munro's. They do not regress to "women's stuff and women's issues," and one of Shields's reviewers comes to the conclusion that, in general, women are the ones who have the more interesting stories to tell: "In regard to careers and accounting, men may leave women far behind, but in the novel, women rule," claims Rutschky. And they rule with "the material that makes a woman's novel ... : letters, floriculture, family secrets, recipes, and fragments of conversations." In contrast to Atwood and Munro, Shields found her German readers during a time of neoconservatism in Germany, when anxiety about "individualization" and (the loss of) families as sole social resources outweighed debates over feminism and women's independence. This may well have provided her with an all-the-more-interested readership.

**CONCLUSION**

Atwood, Munro, and Shields were the women writers whose works were most widely discussed in Germany in the 1980s and 1990s, although numerous others were translated into German during that period too. Barbara Gowdy, Gail Anderson-Dargatz, Joan Barfoot, Jane Urquhart, and Ann-Marie MacDonald are only a few female authors whose public reception also focused specifically on female protagonists and women's roles in Western societies.

The translations and publications of Atwood's novels stood at the onset of, and helped to trigger, an avalanche of Canadian writing in German translation and a rising awareness of Canadian writing, which was financially supported and promoted by both Canadian and German institutions and agents and praised by a group of faithful reviewers. Summing up, we can say that the female models provided by Canadian women writers, models of women who are "different" as well as those who lead a "normal" life, were met with enthusiasm and a certain feeling of relief. Atwood's struggling women and, in the next decade, her devilish women, Munro's dignified women in their daily subtle fights for independence, and Shields's down-to-earth women with their fractured families and womanly labours—the German press discussed all of them as providing surprising new inspirations for contemporary women's lives. These Canadian writers were obviously able to fill a gap in German writing, where radical feminism and semi-autobiographical "problem" novels had saturated the market and tired even the

---

37. Elmar Krekeler, "Alles über Larry," *Die Welt*, 24 April 1999.

professional readers. Canadian women writers were read for their refreshingly told "stories"—stories that drew the German readers' attention away from their everyday world, stories that offered them new geographical and psychological landscapes. For a period of about fifteen years, Canadian novels featuring women who are strong and complex and anchored in a real life that is mysteriously and subtly different from everyday life in Germany, yet familiar enough for identification, were much-discussed commodities.

## REFERENCES

Arnold, Armin, and Walter Riedel, eds. *Kanadische Erzähler der Gegenwart*. Zurich: Manesse, 1967.

Bammer, Angelika. *Partial Visions: Feminism and Utopianism in the 1970s*. New York: Routledge, 1991.

Bartsch, Ernst, ed. *Die weite Reise: Kanadische Erzählungen und Kurzgeschichten*. Berlin: Volk und Welt, 1974.

El-Hassan, Karla, ed. *Kolumbus und die Riesendame*. Berlin: Aufbau, 1992.

Even-Zohar, Itamar. "Factors and Dependencies in Culture: A Revised Draft for Polysystem Culture Research." *Canadian Review of Comparative Literature/Revue Canadienne de Littérature Comparée* 24 (March 1997): 15–34.

———. "Polysystem Studies." *Poetics Today* 11.1 (1990) [Special Issue].

Gottfried, Friedrich, and Walter E. Riedel, eds. *Gute Wanderschaft, mein Bruder: Eine kanadische Anthologie*, Leipzig: St. Benno Verlag, 1986.

Riedel, Walter, ed. *Moderne Erzähler der Welt*. Tübingen: Erdmann, 1976.

Sabin, Stefana, ed. *Kanada erzählt: 17 Erzählungen*. Frankfurt: Fischer Taschenbuch, 1992.

Stefan, Verena. "Foreword" to *Häutungen*, transl. Johanna Moore and Beth Weckmueller. In *German Feminism: Readings in Politics and Literature*, ed. E. H. Altbach, J. Clausen, D. Schultz, and N. Stephan. Albany: SUNY Press, 1984. 53–54.

von Flotow, Luise. "Internationale Bastarde ... irgendwo im weiten Kanada: Canadian Writing Tempered by Austrian Reception." *canadiana oenipontana* 6 (2004): 269–84.

Weaver, Robert, ed. *Stories from Canada/Erzählungen aus Kanada*. Munich: Langewiesche-Brandt/dtv, 1969.

# Margaret Atwood in German/y: A Case Study

*Stefan Ferguson*
*University of Constance*

**INTRODUCTION**

There can hardly be a more appropriate subject for a case study of Canadian literature in German translation than Margaret Atwood.[1] As a novelist, poet, short-story writer, and literary and cultural critic, Atwood has, for the best part of four decades now, been Canada's most prominent and admired literary figure, both in her home country and abroad. Indeed, through her literary oeuvre as well as her charismatic personality, she has become a genuine literary and media icon, symbolizing not only Canadian literature but also in many respects Canadianness itself. Atwood's high renown in her native country—the phenomenon of "Atwood bashing" notwithstanding—comes as no surprise, since her works, for all their universality, are rooted in a strong sense of Canadian locality, both wild and urban, and often involve deeply cogitated negotiations with Canadian identity. Similarly, Atwood's success in the rest of the English-speaking world, and specifically in the United Kingdom and the United States, though remarkable, is hardly unexpected given the shared linguistic and cultural backgrounds of the countries involved.

What is more thought-provoking is the success of Atwood's works in translation, in cultural and linguistic environments often radically different from those of her original texts. Remarkably, Atwood's works have been translated into over thirty languages (see Nischik 2002, 273), a sure sign of their ability to cross literary and cultural borders. Among the many languages and cultures into which her works have been transferred, Germany occupies a special position. In hardly any other country—the anglophone world not

---

1. At various points in this chapter, I quote sources originally written in German. For the convenience of the reader, I have provided my own translations of such passages. Page references are to the original German texts.

excepted—is Atwood so admired and so popularly successful, hardly anywhere else so prominent on syllabi and curricula, so well represented in academic research.[2]

This chapter explores the reasons for Atwood's outstanding success in Germany, placing it in the context of Germany's fascination with Canadian literature in general and examining aspects of German and Canadian culture that help to explain the phenomenon. It also provides an analysis of two German translations of Atwood's seminal novel *Surfacing* as a case in point for cultural processes at work in the translation of Canadian literature into German.

## THE STATUS OF MARGARET ATWOOD'S WORKS IN GERMANY

What exactly does it mean when we talk about Atwood's "success" and "popularity" in Germany? Her prominence as a best-selling author represents just one facet of her status in Germany, though a significant one. Her continued success in this respect is all the more remarkable when compared with that of other prominent North American writers. As German publisher Arnulf Conradi states, "American writers like Saul Bellow, John Updike, Philip Roth or our own Richard Ford are highly respected, but they very rarely reach the bestseller lists in our country. Margaret Atwood does it every time" (2000, 35).

However, other indicators of Atwood's success in Germany are equally revealing: the database of the Canadian Embassy in Germany, *Kanadische Autoren in deutscher Übersetzung*,[3] lists twenty-eight translations of works by Atwood. Excluding reprints of individual short stories or poems, there are thirteen translations of novels (including two versions of *Surfacing*)—the entire novelistic oeuvre has thus been translated; three of Atwood's five short-story collections have appeared in German, representing fairly good coverage of the genre; all three of Atwood's prose-poetry/short-prose collections have been translated; three of her five works of children's fiction have been translated; however, only two of her volumes of poetry (*True Stories/Wahre Geschichten* and *Morning in the Burned House/Ein Morgen im verbrannten Haus*) out of a total of eleven (excluding anthologies) have been translated. These figures suggest two things. First, they clearly demonstrate the extent to which Atwood's works (with the exception of her poetry) have been made available in German translation, a good indicator

---

2. The special status of Germany in the reception of Atwood is suggested by the order in which the nationalities are listed in the following statement by Robert Fulford: "For a long time she's been a grand international figure, loved by the Germans, the English, the Japanese and God knows who else"; "Toronto and Margaret Atwood," *National Post*, 24 August 2000.
3. The database can be accessed at www.dfait-maeci.gc.ca/canada-europa/germany/cultureincanada2a-de.asp [consulted 18 February 2007].

of her prominent position in the German-speaking world, even if translations are seen as an enabler rather than a reflection of an author's reception.[4] Second, it is also possible, based on these statistics, to postulate a generic hierarchy of translations of Atwood, comprising, in descending order, novels, short-prose texts (short stories, shorter fictions, and prose poems), and poetic texts.

Atwood's importance in teaching at school and university levels is also a measure of her popularity in the German-speaking countries. Caroline Rosenthal has surveyed Atwood's representation on syllabi and curricula and has concluded that, as well as "being taught increasingly in high schools" (2000, 44), Atwood has "been taught more often than any other Canadian writer" at the university level (43), having been included in at least fifty-one courses at German universities between 1981 and 1999. As Rosenthal points out, this figure probably constitutes an underestimate, and if the University of Constance is anything to go by it must have increased considerably in recent years, reflecting the continuing canonization of Atwood's works in a German context.

Similarly, the prominence of Germany in scholarly research on Atwood is clear testimony to the author's status in that country. Remarkably, nine of the forty-seven major book publications on Atwood listed in a recent Atwood bibliography (Nischik 2000, 321–323) were published in Germany or with heavy involvement by German scholars (with a further work published in Bern, Switzerland), a figure far in excess of any other non-English-speaking country.

Taken together, these indicators, along with other factors such as the overwhelmingly positive reviews that greet the publication in German of every new Atwood novel or the author's appearance at the international book fair in Frankfurt, paint a vivid picture. Atwood is clearly a literary figure of considerable, and increasing, status in the German-speaking world and appeals both to a broad readership and to a scholarly and academic clientele, which reflects the situation in the English-speaking world. The only caveat regards the fact that Atwood is received in the German-speaking world almost exclusively as a prose writer, specifically as a novelist. Unfortunately, the bulk of her outstanding poetic work as yet remains unavailable to a reading public not fluent in English.[5]

---

4. In its early stages at least, an author's reception in a foreign country is to a large extent dependent on the existence of translations; in other words, the translations enable the reception of an author's work. At a later stage, once the writer's reputation has been established, the situation is turned around, and the status of the writer leads to the production of translations. Of course, the reality is not quite as clear-cut as this differentiation suggests. At all stages, both aspects feed off each other to a greater or lesser degree.
5. In the English-speaking world, too, Atwood's poetry is often unjustly neglected compared to her prose works.

## REASONS FOR ATWOOD'S PROMINENCE IN GERMANY

That Atwood should appeal in Germany to a broadly based reading public akin to that in the United States or Canada, for instance, is highly unusual. It can be argued that her works in translation suffer from a double handicap: first, translated works tend to occupy a peripheral position in the literary systems into which they have been transferred; second, Canadian literature, and indeed Canada in general, have not enjoyed a particularly prominent profile abroad (although this situation may well be in the process of changing).

The first problem can be addressed with reference to a poll of Germans' favourite books conducted by the German television channel ZDF in 2004, in the course of which a quarter of a million readers cast their votes. In contrast to similar polls conducted in English-speaking countries, which are invariably dominated by home-grown authors and books, the result of the German poll indicated that only two of German readers' ten favourite works had been written by German authors, the others originating in, among other countries, Britain, the United States, and France.[6] Any attempt to explain the startlingly non-nationalistic tastes of the German reading public must be very tentative, but a plausible link can be made to Germany's general rejection of all kinds of nationalism (and even to a great extent more moderate patriotism) since World War II. Whatever the reason, the quoted poll at the least provides an interesting insight into how readily translated works such as those of Atwood can access the centre of German literary culture.

The solution to the second problem should be sought in the context of the remarkable change in fortunes of Canadian literature in Germany in the past four decades. Canadian literature has developed from a position of almost complete obscurity in the 1970s to a situation where at present it not only enjoys considerable popularity but also has a clearly defined profile—a process in which Atwood herself has been one of the crucial factors. In trying to explain this dramatic increase in popularity, it is necessary to look for fundamental cultural correspondences that explain the unusual empathy that German readers seem to have developed with Canadian literature and above all with Atwood. Conradi (2000, 35) has suggested that the "irony and reflection" inherent in Canadian literature, and its "consciousness of historical continuity" (both "European" qualities not to be found to the same degree in American literature), make it so attractive to German readers. Indeed, one might go even further and ask whether the Canadian search for a distinctive identity in the second half of the twentieth

---

6. Details of the poll can be found at www.zdf.de/ZDFde/inhalt/7/0,1872,2181735,00.html [consulted 18 February 2007].

century and the country's readiness to question itself do not constitute a direct parallel to Germany's attempts to define a new identity for itself since World War II and to its continuing self-doubt. Insofar as these qualities are reflected in Canadian literature, one can argue that they foster a literary atmosphere that touches a chord among specifically German rather than just European readers. Similarly, the important role played by the environment and the natural world in many Canadian works of literature—subjects that take on particular prominence in Atwood's oeuvre—is paralleled by the extreme concern for environmental issues that has developed in Germany more than in any other European country in the postwar era, particularly since the 1960s.[7] Or again, the concern and skepticism, not to say outright hostility, felt by Canadian writers such as Atwood toward the looming presence of their country's southern neighbour may well have found a receptive audience, particularly among the German liberal intelligentsia with its traditionally anti-American stance.

This focus on broad cultural explanations, however, should not blind us to the importance of individuals who have done great service to Canadian literature in Germany. For example, a considerable contribution to Atwood's—and other Canadian authors'—discovery and rise to prominence in Germany has been made via the efforts of a number of publishers in promoting individual Canadian authors:

> Margaret Atwood's success, for example, is unthinkable without the efforts of Arnulf Conradi. Michael Klett and his copy editor Ulrike Killer are synonymous with the success of Alice Munro. Antje Kunstmann is behind the success of Barbara Gowdy. Michael Ondaatje's success is linked to the publishing house Hanser Verlag and to his friendship with its publisher, Michael Krüger (Holzamer 2000, 11).[8]

Similarly, prominent Canadianists and an increasing number of departments

---

7. See the following comment by German critic Walter Riedel: "What is more, in the present climate, dominated as it is by mechanization, progress, and overpopulated cities, the interest in or rediscovery of nature that is embodied in images of Canada offers modern people something approaching the fulfillment of their subconscious desire for a natural paradise" (1980, 105). Riedel also makes the point that mainly nature-oriented Canadian texts have been translated into German, to the exclusion of texts with other, especially urban, settings: "In Canadian literature that has been translated into German, the dominant themes are the landscape, Native peoples, the animal world, and the interaction of humans with nature. On the other hand, books that deal predominantly with the problems of life in the city or with political and social ... questions have hitherto been underrepresented in translation and on the German book market" (104).
8. For Conradi's recollections of his "discovery" of Margaret Atwood, see Conradi (2000, 27–35).

at German universities have contributed to passing on an interest in Canadian literature and culture to new generations of students and readers. Suffice it here to mention the late Walter Pache or the important research and teaching being carried out at the Universities of Constance and Marburg. In addition, the role of the media in promoting Canadian literature in Germany should not be underestimated. In this context, one should mention Susanne Becker, editor in the Culture Department of German television channel ZDF in Mainz. She herself describes the importance of her first interview with Atwood on 6 March 1979:

> In my first media encounter with Margaret Atwood, she walks through the snow, purposefully, dreamily, with her hands in the pockets of a dark coat, along high, snow-covered pines, while a disembodied dark female voice recites, in German, the famous last paragraph from *Surfacing* ... Then—cut—Margaret Atwood is joined by writer-husband Graeme Gibson ... while a male commentator explains that she is the representative of a small but important literature, from Canada, that the German readership tends to forget because of U.S.A. cultural imperialism. An interview about nationalism, nature, and feminism follows, during which Atwood sits with her back to a brooding winter landscape.... Years later, I spoke to Graeme Gibson about that scene ... They had played the game and it worked: to her German readers, it established Margaret Atwood firmly as a Canadian figure—never to be confused with American writers. (2000, 32)

Finally, we should not forget that much of Atwood's success, around the world and in Germany, can simply be attributed to the sheer quality of her work. Works like hers that combine thematic complexity with entertaining, plot-driven narratives, humour with stylistic precision and elegance, are almost predestined to appeal to a wide-ranging public, from the casual to the academic reader.

**ATWOOD'S NOVEL *SURFACING* IN GERMAN**

I will now take a closer look at how an individual work of Atwood's has fared in German translation. My aim is not only to chart some of the individual translation decisions made in rendering Atwood's English into a German linguistic and cultural context but also to explore the central underlying issue of how an author's—in this case Atwood's—reception in a particular country is influenced by decisions made by translators and publishers. The work on which I have chosen to base my analysis is Atwood's early novel *Surfacing* (1972), which for a number of reasons is ideal for my present purposes. Not only is it one of her major achievements in any genre, but it also encapsulates a wide range of her central thematic concerns (e.g., Canadian identity and environment, gender relations, U.S. cultural imperialism), many of which, in their cultural specificity, provide tricky challenges for the translator. Most importantly, the existence of two German translations of the novel by the same translator, published in the western and eastern parts of the then-divided Germany, makes possible a comparison of them as well as an examination of the factors influencing their production and their reception in the target cultures.

*Production History of the Translations*

It is worth examining the circumstances in which two different though textually related translations of *Surfacing*, both by the East German translator Reinhild Böhnke, appeared more or less simultaneously in 1979 in West and East Germany respectively.[9] The process of translation, as Böhnke has related to me,[10] began with her being offered the job of translating the novel by the East German publisher Philipp Reclam of Leipzig. While the work of translation was in progress, the West German publishing house Claassen showed interest in the project, at which point Reclam, eager for Western currency, pressured Böhnke to complete her work as quickly as possible. Eventually, a not fully revised version of the translation was passed on to Claassen, where it was edited and modified by Arnulf Conradi, not yet the prominent publisher that he would later become.[11] Conradi's involvement at this stage was of paramount importance since, voluntarily or not, as a West German he would be working with West German cultural assumptions, which may have influenced the final form of the text. Meanwhile, Böhnke herself completed and revised her version for the East German publisher. The West German translation was finally published as *Der lange Traum* ("The Long Dream"), the East German under the title *Strömung* ("Current" or "Flow"). This unusual story not only provides a snapshot of the machinations of the publishing industry in pre-reunification Germany but also sheds light on the production of a translation that was to a significant extent to mark the breakthrough of Atwood, and with her the whole of Canadian literature, into the German cultural environment. The significance of the translation is underlined by Astrid Holzamer, who at the time was already working for the Canadian embassy in West Germany: "*Der lange Traum* was published in 1979, and Margaret Atwood came to the Frankfurt Book Fair ... We were soon riding on the crest of a wave that Atwood had set in motion" (2000, 17–18).

---
9. The bibliographical information concerning the date of publication provided by the East German version is ambiguous. Although the copyright date for the translation is given as 1978, the date of the first printing is 1979. Private correspondence with the translator (dated 28 May 2003) confirms that the translation did not appear until 1979.
10. Personal correspondence, 28 May 2003.
11. In fact, Conradi has stated in personal correspondence with Reingard M. Nischik that this was the first book he worked on for Claassen.

## Cultural Factors Influencing the Production of the Translations

The double publication of translations of *Surfacing* in East and West Germany meant that Atwood's work was being made available to two highly different reading publics, representing two cultural spheres with divergent sets of cultural and ideological assumptions and standardizations. Not surprisingly, such parameters place powerful constraints on both the production and the reception of a translation. This was most obviously the case in the German Democratic Republic (GDR),[12] where the political and ideological climate was generally inimical to the free expression of ideas. However, contrary to what might be expected given the nature of the regime, the translator, in making her East German translation, seems to have come under no explicit pressure to modify its content in any way: "At the publishing houses for which I worked no one ever prescribed the content of the translations ... I was never faced with politically motivated preconceptions about my translations" (personal communication, 28 May 2003). That is not to say that there was no control over the content of books or translations published in East Germany. Rather, the control was carried out prior to translation by a censorship commission that authorized books for publication. Only after this approval was the translator free to do his or her work: "After the book had been approved for publication, my task was to translate the text as faithfully as possible into German" (personal communication, 28 May 2003). In the case of *Surfacing*, with its anti-American tendencies and its critical dialogue with the norms and conventions of Western civilization in general, it is easy to see why the novel would pass the scrutiny of the censors.

A more subtle form of censorship practised in the GDR is apparent in Böhnke's East German translation of *Surfacing*: namely, the inclusion of an "explanatory" afterword to nudge the reader's interpretation of the text in the desired direction: "A fore- or afterword was often used to 'explain' to readers—who were considered politically immature—how the text should be interpreted" (personal communication, 28 May 2003). I will discuss below how the afterword to the East German translation of *Surfacing* (written, interestingly, not by the translator but by copy editor Gabriele Bock) attempts to influence the reader's perception of the novel.

By her own account, Böhnke's approach to translating *Surfacing* seems not to have been particularly influenced—at least consciously—by considerations of the cultural differences between source and target culture or by the need to clarify these differences for the target readership. Although clearly aware of the

---

12. For an overview of Canadian literature in the GDR, see Barbara Korte's chapter in this volume.

problems of cultural transfer, and of the difficulties of making the Canadian context of Atwood's novel comprehensible for a reader in the GDR (and also, though arguably to a lesser extent, to a West German reader), the translator maintains that they were not the main focus during her work on *Surfacing*: "As far as I can remember [such considerations] played no part in the translation of *Surfacing*" (personal communication, 28 May 2003). Böhnke's statement, however, although it is no doubt representative of her general approach to the translation, need not be taken entirely at face value. Evidence from the text itself confirms that the work cannot have been that simple. One need only cite the endnotes that accompany the East German translation, providing explanations (though not always satisfactory ones) for numerous culturally specific terms that would otherwise have been incomprehensible to an East German reader.

In contrast to the situation in East Germany, where the external influences on the translator, if not always openly stated, were palpable and real, the situation in the free market of West German publishing was, and is, considerably different. Whereas it is much less likely—though not fully excluded—that ideological considerations should influence the production of the translation, the fact that it was published not, as in the GDR, for a deliberately restricted market, but as a mainstream publication designed to sell as many copies as possible, brings with it its own set of constraints. The choice of title, for example, which forms the reader's first introduction to the novel, may be influenced not simply by an attempt to produce as accurate a translation of the original as possible but also by a desire to catch the attention of potential buyers. Additionally, the use of a paratextual apparatus, in particular foot- or endnotes (as employed in the East German but not in the West German translation), is by convention highly restricted in a mainstream, as opposed to a scholarly, publication, no doubt since they would detract from the illusion of reading an "original" text. This constraint makes it difficult for the translated text to convey the culturally specific references contained in Atwood's work. Or again, the nature of the translation itself is highly circumscribed: the buyer of a mainstream translation expects a faithful rendering of the source text, so that the translator is hardly at liberty to attempt more re-creative or non-standard forms of translation.

## *Analysis of the Translations*

The most visible sign of a conscious desire to manipulate the reader's reception of the text, and to mould it in a particular direction, is provided by Gabriele Bock's[13]

---

13. As Böhnke has informed me (personal communication, 25 March 2004), Gabriele Bock was the copy editor (*Lektorin*) for English-language literature at Philipp Reclam of Leipzig from the

afterword to *Strömung*, the East German translation of *Surfacing*. Although written in a superficially scholarly tone, and exuding a surface air of normality, the afterword repeatedly takes Atwood's works as a starting point for a wide-ranging and scathing ideological critique of Western capitalist culture and society. In doing so, it employs two main discursive strategies. On the one hand, Atwood's oeuvre in general, and *Surfacing* in particular, are praised for their criticisms of what are perceived to be the moral failings of the West, particularly as encapsulated by America. On the other hand, those aspects of Atwood's work that do not fit into the writer's ideological framework are played down or twisted into shape. Inevitably, Bock's desire to criticize Atwood's cultural background, while at the same time praising the author herself, leads to contradictions in her argument.

One of the most noteworthy examples of Bock's approach appears in a passage (1979, 194) in which Bock touches upon Atwood's treatment of war and politics. Contrary to the usual interpretations of Atwood's stance on this matter, which take note of her strong, active views on human rights and power politics, Bock portrays Atwood as a passive figure, observing from the outside ("observer") but not rebelling or attempting to (re)form society ("does not interfere in social processes"). Indeed, Atwood's individuality as a whole is played down; instead, in tried and true Marxist tradition, Atwood is presented as merely a part of society as a whole ("an element of the society in which she lives") and thus unable as a mere individual to influence it. The author of the afterword thus attempts to defuse Atwood's potential political and ideological explosiveness. By presenting the reader with an unusual, not to say marginal, interpretation of Atwood's politics—an interpretation lent authority by its very presence in the afterword—Bock manipulates the reader's reception of Atwood's novel, leading it in a more ideologically acceptable direction.

In another passage dealing with the role of women in *Surfacing*, Bock explicitly criticizes the "aggressive feminism" that she perceives in "countless" Western novels and that, she argues, leads to a fruitless conflict between men and women. Western culture, then, is explicitly linked with such negative qualities as aggression and conflict, hardly surprising within the context of a culture that conceived of itself as the front line against Western "imperialism" and "fascism." In this passage, Atwood, in her treatment of issues relating to women, is implicitly praised for not

---

mid-1970s to the early 1990s. It was therefore, as Böhnke points out, unusual that Bock should have written the afterword: "Usually, English specialists from university ... were charged with the task." Böhnke also provides a plausible explanation for this anomalous situation: "She [Bock] probably felt that she should provide some ideological justification for publishing the novel in the GDR. I know, for example, that she encountered serious problems with the publication of Kerouac's *On the Road*."

conforming to Western norms and is thus subtly brought closer to acceptability within an East German cultural context. Atwood is good, implies Bock, because she is un-Western: "Although the events of this book are seen through the eyes of a woman, we should thank Atwood that it is not one of the countless aggressively feminist Western novels. The solution to the problems of human existence and coexistence does not lie in the conflict between men and women" (1979, 198). The last sentence quoted is particularly subtle since in its context—and particularly in the original German—it is unclear whether Bock is presenting her own opinion or that of Atwood—East German critic and Canadian novelist become one. Atwood is implicitly portrayed as supporting and "authorizing" the East German point of view and rejecting the Western perspective. This sleight of hand involves not only a reassessment of Atwood's ideological stance but also a misrepresentation of Western feminism. Bock deliberately reduces the attitudes of the movement to a mere war of the sexes, ignoring the many varieties of feminism current at the time that Atwood was writing.

Bock launches a further attack on gender relations in Western society at another point in the afterword. She praises Atwood for not conforming to the supposed tendency of Western writers to deal only with what Bock sees as the problems of women in the West:

> Unlike many other writers, she is not simply interested in the superficial problems of the majority of women in Western society: sexual repression, discrimination in their choice of profession and in the job market. More important is the question of what goes beyond this, since money, employment, and independence do not lead automatically to fulfillment—either for women or for men. (1979, 198)

Once again the reader is presented with a highly negative view of the West. Western women are portrayed as being disadvantaged both sexually and in the workplace, a situation which, it is implied, exists only in the West and is entirely absent from East Germany. Quite apart from the dubious validity of such an assertion, a closer look at the final sentence of the above quotation suggests that it undermines what has been said in the remainder of the extract. Again it is not entirely clear whether Bock is expressing her own opinion or that of Atwood. In any case, this sentence states that the very aspects of life that, according to Bock, are problematic for women in the West and therefore positive for women in the East (i.e., money, work, independence) do not suffice to make women happy. If the statement reports Atwood's opinion, then it inadvertently shows Atwood undermining Bock's presentation of the supposed advantages of Eastern society.

If it is Bock's, then Bock herself is proving the irrelevance of her previous critique of Western society.

Bock's afterword also contains clear expressions of anti-Americanism. The most extended treatment of the subject comes toward the end of the afterword (1979, 198–199), in a passage highlighting Atwood's own anti-Americanism in *Surfacing*. A strong current of anti-Americanism is certainly present in the novel and provides ideal material for an East German who is geared to such attitudes. Bock is careful, however, to note that Atwood's attitude to America is ambivalent rather than downright hostile: "Hostility or admiration alone are equally dangerous for the weaker nation [i.e., Canada]" (198). Nevertheless, anti-Americanism of a particularly hostile kind is implied in Bock's subsequent mentioning of Hitler and the United States in one sentence, with the clear intention that the reader should see parallels between the two and with the equally clear implication that Atwood, too, intends the reader to do so: "The narrator realizes that death and evil cannot be ignored as something belonging exclusively to Hitler ... or to modern Americans" (199). This is the final, and perhaps the most extreme, case of the East German critic's (deliberate) misinterpretation and decontextualization of aspects of Atwood's texts with the purpose of harnessing the author to the exigencies of a particular political ideology.

The aims of the afterword are clear enough, but we must ask ourselves how it was received by the East German reading public and more specifically how it might have affected their approach to Atwood's novel. Up to a point, one must trust the critical judgment of East German readers and assume that they were able to ignore what was easily identifiable as government propaganda. This supposition is supported by the fact that, as Reinhild Böhnke has pointed out (personal correspondence, 19 June 2003), translations of English-language books sold very well in spite of being published only in small, censored editions. Buying a translation of an English-language book, then, may have been a somewhat subversive activity, as the reader was aware that he or she was buying something that was not easy to obtain and of which the authorities were suspicious. On the other hand, if a reader, no matter how critically versed, is repeatedly confronted with texts of a particular ideological slant, it is inevitable that at least some influence will rub off. Ideas that seem problematic to an outsider are thus accepted as cultural standardizations. At least to some extent, then, the afterword may have fulfilled its intended function and modified readers' reception of the text.

The best place to compare ways in which the two translations may have been influenced by the ideological climates in which they were produced is in their treatment of Americans, who were, needless to say, viewed rather differently in

East and West Germany. As we have seen, the afterword to the East German translation contains several instances of anti-Americanism. But to what extent is it reflected in the translation itself?

One case in which the divergent approach of the two translations is immediately noticeable occurs in the rendering of the narrator's striking statement, "I was asking Are the Americans worse than Hitler?" (Atwood 1979 [*Surfacing*], 123), which, by not only mentioning Americans in the same breath as Nazism[14] but also entertaining the possibility that the former are the more despicable of the two, is almost shockingly anti-American. Böhnke's East German translation offers a rendering that closely follows the English source text: "fragte ich mich: Sind die Amerikaner schlimmer als Hitler?" ("I asked myself: are the Americans worse than Hitler?") (Atwood 1979 [*Strömung*], 130); the West German version, on the other hand, departs subtly, but nevertheless with radical consequences, from Atwood's original English: "Ich fragte mich: Sind die Amerikaner jetzt, was früher Hitler war?" ("I asked myself: are the Americans now what Hitler used to be?") (Atwood 1979 [*Der langue Traum*], 168).

It is clear after even a relatively superficial analysis that this West German translation of Böhnke's presents the Americans in a more favourable light than either the original English or her own East German translation. Whereas in the original and in the East German version the narrator asks herself whether the Americans are worse than Hitler, this has been toned down in the West German version to wondering whether they are as bad as the Nazi dictator once was, a considerable difference that takes some of the sting out of Atwood's statement and leaves the West German reader with a more positive (or less negative) image of the Americans than his or her East German counterpart or a reader of the original English.

Another instance in which the West German text seems to show the Americans in a more positive light than either the East German version or the source text is fascinating in its subtlety. It involves the assertion by David, one of the main characters, that Canada would be a better country "if we could only kick out the fascist pig Yanks and the capitalists" (Atwood 1979 [*Surfacing*], 33). The two translations are almost identical apart from one comma: "Wenn wir nur die Yanks, die Faschistenschweine, und die Kapitalisten rauswerfen könnten" (Atwood 1979 [*Strömung*], 38); "Wenn wir nur die Yanks, die Faschistenschweine und die Kapitalisten hinauswerfen könnten" (Atwood 1979 [*Der langue Traum*],

---

14. This is clearly the passage that Bock is playing upon in her comparison, in the afterword, of Hitler and Americans (see above). By taking it out of context, however, the East German writer lends it a spurious aura of general validity, which is at odds with Atwood's more nuanced approach to anti-Americanism.

48). While the extra comma in the East German translation makes it clear that the term "Faschistenschweine" ("fascist pigs") is in apposition to the "Yanks" and thus descriptive of them as in the source text, its absence in the West German version makes the sequence appear like a list with three separate elements, thus suggesting that the "Faschistenschweine" are a different group from the Americans. We must at least entertain the possibility that the West German copy editor was intentionally attempting to defuse some of the opprobrium heaped on the Americans (as is also the case in the previous example), perhaps because the suggestion that Americans are "fascist pigs" might be considered unpalatable for a West German audience.

Another passage, however, shows a different tendency from what has been hitherto observable. One of the most venomous attacks on the Americans in the whole of *Surfacing* occurs shortly before the comparison with Hitler discussed above and in fact builds up to it. During the passage in question ("But they'd killed the heron anyway"—"a language is everything you do"), the Americans (actual or honorary) are, among other things, scathingly compared to a "virus," a "disease," and alien "body-snatchers" (Atwood 1979 [*Surfacing*], 123). An examination of the two translations (Atwood 1979 [*Strömung*], 129; Atwood 1979 [*Der langue Traum*], 167–168) reveals very little difference. One exception, however, is the translation of the English "disease," used as a metaphor for the Americans. It is rendered as "Krankheit," a reasonable equivalent, in Böhnke's East German translation; the West German translation, however, has "Seuche." Although it is also an acceptable translation, the German word might be considered stronger and more unappealing than the original English—indeed, a correct translation of "Seuche" into English would produce "plague" or "pestilence"—thus making Americans seem even more unpleasant than they are in Atwood's original text.

Again, then, this is an example of a discrepancy between the two translations, and again it is the West German translation that deviates from the original English; the East German version remains as faithful as on other occasions. This time, however, the West German text modifies the original in the diametrically opposite direction to what has been observed previously. This example is important in that it highlights the fact that any attempt to discern a specific culturally motivated tactic in the translations of passages pertaining to the Americans must proceed with caution.

The passage under discussion contains one further, particularly culturally revealing piece of translation that indirectly and subtly highlights the differences in attitude toward Western—specifically American—culture in the two target cultures. The phrase in question is "late show sci-fi movies" (Atwood 1979 [*Surfacing*], 123), representative of American culture in that both movies and the science fiction genre are associated with the United States. The West German translation, "Science-fiction-Spätfilmen" (Atwood 1979 [*Der langue Traum*], 167), here reveals, if not an attitude of approval, at least absolute familiarity with the genre in question and its conventions, hardly surprising given the currency and popularity of science fiction films in West Germany and in Western Europe in general. Cultural transfer is thus relatively easy to achieve in this case, since the medium, the genre, and its standardizations and cultural implications are as familiar to readers in the target culture as to those in the source culture.

In the case of Böhnke's East German translation, the approach and its implications are very different. Here Atwood's original English is rendered as "den letzten utopischen Monumentalfilmen" (Atwood 1979 [*Strömung*], 129) ("the last monumental utopian films"). What is immediately striking about this version is its translation of "sci-fi movies" as "utopischen Monumentalfilmen." This demonstrates at the least the translator's unwillingness, in an East German context, to leave the English genre designation untranslated, perhaps because it would be considered inappropriate to use such an ostentatiously American term. It also suggests, however, unfamiliarity with, and perhaps disapproval of, the genre itself within the context of East German culture. Although the "utopischen Monumentalfilmen" may be an adequate description of some science fiction films, it is inaccurate as a description of the genre as a whole. On the one hand, it plays down the elements of pure entertainment, fantasy, and frivolity inherent in the genre; on the other hand, it lends it the aura of a massively serious and rather grim Soviet-era film on the social aspirations of the proletariat. Certainly, it presents the genre, probably deliberately, as very different from its typical Hollywood manifestation in the United States. This may well be a reflection of official attitudes toward the genre in communist Eastern Europe and the specific cultural assumptions concerning it.

Suggestions of disapproval of the genre, at least in its typical American guise, can perhaps also be detected in the use of the adjective "letzten" ("last"). This is apparently intended to translate the original English "late show," implying that science fiction films are often shown in late-night projections, but the East German translation does not at all correspond to this meaning. It is possible that the German is intended to carry the meaning of "recent," which would make sense but is not justified by the original. It is all the more interesting, then, that the word in German can convey the sense of worthlessness or uselessness. Would it be going too far to suggest that Böhnke's East German translation in this instance constitutes a (deliberate) rejection of the quintessentially American genre of science fiction, perhaps as a result of official policy in East Germany? The evidence from the translations of both parts of the English phrase certainly seems to suggest a general rejection of the genre as practised in North America. This particular phrase may constitute an interesting example, then, of the imposition of cultural standardizations of the target culture onto the content of the source text, thus entirely changing its meaning.

However, we should note, in contrast, the totally neutral treatment in the East German translation (Atwood 1979 [*Strömung*], 113) of the reference to Superman ("neither of us would put on the cape and boots and the thunderbolt sweatshirt" [Atwood 1979 (*Surfacing*), 106]), an aggressively self-confident icon of American culture, where a negative portrayal might have been expected. The West German translation, while also adopting a neutral stance, interestingly makes the reference to Superman explicit ("keiner von uns wollte Supermann [sic; this Germanization of the name is in itself an interesting example of cultural appropriation] sein" [Atwood 1979 (*Der langue Traum*), 144]), as if a West German audience were in more need of an explanation here than an East German one.

## CONCLUSION

In the opening sections of this chapter, I provided a sketch of the status of Margaret Atwood's works in Germany and suggested reasons for the author's prominence in that country. The overview I have given of the two German translations of Atwood's novel *Surfacing* highlights the important point that an author's reception in a particular country is dependent not only on factors inherent in her or his works but also on the many constraints and norms in the target culture that shape the way in which translations are produced and received. As the comparison of two German-language versions of the same work suggests, these factors are cultural rather than primarily linguistic; indeed, one might go as far as to say that they are only linguistic to the extent that language is a constitutive element of culture.

I have tried to show, then, that cultural concerns specific to East and West Germany respectively undoubtedly governed aspects of the production and content of the two translations. From the few examples that I have provided in the context of this chapter, it should be clear, however, that discerning and quantifying these influences is a hazardous process and must be approached with considerable caution. On one immediately obvious level, the influence of the target cultures is visible in the physical appearance of the translations. Whereas the West German version, like the English original, is a typically "Western" book production, with a glossy cover, printed on reasonably good-quality paper, of comfortable dimensions, and containing no paratextual apparatus, the East German edition is a small, grey-looking paperback printed on low-quality paper, with a print size and spacing that are inimical to comfortable reading, but containing endnotes and an afterword. This is clearly a result of the differing market circumstances in which the books appeared. As far as the content is concerned, however, specific influences of the target cultures are harder to quantify. A number of cases have been noted, in the treatment of the Americans, for instance, where a culturally specific antipathy in the East German translation, and a greater acceptance in the West German version, are apparently discernible. Before jumping to any conclusions, however, we must remember that examples can nearly always be adduced that refute these tendencies.

There are, however, points in the text at which the cultural influence of the target culture is indubitably at work, for example in a rendering such as "utopischen Monumentalfilmen," where an item of specifically East German vocabulary with its own set of cultural implications is employed in the East German translation but not in its West German counterpart. More importantly, there is the afterword to the East German translation, which is the major tool for the imposition of the values of the target culture onto the source text and culture. By means of the afterword, the East German reader's perception of the text is guided in such a way as to conform to the norms of East German culture. Significantly, the West German text has no equivalent to this "interpretative" text; the readers are left to decide for themselves.

Aside from matters of cultural influence, however, we should not forget that the great success of Atwood's works in Germany—in a cultural environment that, the many similarities notwithstanding, is also profoundly different from that in which Atwood writes—is testimony to their remarkable ability to speak to readers from a wide variety of cultural backgrounds.

**REFERENCES**

Atwood, Margaret. *Surfacing*. London: Virago, 1979 [1972].
———. *Strömung*, transl. Reinhild Böhnke. Leipzig: Reclam, 1979.
———. *Der lange Traum*, transl. Reinhild Böhnke. Düsseldorf: Claassen, 1979.
Becker, Susanne. "Celebrity, or a Disneyland of the Soul: Margaret Atwood and the Media." In Nischik 2000, 28–40.
Bock, Gabriele. Afterword. In *Strömung*, by Margaret Atwood. Trans. Reinhild Böhnke. Leipzig: Reclam, 1979.
Conradi, Arnulf. "Canadian Literature in Germany." In Kuester and Wolf 2000, 27–35.
Fulford, Robert. "Toronto and Margaret Atwood." In *National Post*, 24 August 2000. Available electronically at: http://robertfulford.com/Ravines.html (date of access 18 February 2007).
Holzamer, Astrid H. "Zur Rezeption kanadischer Literatur in Deutschland: Vom garstigen Haarball zum süßen Zimtschäler." In Kuester and Wolf 2000, 10–26.

Kuester, Martin, and Andrea Wolff. *Reflections of Canada: The Reception of Canadian Literature in Germany*. Marburg: Universitätsbibliothek, 2000.

Nischik, Reingard M. "Margaret Atwood, *Power Politics*, oder: Vom Ende romantischer Liebe bzw. Liebeslyrik?" In *Schwellentexte der Weltliteratur*, ed. Reingard M. Nischik and Caroline Rosenthal. Konstanz: Universitätsverlag Konstanz, 2002. 273–301.

———, ed. *Margaret Atwood: Works and Impact*. Rochester, N.Y.: Camden House, 2000.

Riedel, Walter E. *Das literarische Kanadabild: Eine Studie zur Rezeption kanadischer Literatur in deutscher Übersetzung*. Bonn: Bouvier, 1980.

Rosenthal, Caroline. "Canonizing Atwood: Her Impact on Teaching in the US, Canada, and Europe." In Nischik 2000, 41–56.

# The "AlterNative" Frontier: Native Canadian Writing in German/y[1]

*Eva Gruber*
*University of Constance*

Literature in translation constitutes a highly visible form of cultural representation and plays a substantial role in shaping the image of a cultural group as it presents itself or is presented to others. The kind of literature by or about a specific cultural group that appears in translation, as well as when and in which ways these translations are conducted, have an impact on the perception of this group abroad. This chapter undertakes an empirical survey of existing German translations of Canadian First Nations literature. In addition, it explores the reciprocal influence that the image of "the Indian"[2] and the literature appearing in German translation exert on each other, trying to detect possible underlying patterns in the selection of literature by Native Canadian writers for translation. The chapter concludes with a discussion of some of the idiosyncrasies inherent in the translation of English-language First Nations literature into German with regard to the processes of cultural transfer.

Most German readers' first contact with Canadian Indians happens through literature *about* them rather than *by* them. While translations of works by Canadian First Nations writers are still scarce, books about Indians have been available to German readers and very much in demand since the end of the

---

1. *AlterNatives* is the title of a play (2000) by Ojibway playwright Drew Hayden Taylor.
2. I use the term "Indian" when referring to the stereotypical construct—that is, the simulacrum of Native identity—but "Native Canadian" or "First Nations" for Canada's indigenous population. German readers usually do not differentiate between American and Canadian Natives but subsume them under the general category "Indian." North America's indigenous population itself often does not acknowledge the American-Canadian border as a valid line—a fact that makes the distinction between Native American and Native Canadian literature problematic to some degree—regarding it as an artificial classification imposed on them by European colonizers. The conflation within the German readership's imagination is most likely not due to such identity politics but determined by images created by non-Native literature and Hollywood movies.

nineteenth century, when James Fenimore Cooper's *Leatherstocking Tales* appeared in German. This is not really surprising, considering that until recently most Canadians themselves did not read First Nations literature but turned to fictionalized accounts about Indians by white Canadian authors as diverse as Duncan Campbell Scott, E. J. Pratt, Farley Mowat, Fred Bodsworth, Yves Thériault, Rudy Wiebe, Anne Cameron, and W. P. Kinsella (see King 1994, 353; Young-Ing 1996, 165). As Thomas King claims, "Indeed, the list of Canadian authors who have *not* made use of the Native is almost easier to compile than the list of those who have" (1994, 353). Thus, even before the German public was introduced to the Hollywood image of "the Indian," a set perceptional frame with regard to North America's indigenous population had been established both by North American writing in translation and by German writers' works, such as Karl May's novels about Winnetou, a fictional Mescalero Apache chief, or Fritz Steuben's Tecumseh novels, which transported a highly dubious ideological agenda during the Nazi era (see Lutz 2000, 41–43). Writings such as these induced a curious German infatuation with Indians, a phenomenon for which Hartmut Lutz coined the term *Indianertümelei* or "Indianthusiasm" to signify "a yearning for all things Indian, a fascination with American Indians, a romanticizing about a supposed Indian essence" (2002b, 168).[3] Indianthusiasm is, as he points out, a conceptual frame that both racializes and historicizes the image of the Indian in that it stereotypically ossifies Native North Americans as figures of the past and neglects contemporary Native North American realities. In extending the physical and material colonization practised by Europeans, some Germans even try to appropriate the identities of North America's indigenous population by "playing Indian" in special clubs on weekends (see Carlson 2002)—a romanticizing practice that quite clearly has more to do with the participants' national background and personal needs than with real Native North Americans.

Curiously enough, the German fascination with "Indians" is widely known among Canada's First Nations by now, giving rise both to instrumentalization of this interest and to much mirth: Lutz reports that, during a 1998 conference on indigenous art in Ottawa, four out of six indigenous participants in the opening panel discussion "expressly mentioned 'the Germans' or 'Germany' as the most profitable marketing outlets for their cultural productions in writing and

---

3. While Lutz considers this idealizing fascination with Indians and the belief in a special affinity between Germans and Indians a specifically German phenomenon, originating in or at least closely linked to the development of a German national or "ethnic" identity and instrumental in compensatory German self-aggrandizement (see Lutz 1999, 87–88; 2000, 38; 2002b, 179), Christian Feest asserts that "the desire to identify with the Indians is a widespread European phenomenon, rather than just a German aberration" (2002, 29).

publishing, in the visual arts, in music, media arts, theatre, and dance music" (2003, 217–18). Algonquin playwright Yvette Nolan reacted to an invitation to a Canadian Studies conference at Düsseldorf, Germany, by shrugging her shoulders and saying, "Okay, I'll be their annual Indian for the next year" (see Lutz 2003), and Ojibway playwright Drew Hayden Taylor candidly describes his trips to Germany for similar purposes in "Ich bin ein Ojibway" (in *Funny, You Don't Look like One: Observations from a Blue-Eyed Ojibway*, 1998) and "First We Take Turtle Island, Then We Take Berlin" (in *Further Adventures of a Blue-Eyed Ojibway*, 1999). Such awareness of attention from Germany also shows in fictional works (see Eigenbrod 2002), be it in Emma Lee Warrior's short story "Compatriots," in which a German student in search of "authentic Indians" encounters a German wannabe shaman in Alberta, or in Thomas King's novel *Truth and Bright Water*, in which trickster character Monroe Swimmer, on the occasion of Indian Days, dresses up as the stereotypical German, complete with short elk-hide pants and a tuba, pretending to belong to the local German Club.

The idealization of the image of the Indian, which looms so large in the German imagination (and only there, one might add), to some extent also determines the reception of and thus the marketing conditions for Native Canadian literature in Germany. And while the German fascination with "things Indian" might be taken at first sight as an indicator that First Nations literature should do well on the German market, a second glance reveals the situation to be more complex. As Lutz observes,

> the German reception of literature written by Indigenous authors from Canada is informed by a dialectic which *both fosters and impedes it at the same time*. On the one hand, there is the remarkable phenomenon of a very keen and enthusiastic German interest in North American Indians, and on the other, this keen interest has engendered a set of stereotypical notions which predetermine our perception and make it hard for contemporary Aboriginal authors to be read outside existing stereotypes. In other words, our centuries-old traditional interest in North American Indians has determined a perceptional structure which literally serves as a cliché, a cut-out frame, allowing for the reproduction of images fitting that frame, and blocking the vision of images not conforming to its contours. So, while the traditional interest engenders, to this day, a booming "industry" of Indian image-making—books, calendars, toys, advertising iconography, films, New Age meditation music, and dream catchers—that same interest-based image-making industry is also effective in *distorting or even blocking the reception of contemporary Indigenous literatures from Canada*. (2000, 36; emphasis added)

In a self-perpetuating process, what reaches the German market in translation is therefore already filtered through the expectations that German readers bring to literature by/about Indians, which in turn are shaped by previous representations of Native people and determine the marketability of indigenous works in the future. Such writing will obviously appear in German translation only if there is a reasonable chance to sell it (though, with regard to First Nations literature, a certain amount of idealism might enter into the process of publishing, especially with smaller publishing houses—in which case economic considerations tend to be secondary; see below). These mechanisms are not unique to the German market, though, as the following comments from a conversation with Native American writer Sherman Alexie show:

> The dilemma, as Alexie sees it, is that the marketplace defines what works of Native American literature are published and widely marketed; those that receive a broad distribution and readership in the dominant white community have tended to be books that present a romanticized view of Native America that appeals to the expectations of non-Native readers. ... Alexie points out [that] "It's safer to write the Mother Earth, Father Sky stuff," since that's what white America buys. (Brill de Ramirez 1999, 57–58)

If Indian books by non-Native imposters and "wannabes" conform more fully to a German audience's expectations in regard to Indians, then *those* books will be published in translation—rather than books by First Nations writers themselves.[4] Through such processes, translations have contributed to the ahistorical, exoticized image of the Indian and continue to do so. They perpetuate a canon of Canadian Indian literature in Germany that caters to German tastes but does not mirror the existing multifarious literary production of contemporary First Nations writers.

**SURVEY OF NATIVE CANADIAN WRITING IN GERMAN TRANSLATION**

In view of such interdependencies, the following survey of First Nations writing in German translation focuses on the areas of incongruity, shifts of emphasis, and selective patterns that might emerge when comparing the original production of

---

4. Examples of such translations by non-Native writers are Anne Cameron's *Daughters of Copper Woman*, 1981 (*Töchter der Kupferfrau: Mythen der Nootka-Indianerinnen und andere Frauengeschichten*, 1993) and *Dreamspeaker*, 1978 (*Traumdeuter*, 1999); several books by would-be shaman Lynn Andrews with enticing titles such as *Medicine Woman*, 1981 (*Die Medizinfrau: Der Einweihungsweg einer weißen Schamanin*, 1983) and *Jaguar Woman and the Wisdom of the Butterfly Tree*, 1985 (*Die Jaguarfrau und die Lehren des Schmetterlingsbaumes*, 1991), all brought out by large publishers such as Rowohlt, Ullstein, and Goldmann; and several books by the German Canadian would-be shaman Adolph Hungry Wolf, such as *Life in Harmony with Nature*, 1983 (*Vater Sonne, Mutter Erde: Zeugnisse indianischen Lebens im Einklang mit der Natur*, 1984) and *The Spirit at Hidden Valley: A Good Medicine Story*, 1972 (*Das Geheimnis des verborgenen Tales: Eine Mutter-Erde-Geschichte*, 1979).

First Nations writing to its counterpart in German translation. To assess properly which fragment of Native Canadian literature is translated into German, it is indispensable to glance first at the most important developments within Native writing in Canada during the time frame under analysis.

While in the United States the publication of N. Scott Momaday's (Kiowa) *House Made of Dawn* in 1969 is generally taken as the beginning of the so-called Native American Renaissance, in Canada, according to Lutz (2000, 48), it is George Clutesi's (Nootka) *Son of Raven, Son of Deer: Fables of the Tse-shat People* (1967) that marks the beginning of contemporary First Nations writing. From the beginning of the twentieth century until the late 1960s, hardly any Native Canadian writing—apart from contributions to local newspapers and magazines—was published (with the notable exception of Mohawk poet E. Pauline Johnson). In the subsequent decades, however, Canada's First Nations began to claim a literary voice of their own. In the wake of the increased nationalism ensuing from Canada's centennial celebration in 1967, and especially in the aftermath of the 1969 White Paper (a proposal by the Trudeau government to abandon all legal obligations toward Canada's indigenous population and to terminate their relationship based on the treaty and status system), a new interest in Native issues arose (see King 1994). In this atmosphere of heightened awareness, various forms of Native writing boomed and came into critical focus: whereas the political writing or "protest literature" of the time can be considered a direct reaction to the government's plans, less confrontational forms of Native writing, especially from the mid-1970s onward, included autobiographies and memoirs, cultural narratives, and First Nations fiction and poetry. In retrospect, Greg Young-Ing considers the 1970s as "somewhat of a heyday in publishing by Aboriginal authors," pointing out, however, that "this rash of books did not manage to carve a respectable, ongoing niche for aboriginal literature in the Canadian publishing industry" (1993, 183).

The situation for Native writers changed to some extent with another political event: the Oka crisis in 1990 was an extended and at times violent confrontation between Mohawk protesters and provincial police/Canadian military over the expansion of a golf course onto Mohawk lands in Kanesatake and Kahnawake. The extensive media coverage of the matter brought Native presence and the disregard of Native rights in Canada to wider attention in an unprecedented way, the consequences also being felt by Native writers as the interest in Native literature increased. This change in political climate, in combination with the stronger attention that postcolonial and marginalized literatures received in academia (see Lutz 1999, 93), fostered an unparalleled flourishing of Native literature in Canada in the 1990s. Today First Nations writers are "among the most powerful and innovative voices in Canadian writing" (Kuester and Keller 2002, 11) and are starting to be integrated into the Canadian literary canon.

Despite this success, First Nations writing is still marginalized to a substantial degree within the Canadian publishing landscape; with a few notable exceptions discussed below, the works of Native Canadian authors continue to be published by small, independent, often Native-run presses,[5] while books about Canada's Natives by non-Native authors fill the catalogues of large publishing houses (see Young-Ing 1993, 184–85). In addition, the Native literary scene now faces the danger of tokenism, "the foregrounding of a few selected 'pet' authors ... whose works may be more amenable to established literary tastes and perhaps more manageable in postmodern theories" (Lutz 1999, 93). Such a celebration of selected "academically compatible" authors blocks both the quantity and the heterogeneity of contemporary First Nations writing. Apart from these impairments, though, it can safely be said that the publishing situation for First Nations writers in Canada has greatly improved during the past decade.

The question of interest within the framework of this analysis is, of course, to what extent these developments, in confluence with German market conditions, are reflected in the number and kind of works by Native Canadian writers available in translation. Ironically, the first "authentically Indian" authors from Canada to be published in German, Grey Owl and Buffalo Child Long Lance, turned out to be imposters who merely marketed themselves as Canadian Indians in order to cater to the tastes of a Euro-American public (would-be shamans such as Adolph Hungry Wolf and Lynn Andrews happily continue this "tradition" today). Regarding works by First Nations writers after 1967, one should keep in mind that a substantial part of Native writing blurs the boundaries not only between disciplines (for instance, ethnography, cultural studies, history, and literature) but also between the various Western categories of genre (autobiography and fiction coming together in various forms of life writing, prose poetry or short fiction merging with originally oral forms of narrative or song). For the sake of clarity, the following survey is nonetheless structured roughly along generic lines, with qualifying comments wherever necessary.

Autobiography or life writing is usually among the first forms to emerge in the literature of marginalized groups. This is also the case with Native Canadian literature, many early instances being produced in an "as told to" format in collaboration with non-Native ethnographers, anthropologists, or editors, while later texts were authored independently. It comes as no surprise, then,

---

5. These are the Native-owned Pemmican Publications (Saskatoon) and Theytus Books (Penticton, BC), both founded in 1980, as well as Kegedonce Press (Wiarton, ON), Press Gang (Vancouver), Women's Press (Vancouver), Write-on-Publishers (North Vancouver), Fifth House (Calgary), Sister Vision (Toronto), Talonbooks (Burnaby, BC), Brick (London, ON), Seventh Generation Books (Toronto), Gabriel Dumont Institute Press (Regina), and Coteau Books (Regina).

that the first book by a First Nations author to appear in German translation was an autobiography, Lee Maracle's *Bobbi Lee: Struggles of a Native Canadian Woman* (1975), published as *Bobbi Lee, Indian Rebel: Das Leben einer Stadtindianerin aus Kanada* as early as 1977. It was followed in 1981 by Maria Campbell's *Half-Breed* (1973)—by now a Canadian classic—which appeared as *Cheechum's Enkelin: Autobiographie einer kanadischen Halbindianerin*, as well as Ted Poole and Wilfred Pelletier's collaborative volume *No Foreign Land: The Biography of a North American Indian* (1973), with the German title *Frei wie ein Baum: Ein Indianer erzählt sein Leben*. Both Beatrice Culleton's *In Search of April Raintree* (1983) (*Halbblut! Die Geschichte der April Raintree*, 1994) and Tomson Highway's *Kiss of the Fur Queen* (1999) (*Der Kuss der Pelzkönigin: Ein indianischer Lebensweg von heute*, 2001), while clearly based on the authors' personal experiences, are often considered novels rather than autobiographies in the strictest sense—the term "fictionalized autobiography" would probably characterize them best. Two brief autobiographical sketches—Howard Adams's "The Colonized Halfbreed" ("Das kolonisierte Halbblut") and Lenore Keeshig-Tobias's "One School Day Afternoon" ("Eines Schulnachmittags")—are also included in the bilingual anthology *Four Feathers* (edited by Lutz; see below).

While it is hardly possible to tell what prompted the translation of these texts rather than any of the other numerous First Nations autobiographies,[6] one potential explanation for the general tendency to translate autobiographies lies in the genre's aura of "authenticity," which, in connection with Native writing, seems to be a catch-all magic phrase ensuring a large readership. A further reason for the success of Native autobiographies may be their assertion of cultural distinctiveness, their description of racial discrimination, and their situating of the individual within the wider context of Native/Métis history and culture. While life writing is not as openly political as what is usually termed "protest writing," it nonetheless constitutes a form of criticism of the Euro-Canadian mainstream by making the personal political. As briefly mentioned above, Trudeau's 1969 White Paper triggered a number of politically oriented non-fiction works ("protest literature") by Native Canadian writers and activists. In publications such as Harold Cardinal's *The Unjust Society* (1971) and *The Rebirth of Canada's*

---

6. Starting with John Tetso's *Trapping Is My Life* in 1964 and James Sewid's *Guests Never Leave Hungry* in 1969, writing of this kind was published in a steady stream, reaching its peak in the 1970s with works such as Alma Greene's *Forbidden Voice: Reflections of a Mohawk Indian* (1971), James Redsky's *Great Leader of the Ojibway: Mis-Quona-Queb* (1972), Dan Kennedy's *Recollections of an Assiniboine Chief* (1972), and Jane Willis's *Geniesh: An Indian Girlhood* (1973), to mention but a few. More recent examples include James Tyman's *Inside Out: An Autobiography by a Native Canadian* (1989), Shirley Stirling's *My Name Is Seepeetza* (1992), and Gregory Scofield's recent *Thunder through My Veins: Memories of a Métis Childhood* (1999).

*Indians* (1977), Henry Pennier's *Chiefly Indian* (1972), and Howard Adams's *Prison of Grass: Canada from the Native Point of View* (1975), to name but a few, Native Canadian authors spoke up for themselves for the first time, openly criticizing a Canadian policy that implicitly fostered racism and marginalization. But as important as these publications were for asserting the continued Native presence in a country that had long ignored its indigenous population, German publishers obviously did not consider them interesting enough for their readership: none was translated into German. This is rather surprising since, according to Lutz, "in the seventies, AIM [American Indian Movement] support groups sprouted in both East and West Germany, converting *Indianertümelei* into well-meant but often puerile and patronizing solidarity with Native Americans" (2002b, 179). It is conceivable that this "gap" with regard to sociopolitical writing by First Nations authors is partly accounted for by autobiographies such as those by Maracle and Campbell, which, through the descriptions of their authors' experiences with poverty and racism, also implicitly critique Canada's Indian policy. By catering to sociopolitical interests in a less abstract way, they may have been deemed capable of satisfying a German readership's romanticizing expectations more fully than other forms of non-fiction writing, enabling a patronizing empathy with "the poor Indian victims." (This is, admittedly, highly speculative and not meant to disparage these works in the least.)

Much of the early (1970s) Native Canadian poetry was political in content and angry in tone, taking the form of what is now referred to as "Indian lament" in deploring the injustices experienced by Canada's First Nations and their loss of traditional culture. Since then, the genre has moved a long way from such narrowly functional aspects. While the authors' Native identities and respective cultural backgrounds are still recognizable and determining factors in most of the texts, the themes and formal realizations of Native poetry today cover a wide spectrum. Poetry is the genre in which Native writing on both sides of the U.S.-Canadian border appears to be most prolific. This fact can be attributed to the economic situation of Native writers, only a few of whom can afford to devote their time to longer works, but also to the formal closeness of poetry to various kinds of oral expression (see Lutz 2002a, 118). The large production of Native poetry (best reflected in *Native Poetry in Canada: A Contemporary Anthology*, edited by Jeannette Armstrong and Lally Grauer in 2001) is not, however, reflected in translation; though numerous First Nations writers have published poetry collections, few of these volumes have appeared in German. Works by a single author are restricted to Chief Dan George's collections of prose poetry, *My Heart Soars* (1974) (*Und es jubelt mein Herz*, 1991) and *My Spirit Soars* (1982) (*Und es jubelt mein Geist*, 1993), possibly spurred by his prominence as an actor, and Peter Blue

Cloud's bilingual collection of poems, songs, and stories, *Ich bin Schildkröte/I Am Turtle: Gedichte—Lieder—Geschichten/Poems—Songs—Stories,* in 1991, as well as the translation of his 1990 collection *The Other Side of Nowhere: Contemporary Coyote Tales* (*Die andere Seite von Nirgendwo: Zeitgenössische Coyote-Geschichten* [1992], which can also be considered prose poetry. To my knowledge, only poems by Marie Annharte Baker and Duke Redbird have appeared in translation, in an anthology of women's writing and an illustrated book about Canada respectively (see bibliography).

It is thus only *Four Feathers,* a bilingual anthology edited by Hartmut Lutz in 1992, that somewhat mitigates the gross underrepresentation of contemporary Native poetry in German translation by making available to a German-speaking readership selected examples of poetry by Anne Acco, Jeannette Armstrong, Joy Asham Fedorick, Beth Cuthand, Greg Daniels, Rita Joe, Lenore Keeshig-Tobias, Emma LaRocque, Leah Messer, Daniel David Moses, Jo-Ann Thom, and Greg Young-Ing. While some of the best-known and most successful contemporary Native Canadian poets—Armstrong, Baker, Cuthand, Joe, and Moses—are represented in (albeit minute) excerpts in German, others among the first voices in First Nations poetry (especially those with more recent publications) have not been translated: Joan Crate, Kateri Damm, Marilyn Dumont, Connie Fife, Louise Halfe, Lee Maracle, Armand Garnet Ruffo, and Gregory Scofield have made names for themselves in Canada but have not appeared in translation. Possible reasons for the incongruity between the large production of poetry by First Nations writers on the one hand and the lack of translations on the other may lie in the linguistic difficulties that the more condensed format of poetry poses for translation in general. Moreover, in Native poetry, due to its proximity to the oral tradition, cultural specificity seems to figure even more prominently than in prose writing. Already limiting the accessibility of this kind of writing for a non-Native, English-speaking readership, the problem might even be exacerbated in translation. By far the best solution for poetry is thus the bilingual format chosen by Lutz, in which both the original version and its translation are available to the reader.

The discrepancy between original productions and their availability in German translation shows up most drastically, however, in the genre of Native Canadian drama. Hartmut Lutz's observations that "in no other field have Native authors from Canada been so successful internationally as in drama" and that "Native plays have repeatedly been chosen to represent Canadian culture abroad" (2002a, 212) are by no means indicative of the number of translated plays by First Nations authors. Despite the vibrancy and popularity of Native drama in Canada (see also King 1994, 363–64)—especially in comparison with Native drama's meagre existence in the United States—not a single play by a First Nations author has appeared in German translation. Even before Tomson Highway's play *The Rez Sisters* sparked a boom in Native theatre in 1987, performing arts had been a favoured form of Native artistic expression—George Kenny's *October Stranger* (1977) and Maria Campbell's *Jessica* (first performed in 1983) being only two examples. While Highway is still the most prominent figure in Canada's Native theatre scene, he has been joined by a wide range of other dramatists, including the prolific Drew Hayden Taylor (with no fewer than eleven published plays and over sixty professional productions of his plays to his credit), Daniel David Moses, Monique Mojica, and actresses/playwrights Shirley Cheechoo and Margo Kane. Throughout Canada, theatre companies such as Native Earth Performing Arts in Toronto, De-ba-jih-mu-jig Theatre Group on Manitoulin Island, Spirit Song Native Indian Theatre Company in Vancouver, and Saskatoon Native Theatre in Saskatoon (see King 1994, 363) testify to the genre's vitality.[7] In a German literary context, however, Native theatre from Canada appears only in Albert-Reiner Glaap's edition of Taylor's play *Toronto at Dreamer's Rock* for use in secondary school teaching (including an accompanying teacher's book) and in the inclusion of three plays by First Nations playwrights (Highway's *The Rez Sisters,* Taylor's *Someday,* and Moses' *Almighty Voice and His Wife*) in Glaap's *Stimmen aus Kanada: 25 kanadische Dramen für deutsche Bühnen* ("Voices from Canada: 25 Canadian Dramas for German Stages," 1997), a reference book on Canadian theatre with short summaries, background information on the authors and the plays' central themes, cast, setting, productions, and reception in Canada. Lutz partly attributes the Native Canadian emphasis on the performing arts to the genre's proximity to the oral tradition, regarding even modern drama as a continuation of oral narrative (see 2002a, 125).[8]

Considering the popularity of translated Indian tales, which are probably presumed to be closest to ancient oral traditions by the general reading public (though the versions available are often grossly distorted), the question arises why translations of Native Canadian drama do not exist—even when taking into consideration that drama in general is the genre that appears least often in translation. The varied productions of Native drama seem to indicate that contemporary plays focus mostly on contemporary Native life in Canada,

---

7. See also the recent *Staging Coyote's Dream: An Anthology of First Nations Drama in English* (2003), edited by Monique Mojica and Ric Knowles.
8. This position is supported by Drew Hayden Taylor, who also attributes the popularity of Native theatre in Canada to the fact that "theater is the next logical progression in traditional storytelling—the ability to take the audience on a journey using your voice, your body, and the spoken word, and also the fact that unlike other media you don't need secondary knowledge" (in Däwes 2003, 6–7).

sometimes in combination with Native mythic or magical elements or integrating Euro-American historical conceptualizations. Highway's sometimes bitterly sarcastic and realistic depictions of reservation life in *The Rez Sisters* (1987), Mojica's subversive debunking of presumed white superiority in *Princess Pocahontas and the Blue Spots* (1990), and Taylor's satiric comments on white liberal ideas about Canada's First Nations in *AlterNatives* (2000) may simply shatter the expectations of a German audience about Indians. The classic collections of "tales" to be discussed below preserve the "exotic" aspects of the Indian from a safely distant past and are thus fascinating not in spite of but possibly because of their inaccessibility to a German readership. The contemporary Natives depicted by these playwrights, however, sometimes aggressively speak their own minds, thus defying any tendencies toward stereotyping from their audiences.

Due to the economics of its production, the short story, like poetry, is a format frequently chosen by Native Canadian writers. Most of the short fiction by First Nations writers is published in magazines and/or collected in anthologies such as *Achimoona* (1985), edited by Maria Campbell; *All My Relations: An Anthology of Contemporary Canadian Native Fiction* (1990), edited by Thomas King; and the extensive *Anthology of Canadian Native Literature in English* (1992, 2nd ed. 1998), edited by Daniel David Moses and Terry Goldie. Short-fiction author collections include George Kenny's *Indians Don't Cry* (1977) and Beth Brant's *Mohawk Trail* (1985), both of which contain stories and poetry; Jordan Wheeler's *Brothers in Arms* (1989); Lee Maracle's *Sojourner's Truth and Other Stories* (1990); Thomas King's *One Good Story, That One* (1993) and *A Short History of Indians in Canada* (2005); Eden Robinson's *Traplines* (1997); Drew Hayden Taylor's *Fearless Warriors* (1998); and Richard Van Camp's *Angel Wing Splash Pattern* (2002). Of these works, only Robinson's *Traplines* is available in German translation (*Fallen stellen: Kurzgeschichten*, 2002), a fact that is not easy to understand given that most of the short stories are not only of high literary quality but also deal with subject matter and themes of general relevance. Furthermore, besides *Four Feathers*, which concentrates mainly on poetry, there is no German-language anthology of contemporary Native Canadian fiction to date.[9] Considering that even English-

---

9. There are numerous anthologies by German editors, though, that cater specifically to New Age interests, usually idealizing and romanticizing North American "Indian philosophy" or "wisdom" in spiritual and ecological contexts. Examples are Maria Otto's *Worte wie Spuren: Weisheit der Indianer*, 1985 ("Words like Traces: Indian Wisdom"), Peter Baumann's *Der Wind ist unser Atem: Harmonie mit der Erde—Indianische Weisheitstexte*, 1989 ("The Wind Is Our Breath: Harmony with the Earth—Indian Wisdom Texts"), and Käthe Recheis's *Weißt du dass die Bäume reden: Weisheit der Indianer*, 1985 ("Do You Know that the Trees Talk? Indian Wisdom"), which states on its back cover that "The Indians' wisdom is an important experience for the Western, overcivilized man, which shows him how one can live in harmony with Nature and how body, soul, and spirit can

language anthologies of this kind, numerous as they are now, are a relatively recent phenomenon, this should not come as a surprise. Deplorably, contemporary Native Canadian short fiction is also hardly ever included in general German-language anthologies of Canadian writing; while the early *Moderne Erzähler der Welt: Kanada* (1976) and *Gute Wanderschaft, mein Bruder: Eine kanadische Anthologie* (1986), edited by Walter Riedel, and Riedel and Gottfried Friedrich, respectively, at least include excerpts from George Clutesi's *Son of Raven, Son of Deer*, later collections such as *Kanada erzählt: 17 Erzählungen* (1992), edited by Stefana Sabin, or *Kolumbus und die Riesendame: Kurzgeschichten aus Kanada* (1992), edited by Karla El-Hassan, contain no contributions by First Nations writers. The latter even follows a familiar practice of exclusion: with W. P. Kinsella's "Born Indian" ("Von Geburt Indianer"), it presents a story by a non-Native author who has frequently been accused of appropriating Native voice and culture in his writing but includes no story by First Nations authors. An exception to this pattern is Birgit Herrmann's anthology *Frauen in Kanada: Erzählungen und Gedichte* (1993), which contains Lee Maracle's "Who's Political Here? " ("Wer ist hier eigentlich politisch?") from *Sojourner's Truth* and Beth Brant's "A Death in the Family" ("Ein Todesfall in der Familie") from *Food and Spirits*.

There are many collections of so-called Indian myths, legends, or tales in English and several in German translated from English or assembled by German editors in the first place.[10] The material for such collections of traditional narrative is

---

form a unity" (my translation). In addition to patronizingly nourishing the cliché of the noble but vanishing Indian, these collections unquestioningly appropriate cultural texts. While some of the texts are attributed to specific sources, the majority of the *Weisheiten* are simply ascribed to a tribe or nation—*Gebet der Kwakiutl* ("prayer of the Kwakiutl"), *Lied der Odschibwä* ("song of the Ojibway")—or to generic categories such as *Haida-Indianer* ("Haida Indian") or *Irokesenfrau* ("Iroquois woman"; examples taken from Recheis 1985). Baumann justifies this practice at the end of his "list of sources" by simply declaring, "The texts given without sources stem from oral traditions, which are not commonly accessible in books, magazines, or research reports, or from conversations with the editor" (1989, 143; my translation). Such direct acts of appropriation are aggravated when the transcripts are utilized within a foreign ideological framework: Maria Otto (1985), for instance, links her examples of "Indian" philosophy and wisdom to biblical ideas, stating on the back cover that "Indian wisdom breathes the spirit of the Bible" (my translation).

10. Examples of such collections available in the German language are *Die schönsten Sagen aus der Neuen Welt* (1972), edited by Inge Dreecken and Walter Schneider; *Bärenmann und Büffelgeist: Indianermärchen aus Nord- und Südamerika* (1973), edited by Ulf Diederichs; and more recent translations of Lewis Spence's (ed.) 1993 *Illustrated Guide to North American Mythology* (*Mythen der Indianer*, 1995) and Colin C. Taylor's (ed.) 1995 *Myths of the North American Indians* (*Mythen der nordamerikanischen Indianer*, 1995). Two examples that focus explicitly on Canadian material are Fredrick Hettmann's (ed.) 1978 *Indianermärchen aus Kanada*, relying mostly on originals taken from Bureau of Ethnology reports or material collected by Franz Boas and Silas Rand, and the

either provided by members of a First Nations culture in volumes brought out by themselves or gathered by non-Native anthropologists or ethnologists. In the latter case, the danger of generalization, appropriation, and misinterpretation looms large. In addition to the editing that these stories were subjected to at the time of collection (for example, condensation of the longer oral version, cutting out of material perceived to be obscene) or during translation into English, modern compilations usually sort the material according to tribe and to (imposed) functional categories that may not mirror the original context. This distortion, carried out to fit Euro-American frames of reference, is reflected in the German titles of the popular collections that refer to the stories as *Märchen* ("fairy tales") or *Legenden* ("legends"). When put into writing by members of a Native culture themselves—that is, without intercultural modification—the stories are often even less accessible to readers unfamiliar with the respective culture, with basic practices, characteristics, and functions of oral transmission, or with concepts such as story cycles (again these difficulties are primarily located not within the German translations of the texts but within the transmission from Native to Euro-North American culture). Nonetheless, several of the approximately twenty Native-authored collections of traditional stories and cultural beliefs known to me to date are available in German translation: George Clutesi's 1967 *Son of Raven, Son of Deer* (*Sohn des Raben, Sohn des Rehs*, 1987) and no fewer than three volumes on Ojibway culture by Basil Johnston (see bibliography); furthermore, Ethel B. Gardner's "Ka-ims's Gift: A Sto:lo Legend / Ka-ims Geschenk: Eine Legende der Sto:lo" and George Kenny's "Whee-skay-chak and Kah-kah-ge / Whee-skay-chak und Kah-kah-ge" are included in translation in *Four Feathers*. Whether these translations are primarily intended for an anthropologically / ethnologically interested readership, or are deemed attractive to a mainstream audience because of their "exoticism," remains a matter for speculation.

As pointed out above, it is not always possible or desirable to distinguish between (re)tellings of traditional tales, prose poetry, contemporary short fiction, or autobiographical episodes (writers such as King and Brant, for instance,

---

1982 volume *Legenden der kanadischen Indianer*, "collected and renarrated" by Meta Regehr-Mirau. The information given by the book's publisher, A. E. Johann, on his homepage speaks for itself: "If the European wants to access this foreign, almost lost world, these old Indian tales will have to be presented in his language, his tonality; it is not only the words, plot, and atmosphere that will have to be reshaped into a form comprehensible to the European so they can be experienced according to our environs. Thus, one will have to transmit Indian tales in a style approaching the manner of German fairy tales. Only then will the European fully comprehend the warmth and depth of a possible ancient legend from North American Indians, will it 'resonate' within him. The adaptations of Indian legends presented by Meta Regehr in her book most favourably fulfill the criteria just called for" (my translation).

amalgamate traditional stories and contemporary elements in their short stories). Peter Blue Cloud's writing, three volumes of which are available in German translation (see bibliography), merges traditional stories and tribal history with personal memoir and current observations, oral style with an elaborate written format, using poetic frames and prose narrative to tell about his culture. So far, Blue Cloud's writings (and arguably Beverly Hungry Wolf's *The Ways of My Grandmothers,* 1980) are the only instances of such "culture narrative" in German translation. It will be interesting to see whether other examples, such as Maria Campbell's *Stories from the Road Allowance People* (1995), Basil Johnston's *Moose Meat and Wild Rice* (1978), Wayne Keon's *Storm Dancer* (1993), or Harry Robinson's *Write It on Your Heart* (1989) and *Nature Power* (1992) will someday be considered for publication in the German-speaking market.

In comparison to the United States, where the novel was the genre that, from the beginning of the Native American Renaissance, firmly established Native writing within the canon, the development of the First Nations novel in Canada was slow at first (see Lutz 2002a, 121) but has gained momentum during the past decade and a half since the Oka crisis. This may serve as an explanation for the fact that (leaving aside *In Search of April Raintree* as fictionalized autobiography) the only First Nations novel from the 1980s in German translation is Jeannette Armstrong's *Slash* (1985), published under the same title in Germany in 1997. This historical novel, partly resulting from Armstrong's need to teach her Native students their recent history, has its fictional protagonist Slash participate in political events during the 1960s and 1970s Red Power movement. Other prominent Native novels from the 1980s, Ruby Slipperjack's *Honour the Sun* (1987), Thomas King's episodic *Medicine River* (1989), and Joan Crate's *Breathing Water* (1989), all with a more personal slant and stronger focus on the characters' respective First Nations culture, have not (yet?) been translated; neither have recent novels by previously translated authors Armstrong (*Whispering in the Shadows,* 2000) and Culleton (*In the Shadow of Evil,* 2000). As a matter of fact, the vast majority of successful First Nations novels from the past fifteen years share this fate: Lee Maracle's *Sundogs* (1992) and *Ravensong* (1993); Ruby Slipperjack's *Silent Words* (1992), *Weesaquachak and the Lost Ones* (2000), and *Little Voice* (a novel for young readers, 2001); Lorne Simon's *Stones and Switches* (1994); Thomas King's *Truth and Bright Water* (1999); Warren Cariou's *Lake of the Prairies* (2002); and Richard Wagamese's *A Quality of Light* (1997). The few novels that are available in German are King's *Green Grass, Running Water,* 1993 (*Wenn Coyote tanzt,* 2003), Eden Robinson's *Monkey Beach,* 2000 (*Strand der Geister,* 2002), Richard Wagamese's *Keeper 'n Me,* 1994 (*Hüter der Trommel,* 1997), and Richard Van Camp's *The Lesser Blessed,* 1996 (*Die ohne Segen sind,* 2000), which even won the Deutscher Jugendliteraturpreis at the Frankfurt Book Fair in 2001.

Interestingly, in looking at which part of contemporary First Nations fiction has been translated and at what, in contrast, has not appeared in translation, a tentative correlation emerges between the size of the Canadian publisher of a book and the probability of its translation into German: all of the aforementioned novels in German translation are rather exceptional in the First Nations literary landscape in that they have appeared with large publishing houses and not with the smaller, independent presses with which Native authors are usually affiliated.[11] This does not necessarily imply that being published by a large Canadian or American press automatically guarantees that the rights for a First Nations work will be sold to the German market; still, it shows that the larger Canadian publishing houses are more successful than smaller presses in marketing their products abroad—as is to be expected. A further noticeable issue is the selection of works from within the corpus of writing by a single author: what is behind the fact that distinguished writer Lee Maracle's autobiography *Bobbi Lee* came out in translation two years after its publication in Canada but that none of her poetry, novels, short stories, or other non-fiction writing ever appeared in translation? The same question could be asked with respect to Tomson Highway, Canada's most successful, award-winning playwright: none of his widely known dramatic work has been translated, while his autobiographical novel *Kiss of the Fur Queen* came out in Germany only two years after its original publication as *Der Kuss der Pelzkönigin: Ein indianischer Lebensweg von heute* (2001). It may well be the lure of authenticity that makes the autobiographical part of an author's oeuvre more attractive to a German readership.

In this context, it is also worth mentioning that in several cases the titles of books by First Nations authors have been "adjusted" to fit the German market (see Lutz 2000, 47–51). Wilfred Pelletier's *No Foreign Land* was turned into the harmless *Frei wie ein Baum* ("Free as a Tree"), shedding its confrontational connotations, which assert ancient Native presence in times of Euro-American colonization; Beatrice Culleton's *In Search of April Raintree* was modified to *Halbblut: Das Mädchen April Raintree* ("Halfblood: The Girl April Raintree"), possibly to make it sound more spectacular;[12] and curiously, Beverly Hungry Wolf's *The Ways of My Grandmothers*

---

11. In Canada, King's *Green Grass, Running Water* was published by HarperCollins; Robinson's *Traplines* and *Monkey Beach* by Knopf; Wagamese's *Keeper 'n Me* by Doubleday; and Van Camp's *The Lesser Blessed* by Douglas and McIntyre. The correlation does not hold for the earlier *Slash* by Armstrong, published by Theytus, and *In Search of April Raintree* by Culleton, published by Pemmican; both of these books, however, were taken on by German publishing houses at the initiative of the OBEMA group (Osnabrück Bilingual Editions of Minority/Marginalized Authors), which prepared translations of these volumes.
12. See Lutz (2000, 51): "In this case, the choice of an 'exoticizing' title backfired on the publishers: they were sued by the Karl May Verlag, because of the Karl May novel of the same title, *Halbblut*.

(1980) in its first German edition of the same year appeared as *Das Tipi am Rand der großen Wälder: Eine Schwarzfuß-Indianerin schildert das Leben der Indianer, wie es wirklich war* ("The Tipi on the Edge of the Great Woods: A Blackfoot Indian Describes the Indians' Life as It Really Was"), just to be subsequently renamed *Die weisen Frauen der Indianer: Hüterin des Hauses, Jägerin, Medizinfrau—eine Schwarzfußindianerin schildert das Leben ihrer Vorfahren* ("The Wise Women of the Indians: Keeper of the House, Hunter, Medicine Woman—a Blackfoot Indian Describes the Life of Her Ancestors") in a second edition in 1994. This may reflect changes in taste and in envisioned readership, as the latter title apparently hints more toward "spiritual" or "feminist" tendencies. In addition to such modifications, anthologies put together by German editors, as Lutz correctly observes, "even if containing contemporary and very political texts, often use titles evoking the quaint, sometimes with a decisive ecological and especially an esoteric touch" (2000, 47): *Der Erde eine Stimme geben* ("To Give Voice to the Earth," Biegert 1987) or *Flüstere zu dem Felsen* ("Whisper to the Rock," Ludwig 1993) are but two examples here.

Finally, in looking at translations of First Nations literature, one should also consider a book's domestic success and the span of time that passes between the appearance of the original and the translation. While one reason for the general time lag that Native Canadian literature experiences on the German-speaking market is that much of the material originally appeared in Canadian magazines, journals, and newspapers (some specifically addressing a Native audience), this cannot account for the fact that it took twelve years for Jeannette Armstrong's successful novel *Slash* to appear in translation. And what kept the best-selling Governor General's Literary Award nominee *Green Grass, Running Water* by Canada's most established Native writer, Thomas King, off the German market for ten years? While it is impossible to answer such questions conclusively, factors determining whether or not a book by a First Nations writer is translated tend to exceed purely economic considerations. Peter Baum's publication of Native material is certainly spurred by his personal enthusiasm for Native writing rather than by the hope for financial success. Similarly, the OBEMA series (Osnabrück Bilingual Editions of Minority/Marginalized Authors), which publishes bilingual editions of works by authors from marginalized groups for a German-speaking readership, was launched in 1989 by Lutz, among others, out of his interest in Native literature and "out of frustration with another publishing project." He explains that "helping translate and disseminate texts by Native authors has been one of the most important, most time-consuming and often least successful projects in Native American and Canadian First Nations studies [he has] ever

---

… A second edition, now under the more adequate title *Auf der Suche nach April Raintree*, according to the publisher, is in the pipeline."

been involved in" (2002a, 8). Still, he considers it the task of Native American Studies (NAS) scholars to select texts by First Nations writers for translation and publication and thus make them available for a German-speaking readership:

> Who but scholars in NAS could or should select texts by Aboriginal authors for translation and publication in Europe? Who but we should or could be engaged in recommending texts and materials for the use in schools? All too often such work is left to editors scantly aware of the perceptional structures of *Indianertümelei* and helpless to avoid immediate shortcuts the market may dictate. There is much more stuff written about Indians, often ludicrous and sometimes downright racist, than there are translated texts by Native American authors. I think it behooves us to leave the ivory tower and become active in this field. (2002a, 106)

It is owing to such activity that Culleton's *April Raintree* and Armstrong's *Slash* appeared in German translation—which to some extent explains the time lag of nine and twelve years, respectively, since it was not an original interest of the publishing houses that got these projects going but the initiative and dedication of the scholars involved in them (see Lutz 1999, 99).

As has become obvious from this overview and the questions raised, the politics of translation often remain opaque. With the limited amount of research so far in this field,[13] one is frequently left to speculate on the factors that influence the decisions of authors, publishers, or readers. While Canadian literature from the 1960s onward was subsidized for (international) publishing and promotion by programs established in the wake of the Massey Commission's finding that Canada lacked a national identity, Native literature seems not to have profited from this rise of national awareness.[14] The reception of those works that have been translated into German seems positive, but it is obviously difficult

---

13. Apart from Lutz's comments on Native writing in German translation in "Receptions of Indigenous Canadian Literature in Germany" (2000, 46–55) and scattered throughout "'Okay, I'll Be Their Annual Indian for the Next Year': Thoughts on the Marketing of a Canadian Indian Icon in Germany" (2003), there are no academic insights into the topic. Tellingly, Riedel's (1980) chapter on "Die Ureinwohner: Indianer und Eskimos" in his study on the reception of Canadian literature in German translation concentrates on literature written about Canada's indigenous population rather than by it and on "legends" collected and edited by non-Natives. The Native Canadian authors whom Riedel does mention are George Clutesi and Duke Redbird as well as "Büffelkind Langspeer," who by now is known to have been an imposter posing as a Blood Indian from Alberta.
14. Tellingly, none of the brochures on *Kanadische Verlage und Autoren in Deutschland* ("Canadian Publishing Houses and Authors in Germany"), three of which have so far been published by the culture department of the Canadian Embassy (fall 2002, spring 2003, and spring 2004), contained a single First Nations writer, let alone publisher.

to get books by First Nations writers accepted into the programs of German publishers.[15] Apparently, the traditions and products of First Nations cultures, and thus First Nations literature in German translation, are still in constant jeopardy of being instrumentalized for various extrinsic purposes. Karl May's deployment of Indians as a means of German self-aggrandizement and Fritz Steuben's books about the "heroic" figure of Tecumseh as a forum for Nazi propaganda are luckily outdated, but they have been replaced by more contemporary causes. Today the adoption of Native literature and culture by feminist, ecological, or esoteric/New Age movements also reeks of appropriation and commodification for very specific purposes rather than real interest in a foreign culture. This is especially the case wherever the contents and messages of Native writing and cultures are simplified or grossly distorted to fit the respective agenda but can also take place on a much less dramatic level. Métis author Maria Campbell, for instance, in *The Book of Jessica,* an account of the joint Native-white production of a play based on her novel *Halfbreed,* describes her massive struggles with a white liberal feminist stance. She indicates that she cannot relate to the concept of feminism and that she resents the feminist movement's appropriation of Native/Métis culture. Nonetheless, the translation of *Halfbreed* was published by a small German feminist publisher, Frauenoffensive.

On the whole, the publishing landscape for First Nations literature in German-speaking countries is rather heterogeneous, ranging from small publishing enterprises specializing in Native (Baum Publications), feminist (Frauenoffensive), or religious (Missio, Diederichs) publications, publishers of juvenile literature (Ravensburger) and publishers with an ethnological or "world literature" orientation (Diederichs, Peter Hammer, Frederking & Thaler, and the small Husum-Verlag), to large German publishers such as Fischer and Rowohlt. As in the Canadian market, though, the size of the publisher seems crucial with regard to the sales of a particular work. This correlation is due mostly to the large booksellers' acquisition and sales policy, according to which works brought out by

---

15. In scanning the major German newspapers for reviews, I could only find an enthusiastic discussion of Thomas King's *Wenn Coyote tanzt* ("Unbedingt Lesen!" *Die Welt,* 6 December 2003). Further information on First Nations books in translation—which, however, should not be considered impartial—is to be found on the publishers' homepages and other online forums. Correspondence with some of the Canadian publishing houses that hold First Nations titles (out of eleven publishers that I directed my inquiries to, only Coteau, Brick, Tundra, and McClelland and Stewart responded) indicated that the German interest in First Nations culture is vivid but still seems to be based on a romanticized view of "Indians" rather than genuine interest in contemporary Native life; contacts established via agents at the Frankfurt Book Fair were said to hardly ever lead to any mentionable results. Often coincidence and personal interest seem to enter into the decision whether a book will appear in translation or not.

small publishers are restricted to special order at specific customer request, while books brought out by the larger publishing houses are more or less automatically accepted into the bookstores' assortment.[16]

## IDIOSYNCRASIES OF TRANSLATING NATIVE CANADIAN LITERATURE INTO GERMAN

In the remainder of this chapter, I concentrate on difficulties arising from translating First Nations literature into German to see to what extent translation as cultural transfer can succeed in this constellation. In view of recent cultural studies paradigms, it is no longer justifiable to uphold a clear-cut distinction between categories such as "cultural content" and "linguistic form," since they clearly affect each other to a substantial degree. Nonetheless, one can probably distinguish between more culturally and more linguistically determined issues, which crop up in the process of translating texts that are not only written in a different language but also originate from vastly different cultural spheres. Since First Nations writers mostly—though not exclusively—write from either a general Native or a specific tribal/national perspective, any non-Native translator is first of all a cultural outsider. While this position is shared by all other non-Native and thus by English-speaking readers, the translator's task is further complicated by transferring the work to a culture that is even further removed from the source culture—Germany lacks the geographical and limited sociocultural proximity that connects Euro-Canadians with the country's Native inhabitants.[17] These circumstances highlight the fact that translation constitutes both a linguistic and a cultural contact zone, a process of cultural transposition that exceeds the mere technical aspect of converting a work of literature from one language to another. Within this contact zone, the translator has to find a precarious balance between

> a fairly aggressive presentation of unfamiliar cultural elements in which differences, even ones likely to cause problems for a receiving audience, are highlighted ... [and] an assimilative presentation in which likeness or

---

16. See Wieland Freund (2004), who uses King's *Wenn Coyote tanzt*, brought out by the small A1-Verlag, as an example.
17. This sometimes shows in minute details; the reference by an American police investigator to a black female witness as "Aunt Jemima" (King 1993, 54), a black nanny character, which in the American cultural sphere is a well-known advertising icon, clearly conveys a racist, degrading intention to North American readers. German readers will be unfamiliar with the advertising figure—the products are not available on the German market—which is probably why the translator chose the German *Märchentante* (King 2003, 50) instead. While this term implies that the black woman is spinning a tale rather than telling the truth, it lacks the specific racist implications conveyed by the original.

"universality" is stressed and cultural differences are muted and made peripheral to the central interests of the literary work. Similarly, linguistic features related to the source culture (such as dialect or unfamiliar lexical items) can be highlighted as defamiliarized elements in the text, or be domesticated in some way, or be circumvented altogether. (Tymoczko 1999, 21)

Moving too far in either direction proves risky, resulting either in alienating the audience of the target culture or in compromising the text with regard to its culturally specific content. One avenue toward at least mitigating this problem is bilingual editions (for instance, the publications within the OBEMA series), which present the reader with both original and translation and thus take some of the representational responsibility off the translator's shoulder:

While creating an intertextual space between the two versions, in which the readers may become (inter)active, the bilingual format guarantees the integrity of the author's own work. Thus, bilingual editions seem particularly appropriate in an intercultural context in which authors and translators belong to radically different cultural contexts, and in which the conflicting author-translator relationship is additionally implicated by legacies of colonialism and inequalities in agency, access, and power. (Lutz 2000, 48)

Keeping these intricacies in mind, in the following I point to some selected features that in the context of translation into German appear to be rather distinctive of First Nations literature in comparison to the mass of texts originating from a Euro-Canadian background. With regard to a text's cultural content, as Maria Tymoczko observes, "often unfamiliar cultural information does not simply reside in lexical items, but is a more diffuse presence in a source text" (1999, 27). Knowledge of the source culture's myths and traditions may therefore change a reading completely. Without at least some acquaintance with the Native oral tradition and Native mythology and cultural transmission, the translations of George Clutesi's or Peter Blue Cloud's writing may be disqualified as flat, naive, or reminiscent of children's literature by German readers due to the unfamiliar style of presentation and content. Similarly, the uncommented inclusion of various Native creation myths in Thomas King's *Green Grass, Running Water* at best creates the intended mildly puzzling reading experience but may also be downright alienating to a German audience unfamiliar with Native cultures. There is, of course, always the possibility of including background information not provided by the author in the text itself "either through explicit inclusion in the translation or through paratextual devices" (Tymoczko 1999, 27). Both strategies constitute a massive intrusion on and interference with the original source text, however.[18] With other translated contemporary texts, the process of cultural transmission is eased as a "side effect" of their plots; in both Jeannette Armstrong's *Slash* and Richard Wagamese's *Keeper 'n Me*, the reader gradually comes to learn about the Red Power movement and reservation life, respectively, along with the novels' young protagonists. The extent to which contemporary First Nations literature lends itself as a medium for cultural transfer is therefore only to a lesser degree determined by its recurrent thematic focus on First Nations cultural identity and contemporary Native realities. Instead, the question of whether the cultural information included in a Native Canadian text is accessible to a German-speaking readership depends on the author's mode of presenting the idiosyncratic First Nations material, on his or her (un)willingness to comment and explain.

In regard to cultural content, the opportunity for cultural transfer lies mostly with the author; however, the emphasis shifts toward the translator when the linguistic details of the text come up. The transitions are gradual, though, as can be exemplified through the phenomenon of code-switching. The inclusion of fragments (words, sentences, or longer passages such as stanzas in poetry or whole conversations in drama) in the writer's original Native language into otherwise English-language texts is one way of introducing original Native cultural expression into contemporary writing. A method employed by George Clutesi, Tomson Highway, Louise Halfe, Marilyn Dumont, Monique Mojica, Richard Wagamese, and Thomas King, it serves as a linguistic assertion of Native identity and a link to traditional heritage but also as a challenge to notions of dominance and universality associated with English. Most often translators simply take over the Native expressions without modifying them or presenting paratextual explanations. This is the way in which the Ojibway phrases and sentences in Wagamese's *Keeper 'n Me* are handled as well as the Cherokee expressions in King's *Green Grass, Running Water* (particularly the beginning formulas of its four parts, which are even less accessible since they are written in Cherokee syllabary).

The practice of code-switching, which also represents a challenge for English-speaking readers, is only one component in a whole cluster of complexities that arises in the translation of contemporary Native literature. Further intricacies include, for instance, the use of "Red English" and of narrative features originating from the oral tradition as well as a pronounced delight in wordplay. Red English (also called Rez English), used, among others, by Marie Annharte Baker, Louise

---

18. See in this context Lutz in his preface to *Four Feathers:* "For many readers, a few passages in some of the texts may seem obscure or remain inaccessible.... Despite such foreseeable difficulties, we have refrained from including explanatory notes but trust that those readers who are touched by these texts will themselves gradually gain the experience and the knowledge that will eventually provide readier access across this transatlantic and transcultural bridge" (in Lutz et al. 1992, 10).

Halfe, and Richard Wagamese, is a pan-Indian, demotic, non-standard variant of English, the idiom spoken by most Natives on the reserves. Differences from standard English include not only changes in phonetics and inflection but also grammatical and syntactical modifications. In *Keeper 'n Me,* the translator captures the paratactic aspects of elder Keeper's direct speech quite well, whereas his contractions, slurs, and occasionally haphazard syntax are ignored:

> Get a lotta tourists this way now. Never used to be. When I was a boy this here country was still Ojibway land. Anishinabe we called ourselves. Lottsa huntin' and trappin', fishin' still good in the rivers. Not like now. ... Okay for me, I'm an old man now. I just play dumb Indian and they leave me alone. But it's hard on the young ones. Kinda caught between two things them. (Wagamese 1994, 1)

> Jede Menge Touristen kommen jetzt hierher. Gab's hier früher nicht. Als ich ein Junge war, war die ganze Gegend hier Ojibwaland. Anishinabe nannten wir uns. Genug Wild zum Jagen und Fallenstellen, viele Fische in den Flüssen. Nicht so wie jetzt. ... Für mich ist das nicht so schlimm, ich bin ein alter Mann. Ich spiel den blöden Indianer und sie lassen mich zufrieden. Aber für die Jungen ist es schwer. Die sind irgendwie zwischen zwei Sachen hin- und hergerissen. (Wagamese 1997, 9–10)

Protagonist Garnet's way of talking also displays a different, less colloquial register in German translation and, in comparison with the English original, sounds rather wooden and less alive: "Most people never hearda the Ojibway. Probably because we never raided wagon trains or got shot offa horses by John Wayne. The Ojibway's big claim to fame is a few centuries back when we chased the Sioux outta Minnesota" (Wagamese 1994, 5) is translated as "Die meisten Leute haben noch nie von den Ojibwas gehört. Das liegt wahrscheinlich daran, dass wir nie Wagenkolonnen überfallen haben oder von John Wayne aus dem Sattel geschossen worden sind. Das Einzige, womit die Ojibwas sich brüsten können, ist, dass wir vor ein paar Jahrhunderten die Sioux aus Minnesota vertrieben haben" (Wagamese 1997, 16). In the case of Wagamese's novel, the translation in my opinion has not transferred much of the specific flavour conveyed by Red English into the German version.

Oral influences on First Nations literature become apparent in (structural) features on the textual level—for instance in repetitions or the use of imagery—but also, as with Red English, on the clause and word level in particular sounds, rhythms, or constructions (for instance, parallelisms). They are most apparent in Harry Robinson's writing but also show in Thomas King's works—which are, by his own admission, influenced by Robinson's style—and in Peter Blue Cloud's poems. In King's case, some of the texts' oral characteristics can be imitated reasonably well in German (see King 2003, 5), for example, by directly addressing the reader, making syntactic changes, and using colloquial style. Other elements contribute to the "oral impression" of King's texts in that they become meaningful only in actual articulation. These devices pose more difficulties for translators: "Dr. Joe Hovaugh," a character in *Green Grass, Running Water,* clearly reveals himself as "Jehovah" in the original due to the phonetic proximity and several other clues as to his hierarchical Judeo-Christian world view. In German, the name of the Judeo-Christian God is pronounced differently, however, and it is hard to imagine that readers of the translated version establish any connection, since the name is not modified in translation.[19] Then again, with regard to Blue Cloud's writing, it is precisely the rhythmic flow and the sound patterns that are hard to transfer into German, and translators are hard pressed to retain both the semantic precision and the phonetic character of the original. In some cases, however, the relative proximity of German and English helps:

| Hailstones falling like sharp blue sky chips | Hagel fällt wie spitze blaue Himmelssplitter heulende Winde braunes Gras biegt, während |
| Howling winds the brown grass bends, while Buffalo paw and stamp ... | Büffel stampfen und strampeln ... |
| | (Blue Cloud 1991, 16–17) |

In other cases, the smooth loping rhythm of Blue Cloud's writing, which is reminiscent of a storyteller's pacing, is lost in stumbling and awkward German translations.

Wordplay, finally, one of the prominent features of Native writing, proves one of the most challenging tasks for a translator. The reason is that wordplay and especially puns are based on the binary nature of the linguistic sign but at the same time transgress it. One signifier (or homophonic signifiers) correspond to two or more distinctly different signifieds, allowing for secondary meanings and ambiguities. The identity or similarity of signifiers usually works only in the

---

19. The translation of proper names in general is a challenging task for translators wherever the original name is allusive or conveys a specific meaning (for instance, when King transforms Cooper's Nathaniel "Natty" Bumppo into the telling "Nasty" Bumppo). Cornelia Panzacchi tackles the problem quite well by translating "Ahdamm," an allusion to Adam, as German *Ahverdamm;* but then again she does not convert A. A. (that is, "Arch Angel") Gabriel into E. E. (*Erz-Engel*) Gabriel in German (King 2003, 63), which would have been fairly easy. There are countless other examples that would, however, exceed the scope of this chapter.

source language, and a direct translation loses its ambiguity and comic effect. The pun on the Canadian national anthem—"O Canada, our home and native land"—in the first stanza of Lenore Keeshig-Tobias's "Canada" (Lutz et al. 1992, 126–27) works in English, while the comically subversive undertone achieved through the diverging meanings of "Native" is to a large degree lost in translation:[20]

| O Canada—your provinces shout | Oh Kanada—deine Provinzen rufen |
| O Canada—your country shouts | Oh Kanada—dein Land ruft |
| O Canada—your people shout | Oh Kanada—deine Menschen rufen |
| Our home and native land. | Unser Heim und Heimatland. |
| (Our home, your settled land) | (Unser Heim, euer Siedlerland) |

Similarly, a pun on the two diverging usages of reservation—as "something set aside for someone" on the one hand and as restricting a people's space to a defined area of land on the other—has to be modified in the German translation of *Green Grass, Running Water*: protagonist Lionel tells an AIM (American Indian Movement) activist that he will not be able to join their protest because he has to "'fly back. I've got a reservation.' The man took Lionel by the shoulders, looked at him hard, and said, 'Some of us don't'" (1993, 58). In German, this quip turns out as "'Ich habe einen gebuchten Flug. Ich muss zurück.' Der Mann packte Lionel bei den Schultern, sah ihm fest in die Augen und sagte: 'Manche von uns können nicht zurück'" (King 2003, 54). While this translation through the repetition of "zurück" at least tries to re-create some of the effects of the original wordplay, the issue that it centres on is completely changed.[21]

A far more drastic loss of meaning due to the untranslatability of wordplay, however, occurs in this novel on the translation's first page. In the original version, during an account of how the world came into being, a Coyote dream turned loose develops a mind of its own and transmutes into a dog. Then, because it "gets everything backward," it ends up being "god," eventually even a big "GOD." Together with Coyote's comment that "that Dog Dream is a contrary. That Dog Dream has everything backward" (King 1993, 2), King's use of palindrome opens

---

20. A similar passage in King's *Green Grass, Running Water* suffers the same fate. The swipe at Canada's colonial policy inherent in the first-person narrator's corrections of Coyote's attempt to sing—"You got the wrong song. ... This song goes 'Hosanna da, our home on Natives' land" (1993, 270)—in Panzacchi's translation ends up as "Hosanna da, unser Haus auf Eingeborenenland" (King 2003, 258) ("our house on indigenous peoples' land"; my translation).

21. Luckily, the translator of this novel seems to share King's sense of humour. A brief biography of Panzacchi provided at the end of the book includes the comment, "Bei der vorliegenden Übersetzung fiel es ihr nicht leicht, immer mit vollem Ernst bei der Sache zu bleiben" (King 2003, 413) ("with the present translation, she was sometimes hard pressed to keep her mind on the work in dead earnest"; my translation).

up a whole cultural sphere here, the world of Native tricksters, contraries, and clowns. Coyote is the prototypical Native trickster; he is both a promethean hero and a situation inverter. Contraries, on the other hand, are seriocomic "clowns" existing in several Native cultures. They do everything backward and behave contrary to normal and appropriate social behaviour and expectations. Part of their mission is to shake up the moral values and traditional codes of conduct of a culture by demonstrating to people what happens when such conventions are flouted. Their role, obviously, is like that of trickster Coyote himself, which implies that the relation between dog and Coyote is not only of a biological nature here and, in a further step, that the Judeo-Christian God is actually a chaotic contrary sprung from a Coyote's dream (via dog and god to GOD). This beginning introduces in a nutshell the issues that dominate the novel, in which Native cultural heritage is brought into dialogue with Christian tradition and in which the creative power of words can change the world. Sadly, much of what this artful overture conveys in English is lost in German translation because the German words for dog and god, *Hund* and *Gott*, do not form a palindrome. The translator tries to save some of it by introducing the English words into the text, but the concept of the contrary is completely left out: "That Dog Dream is a contrary. That Dog Dream has everything backward" (King 1993, 2) becomes "Dieser Hundetraum macht alles verkehrt herum. Der Hundetraum hat alles umgedreht. Dog. God" (King 2003, 6). While not every reader of the original may be aware of the complex scenario's full meaning, readers of the translation are thus deprived of even the option of grasping everything that King offers, however well versed in Native cultural traditions they may be. As a consequence, later references to the dog-god interconnection, such as the restaurant name "Dead Dog Café" alluding to Nietzsche's "God is dead," are also lost in the German translation. Fortunately, though, as far as I can tell, there are only isolated instances where linguistic limitations severely hamper the successful transmission of cultural subject matters. On the whole, the translation of First Nations literature from Canada into German, especially with regard to its potential for transmitting cultural particularities, proves challenging but possible.

## CONCLUSION

In 1999, Hartmut Lutz stated that, "heard from abroad, the Native Voice from Canada is growing in volume and articulation" (100). Although I agree with him on the basic direction of this development, the above survey of Native Canadian writing in German translation shows that only a limited body of writing by First Nations authors has appeared in German so far. In general, there may be some truth to Walter Riedel's observation that a work's translation can be taken as an indication of its transnational and timeless relevance (1980, 13) and thus implicitly of its quality. As I have argued, however, in the case of First Nations writing, the major factors responsible for the limited number of works available in translation are marginalizing publishing politics and especially stereotypical perceptual frames rather than lack of quality.[22] Translation, as Lawrence Venuti observes,

> wields enormous power in constructing representations of foreign cultures. The selection of foreign texts and the development of translation strategies can establish peculiarly domestic canons for foreign literatures, canons that conform to domestic aesthetic values, and therefore reveal exclusions and admissions, centres and peripheries that deviate from those current in the foreign language. (1995, 10)

The recent translation of works that break stereotypical patterns of expectation toward *Indianer*—especially the novels by Thomas King, Eden Robinson, Richard Wagamese, and Richard Van Camp—raises hopes that the fixed frames of reference with which a German readership may have approached First Nations literature in the past will finally shift toward a more open perception. An increasing number of contemporary First Nations works in translation (especially in the so far totally neglected field of contemporary short fiction) might not only halt but actually reverse the self-perpetuating canonization process that once cemented preconceived notions about the "Indian other." They may even set in motion a self-intensifying cycle in which new First Nations literature "educates" and thus creates and/or widens its potential audience. It will take further research in this highly complex field to arrive at more definite and more encompassing conclusions than those presented within the framework of this first study. Such further research in connection to translation should also assess the situation of the discipline of Native Studies in German-speaking countries and take stock of the Native literature courses taught at German universities and the German library holdings of First Nations literature in translation. This research should ask German publishers of First Nations literature about the politics of translation and publication, find out about possible (English or German) performances of First Nations drama on German stages, and possibly compare First Nations literature in translation to translations of Native American writing, with regard

---

22. How else could Fred Bodsworth's sentimental and mediocre *The Sparrow's Fall* (1967) appear in five different editions as *Lauft, Füße lauft! Ein Indianerschicksal* with various *Buchgemeinschaften* ("reading clubs") catering to the tastes of German-speaking readers, while Ruby Slipperjack's *Honour the Sun* (1987) and Lee Maracle's *Ravensong* (1993) have never been translated?

to both the number and the kind of texts that have been selected for translation. Since translation "is not an isolated act, it is part of an ongoing process of intercultural transfer" (Bassnett and Trivedi 1999, 2), it is to be hoped that, even with the challenges and limits posed by texts from a First Nations cultural background, more contemporary Native Canadian literature will reach the German market. At this "alterNative frontier," a genuine attempt at intercultural contact, cultural transfer, and human respect constitutes the best chance for the First Nations to counter German *Indianertümelei*.

## REFERENCES

Bassnett, Susan, and Harish Trivedi. "Introduction: Of Colonies, Cannibals, and Vernaculars." In *Post-Colonial Translation: Theory and Practice*, ed. Susan Bassnett and Harish Trivedi. London: Routledge, 1999. 1–18.

Baumann, Peter. *Der Wind ist unser Atem: Harmonie mit der Erde—Indianische Weisheitstexte.* 1989 [reprinted 1998].

Blue Cloud, Peter. *Ich bin Schildkröte/I am Turtle: Gedichte—Lieder—Geschichten/Poems—Songs—Stories.* Ed. and trans. H. J. Vollmer et al. OBEMA: Osnabrück Bilingual Editions of Minority Authors 5. Osnabrück: VC-Verlagskooperative, 1991.

Brill de Ramirez, Susan Berry. "Fancydancer: A Profile of Sherman Alexie." *Poets & Writers* 27.1 (Jan. 1999): 54–59.

Carlson, Marta. "Germans Playing Indian." In *Germans and Indians: Fantasies, Encounters, Projections*, ed. Collin G. Calloway, Gerd Gemünden, and Susanne Zantop. Lincoln: University of Nebraska Press, 2002. 213–16.

Däwes, Birgit. "An Interview with Drew Hayden Taylor." *Contemporary Literature* 44.1 (Spring 2003): 1–18.

Eigenbrod, Renate. "'Stranger and Stranger': The (German) Other in Canadian Indigenous Texts." In *Germans and Indians: Fantasies, Encounters, Projections*, ed. Collin G. Calloway, Gerd Gemünden, and Susanne Zantop. Lincoln: University of Nebraska Press, 2002. 259–80.

Feest, Christian. "Germany's Indians in a European Perspective." In *Germans and Indians: Fantasies, Encounters, Projections*, ed. Collin G. Calloway, Gerd Gemünden, and Susanne Zantop. Lincoln: University of Nebraska Press, 2002 <Author: given as 2000 in the text.>. 25–43.

Freund, Wieland. "Kalte Ökonomie und nackte Angst: Wie der deutsche Buchhandel seine Vielfalt verliert." *Die Welt*, Oct. 2004: 4.

King, Thomas. *Green Grass, Running Water.* Toronto: HarperCollins, 1993.

———. "Native Literature of Canada." In *Dictionary of Native American Literature*, ed. Andrew Wiget. Garland Reference Library of the Humanities. Vol. 1815. New York: Garland, 1994. 353–69.

———. *Wenn Coyote tanzt.* Aus dem Englischen von Cornelia Panzacchi. München: A1

Verlagsgesellschaft, 2003 [*Green Grass, Running Water*. Toronto: HarperPerennial, 1993].

Kuester, Martin, and Wolfram R. Keller. "Beyond *Fleur de Lis* and *Maple Leaf*: Ethnicity in Contemporary Canadian Literature." In *Writing Canadians: The Literary Construction of Ethnic Identities*, ed. Martin Kuester and Wolfram R. Keller. Marburger Kanada-Studien 1. Marburg: Universitätsbibliothek Marburg, 2002. 9–27.

Lutz, Hartmut. *Approaches: Essays in Native North American Studies and Literatures*. Augsburg: Wißner, 2002a.

———— et al., eds. and trans. *Four Feathers/Vier Federn: Poems and Stories by Canadian Native Authors/Gedichte und Geschichten kanadischer Indianer/innen und Métis*. OBEMA: Osnabrück Bilingual Editions of Minority Authors 7. Osnabrück: VC-Verlagskooperative, 1992.

————. "German Indianthusiasm: A Socially Constructed German National(ist) Myth." In *Germans and Indians: Fantasies, Encounters, Projections*, ed. Colin G. Galloway, Gerd Gemünden, and Susanne Zantop. Lincoln: University of Nebraska Press, 2002b. 167–84.

————. "Nations Within as Seen from Without: Ten Theses on German Perspectives on the Literature of Canada's First Nations." In *Native North America: Critical and Cultural Perspectives*, ed. Renée Hulan. Toronto: ECW Press, 1999. 83–108.

————. "'Okay, I'll be their annual Indian for the next year': Thoughts on the Marketing of a Canadian Indian Icon in Germany." In *Imaginary Relocations: Tradition, Modernity, and the Market in Contemporary Native American Literature and Culture*, ed. Helmbrecht Breinig. Tübingen: Stauffenburg, 2003. 217–45.

————. "Receptions of Indigenous Canadian Literature in Germany." In *Reflections of Canada: The Reception of Canadian Literature in Germany*, ed. Martin Kuester and Andrea Wolff. Marburg: Universitätsbibliothek Marburg, 2000. 36–63.

Otto, Maria. *Worte wie Spuren: Weisheit der Indianer*, 1985.

Recheis, Käthe. *Weißt du dass die Bäume reden: Weisheit der Indianer*, 1985.

Riedel, Walter. *Das literarische Kanadabild: Eine Studie zur Rezeption kanadischer Literatur in deutscher Übersetzung*. Bonn: Bouvier, 1980.

Taylor, Drew Hayden. "First We Take Turtle Island, Then We Take Berlin." In Taylor, *Further Adventures of a Blue-Eyed Ojibway: Funny, You Don't Look Like One, Too Two*. Penticton, B.C.: Theytus, 1999. 5–7.

————. "Ich bin ein Ojibway." In Taylor, *Funny, You Don't Look Like One: Observations from a Blue-Eyed Ojibway*. Revised edition. Penticton, B.C.: Theytus, 1998. 36–39.

Tymoczko, Maria. "Post-Colonial Writing and Literary Translation." In *Post-Colonial Translation: Theory and Practice*, ed. Susan Bassnett and Harish Trivedi. London: Routledge, 1999. 19–40.

Venuti, Lawrence. "Translation and the Formation of Cultural Identities." In *Cultural Functions of Translation*, ed. Christina Schäffner and Helen Kelly-Holmes. Clevedon: Multilingual Matters, 1995. 9–25.

Wagamese, Richard. *Hüter der Trommel*. Aus dem Amerikanischen von Ingrid Kran-Müschel. Hardcover: Munich: Schneekluth, 1997; paperback: Bastei Lübbe, 2000 [*Keeper 'N Me*. Toronto: Doubleday, 1994].

Young-Ing, Greg. "Marginalization in Publishing." In *Looking at the Words of Our People: First Nations Analysis of Literature*, ed. Jeannette Armstrong. Penticton, B.C.: Theytus, 1993. 178–87.

———. "An Overview of Aboriginal Literature and Publishing in Canada." *Australian-Canadian Studies* 14.1/2 (1996): 157–71.

## RESOURCES: NATIVE CANADIAN WRITING IN GERMAN (1967–2001)

### Autobiography

Campbell, Maria. *Cheechum's Enkelin: Autobiographie einer kanadischen Halbindianerin*. Transl. Roswitha McCoppin. Munich: Frauenoffensive, 1981 [*Halfbreed*. Toronto: McClelland & Stewart, 1973].

Culleton, Beatrice. *Halbblut! Die Geschichte der April Raintree*. Transl. Annette Kohl-Beyer. Wuppertal: Hammer, 1994 [*In Search of April Raintree*. Winnipeg: Pemmican, 1983].

Highway, Tomson. *Der Kuss der Pelzkönigin: Ein indianischer Lebensweg von heute*. Transl. Thomas Bauer. Munich: Frederking & Thaler, 2001 [*Kiss of the Fur Queen*. Toronto: Doubleday, 1998].

Maracle, Lee. *Bobbi Lee, Indian Rebel: Das Leben einer Stadtindianerin aus Kanada*. Transl. Werner Waldhoff. Munich: Trikont, 1977 [*Bobbi Lee: Struggles of a Native Canadian Woman*, rec. and ed. Don Barnett and Rick Sterling. Richmond: LSM, 1975].

Pelletier, Wilfred, and Ted Poole. *Frei wie ein Baum: Ein Indianer erzählt sein Leben*. Düsseldorf: Diederichs, 1981 [*No Foreign Land: The Biography of a North American Indian*. New York: Pantheon, 1973].

### Poetry

Baker, Annharte Marie. "Hurenmond." In *Frauen in Kanada—Erzählungen und Gedichte*, ed. Birgit Herrmann. Munich: dtv, 1993 ["Hooker Moon" from *Being On the Moon*. Victoria: Polestar Press, 1991].

Blue Cloud, Peter. *Ich bin Schildkröte/I am Turtle: Gedichte—Lieder—Geschichten/Poems—Songs—Stories*. Ed. and trans. H. J. Vollmer et al. OBEMA: Osnabrück Bilingual Editions of Minority Authors 5. Osnabrück: VC-Verlagskooperative, 1991.

George, Chief Dan. *Und es jubelt mein Geist*. Aachen: Missio Aktuell, 1993 [*My Spirit Soars*. Surrey, B.C.: Hancock House, 1982].

———. *Und es jubelt mein Herz*. Aachen: Missio Aktuell, 1991 [*My Heart Soars*. Surrey, B.C.: Hancock House, 1974].

Redbird, Duke. "Meine Mokassins," "Ich bin der Rote Mann," "Indianertreffen in Banff," "Alte Frau," "Meine Art." Transl. Dieter Curths and Karin Schreiner. In *Kanada: Bilder aus einem Großen Land*, ed. Jürgen F. Boden and Hans Scherz. Frankfurt: Umschau, 1976. ["My Mocassins," "I Am the Redman," "Banff Indian Seminar," "Old Woman," "My Way" from *Loveshine and Red Wine*. Cutler, Ont.: Woodland Studios, 1981].

The bilingual anthology *Four Feathers* (ed. Lutz et al. 1992, see below) contains the following poems:

Acco, Anne. "Baja Bound/Unterwegs nach Baja," "Speed/Speed," "Elizabeth/Elizabeth."
Armstrong, Jeannette. "I Study Rocks/Ich betrachte Steine."
Cuthand, Beth. "Four Songs for the Fifth Generation/Vier Lieder für die fünfte Generation."
Daniels, Greg. "Sky Woman/Himmelsfrau," "Yesterday/Gestern," "Today/Heute," "Tonight/Heute Nacht," "His Horse Danced/Sein Pferd tanzte."
Fedorick, Joy Asham. "To the Grandmothers/An die Großmütter," "It Was No Surprise to Me/Es hat mich nicht überrascht."
Joe, Rita. "Oka/Oka," "The Wishing Figure/Die Wunschgestalt."
Keeshig-Tobias, Lenore. "Running on the March Wind/Rennen auf dem Märzwind," "Canada/Kanada."
LaRocque, Emma. "Brown Sister/Braune Schwester," "Eulogy for Priscilla/Lobrede für Priscilla," "The Geese Over the City/Die Gänse über der Stadt."
Messer, Leah. "Thank You for Oka/Danke für Oka," "Mother Earth Is Crying/Mutter Erde weint," "I Have Hope/Ich habe Hoffnung."
Moses, Daniel David. "Paper Eclipse/Papierfinsternis," "Song of Bear's Breakfast/Lied vom Bärenfrühstück."
Thom, Jo-Ann. "Half-breed Lost in Academia/Halbblut verloren in Akademia," "What I Don't Know About Mayan Indians/Was ich nicht über die Mayas weiß," "Thank You, Mr. Hughes/Danke, Herr Hughes," "My Room/Mein Zimmer," "Training For Motherhood/Training für die Mutterschaft."
Young-Ing, Greg. "Reflections on Oka/Nachdenken über Oka," "Expression/Ausdruck," "Expression II/Ausdruck II," "Heart/Herz."

**Prose Fiction**

Armstrong, Jeanette. *Slash*. Transl. Audrey Huntley. Münster: Unrast, 1997 [*Slash*. Penticton: Theytus, 1985].
Brant, Beth. "Ein Todesfall in der Familie." Transl. Sophie von Lenthe. In *Frauen in Kanada—Erzählungen und Gedichte*, ed. Birgit Herrmann. Munich: dtv, 1993 ["A Death in the Family" from *Food and Spirits*. Vancouver: Press Gang Publishers, 1991].
King, Thomas. *Wenn Coyote tanzt*. Transl. Cornelia Panzacchi. Munich: A1 Verlagsgesellschaft, 2003 [*Green Grass, Running Water*. Toronto: HarperPerennial, 1993].
Maracle, Lee. "Wer ist hier eigentlich politisch?" Transl. Ursula Flitner. In *Frauen in Kanada—Erzählungen und Gedichte*, ed. Birgit Herrmann. Munich: dtv, 1993 ["Who's Political Here?" from *Sojourner's Truth and Other Stories*. Vancouver: Press Gang Publishers, 1990].

Otto, Maria, ed. and introd. *Worte wie Spuren: Weisheit der Indianer*. 8th ed. Freiburg: Herder, 1994.

Recheis, Käthe, ed. *Weißt du, daß die Bäume reden: Weisheit der Indianer*. 19th ed. Freiburg: Herder, 1992.

Robinson, Eden. *Fallen stellen*. Transl. Sabine Hedinger. Reinbek: Rowohlt, 2002. [*Traplines*. Toronto: Knopf Canada, 1996]

———. *Strand der Geister*. Transl. Sabine Hedinger. Reinbek: Rowohlt, 2002 [*Monkey Beach*. Toronto: Knopf Canada, 2000].

Van Camp, Richard. *Die ohne Segen sind*. Transl. Ulrich Plentzdorf. Ravensburg: Ravensburger, 2000 [*The Lesser Blessed*. Vancouver: Douglas & McIntyre, 1996].

Wagamese, Richard. *Hüter der Trommel*. Transl. Ingrid Krane-Müschen. Hardcover: Munich: Schneekluth, 1997; paperback: Bergisch Gladbach: Bastei Lübbe, 2000 [*Keeper 'N Me*. Toronto: Doubleday, 1994].

**Miscellaneous Monographs (Stories, Ethnographic and Semi-Autobiographical Texts, Essays)**

Blue Cloud, Peter. *Die andere Seite von Nirgendwo: Zeitgenössische Coyote-Geschichten*. Idstein: Baum Publications, 1992 [*The Other Side of Nowhere: Contemporary Coyote Tales*. Fredonia, N.Y.: White Pine Press, 1990].

———. *Ein sanftes Erdbeben*, ed. Thomas Kaiser, transl. Helmut Salzinger. Munich: Dianus-Trikont, 1986 [*A Gentle Earthquake*. Brunswick, Maine: Blackberry, 1983].

Clutesi, George. *Sohn des Raben, Sohn des Rehs*. Transl. H. Holle-Scherer. Aachen: Missio, 1987 [*Son of Raven, Son of Deer: Fables of the Tse-shaht People*. Sidney, B.C.: Gray's, 1967]; excerpts are also anthologized in *Gute Wanderschaft, mein Bruder* (Leipzig: St. Benno-Verlag, 1986) and *Moderne Erzähler der Welt* (Tübingen: Erdmann, 1976), both edited by Walter Riedel.

Hungry Wolf, Beverly. *Büffel und Beeren: Die Küche der Blackfoot-Indianer*. Transl. Claus Biegert. Nördlingen: Greno, 1988.

———. *Das Tipi am Rand der großen Wälder: Eine Schwarzfuß-Indianerin schildert das Leben der Indianer, wie es wirklich war*. Munich: Knaur, 1980; new edition as *Die weisen Frauen der Indianer: Hüterin des Hauses, Jägerin, Medizinfrau—eine Schwarzfußindianerin schildert das Leben ihrer Vorfahren*. Bern: Scherz, 1994 [*The Ways of My Grandmothers*. New York: Morrow, 1980].

Johnston, Basil. *Großer weißer Falke: Der Lebenskreis eines Ojibway*. Transl. Jochen Eggert. Cologne: Diederichs, 1987 [*Ojibway Ceremonies*. Toronto: McClelland & Stewart, 1982].

———. *Nanabusch und großer Geist: Geschichten der Odschibwä-Indianer*. Transl. Käthe Recheis. Mödling: Verlag St. Gabriel, 1985 [*Tales the Elders Told: Ojibway Legends*. Toronto: Royal Ontario Museum, 1981].

———. *Und Manitu erschuf die Welt: Mythen und Visionen der Ojibwa*. Transl. Jochen Eggert. Munich: Diederichs, 1979 [*Ojibway Heritage*. New York: Columbia University Press, 1976].

## Anthologies

Biegert, Claus, ed. *Der Erde eine Stimme geben: Texte von Indianern aus Nordamerika.* Reinbek: Rowohlt, 1987.[23*]

Diederichs, Ulf, ed. *Bärenmann und Büffelgeist: Indianermärchen aus Nord- und Südamerika.* Düsseldorf: Diederichs, 1973.[*]

Dreecken, Inge, and Walter Schneider, ed. *Die schönsten Sagen aus der Neuen Welt.* Munich: Südwest, 1972.[*]

Hetmann, Frederik, ed. and transl. *Indianermärchen aus Kanada.* Frankfurt/M.: Fischer, 1978.

Kaiser, Rudolf, ed. and transl. *Indianische Reden: Dies sind meine Worte.* Münster: Coppenrath Verlag, 1987.[*]

Laboucan, Eduard et al., eds. *Unsere Kindheit—unsere Zukunft: Indianische Stimmen aus Kanada und den USA.* Frauenfeld: Verlag im Waldgut, 2001.[*]

Ludwig, Klemens. *Flüstere zu dem Felsen: Die Botschaft der Ureinwohner unserer Erde zur Bewahrung der Schöpfung.* Freiburg: Herder, 1993.[*]

Lutz, Hartmut et al., eds. and trans. *Four Feathers/Vier Federn: Poems and Stories by Canadian Native Authors/Gedichte und Geschichten kanadischer Indianer/innen und Métis.* OBEMA: Osnabrück Bilingual Editions of Minority Authors 7. Osnabrück: VC-Verlagskooperative, 1992.

Regehr-Mirau, Meta. *Legenden der kanadischen Indianer.* Collected and renarrated by Meta Regehr Mirau. Husum: Husum Verlag, 1982.

Spence, Lewis. *Mythen der Indianer.* Transl. Hildegard Doerr. Augsburg: Pattloch, 1995 [*The Illustrated Guide to North American Mythology.* London: Studio Editions, 1993].[*]

Taylor, Colin C. *Die Mythen der nordamerikanischen Indianer.* Transl. Eva and Thomas Pampuch. Munich: C. H. Beck, 1995 [*Myths of the North American Indians.* London: Lawrence King, 1995].

---

23. [*] Includes texts of Native Canadian and Native American origin.

# From *Beautiful Losers* to *No Logo!* German Readings of Jewish Canadian Writing

*Fabienne Quennet*
*University of Marburg*

The main thesis that Michael Greenstein expounds in his seminal study *Third Solitudes: Tradition and Discontinuity in Jewish-Canadian Literature* (1989) is that the work of the poet and novelist A. M. Klein (1909–1972) constitutes the beginning of Jewish Canadian writing in Canada. According to Greenstein, texts of writers coming after him are revisions and reinscriptions of Klein's work and are, in particular, preoccupied with his novel *The Second Scroll* (1951). Such authors, of whom Norman Levine (1923–2005) and Mordecai Richler (1931–2001)[1] have been translated into German, "construct texts that in their rewriting of other texts transmute the world into a scene of eternal Diaspora ... where meaning can only be construed as a patchwork of trajectories" (Blodgett 2003, 227). Unfortunately, Klein's novel has not been translated into German, so that the tradition and discontinuity typical of Jewish Canadian writing—and inherited from Klein—cannot be fully grasped when we look at the body of German translations of Jewish Canadian authors. Nonetheless, those titles that were translated into German between 1967 and 2000 can indeed be considered representative of Jewish Canadian writing in Canada.

The transfer of Jewish Canadian literature to Germany always entails a cautious handling of European, Jewish, and Canadian sensibilities, an approach that is of central significance, for example, in the case of Anne Michaels's Holocaust survivor novel *Fugitive Pieces,* 1996 (*Fluchtstücke,* 1996). The intricacies affecting this transfer can be seen when we look at the reception of the German translations of Jewish Canadian authors. Writers such as Mordecai Richler and

---

1. These authors, along with Matt Cohen (1942–1999), are those whom Greenstein considers. Of course, authors such as Leonard Cohen and Anne Michaels have also been influenced by A. M. Klein.

Anne Michaels have been recognized specifically as Jewish writers (although not all the reviews stress this fact). Others, such as Leonard Cohen and Naomi Klein, have been regarded as international authors whose topics and success transcend regional or national boundaries and book markets. Norman Levine, along with Howard Engel and Matt Cohen, however, are seen first and foremost as *Canadian* writers.

There are a number of questions underlying the reception of these writers. One might ask whether German reviews in any way reflect the Jewish Canadian aspect of the writing and, if so, which factors are singled out and defined as either Canadian or Jewish or both. Another question might address the way in which the German reception accounts for the success of Jewish Canadian writing on the German book market. This chapter explores which authors and books have been published in German and how they have been reviewed. It concentrates on English-language Jewish Canadian prose works, with the exception of Leonard Cohen's translated poetry collections. Only one poem by Irving Layton has been published in German, "In the Midst of My Fever," 2000 ("In der Mitte meines Fiebers"; see Layton 2000). Anne Michaels's poetry collections have not been translated at all. Nor has Jewish Canadian work been translated from French.

The term "Jewish Canadian literature," as a generic definition, never occurs in reviews. However, although the term is not used to designate a genre or type of writing in Germany, I contend that it needs to be used. Interestingly, the most outspoken and visible Jewish writers, such as Richler, Michaels, and—to a much lesser extent—Levine, are the most successful in terms of public attention and number of books sold in Germany, even though their Jewish origins are more or less ignored by the public. Cohen is in a different category since his success is based on his international popularity as a musician. By showing how Jewish Canadian writing has been received by German publishers, critics, and readers, I seek here to define the body of works translated into German as an entity that reveals the diversity of this particular kind of Canadian literature.

**EARLY TRANSLATIONS**

As early as 1955, Mordecai Richler's novel *The Acrobats*, 1954 (*Die Akrobaten*), was published by the German publisher Kindler. It was followed in 1958 by *Der Boden trägt mich nicht mehr*, 1957 (*A Choice of Enemies*), and in 1963 by *Sohn eines kleineren Helden*, 1955 (*Son of a Smaller Hero*), both by Kindler. There are no reviews available for the early editions of Richler's novels, and, interestingly, there was a substantial publication pause of seventeen years before his novel *St. Urbain's Horseman*, 1971 (*Der Traum des Jakob Hersch*), came out in Germany in 1980, and *Joshua damals und jetzt,* 1980 *(Joshua Then and Now),* appeared a year later. However, during this period of silence for Richler, other Jewish Canadian authors appeared in German. In 1967, Norman Levine entered the German literary scene with his book *Canada Made Me,* 1958 *(Kanada hat mich gemacht),* published by Claassen in Hamburg and Düsseldorf. Levine is known as a master of the short story, and some of his stories were translated by the German Nobel Prize–winner Heinrich Böll and his wife Annemarie, both established as excellent translators of English literature, a fact that was exploited for marketing purposes and noted in some reviews (Riedel 1980, 77). The first review that deals with Levine's work dates from 1968[2] and introduces Levine's non-literary book *Kanada hat mich gemacht* to a German-speaking readership. Since Levine does not foreground his Jewishness in this book, it is not surprising that the reviewer never mentions his Jewish background. Instead, he compares Levine's description of Canada, which celebrates the diversity of the Canadian regions and people, with Egon Erwin Kisch's observations on America. Indeed, these descriptions of the country and people seem to support the image of Canada that is ingrained in the German public imagination, making the book representative of what Germans at the time expected to read in Canadian literature. This is probably also the reason why the short piece "Eine kanadische Jugend" ("A Canadian Youth"), translated by the Bölls, was anthologized in *Kanada erzählt: 17 Erzählungen* (see Sabin 1992). This collection was part of a series of short-story collections from around the world, and Levine is introduced as the author translated by Heinrich Böll (Sabin 1992, 266); the story itself centres on the (semi-autobiographical) experience of an expatriate who has had to leave Canada.

**NORMAN LEVINE IN GERMAN**

When Norman Levine's short-story collection *One Way Ticket: I Don't Want to Know Anyone Well* (1961) was published by Claassen in 1971 as *Ein kleines Stückchen Blau* (a title taken from Levine's story "A Small Piece of Blue"), also translated by the Bölls with Reinhard Wagner, the review in the *Frankfurter Allgemeine Zeitung (FAZ),* "Büchertagebuch" ("Book Diary"), called Levine a Canadian Jewish author who had lived in England for many years. According to reviewer Gertrud Mander,[3] the classic alienation of the artist from society is doubled or even tripled in Levine, who is also a "colonial" and Jewish, somebody who is at home everywhere and nowhere, a permanent exile. Mander stresses Levine's

---
2. Walter Kyburz, "Kanada: Ein ungeschminkter Bericht," *Frankfurter Allgemeine Zeitung,* 25 March 1968: 19.
3. "Lakonisch: Norman Levine, 'Ein kleines Stückchen Blau,'" *FAZ,* 1 November 1971.

position as an observer who, in a laconic and almost objective way, describes the changing places in Canada and people at the edge of "normal life," living from hand to mouth, trying to give expression to their personal experiences and their aesthetic visions.[4]

Levine's third collection translated into German, *Django, Karfunkelstein, and Rosen* (1987) was also published by Claassen. The Swiss review of the collection (in *Neue Zürcher Zeitung*, 23 September 1987), mentions Levine's literary agent Ruth Liepman, whom Levine visited in Zurich in 1979 on the occasion of her seventieth birthday. Liepman had been highly influential in promoting Levine's work for a German-speaking readership since the mid-1960s, and the title story recalls his first visit to Zurich. Apparently, Levine picked the Liepman agency by pure chance, but according to editor Ruth Weibel, Liepman, a German Jew and antifascist, who had survived Nazi Germany only by hiding with a Calvinist worker's family in the Netherlands, "always had a soft spot for Canadians, because she witnessed the liberation of Holland, mainly by Canadian soldiers."[5] Among her good friends, Liepman counted Hilde and Eugen Claassen, the publishers who eventually brought out Levine's work.[6] Another reviewer of Levine's *Django, Karfunkelstein, and Rosen*, Elisabeth Kaiser, stresses Levine's method of "fictional autobiography," a term that Levine himself used to describe his writing (*FAZ*, 10 October 1987). Still another review praises Levine as one of Canada's most prominent authors: Cornelia Staudacher briefly describes his youth spent in Ottawa and the influence of the French Canadian neighbourhood, along with the Jewish tradition of his family, but her emphasis is on the stories themselves, which she calls "minimalist narrations" (*Tagesspiegel*, 14 February 1988).

While only a few reviews identify Levine as a Jewish Canadian author, all of them stress his position as one of Canada's most important short-story writers. What seems to make him especially attractive for a European and German readership is his life in exile. As an expatriate, he is a traveller between the Old World and the

---

4. The title story "Ein kleines Stückchen Blau" was also included in a collection of Canadian tales and short stories called *Die weite Reise: Kanadische Erzählungen und Kurzgeschichten*, published by Volk und Welt in East Germany in 1974. Another East German publication, *Der Mann mit dem Notizbuch* (Leipzig: Reclam, 1979), collected stories from Levine's *In Lower Town* (1971), again translated by the Bölls, Gabriele Bock, and Reinhard Wagner. See the chapter by Barbara Korte in this volume on the East and West German translations of Canadian texts.
5. Personal communication with Ruth Weibel, 23 August 2004.
6. The Liepman agency, established in Zurich in 1961, was extremely important for the German book market in postwar Germany. It was responsible for Norman Mailer's *The Naked and the Dead*, J. D. Salinger's *The Catcher in the Rye*, and *The Diary of Anne Frank*. Today it represents Les Éditions du Boréal, McClelland and Stewart, Bella Pomer Agency, Random House Canada, and Westwood Creative Artists.

New World, with intimate knowledge of both and thus an international outlook. Indeed, exile in Europe was a way in which many Canadian authors of Levine's generation could gain international reputation and be picked up by publishers in London, New York, or Paris.[7]

Generally, literature departments at German universities have played an important role in mobilizing the cultural transfer between Canada and Germany, primarily by establishing Canadian literature and Canadian Studies as valid interests for scholarly work. In the former German Democratic Republic, individual scholars were also engaged in the field. Levine's work was promoted by Karla El-Hassan, University of Jena, who edited a collection of his short prose in 1975 (*Der Mann mit dem Notizbuch: Erzählungen*) and brought out a second, revised edition in 1979, both published by Reclam Leipzig (Nischik 1982).

Other Jewish Canadian authors whose short stories have been published in German anthologies include Howard Engel, Matt Cohen,[8] Irving Layton, Helen Weinzweig, Jack Ludwig, Henry Kreisel, and Miriam Waddington, with the latter three representing Jewish Canadian writers of the Prairies.[9] Since anthologies are only rarely reviewed, little can be said about the reception of the stories within these collections. However, we do know that Kreisel was delighted to have his best-known story, "The Almost Meeting" (1981), published in the weekly extra of the daily Austrian paper *Die Presse* in the late 1980s.[10] Kreisel (1922–1991), who was born in Austria, fled to England in 1938, came to Canada as an "enemy alien," and was interned in a Canadian camp in 1940.[11] He then decided to write exclusively in English, and, although his two novels *The Rich Man* (1947) and *The Betrayal* (1964) have not been translated into German, some of his short stories have appeared in German short-story collections.[12]

---

7. Exile or *Ortlosigkeit* ("placelessness"), I would argue, is the reason for much of the German readership's fascination with Jewish Canadian literature; it is an attraction to experiences that we do not share. See Hahn (2005), who comes to the same conclusion regarding the reception of Israeli literature in Germany.
8. Engel's and Cohen's works have been translated into German; however, Cohen and Engel have not been perceived as Jewish Canadian authors (Engel has even been called an American crime writer), so only the German translations of their shorter works are listed in the bibliography (most of their novels have been published in German, although Engel's are out of print).
9. For a detailed study of the Jewish prairie writers, see Klooß (1998).
10. Personal communication with Eugen Banauch from the University of Vienna, 23 June 2004 and 2 February 2005. The letter from Kreisel to Professor Zacharasiewicz, who was responsible for the publication, can be found in the Archives and Special Collections of the University of Manitoba, which houses Kreisel's collected papers.
11. Biographical information is taken from www.athabascau.ca/writers/kreisel/hkreisel.html [consulted 26 January 2004].
12. See the list of short stories in the bibliography.

## LEONARD COHEN

Judging by the number of reviews, Leonard Cohen (born 1934) is the most popular Jewish Canadian author in Germany. This probably has more to do, however, with his fame as a songwriter and musician than with his literary career, although he was successful as a writer before he achieved worldwide success with his music. Born as the son of a wealthy Jewish family from Westmount, Montreal, he published two novels and four poetry collections before he turned to music and became a songwriter at the age of thirty-two. In 1966, during a poetry reading in New York, he sang two of his poems, "Suzanne" and "Stranger," and soon his readings evolved into concerts. Since then, Cohen has regularly brought out new albums and CDs and has been on concert tours around the world. In Europe, he made his name as a musician during his tours in 1970 and 1972.

Two men in particular have been responsible for Cohen's long-lasting reputation in German-speaking countries: publisher Jörg Schröder, and Cohen expert Christof Graf. Schröder is the owner of März Verlag,[13] a publishing company that leaned toward the political and cultural left in the 1960s and 1970s, representing a part of Germany's literary "subculture." März Verlag published four of Cohen's works in non-chronological order: his second novel, *Beautiful Losers* (1966), came out first in Germany as *Schöne Verlierer* in 1970; the poetry collection *Blumen für Hitler* (*Flowers for Hitler*, 1964) in 1971 and in another edition in 1982; his first novel, *Das Lieblingsspiel* (*The Favorite Game*, 1963), in 1972; and the poetry collection *Wem sonst als Dir/Book of Mercy* (1984) in 1985; both poetry collections were published in bilingual editions. Clearly, these translations, which began to appear in the year of his first concert tour, are the direct result of his sensational popularity as a songwriter and singer in Germany (Riedel 1980, 87). According to Schröder, Cohen's novels and poetry collections have sold comparatively well. By 1973, approximately 5,000 copies of each of the three books (*Das Lieblingsspiel, Schöne Verlierer, Blumen für Hitler*) had been sold; from 1974 to 1978, März Verlag sold all three books in a package (a so-called *Omnibus*) through the mail-order music and bookstore Zweitausendeins, which resulted in twenty editions of approximately 100,000 books. The last poetry book, *Wem sonst als Dir,* sold only 3,000 copies.[14]

Other poetry collections published in Germany with Zweitausendeins include *Parasiten des Himmels: Gedichte aus zehn Jahren* (1976), a bilingual edition of Cohen's early poetry collections, including *Let Us Compare Mythologies* (1956), *The*

---

13. In 1987, the archive of März Verlag was handed over to the Deutsche Literaturarchiv (German Literature Archive) in Marbach, near Stuttgart, where all the materials, reviews, and letters related to the publication of the Leonard Cohen books are stored. März Verlag still exists in Augsburg.

14. Personal correspondence with Jörg Schröder, 10 December 2003.

*Spice-Box of the Earth* (1961), and *Parasites of Heaven* (1966). One year earlier, in 1975, Zweitausendeins had brought out *Die Energie von Sklaven* (*Energy of Slaves*), translated by Harry Rowohlt, who is well known for his intriguing translations of authors such as A. A. Milne, William Kotzwinkle, Flann O'Brien, and Kurt Vonnegut. By 1977, this collection had appeared in its seventh edition. In 1982, Zweitausendeins published the prose-poem collection *Death of a Lady's Man* (1978) under the title *Letzte Prüfung;* Rowohlt Taschenbuch Verlag brought out *Blumen für Hitler* in a bilingual edition in 1984 and *Das Lieblingsspiel* in 1983; and a new German translation and hardcover edition of *Das Lieblingsspiel* appeared with Triptychon in 2005.

Any event in Cohen's life, a new album, a new tour, an important anniversary, causes a plethora of previews, reviews, and interviews to appear in German papers and magazines. The "Internet is ... afire with his name," writes critic Norman Ravvin (1998), and this is especially true in Germany. German editions of Cohen's literary works have been reviewed regularly over the years, though not as extensively as his albums and CDs. Focusing on the reception of his literary output, it is interesting to note that the scope of the reviews ranges from critiques in serious and prestigious papers and magazines such as *FAZ, Der Spiegel,* and *Die Zeit* to many shorter reviews and previews in less well-known local papers and small magazines, including high school publications. The evaluation of his literary output is as diverse as the sites where the reviews appear. The reactions to Cohen as a person, a writer, and a musician oscillate between "success and annoyance" (Riedel 1980, 83). Cohen polarizes public opinion, and many clichés have been used to characterize his person and his music: he is "the poet of broken hearts," "the melancholic of pop," and the "Eichendorff of the twentieth century." In 1980, Walter Riedel argued that there is hardly another contemporary author who has earned so many contradictory epithets (84), and he claimed that there had so far been no serious academic reception of Cohen's work in Germany (86). Criticism was limited to the pop star Cohen and had circled around one question only: how can someone who claims that he cannot sing and has nothing to say still achieve such sensational success (86)?

Although Cohen's two novels have often been regarded as outstanding, the reviews that appeared when they were published were not nearly as enthusiastic. One of the earliest reviews of *Schöne Verlierer* (*Beautiful Losers*) was entitled "Sankt Porno" ("Saint Porno"; *Der Spiegel,* 13 July 1970).[15] Cohen is described as a

---

15. Cohen was first introduced to the German public in an article in *Der Spiegel* (fall 1969) on the occasion of his first European tour. Entitled "Anarchist without a Bomb," the article portrays him as a successful North American poet whose melancholic songs and verses deal primarily with love and sensuousness.

Canadian Jewish poet, novelist, and world-famous pop singer whose imagination borders on the pedantic. The book is described as a kind of pornographic life story of a saint, in which a nameless anthropologist reconstructs the sex life of his First Nations wife, Edith, by interpreting sources concerning the legend of Catherine Tekakwitha, the historical Iroquois girl. The reviewer notes Cohen's ability to write simple poetry, whose simplicity is disguised, however, in this novel. *Schöne Verlierer*, written in a drug-induced state on the island of Hydra, Greece, has aroused ambivalent responses. Generally, the book has been discussed as an example of pop literature, at the time a new concept that emphasized the originality, fantasy, and documentary qualities of literature with a postmodern approach. Cohen's novel is said to reflect the spirit of the counterculture of the 1960s.

Yet not all German reviews hailed the book as a postmodern breakthrough. In December 1983, when a new paperback edition appeared with Rowohlt Taschenbuch Verlag, the reviewer, Gila Winkel, reading it for a centre for youth literature, still finds it ahead of its time and praises, among other things, its detailed and knowledgeable account of Native Canadians' lives. However, she does not recommend it as reading material for young people since it is marked by a rather complicated form and includes many brutal and perverted scenes. Although some reviews mention that Cohen is a Jewish writer from Montreal, the novel itself is rarely read as a particularly Jewish book. Whereas Jewish Canadian scholar Michael Greenstein argues that *"Beautiful Losers* is about a lost Jewish folk" and about the invention of the "New Jew, a beautiful loser who plays favourite games" and "loses his mind gracefully" (1989, 137), German reviews do not focus on themes that might be linked to Cohen's Jewish background. As late as 2002, the novel was mentioned in an article by Georg Klein in the *Frankfurter Rundschau* (14 December 2002) in a series called "Aus einem kleinen Kanon schlechter Bücher" ("From a Small Canon of Bad Books"). Klein refers to Cohen as a "Schundautor," a "trash author," and discusses his novel as an example of pop literature. He claims that Cohen possesses the highest credentials that a pop author can achieve: for the past three decades, he has been an icon of international mass culture as a singer and songwriter. The fact that the lives of the protagonists of *Schöne Verlierer* revolve around the unholy trinity of sex, drugs, and music marks the book as true pop/trash literature. The reviewer has a sentimental attachment to it, however, and finds it a literary classic of the 1960s and early 1970s.

When Cohen's autobiographical novel *Das Lieblingsspiel* (*The Favorite Game*) came out in Germany in 1972, Cohen was described as a "new J. D. Salinger" (*FAZ*, 28 November 1972) who uses the "psychedelic" language of and for a new generation. Wilfried Wiegand sees a relation between Cohen as a singer, a youth idol singing sentimental songs, and a mystic writer who believes in the beauty of life. Cohen's philosophical conviction that beauty exists is apparently the reason for his success. Again there is no mention of the modern Jewish Canadian experience, which is a major theme in *Das Lieblingsspiel*. None of the reviewers comments on Cohen's portrayal of the ambiguities of Jewish Canadian identity, which "remain unresolved" for his protagonist (Greenstein 1989, 124). The utter silence on the topic of Cohen's religious and cultural background may be accounted for by the fact that, at the beginning of his musical success in Germany, the greater audience was aware of neither his Jewish background nor his reputation as an author in the English-speaking world. Furthermore, one may speculate that not much was known about Jewish Canadian history and experience in the early 1970s and that Cohen's "Jewishness" was a feature that many German journalists felt uncomfortable with or did not consider worth mentioning.

To some in Canada, Cohen represents the poet-troubadour whose poetry reflects the fact that "the Holocaust is the central theme of Jewish Canadian poetry" (Blodgett 2003, 226). However, the poems in which this central theme features prominently and which have been collected in *Die Energie von Sklaven, Parasiten des Himmels,* and *Blumen für Hitler* have not received much attention. The later collection *Wem sonst als Dir* got a number of reviews, many of which appeared in small magazines and local papers such as high school magazines, city journals, and music journals.[16] All of the reviews comment on the personal quality of the poems, though not all of them like the mix of Augustine's confessions with the Cabbala and Schma Israel (see *Münsters City Magazine*, September 1985). Some reviews suggest that Cohen seems to have suffered from religious mania in a manner similar to Bob Dylan (to whom he has been constantly compared; see *Stadtblatt Münster*, October 1985).

Since the publication of *Wem sonst als dir/The Book of Mercy*, public and critical attention has shifted to books about and studies on Cohen. Christof Graf, a professor of marketing at the University of Saarbrücken, is the author and editor of many books on the life and works of Leonard Cohen: *So Long, Leonard: Leben und Lieder von Leonard Cohen* (1990); *Leonard Cohen: Partisan der Liebe* (1996); *Ich kenne deine Träume: Songs und Gedichte mit Illustrationen von Jürgen Jaensch* (1997); and *Leonard Cohen: Songs of a Life* (2002). Graf is also the webmaster of the German Leonard Cohen homepage (www.leonardcohen.de). Despite Graf's achievement in keeping the interest in Cohen alive and catering to fans' desires (his books

---

16. These generally free magazines had titles such as *uns doch egal, Harpune, Tips Ostwestfalen, Stuttgart Live, Münsters City Magazine,* et cetera.

often include interviews with Cohen and a thorough and usable collection of his lyrics as well as listings of albums and films, tour lists, bibliographies, and Internet references), his monographs have certain weaknesses and have not always been treated kindly. In a review of *Leonard Cohen: Partisan der Liebe*, for example, Manfred Papst calls the book an uncritical Leonard Cohen monograph whose biographical and interpretative part is marked by unreserved enthusiasm and a sycophantic tone (*Neue Zürcher Zeitung*, 10 February 1997).

In many ways, German interest in books on Cohen's life and his songs and music seem by far to have surpassed the interest in his literary production. Canadian literary critic Ira B. Nadel's biography *Various Positions: Das Leben Leonard Cohens: Eine Biographie* came out instantly in a German edition in 1997, and the prestigious *Frankfurter Allgemeine Zeitung* devoted a long review to it (14 October 1997). Critic Burkhard Spinnen points to the weaknesses of these kinds of biographies, written when the subject is still alive, and comments that the biographer often approaches his topic with veneration and apology rather than scholarly interest. Other reviews concur: Ralf Schuler in *Die Welt* (25 October 1997) admits that Nadel's biography has closed a gap, but he asserts that no serious biography in German is yet available and that this particular book is a fan book that does not offer any real assessment of Cohen's personality and artistic achievements. Other reviews criticized Nadel's book for the same reasons ("hero worship," Birgit Weidinger comments in *Süddeutsche Zeitung*, 19 November 1997). Only one reviewer refers to Cohen's Jewish background. Again, "avoiding" the fact of Cohen's Jewishness is symptomatic of the German reception of Cohen, in this case even as the subject of a biography.

### MORDECAI RICHLER

Mordecai Richler (1931–2001) is one of Montreal's most celebrated Jewish men of letters. "After Klein, there is no one who lords over JewCanLit like Richler," claims Jewish Canadian poet Glen Rotchin, and he is only one among many who have commented on Richler's role as a literary "father figure" (see Heft and Rotchin). Although Richler may almost epitomize Jewish Canadian literature, he was in no way dogmatic and prescriptive with regard to what it means to be Jewish or what has constituted the Jewish experience in Canada or elsewhere. His preoccupation with Canadian identity, and Jewish Canadian identity in particular, is a hallmark of his writings, but in German reception this has been overlooked to a large extent in favour of other elements of his work.

As mentioned earlier, Richler's novels have been published in German since 1955. Kindler Verlag brought out five novels, most recently *Der Traum des Jakob Hersch* (*St. Urbain's Horseman*, 1971) in 1980 and *Joshua damals und jetzt* (*Joshua Then and Now*, 1980) in 1981. Richler's children's books, *Ein Geschenk für Jacob Zweizwei* (*Jacob Two-Two and the Dinosaur*, 1987) and *Jacob Zweizwei in Gefahr* (*Jacob Two-Two Meets the Hooded Fang*, 1975), both appeared in 1994 with Eichborn. His last two novels, *Solomon Gursky war hier*, 1992 (*Solomon Gursky Was Here*, 1989), and *Wie Barney es sieht*, 2000 (*Barney's Version*, 1997) were released by the prestigious Carl Hanser publishing house in Munich. Hanser sold 11,000 hardcover copies of *Solomon Gursky* and 5,500 of *Wie Barney es sieht*. The latter was reissued in paperback by BLT Lübbe in 2002. Paperback editions of the children's books and other novels, with the exception of *Die Akrobaten* (1955) and *Der Boden trägt mich nicht mehr* (1958), were published by Fischer Taschenbuch in the 1990s. Several of Richler's short stories published in *The Street* (1969) appeared in German translation in various short-story anthologies.[17]

Richler's works have elicited mixed responses in Germany; his early novels in particular provoked ambivalent commentaries. Interestingly, the only review of *Der Traum des Jakob Hersch* begins with the rhetorical question of whether Canada now wants to have its Jewish novel too (*FAZ*, 20 November 1980), although reviewer Egon Schwarz also praises Richler's satirical exploration of Montreal's Jewish subculture and London's expatriate Canadian community. In contrast, the review of *Joshua damals und jetzt* by Gerhard Kirchner finds fault with Richler as a Jewish author who is viewed as masochistically catering to the cliché of the lewd, sex-obsessed, and stingy Jew, an image often commercially exploited by American Jewish authors. The only review of the paperback edition of *Sohn eines kleineren Helden*, 1994 (*Son of a Smaller Hero*, 1955), is equally critical (*Deutsches Allgemeines Sonntagsblatt*, 17 June 1994). Reviewer Boike Jacobs refers to Richler as a renowned Jewish Canadian author whose depiction of the "ghetto" in Montreal between 1952 and 1954 is a depressing portrait of morals and values that remains inaccessible to the reader.

The most important books in Germany by Richler were *Solomon Gursky war hier*[18] and *Wie Barney es sieht*, results of the productive relationship between the Carl Hanser publishing house and Richler. Publisher Michael Krüger, the public relations department, and reader Dr. Anna Leube often met Richler and accompanied him on reading tours through Germany.[19] Richler was also present at the Frankfurt Book Fairs of 1992 and 1995.

---

17. "Bambinger" appeared in Riedel (1976); "Wasser auf Mervyn's Mühle" appeared in Bartsch (1974) and Sabin (1992).
18. In an article in *Die Zeit* in 2003, young author Max Küng calls *Solomon Gurksy war hier* the best book that he has ever read. See www.zeus.zeit.de/text/2003/42/B_9fcherkauf._42 [consulted 19 February 2005].
19. Personal communication with Dr. Anna Leube, 31 August 2004.

Most reviews of *Solomon Gursky war hier* focus on the wealth of material, which includes countless episodes with equally countless characters, various observations, and flights of fancy, which Richler combines with his own brand of satire, humour, and irony. When the novel was published, all the major newspapers and magazines ran book reviews, wrote portraits, and published interviews with the author. Shortly before the Frankfurt Book Fair, the weekly *Zeitmagazin* featured a portrait of Richler for which Jutta Duhm-Heitzmann went to Montreal to meet the author in his favourite bar in the Ritz Hotel; she assigns him the position of Canada's most eminent novelist along with Margaret Atwood. When introducing Richler to a German readership, she inevitably repeats the anecdote of his first reading experience: Erich Maria Remarque's *Im Westen nichts Neues*, 1929 (*All Quiet on the Western Front*). Richler, who hated all Germans at the time, realized how ignorant he was when he discovered that he shared the protagonist's favourite food, potato latke, which, he found out, is not of Jewish but German origin. Thus, he learned as a young boy that Jews and Germans have something in common.[20]

Richard C. Schneider in "Die Stimme Kanadas" ("Canada's Voice") regards Richler as the most important Canadian author to have achieved worldwide success with his novels *A Choice of Enemies* (1957) and *Duddy Kravitz* (1959), but he admits that Richler has never enjoyed great success in Germany (*Profil*, 2 November 1992). Grouping him with Philip Roth and Saul Bellow, he sees a similarity in their treatment of Jewish European traditions and North American reality. The reviewer attests that Richler gives Canada its own history, voice, and identity by linking his works to the Jewish tradition of constantly repeating Jewish history and retelling Jewish myths. In the alternative newspaper *taz*, Stefana Sabin discusses *Solomon Gursky* along with Jane Smiley's, Cormac McCarthy's, and T. C. Boyle's novels in a longer article on antiheroes in contemporary American (!) literature (*FAZ*, 30 September 1992). She reads it as a successful family history that portrays the mixture of different cultures—of Christians, Inuit, Natives, and Jews—so typical of Canadian society.

There are also negative reviews, such as Lothar Baier's "Gursky Was Here" published in *Die Zeit*, 2 October 1992, in which Baier unfavourably compares Richler to Charles Bukowski and Thomas Pynchon, and Eckart Klessmann's "Dichte Schnapswolke" ("Thick Alcohol Cloud") in the *FAZ*, 19 November 1992, in which the reviewer calls *Solomon Gursky war hier* boring, fussy, circumstantial, and too long. Although never commenting directly on the fact that Richler is a

---

20. In another favourable review of *Solomon Gursky*, Anton Thuswaldner also mentions Richler in the same breath as leading Canadian authors Atwood and Munro; see *Salzburger Nachrichten*, 7 November 1992.

Jewish Canadian author, Klessmann states that only anti-Semites may find the novel a dubious pleasure to read.

The German edition of Richler's last novel, *Barney's Version*, "the memories of a mean old man" (*Ultimo*, 22 May–4 June 2000), have received a rather positive echo in the German press. For example, Tilman Urbach calls *Wie Barney es sieht* Richler's "last great novel" (*Neue Zürcher Zeitung*, 7 July 2001), considering it a satirical portrait of the decay of morals and values. Another review, published in the *FAZ*, 25 July 2000, by Egon Schwarz, interestingly reflects on the "Jewishness" of Richler's novel, which none of the other reviewers singles out as an essential element of his writing. Schwarz sees all kinds of Jewish aspects in the background. However, for him, *Wie Barney es sieht* surpasses anything that Richler has written before with regard to humour and complexity and is a masterpiece. His achievement is to reflect on the post-Holocaust representation of Jewishness by writing within the genre of the Jewish novel, for which Malamud, Bellow, and Roth have found worldwide recognition; whether Canadian author Richler will do the same is left open.

The German reception of Richler as a Canadian author is characterized by a constant reference to other internationally acclaimed Canadian and American Jewish writers. By identifying his literary standing and achievement within the context of the better-known North American authors, the reviewers seem, on the one hand, to be legitimizing their interest in him as well as their evaluations of his works and, on the other hand, seeking to ensure his success and fame by putting him in the same category as other well-known North American authors in Germany. Defining Richler against the backdrop of Roth, Atwood, and the like may help to introduce him to a non-Canadian readership and may be meant as a compliment; however, it more or less ignores his identity as a Jewish Canadian author and his importance to Jewish Canadian literature. The discussion of both his Jewish and his Canadian status is lacking.

## ANNE MICHAELS

This has not been the case with Anne Michaels's novel *Fugitive Pieces*. The Torontonian (born 1958) started as a successful poet; her first poetry collections *The Weight of Oranges* (1986), *Miner's Pond* (1991), and *Skin Divers* (1999) were all nominated for or awarded literary prizes, such as the Commonwealth Prize for the Americas for *The Weight of Oranges* in 1986 and the Governor General's Literary Award for *Miner's Pond* in 1991. Although her poetry collections have been translated and published in Israel, India, and China, none has appeared in German translation. Her reputation in Germany was made with the translation and publication of her first novel, *Fugitive Pieces,* an immediate and widely acclaimed success when it first appeared in Canada in 1996. In September of the same year, the novel topped the *Financial Post* bestseller list. In 1997, the Berlin Verlag published the book with the title *Fluchtstücke,* translated by Beatrice Howeg, and the success was repeated: in just three weeks, almost 50,000 copies were sold (*Die Welt,* 7 March 1997), and the novel was reviewed in all major German newspapers and magazines; a reading tour in the spring of 1997 further increased its popularity.[21] The novel's success in Germany can perhaps also be gauged by the fact that one of the leading literary critics writing in German, Austrian journalist Sigrid Löffler (at the time responsible for the literary and cultural section of the prestigious German weekly newspaper *Die Zeit*), introduced and interviewed Michaels at her reading in the Hamburg Literaturhaus.

The novel hit a nerve with German readers. The story of the Polish Jewish boy Jakob Beer, who, after German soldiers kill his family, hides in the ruins of a sunken town and is rescued by Greek archeologist Athos, with whom he later moves to Toronto, captured German readers' attention and triggered a lively discussion in the book review sections of papers and magazines. The story deals with memory, loss, exile, Holocaust survival, and, as many reviews have pointed out, belief in the power of love. Since the novel is concerned with how to live with the memory of the Holocaust (in the second part, after Jakob and his second wife have died in a car accident, his friend and student Ben travels to Greece and retrieves Jakob's lost diary) and how to remember it in the first place, it is as much about redemption through love as it is about the power of memory. Most reviews single out love and memory as the central topics and draw attention to Michaels's poetic language, which transforms remembrance into a sensual experience.

But reviewers also raise other issues. In the *Spiegel Extra* review of February 1997, Marianne Van Dyck poses a provocative question about the reception of this novel. She wonders whether this book, a Holocaust novel written by a Canadian, will be accepted in Germany, where people, especially those who dominate public discourse, believe that they have the sole right to discuss and interpret the Holocaust. For them, Holocaust memoirs demand respect only if they are legitimated through a person's experience and suffering (Primo Levi's *Is This a Man,* 1965, is apparently the exception). Michaels's novel may thus be highly problematic since it has broken a taboo in producing the imagined life of a Holocaust survivor in "breathtaking metaphors and lyrical pathos." Van Dyck predicts that the novel's critics will find fault with the sentimental abuse of atrocities and categorize the novel as part of so-called "Shoa-business."

---

21. So far, three paperback editions have been published, the most recent in 2004, and one hardcover reprint, published for the women's magazine *Brigitte Edition* in 2006. In 1998, the novel was read onto tape by Germany's leading dubbing voice, Christian Brückner.

Fortunately, Van Dyck's prognosis proved false. Major magazines and newspapers reviewed the novel and/or printed interviews with Michaels, and all of them comment on the courage required to write such a book. Michaels is seen as a Jewish Canadian author who breaks a taboo by writing a novel about Holocaust survivors that is (only) "authentic" in that it is based on stories she has heard from friends and relatives.

The two aspects noted most often in the reviews are Michaels's language and her concern with memory. The review in *Die Welt* (7 March 1997) comments that her language moves the heart; Sven Boedecker, too, praises the beauty of the language and its complexity (*Hamburger Abendblatt*, 25 February 1997). In "Singen für die Toten" ("Singing for the Dead"), Margrit Irgang comments on the novel's powerful language and refers to Michaels as a pre-eminent voice of the second generation, which summons readers to partake in "singing for the dead" in order to redeem them and us (*Süddeutsche Zeitung*, 1 March 1997). Stefanie Schild's interview with Michaels, entitled "Der Erinnerung Sinn verleihen" ("Giving Meaning to Memory"), focuses on both issues: she asks the author about writing a novel full of poetry and collective memory (*Münchner Merkur*, 7 March 1997). One of the most enthusiastic responses is found in John Berger's article in *Die Weltwoche* (13 February 1997), in which Berger calls *Fluchtstücke* the most important book that he has read in the past forty years, a book that finally refutes Adorno's dictum that it is barbaric to write poetry after Auschwitz. Wolfgang Schütte in the *Frankfurter Rundschau* gives a detailed analysis of Michaels's poetics, calling the novel an "ethical-poetic attempt at dialectic rescue and redemption" (15 February 1997). Comparing her novel to Michael Ondaatje's *In the Skin of a Lion* as well as to Thomas Mann's "snow chapter" in *The Magic Mountain*, Schütte argues that Michaels's achievement lies in the "metaphorical corporeality of her prose," which is the only way to talk about the unspeakable. The response to the novel *Fluchtstücke* contributed to and reflected the general discussion about Holocaust remembrance, particularly about the Holocaust memorial in Berlin, which was being planned at the time, and the approach to Holocaust survivors in Germany.

## NAOMI KLEIN: JOURNALIST AND NON-FICTION WRITER

Three years later another young female writer made her appearance in Germany. Naomi Klein's fight against brand names and designer labels began with the publication of her study *No Logo!* in Canada, the United States, and Great Britain in 2000. The book appeared on the German book market in March 2001, published by Riemann Verlag, Munich.[22] By 2001, it had been translated into fourteen

---

22. In 2005, a new paperback edition of the book was published by Goldmann Verlag, Munich.

languages. With publicity coming through the Internet only, *No Logo!* started as a hot tip, eventually selling 100,000 copies worldwide. In Germany, it was reviewed as one of the many new books on corporate globalization or global capitalism published in recent years (*Buchkultur,* April–May 2002). Similarly, it was labelled "a book on globalization" and "a political book" (*Kölner Stadt Anzeiger,* 17–18 March 2001). The *Spiegel* previewed the book as early as 18 December 2000, with reviewer Michael Sontheimer hailing it as a "brilliant mixture of journalism, theory, and autobiographical excerpts," in which Klein does not agitate or moralize but lets the facts speak for themselves. Her in-depth analysis of "the beautiful new world of brand obsession, globalization, and its counterforces" is a powerful statement on the global players' economic strategies, which, as Klein shows, are not only used for gaining power within the market but also have the power to define culture. Mathias Greffrath in *Die Zeit* (22 March 2001) similarly praises the book as a "pleasant and self-confident American [!] combination of non-fiction, analysis, reportage, subjectivity, and moral indignation." Klein's popularity was enhanced by a reading tour in March 2001, during which many prestigious papers and magazines published interviews and photographs. Due to the general and international reception of Klein and her political agenda, Germany's leading popular papers and journals stylized her as an "icon of the anti-globalists" (*Stern,* 6 March 2001), "prophetess of resistance," one of the most influential critics of globalization (*Die Woche,* 9 November 2001), the figurehead of the anti-globalists (*Die Zeit,* 27 December 2001), and "Seattle's darling" (*Frankfurter Rundschau,* 17 March 2001).

Klein, whose Jewish American parents moved to Canada out of protest against the Vietnam War, got involved in politics after a massacre at the University of Montreal in 1989, where an irate gunman killed fourteen women. As a student at the University of Toronto, Klein voiced her opinions on the intifada and attacked Israel for the occupation of Palestine and the repression of women. Her opinions earned her bomb threats and the open disapproval of the Jewish students' union.[23] Most German reviews find it remarkable that Klein still maintains an optimistic outlook on the development of the anti-globalization movement despite the overwhelming evidence that she has amassed on corporations in *No Logo!* She is cited as saying, "I believe in a new political protest movement. ... We have the Internet, demonstrations, we organize protests in small local groups. We are decentralized, this is our power. The global players are vulnerable."[24] Many

---

23. Katherine Viner, "Hand-to-Brand-Combat: A Profile of Naomi Klein," *Guardian,* 23 September 2000.
24. See Mareen Linnartz, "Den Seelenverkäufern auf der Spur," *Frankfurter Rundschau,* 17 March 2001.

reviews emphasize her positive attitude ("Why not try to be an optimist? It is fun"),[25] which is often seen as a characteristic of the Anglo-American mentality that contrasts sharply with the often gloomy outlook of German activists. Her family and religious background are mentioned in various reviews and interviews, though this background plays no role in her book.

## CONCLUSION

Naomi Klein is not the last Jewish Canadian writer to be translated into German. Others, such as novelists Nancy Richler and David Bezmogis, and writers of youth literature such as Karen Levine and Kathy Kacer, have also been successfully introduced into the German book market. Jewish Canadian writers may well be those "whose work has been influenced by Jewish history, the Jewish immigrant experience and eternal Judaic themes" (Weinfeld 2001, 201). However, in Canada the group is as diverse as any Jewish community in the diaspora. The degree of Jewishness in their works varies significantly, as does the attention paid to their Jewishness in the critical and journalistic reception. With the growing popularity of Canadian literature in general, Jewish Canadian writers have found a secure place in the German book market, with many of their books translated.[26] Many have been well received and have figured prominently in the leading German papers and magazines. The notion of Jewish Canadian writing is not, however, used in Germany to denote a certain group of writers. Still, Jewish Canadian literature has established itself in Germany through the publication of successful individual Jewish authors.

Anglophone Jewish Canadian authors who are not explicitly concerned with the Jewish Canadian experience and the portrayal of Jewish people, such as Matt Cohen, Howard Engel, and Naomi Klein, are not usually designated as Jewish Canadian writers. The same holds true for Leonard Cohen, who is in many ways a special case, known more for his songs and music in Germany than as an author. On the other hand, Mordecai Richler is seen as a distinctly Jewish Canadian author, as is Anne Michaels. With the exception of A. M. Klein, the most important and influential anglophone Jewish Canadian authors of the second half of the twentieth century are represented on the German book market, especially those who have been internationally successful.[27] Many of these authors' works enjoy critical attention and positive responses, probably not because they were

---

25. Stefan Schmitz, "Naomi: Klein *No Logo,*" *Stern,* 8 March 2001.
26. Other Jewish writers have not been translated; they include A. M. Klein, Eli Mandel, Adele Wiseman, and Norman Ravvin.
27. Francophone Jewish writers such as Naïm Kattan and Monique Bosco have unfortunately not been translated into German.

written by Jewish authors about Jewish themes but simply because they are good literature.

## REFERENCES

Bartsch, Ernst, ed. *Die Weite Reise: Kanadische Erzählungen und Kurzgeschichten*. Berlin: Volk und Welt, 1974.

Blodgett, E. D. *Five-Part Invention: A History of Literary History in Canada*. Toronto: University of Toronto Press, 2003.

Greenstein, Michael. *Third Solitudes: Tradition and Discontinuity in Jewish-Canadian Literature*. Kingston: McGill-Queen's University Press, 1989.

Hahn, Barbara. "Israel liegt nebenan." *Die Zeit* 21 (19 May 2005): 57.

Heft, Harold, and Glen Rotchin. "Comfort Rings the Death-Knell: Two Poets on the Future of Jewish Canadian Literature." In *Jewish Studies: The Jewish-Canadian Literature Debate*. http://www.vehiculepress.com/jewishlitdebate.html (consulted 3 November 2004).

Klooß, Wolfgang. "Jewish Writers of the Prairies: A Postmodern Reading of the Canadian Diaspora." In *(Trans) Formations of Cultural Identity in the English-Speaking World*, ed. Jochen Achilles and Carmen Birkle. Heidelberg: Winter, 1998. 81–94.

Layton, Irving. "In der Mitte meines Fiebers" ["In the Midst of My Fever"], transl. Hans Thill. In *Anders schreibendes Amerika: Literatur aus Québec*, ed. Lothar Baier, and Pierre Filion. Heidelberg: Verlag Das Wunderhorn, 2000. 185–86.

Nischik, Reingard M. "Zur Behandlung anglo-kanadischer Kurzgeschichten: Tendenzen, Materialien und Hilfsmittel." *Literatur in Wissenschaft und Unterricht* 15.4 (December 1982): 381–98.

Ravvin, Norman. *A House of Words: Jewish Writing, Identity and Memory*. Montreal: McGill-Queen's University Press, 1998.

Riedel, Walter. *Das literarische Kanadabild: Eine Studie zur Rezeption kanadischer Literatur in deutscher Übersetzung*. Bonn: Bouvier, 1980.

———, ed. *Moderne Erzähler der Welt*. Tübingen: Erdmann, 1976.

Sabin, Stefana, ed. *Kanada erzählt: 17 Erzählungen*. Frankfurt: Fischer Taschenbuch Verlag, 1992.

Weinfeld, Morton. *Like Everyone Else ... But Different: The Paradoxical Success of Canadian Jews*. Toronto: McClelland & Stewart, 2001.

## RESOURCES: JEWISH CANADIAN WRITING IN GERMAN

Cohen, Leonard. *Blumen für Hitler: Gedichte und Lieder 1956–1970* [*Flowers for Hitler*, 1964]. Bilingual ed. Frankfurt: März Verlag, 1971.

———. *Blumen für Hitler: Gedichte und Lieder 1956–1970*, transl. Anna von Cramer-Klett and Anja Hauptmann. Hamburg: Rowohlt, 1984.

———. *Die Energie von Sklaven* [*The Energy of Slaves*], transl. Harry Rowohlt. Bilingual ed. Frankfurt: Zweitausendeins, 1975.

———. *Letzte Prüfung* [*Death of a Lady's Man*, 1979], transl. Rudolf Hermstein. Bilingual ed. Frankfurt: Zweitausendeins, 1982.

———. *Das Lieblingsspiel* [*The Favorite Game*, 1970], transl. Elisabeth Hannover-Drück. Frankfurt: März Verlag, 1972.

———. *Das Lieblingsspiel*, transl. Elisabeth Hannover-Drück. Hamburg: Rowohlt, 1983.

———. *Das Lieblingsspiel*, transl. Bettina Hanstein. Munich: Triptychon, 2005.

———. *Omnibus: Schöne Verlierer, Das Lieblingsspiel, Blumen für Hitler*. Frankfurt: Zweittausenddeins, 1974–1978.

———. *Parasiten des Himmels* [*Parasites of Heaven*, 1973], transl. Carl Weissner. Bilingual ed. Frankfurt: Zweitausendeins, 1976.

———. *Schöne Verlierer* [*Beautiful Losers*, 1966], transl. Elisabeth Hannover-Drück. Frankfurt: März Verlag, 1970.

———. *Schöne Verlierer* [*Beautiful Losers*, 1966], transl. Elisabeth Hannover-Drück. Hamburg: Rowohlt, 1983.

———. *Wem sonst als dir / Book of Mercy* [*Book of Mercy*, 1984], transl. Regina Lindhoff and Uve Schmidt. Bilingual ed. Herbstein: März Verlag, 1985.

Cohen, Leonard, and Jürgen Jaensch. *Ich kenne deine Träume*, ed. Christof Graf. Bad Homburg: New Art, 1997.

Cohen, Matt. "Der Auswanderer" ["The Expatriate"], transl. Ekkehard Fabldieck. In *Erkundungen: 26 kanadische Erzähler*, ed. Karla El-Hassan and Helga Militz. Berlin: Volk und Welt, 1986. 60–81.

———. "Kolumbus und die Riesendame" ["Columbus and the Fat Lady"], transl. Elfi Schneidenbach. In *Kolumbus und die Riesendame: Kurzgeschichten aus Kanada*, ed. Karla El-Hassan. Berlin: Aufbau Taschenbuch Verlag, 1992. 108–24.

———. "The Nurse from Outer Space / Die Krankenschwester aus dem All." In *New American Stories, Taut and Strange: Neue amerikanische Erzählungen*, ed. and transl. Ulrike Becker and Claus Varrelmann. Munich: dtv, 1990. 6–27.

Devlin, Jim, ed. *Leonard Cohen: In eigenen Worten*, transl. Clemens Brunn. Heidelberg: Palmyra, 2002.

El-Hassan, Karla. *Kurzgeschichtenensembles: Formen der Verknüpfung anglokanadischer Short Stories*. Bochum: Brockmeyer, 1990.

———. "Die Kurzgeschichten Norman Levines: Ein Beitrag zum Problem des literarischen Zyklus." *Zeitschrift für Anglistik und Amerikanistik* (East Berlin) 29.2 (1981): 154–66.

Engel, Howard. "Ein ruhiges Plauderstündchen." In *Erkundungen: 26 kanadische Erzähler*, ed. Karla El-Hassan and Helga Militz. Berlin: Volk und Welt, 1986. 46–52.

Graf, Christof. *Leonard Cohen: Partisan der Liebe—Eine Biographie*. Cologne: Vgs-Verlag, 1996.

———. *Leonard Cohen: Songs of a Life*. Munich: dtv, 2002.

———. *Leonard Cohen—Un Hommage*. Echternach, Luxembourg: Éditions Phi, 1997.

———. *So long, Leonard: Leben und Lieder von Leonard Cohen*. Heidelberg: Palmyra, 1990.

Klein, Naomi. *No Logo! Der Kampf der Global Players um Marktmacht—Ein Spiel mit vielen Verlierern und wenigen Gewinnern* [*No Logo: No Space, No Choice, No Jobs; Taking Aim at the Brand Bullies*], transl. Helmut Dierlamm. Munich: Riemann, 2001.

Kreisel, Henry. "Chassidische Weise" ["Chassidic Song"], transl. Gottfried Probst. In *Gute Wanderschaft, mein Bruder*, ed. Gottfried Friedrich and Walter Riedel. Leipzig: St. Benno-Verlag, 1986.

———. "Der verbeulte Globus" ["The Broken Globe"], transl. Walter Riedel. In *Moderne Erzähler der Welt: Kanada*, ed. Walter Riedel. Tübingen: Erdmann, 1976. 252–64.

———. "Zwei Schwestern in Genf" ["Two Sisters in Geneva"], transl. Armin Arnold. In *Kanadische Erzähler der Gegenwart*, ed. Armin Arnold and Walter Riedel. 2nd ed. Zurich: Manesse, 1976. 377–90.

Layton, Irving. "Frömmigkeit" ["Piety"], transl. Armin Arnold. In *Moderne Erzähler der Welt: Kanada*, ed. Walter Riedel. Tübingen: Erdmann, 1976. 213–32.

———. "In der Mitte meines Fiebers" ["In the Midst of My Fever"], transl. Hans Thill. In *Anders schreibendes Amerika: Literatur aus Québec*, ed. Lothar Baier and Pierre Filion. Heidelberg: Verlag Das Wunderhorn, 2000. 185–86.

Levine, Norman. *Django, Karfunkelstein & Rosen: Erzählungen* [*Django, Karfunkelstein & Rosen*], transl. Gabriele Bock, Annemarie and Heinrich Böll, and Eike Schönfeld. Düsseldorf: Claassen, 1987.

———. *Kanada hat mich gemacht* [*Canada Made Me*], transl. Heinz Winter. Hamburg: Claassen, 1967.

———. "Eine kanadische Jugend" ["A Canadian Youth"], transl. Annemarie and Heinrich Böll. In *Kanada erzählt: 17 Erzählungen*, ed. Stefana Sabin. Frankfurt: Fischer Taschenbuch Verlag, 1992. 160–67.

———. *Ein kleines Stückchen Blau: Erzählungen* [*One Way Ticket: I Don't Want to Know Anyone Well*], transl. Annemarie and Heinrich Böll and Reinhard Wagner. 2nd ed. Hamburg: Claassen, 1979.

———. "Ein kleines Stückchen Blau" ["A Small Piece of Blue"], transl. Annemarie and Heinrich Böll. In *Die weite Reise: Kanadische Erzählungen und Kurzgeschichten*, ed. Ernst Bartsch. Berlin: Volk und Welt, 1974. 118–34.

———. *Der Mann mit dem Notizblock*, ed. Karla El-Hassan [Stories from *In Lower Town*], transl. Annemarie and Heinrich Böll, Gabriele Bock, and Reinhard Wagner. Leipzig: Reclam, 1979.

Ludwig, Jack. "Requiem auf Bibul" ["Requiem for Bibul"], transl. Armin Arnold. In *Moderne Erzähler der Welt: Kanada*, ed. Walter Riedel. Tübingen: Erdmann, 1976. 266–83.

Michaels, Anne. *Fluchtstücke* [*Fugitive Pieces*], transl. Beatrice Howeg. Berlin: Berlin Verlag, 1996.

Nadel, Ira B. *Leonard Cohen: Ein Leben für die Poesie*, transl. Bernd Oehler. Höfen: Hannibal, 2000.

———. *Various Positions: Das Leben Leonard Cohens*, transl. Hannah Harders. Berlin: Berlin Verlag/Ullstein, 1997/1999.

Nischik, Reingard M. "Zur Behandlung anglo-kanadischer Kurzgeschichten: Tendenzen, Materialien und Hilfsmittel." *Literatur in Wissenschaft und Unterricht* 15.4 (December 1982): 381–98.

Richler, Mordecai. *Die Akrobaten* [*The Acrobats*, 1954], transl. Annemarie Horschitz-Horst. Munich: Kindler, 1955.

———. "Bambinger." In *Moderne Erzähler der Welt: Kanada*, ed. Walter Riedel. Tübingen: Erdmann, 1976. 306–12.

———. "Benny, der Krieg in Europa und Myersons Tochter Bella" ["Benny, the War in Europe and Myerson's Daughter Bella"], transl. Elga Abramowitz. In *Sinn und Form: Beiträge zur Literatur*, ed. Akademie der Künste der Deutschen Demokratischen Republik 37.4 (July/August 1985). Berlin: Rütten & Loening. 765–70.

———. *Der Boden trägt mich nicht mehr* [*A Choice of Enemies*, 1957], transl. Paul Baudisch. Munich: Kindler, 1958.

———. *Ein Geschenk für Jacob Zwei-Zwei* [*Jacob Two-Two and the Dinosaur*, 1987], transl. Reinhard Kaiser. Frankfurt: Eichborn/Fischer Taschenbuch Verlag, 1994/1999.

———. *Jacob Zwei-Zwei in Gefahr* [*Jacob Two-Two Meets the Hooded Fang*, 1981], transl. Reinhard Kaiser. Frankfurt: Eichborn/Fischer Taschenbuch Verlag, 1994/1998.

———. *Joshua damals und jetzt* [*Joshua Then and Now*, 1980], transl. Gisela Stege. Munich: Kindler, 1981.

———. *Die Lehrjahre des Duddy Kravitz* [*The Apprenticeship of Duddy Kravitz*, 1959], transl. Silvia Morawetz. Munich: Verlagsbuchhandlung Liebeskind, 2007.

———. *Sohn eines kleineren Helden* [*Son of a Smaller Hero*, 1955], transl. Paul Baudisch. Munich: Kindler, 1963.

———. *Sohn eines kleineren Helden* [*Son of a Smaller Hero*, 1955], transl. Paul Baudisch. Frankfurt: Fischer Taschenbuch Verlag, 1994.

———. *Solomon Gursky war hier* [*Solomon Gursky Was Here*], transl. Hartmut Zahn and Carina von Enzenberg. Munich/Frankfurt: Hanser/Fischer Taschenbuch Verlag, 1992/1994.

———. *Der Traum des Jakob Hersch* [*St. Urbain's Horseman*], transl. Gisela Stege. Munich/Frankfurt: Kindler/Fischer Taschenbuch Verlag, 1980/1996.

———. "Wasser auf Mervyns Mühle." In *Kanada erzählt: 17 Erzählungen*, ed. Stefana Sabin. Frankfurt: Fischer Taschenbuch Verlag, 1992. 168–98.

———. "Wasser auf Mervyns Mühle." In *Die weite Reise: Kanadische Erzählungen und Kurzgeschichten*, ed. Ernst Bartsch. Berlin: Volk und Welt, 1974. 150–80.

———. *Wie Barney es sieht* [*Barney's Version*], transl. Anette Grube. Munich: Hanser, 2000.

Waddington, Miriam. "Das Halloween-Fest" ["Halloween"], transl. Marlies Juhnke. In *Kolumbus und die Riesendame: Kurzgeschichten aus Kanada*, ed. Karla El-Hassan. Berlin: Aufbau Taschenbuch Verlag, 1992. 274–80.

Weinzweig, Helen. "L'Envoi." In *Frauen in Kanada: Erzählungen und Gedichte*, ed. Birgit Herrmann. Munich: Deutscher Taschenbuch Verlag, 1993. 171–83.

# Contemporary (English) Canadian Plays in German/y: Equivalence in Difference?

*Albert-Reiner Glaap*
*Düsseldorf*

## MOVING CANADIAN PLAYS TO GERMANY

Importing Canadian plays across the Atlantic occurs most frequently when a published text or play script of a Canadian play is translated and converted into a draft for production in Europe. But how do theatres in Germany and their artistic directors get to know about these plays?

Over the past ten years, a number of Canadian playwrights have visited various parts of Germany for readings of their plays and discussions with university students and theatre people; they include Henry Beissel, Michel Marc Bouchard,[1] Ken Gass, Christopher Heide, Tomson Highway, Joan MacLeod, Daniel David Moses, Yvette Nolan, Morris Panych, Sharon Pollock, Rick Salutin, Jason Sherman, Judith Thompson, and Drew Hayden Taylor. With financial support from the Department of Foreign Affairs in Ottawa and the Canadian Embassy in Berlin, some playwrights have also addressed the Annual Conferences of the Association for Canadian Studies in German-Speaking Countries. The cultural section of the Canadian Embassy in Berlin is particularly instrumental in publicizing and promoting Canadian playwrights and plays, as the following excerpts from an interview in November 2004 with Gabriele Naumann-Maerten, Cultural Attaché at the embassy, elucidate:

> **Albert-Reiner Glaap (ARG):** You are very instrumental in bringing Canadian plays to Germany and German theatres on behalf of the embassy. Could you describe how this happens?
>
> **Gabriele Naumann-Maerten (GNM):** Germany has a vibrant and very well-developed theatre system. There are about 2,000 theatres in this country.

---

1. French Canadian plays are discussed by Andreas Jandl in this volume.

These theatres mostly work with ensembles on a project/production basis, but in contrast to other countries they are often hired for the entire season or more. As German theatres produce their own artistic productions and build up repertoires for their audiences, they rarely invite foreign theatre companies. Their focus is on working with texts/plays. This offers opportunities for Canadian playwrights to increasingly come into contact with German theatres and their audiences. Our aim is to draw attention to Canadian playwrights. To do this, we try to bridge the information gap about Canadian playwrights and plays. More often than not, we find that people just do not know how to get access to material, plays, key people, and institutions.

Over the last few years, we have taken a very proactive role with a long-term view. We familiarize ourselves with the artistic profiles and programs of the individual theatres. Personal interaction, communication, and exchange of information [are] the cornerstones. German theatres are very interested and eager to get information about new plays, since this helps them to build up their artistic reputation and increase their *renommé* by introducing new plays and/or new authors to their audiences and to the professionals in the milieu. I must say that artistic profiles vary a lot, and you have to keep abreast of the issues that individual theatres want to reflect on during their season. German theatres are very content-orientated, and as such it can be counterproductive to propose a broad variety of authors to any one theatre. Only when you know your partners well enough will you succeed in proposing an appropriate author or play.

We not only collaborate with theatre directors but also with the respective "heads of dramaturgy" as, in Germany, they are the ones who decide which plays will be staged or introduced to their audiences through readings and how the context of the play will be developed.

Often we start at a much earlier stage: with the translators. For example, we supported research trips for two translators to attend the CEAD (Centre des auteurs dramatiques) translators' workshop in Montreal; they came back with numerous plays for potential staging in Germany. George F. Walker's cycle *Suburban Motel* got introduced to Germany by his translator, who in turn convinced an agent to distribute the play.

But we do not restrict ourselves to launching one particular playwright. We use different kinds of access routes, tools, and channels to provide the theatre community with the kind of information they need so that professionals in the theatres are ultimately able to decide whether the author/the play is of relevance to their respective audiences and fits in with their program. At the embassy, we are constantly trying to keep up to date about current developments and initiatives. We do research on all Canadian plays that have been translated into German to date. So far, we have found as many as seventy-eight plays available in German (see www.international.gc.ca/canada-europa/germany/cultureincanada8-de.asp, "Theaterstücke aus Kanada in deutscher Übersetzung").

We are also participating in an international platform for contemporary theatre between French Canada, English Canada, Germany, and the Netherlands. This project is being developed in several steps, enabling translators and artistic directors to meet, exchange, collaborate, and translate. The idea behind it is, for example, to have one play translated into several languages and launched into different cultures at the same time.

**ARG:** How does the embassy draw the attention of potential theatre audiences to productions of Canadian plays in Germany?

**GNM:** We use our bimonthly cultural magazine *CanadArt,* which reaches about 5,000 readers in Germany, and our website. All our initiatives are carried out in partnerships and collaboration with the professional theatre milieu. When a play is staged or launched, this collaboration is also announced in the program of the respective theatre. The cultural section of the embassy does more promotion in the professional milieu, whereas the wider theatre audiences are mostly reached by the theatres.

**ARG:** The embassy—that is, its theatre department—has proven to be indispensable for promoting Canadian plays in Germany. What are the main priorities of your or the department's various tasks?

**GNM:** Our priorities are to improve the profile of Canada abroad with an image of Canada as a knowledge-based innovative country with profound contemporary artistic cultural diversity. Our main focus in Germany in the arts and in theatre is on cutting-edge productions. Our purpose is to deepen German audiences' knowledge about Canada and to move beyond the existing clichés and prejudices.

Our main objective is to provide opportunities for audiences to discover Canadian playwrights and plays. As a part of that, we are planning to set up an e-newsletter on new Canadian plays. The plays to be promoted will be chosen by a jury which includes German theatre professionals.

Canadian plays written in the wake of Canadian nationalism and realism in the 1970s were of limited interest to European audiences. Most of them were too specifically Canadian, dealing with topics such as ice hockey, the Parti Québécois, or the problems of people living in the Prairies or in the faraway outports of Newfoundland. Since the early 1980s, however, Canadian playwrights have voiced their different cultural experiences and developed innovative concepts: they now write about events, problems, and topics relevant to theatre audiences anywhere, and they address their audiences on two levels—one specifically Canadian and the other universal. A play such as Brad Fraser's *Unidentified Human Remains and the True Nature of Love* (first produced in 1982) is not just a portrait of the Canadian urban jungle but also a compassionate study of the groping search for meaning in a senseless world (see Glaap 2001).

Needless to say, Canadian plays are primarily written for Canadian audiences. However, a considerable number of these plays have also become of interest to European theatres and audiences. These plays are not cast in a specific, traditional mould, and they surprise by their wide variety and their originality. Hence, it is not primarily the fact that they are Canadian that makes them attractive to theatres outside Canada. Theatres everywhere are on the lookout for plays that address substantial issues, use innovative approaches, and develop new dramaturgical concepts.

With respect to current productivity, a handbook for professionals in German theatres was published in German: *Stimmen aus Kanada: 25 kanadische Stücke für deutsche Bühnen* ("Voices from Canada: 25 Canadian Plays for German Stages"; Glaap 1997). The purpose of this book is to familiarize artistic directors and theatres in Germany with a selection of Canadian plays in the form of overviews, providing useful information on each of these plays, such as the date, place, and director of the premiere performance, stage setting, performance rights, and author's agent. Each entry also includes a summary of the play's content, a brief commentary providing information about the context of the play and the author's work, and a list of central themes. An enlarged, revised, and updated English version of *Stimmen aus Kanada* was published by Playwrights Canada Press under the title *Voices from Canada: Focus on Thirty Plays* (Glaap 2003).

It is also a welcome development that some Canadian plays are now being read and discussed in German secondary schools and that annotated editions in English of, among others, Drew Hayden Taylor's *Toronto at Dreamer's Rock* (first produced in 1989) and Anne Chislett's *Flippin' In* (first produced in 1996) are available for classroom work. Clearly, efforts during the past decade to promote Canadian drama have been made at three different levels: university, secondary school, and the theatre.

## STAGING CANADIAN PLAYS IN GERMAN THEATRES

Since 1990, the number of productions of Canadian plays in German translation has greatly increased. Lists of such productions in German theatres, published annually by the Deutscher Bühnenverein (German Theatre Association), give an insight into this development. The following overview of the contemporary situation, based both on the listings of the Deutscher Bühnenverein and on personal research, makes no claim to be complete. Space restraints do not allow for all the productions to be listed here, but the selective list below (data as of 2005) provides details on the names of translators, the number of performances, and the theatres where the respective plays were first produced.

TABLE 8.1

*Canadian Plays Produced in Germany*

| AUTHOR | TITLE IN GERMAN (ORIGINAL TITLE) | TRANSLATOR | NUMBER OF PERFORMANCES* | THEATRES |
|---|---|---|---|---|
| Beissel, Henry | *Inuk und das Geheimnis der Sonne* (*Inook and the Sun*)[1] | Henry Beissel | 12 | Dresden, Theater Junge Generation (2003) |
| Blicker, Seymour | *Verlegtes Glück* (*Never Judge a Book by Its Cover*) | René Freund | 80 | Wien, Theater in der Josefstadt (1991) |
| Bouchard, Michel Marc | *Gefahrenzone* (*Le chemin des Passes-Dangereuses*) | Frank Heibert | 18 | Neuss, Rheinisches Landestheater (2000) |
| Bouchard, Michel Marc | *Die Geschichte von Teeka* (*L'histoire de l'oie*) | Marie-Elisabeth Morf | 153 | Berlin, Carrousel (1996); Heidelberg, Theater der Stadt (1996); Neuss, Rheinisches Landestheater (1997); Salzburg, Theater am Mirabellplatz (1997); Aalen, Theater der Stadt (1998); Braunschweig, Staatstheater (1998); Dortmund, Theater Dortmund (1998) |

1. The title of the play and the spelling of "Inuk" were changed for the 2001 edition of the play in English and French (see References).

| AUTHOR | TITLE IN GERMAN (ORIGINAL TITLE) | TRANSLATOR | NUMBER OF PERFORMANCES* | THEATRES |
|---|---|---|---|---|
| Bouchard, Michel Marc | Die verlassenen Musen (Les muses orphelines) | Frank Heibert | 10 | Neuss, Rheinisches Landestheater (1998) |
| Brassard, Marie | Jimmy, Traumgeschöpf (Jimmy, créature de rêve) | H.-W. Meyer | 32 | Bremen, Bremer Theater (2002); Göttingen, Deutsches Theater in Göttingen (2002) |
| Chaurette, Normand | Der kleine Köchel (Le petit Köchel) | Hinrich Schmidt-Henkel | 14 | Hamburg, Deutsches Schauspielhaus (2001) |
| Danis, Daniel | Das Lied vom Sag-Sager (Le chant du Dire-Dire) | Uta Ackermann | 86 | Berlin, Schaubühne am Lehniner Platz (2000); Leipzig, Schauspiel Leipzig (2001); Mannheim, Nationaltheater (2001); Aachen, Theater Aachen (2002); Osnabrück, Städtische Bühnen (2002) |
| Danis, Daniel | Steinasche Kieselasche (Cendres de cailloux) | Andreas Jandl, Christine Pettinger | 16 | Zürich, Theater Neumarkt (2002) |
| Fraser, Brad | Unidentifizierte Leichenteile & das wahre Wesen der Liebe (Unidentified Human Remains and the True Nature of Love) | Donald Berkenhopp | 31

12

7 | Hamburg, Theater an der Basilika (1993)

Ulm, Ulmer Theater (1997)

Schwerin, Mecklenburgisches Staatstheater (2000) |

| AUTHOR | TITLE IN GERMAN (ORIGINAL TITLE) | TRANSLATOR | NUMBER OF PERFORMANCES* | THEATRES |
|---|---|---|---|---|
| Gow, David | Cherry Docs (Cherry Docs) | Anna Cron | * | Würzburg, Mainfranken-Theater (2004) |
| Laberge, Marie | Der Falke (Le faucon) | Marion Kagerer | 96 | Meiningen, Das Meininger Theater (1997–1998); Bern, Theater an der Effingerstraße (2000); Dresden, Staatsschauspiel (2002); St. Pölten, Theater der Landeshauptstadt (2002) |
| Laberge, Marie | Vaterliebe (L'homme gris) | Paul Bäcker | 209 | Esslingen, Württembergische Landesbühne (1989); Mainz, Mainzer Kammer-spiele (1991); Hannover, Klecks-Theater (1993); Bochum, Schauspielhaus (1994) |
| Laberge, Marie | Vergessen (Oublier) | A. and P. Bäcker | 12 | Krefeld-Mönchengladbach, Vereinigte Städtische Bühnen (2003) |
| Lepage, Robert | Geometry of Miracles (Geometry of Miracles) | | 7 | Salzburg, Salzburger Festspiele (1998) |
| Lepage, Robert, and Marie Brassard | Polygraph (Le polygraphe) | Kristine Hasselmann, Hans-Werner Meyer | 23 | Köln, Bühnen der Stadt (1997); Wuppertal, Wuppertaler Bühnen (2003) |
| Lepage, Robert | Die sieben Ströme des Flusses Ota (The Seven Streams of the River Ota) | Dora Kapurta | 6 | Ludwigsburg, Schlossfestspiele (1996) |

| AUTHOR | TITLE IN GERMAN (ORIGINAL TITLE) | TRANSLATOR | NUMBER OF PERFORMANCES* | THEATRES |
|---|---|---|---|---|
| Murrell, John | Memoiren (Memoir) | Ute Horstmann | 42 | Ingolstadt, Stadttheater (1991); Bregenz, Theater für Vorarlberg (1996); Bamberg, E. T. A.-Hoffmann-Theater (1998) |
| Ondaatje, Michael | Buddy Bolden's Blues (Coming through Slaughter) | Adelheid Dormagen | 38 | Gelsenkirchen/ Wuppertal, Schillertheater (1997); Berlin, Carrousel (1998) |
| Ondaatje, Michael | Die gesammelten Werke von Billy the Kid (The Collected Works of Billy the Kid) | Werner Herzog | 34 | Dortmund, Theater Dortmund (1994); Darmstadt, Staatstheater (2001); Konstanz, Stadttheater (2003) |
| Panych, Morris | Freudige Erwartung (Vigil) | Ulrike Schanko | 14 | Neuss, Rheinisches Landestheater (2003) |
| Scollard, Rose | Feuervogel (Firebird) | Ute Scharfenberg | 24 | Magdeburg, Freie Kammerspiele (2003) |
| Walker, George F. | Das Ende der Zivilisation (The End of Civilization) | Frank Heibert | * | Düsseldorf, Düsseldorfer Schauspielhaus (2003); Mainz, Staatstheater (2003); Lübeck (2003); Karlsruhe, Badisches Landestheater (2004) |
| Walker, George F. | Genie und Verbrechen (Criminal Genius) | Frank Heibert | * | Düsseldorf, Düsseldorfer Schauspielhaus (2003) |

| AUTHOR | TITLE IN GERMAN (ORIGINAL TITLE) | TRANSLATOR | NUMBER OF PERFORMANCES* | THEATRES |
|---|---|---|---|---|
| Walker, George F. | Heaven (*Heaven*) | Frank Heibert | 4 | Magdeburg, Freie Kammerspiele (2003) |
| Walker, George F. | Loretta (*Featuring Loretta*) | Frank Heibert | * | Düsseldorf, Düsseldorfer Schauspielhaus (2003) |
| Walker, George F. | Nur für Erwachsene (*Adult Entertainment*) | Frank Heibert | * | Düsseldorf, Düsseldorfer Schauspielhaus (2003); Darmstadt (2003) |

* Data stated where available.

## PROMOTING AND MARKETING CANADIAN PLAYS

The original English or French versions of the plays listed above are available in Canada as printed texts or as typescripts. The two organizations most prominent in the promotion of Canadian voices for the stage are the PGC (Playwrights Guild of Canada) and its publishing imprint Playwrights Canada Press in Toronto as well as CEAD (Centre des auteurs dramatiques) in Montreal. Both organizations publish Canadian plays and catalogues to market them. PGC, the professional association of more than 450 playwrights, copies and distributes scripts provided by English Canadian playwrights; Playwrights Canada Press produces and publishes printed editions. CEAD's objectives are to develop Quebec plays, primarily in French, but some also in English translation, thereby promoting playwrights at home and abroad. Furthermore, certain Canadian publishing houses, such as Talonbooks in Vancouver, J. Gordon Shillingford (Scirocco Drama) in Winnipeg, and Anvil Press (Anvil Performance Series) in Vancouver, have, over the past fifteen years, rendered Canadian readers and theatrical people great service by making contemporary plays and collections of plays available in print.

The promotion of Canadian plays in Germany, however, was left to chance for a long time. An artistic director from Germany or a theatre agent from some European country might happen to see a production of a play in a Canadian theatre, have it translated, and then find it difficult to place it in a German theatre. Today, some Canadian playwrights or their agents enter into association with a German agent, who establishes contact with theatres in Germany that might want to mount the respective play and who looks for an adequate translator. (In Germany, as a rule, copies of translated play scripts are not published in book form but can be purchased as typescripts from German agents.) It is equally important for artistic directors in German theatres to get in touch with Playwrights Canada Press, Playwrights Guild of Canada, or CEAD to inquire about new plays and ask for their catalogues.

## TRANSLATING CONTEMPORARY CANADIAN PLAYS

Plays are not written for individual readers the way that novels are, which, once they are published, constitute the "end products" of a creative process. Plays are written for directors and actors, who mull them over and develop concepts for productions from the "modelling clay" of the scripts. Play scripts are "blueprints" that mark a transitional phase; they are interim arrangements. The translator of a play is confronted with the kinds of problems that any translator must cope with—problems that ultimately boil down to the overall question of how to approach some semblance of equivalence in difference. Translating a play script, however, makes additional demands on the translator because he or she must always be aware of what could be termed the "third dimension" of the text: that is, the fact that the particular text will be transformed into a production and received by an audience in a theatre.

An excerpt from Scene Two of George F. Walker's play *Risk Everything* (1999),[2] first produced in 1997, lends itself to a contrastive analysis of the English text and its German translation by Frank Heibert; this approach will allow us to tentatively elucidate to what extent the English original is preserved yet at the same time oriented toward present-day colloquial German. In *Risk Everything*, "Walker ... extends the trope of television, continually questioning layers of reality": the main character, R. J., has been in prison; "while incarcerated, [he] has also become addicted to television, especially to daytime talk shows that present ... aberrations in a bourgeois world" (Gilbert 2001, 328–29).

> CAROL is sitting at the table. Eating a bowl of takeout soup. Smoking a cigarette. Drinking from a bottle of Jack Daniels. R. J. is watching television. The program is interrupted by a commercial.
>
> R. J.: <u>Yeah</u>, here it is. Y'know the biggest problem you gotta deal with is the depressing feeling that hits you when the program is interrupted by commercials. I mean if you're really into the show it's <u>like life has stopped</u>. It's that bad. It's

---

2. *Risk Everything* is part of a cycle of plays entitled *Suburban Motel*. Whereas most German theatres have kept the original umbrella title, some of the six titles of the individual plays have been translated.

like God has all of a sudden stopped everything and what are you supposed to do. Just wait? Because that thirty seconds, that minute, that minute and a half is just like forever. And you hate those commercials. If you're really into the show you hate them a lot. And you promise yourself you'll never buy that product. In fact, fuck it, you don't even pay attention. You don't even wanna know what the product is. You feel that intense about it ... (*he turns the TV off*). ... Yeah. Okay. (*smiles*) Anyway it was the sit-com that stopped me from getting really fucked up about that stuff. When the networks started programming a whole evening of funny shows all together. I mean how strung out can you get watching lighthearted family entertainment. I even started liking some of the commercials. Cats in commercials were very big at this time. Anyway, let's not kid ourselves. This wasn't any golden age of television comedy. There were no Barney Millers here. No Rhodas. I've seen those shows on late-night re-runs. And I'm impressed. No, these shows were mostly about families and everybody talked too loud and only a few of the jokes ever worked. But it was enough to chill me out. Now those new cop shows, that's something else. I feel nothing for them. Nothing. Anyway, everything after Colombo is crap. Colombo, McCloud, Hart to Hart, Cagney and Lacey, Magnum P.I. Shows around that time, they had ... class. I've got a friend who has copies of Hart to Hart that he's been watching for ten years. That's five years in prison and five on the outside and he's still a loyal fan. ... My thing is reality. I first turned into a reality fan with the afternoon talk shows. But I got hooked. ... All those people with all those problems. It was too much. I got too emotional. Sometimes I couldn't sleep, thinking about those people. So I moved off the talk shows into cooking and maintenance shows. ... (Walker 1999, 274–75; emphasis added)

CAROL sitzt am Tisch. Isst eine Schüssel Suppe zum Mitnehmen. Raucht eine Zigarette. Trinkt aus einer Flasche Jack Daniels. R. J. sieht fern. Das Programm wird von einem Werbespot unterbrochen.

R. J.: Jawoll, da ist es wieder. Weißt du, was das Allerschlimmste für mich ist? Dieses deprimierende Gefühl, wenn das Programm von der Werbung unterbrochen wird. Also wenn du dich voll auf die Show eingelassen hast, ja, dann ist das, als würde das Leben plötzlich abgeschaltet. So schlimm ist es. So deprimierend. Als hätte Gott urplötzlich den Stecker rausgezogen, und du weißt nicht, was du machen sollst. Einfach abwarten? Weil diese dreißig Sekunden, diese Minute, diese anderthalb Minuten sind die Ewigkeit. Und du kannst diese Werbespots nicht ausstehen. Wenn du dich richtig auf die Show eingelassen hast, kannst du sie auf den Tod nicht ausstehen. Du schwörst dir, dieses Produkt kaufst du nie. Beziehungsweise, scheiß drauf, du achtest gar nicht drauf. Du willst gar nicht wissen, um was für ein Produkt es gerade geht. So heftig reagierst du darauf ... (*schaltet den Fernseher ab*). ... Genau. Okay. (*lächelt*) Jedenfalls habe ich es den Vorabendserien zu verdanken, dass ich über diesem ganzen Stuss nicht völlig verblödet bin. Als die Sender anfingen, den ganzen Abend witzige Shows zu bringen. Weil, ernsthaft, man kann dermaßen süchtig nach heiterer Familienunterhaltung werden! Es ging so weit, dass mir sogar schon ein paar von den Werbespots gefielen. Katzen waren damals in der Werbung echt in. Aber machen wir uns nichts vor. Von wegen Goldene Jahre der Fernsehcomedy. Wo ist denn ein Barney Miller. Eine Rhoda. Deren Sachen hab ich gesehen, als Wiederholungen im Nachtprogramm, und ich war echt beeindruckt. Aber bei diesen Serien heutzutage geht es meistens um eine Familie, alle reden zu laut, und nur ein paar Gags funktionieren wirklich. Aber mir hat's gereicht, <u>um da runterzukommen</u>. Genauso diese neuen Polizeiserien, das ist echt ein anderer Film. Für die hab ich überhaupt nichts übrig. Gar nichts. <u>Alles nach Colombo war sowieso Schrott</u>. Alles nach Colombo, Ein Sheriff in New York, Hart aber herzlich, Cagney & Lacey, Magnum. Die Serien aus der Zeit, die hatten ... Klasse. Ein Freund von mir hat Folgen von Hart aber herzlich auf Video, die guckt er sich seit zehn Jahren an. Fünf Jahre im Knast und fünf Jahre draußen, und immer noch ist er ein treuer Fan. ... Ich steh ja auf Reality TV. Das fing mit den Nachmittags-Talkshows an, dass ich zum Reality-Fan wurde. Da häng ich voll am Haken. Das war zu viel. <u>Ich bin viel zu sehr drauf eingestiegen</u>. Manchmal konnte ich nicht mehr schlafen, weil ich an die Leute denken musste. Deshalb bin ich von Talkshows zu Kochen und Heimwerkersendungen übergegangen. ... (unpublished translation by Frank Heibert, Pegasus Theaterverlag; emphasis added)

For reasons of space, some brief observations, based on a comparison of the two versions of this text, must suffice to elucidate aspects of the translation process.

The more emphatic and colloquial "Jawoll" (not "Jawohl") for the English "Yeah," "beziehungsweise" for "in fact," "this wasn't any golden age" translated as "von wegen Goldene Jahre," and "alles nach *Colombo* war sowieso Schrott" for "anything after *Colombo* is crap"—these examples show that, as often as not, the details are important. Adequate renderings of colloquial expressions will contribute to the impact of the play on audiences and reflect Walker's wry humour: "enough to chill me out" / "mir hat's gereicht, um da runterzukommen"; "is like for ever" / "sind die Ewigkeit"; "you hate them [the commercials] a lot" / "du kannst sie auf den Tod nicht ausstehen"; "I got too emotional" / "Ich bin viel zu sehr drauf eingestiegen"; "I love them all" / "Ich find die alle toll." Moreover, the translator uses some German expressions that underline the context of watching TV, for instance "like life has stopped" / "als würde das Leben plötzlich abgeschaltet" or "like God has all of a sudden stopped everything" / "als hätte Gott urplötzlich den Stecker rausgezogen."

At this point, a revealing statement from the Canadian author and translator Henry Beissel should be taken into consideration because, in this case, the author, himself of German descent and fluent in German, took a particular interest in the translation of his play. His comments (in a letter to the author specifically written for this chapter) on a translation of *Inook and the Sun* (1974) touch on fundamental problems in the translation of Canadian plays. Beissel's play is a dramatized story of initiation based on the Inuit yearning for the coming of spring during the long winter. It tells the story of Inook, an adolescent who sets out to find the sun, and of the many difficulties that he has to overcome before he finally brings it back to his people. He becomes a man because he learns how to tie in with the rhythms of nature and the cycle of the seasons. He sees fundamental patterns of life and death lying open to the mind, patterns that are buried in urban civilization. Here are the author's comments on a few aspects of the translation process:

> In the fall of 1974 I received an inquiry about the availability of the German translation rights to my play *Inook and the Sun* from the Henschel-Verlag in what was then East Berlin. So I wired the Henschel-Verlag and arranged to see them. When I arrived at their offices, I was met by the editor as well as a German translator. To my astonishment, the latter presented me with a copy of the complete translation of *Inook*. The play offers a number of difficulties for any translator on account of its setting in the world of the Inuit in the Arctic and because of the lyrical nature of the text. The resulting difficulties made it desirable, as I had learnt from the French translator, to consult the author on specific issues. I had received no such queries from Berlin.
>
> The translation was as bad as I had feared—with many contextual misunderstandings and a poor grasp of rhythm and image in the poetry. But I felt sorry for the translator who had worked hard to do justice to the original. So I returned the next day and proposed to him that I rework the translation and that it be published in both our names. The revisions involved two categories of corrections:
>
> (1) The text of *Inook and the Sun* has many lyrical passages which can be properly translated only by someone who has experience in writing poetry. It requires a clear sense of the intricacies of rhythm and image. I had to recreate all of these passages entirely. The German translator kept his original, but I recall his "lyrical" passages as clumsy and lacking poetic sensibility. They would have ruined the magic and mythic world of my play.
>
> (2) There were various misunderstandings in content. Here are a couple of examples: In the preface by the translator the reader was informed that the world of *Inook* is "grönländisch." I'm afraid our Canadian Inuit would not recognise themselves as "Greenlanders."
>
> In Episode 2, Inook's father and mother address the Spirit of the Caribou as follows:

> *Großer Geist, erscheine du*
> *Komm, wir erflehen ohne Ruh—*
> *Dein Erscheinen im Iglu.*

(approximate translation: "Great Spirit, we beg you to appear in our igloo.")

Alas, the Spirit of the Caribou doesn't turn up in Inook's igloo but out in the open country where the caribou live. Anyone who has ever been inside an igloo knows that there isn't room in them for a live caribou; it wouldn't even be able to come in. Inook's Father and Mother perform a ritual dance outside the igloo to conjure up the Spirit of the Caribou. In the revised version, they say:

> *Großer Geist, erschein uns hier,*
> *Unser ganzes Verlangen gilt heut dir!*

In Episode 5, Inook's father is killed by a polar bear. Inook is desperately unhappy, but his father had consoled him previously by reminding him that their lives are subject to the irresistible force of fate. For me, this stoic attitude is captured in the Inuit language in the word "Ayorama." A non-native audience requires an explanation for this term. The German translator didn't understand this and had the father say:

> *Sei nicht traurig. Ayorama. Alles ist beschlossen.*

This glances off the fundamental point being made here. It should read:

> *Sei nicht traurig, Inook. Alles geschieht, wie es bestimmt ist. Ayorama.*

There were also misunderstandings concerning the staging of the play. For instance, at the end of Episode 6, a seal that Inook has harpooned pulls him down into an ice hole. Intermission. The second part of the play takes place under water. To give the audience a sense of this setting, the script calls for black lighting. This requires the use of ultraviolet light which makes only objects and characters that have been prepared with phosphorescent paint appear on the dark stage. The Berlin translator had turned my *black lighting* (a technical term) into *düstere Beleuchtung,* thereby casting my magical underwater world into murky darkness.

The translator also produced a very awkward translation of the title of the play. He called it *Inook holt die Sonne zurück* ("Inook brings back the sun") which he later changed to *Inook jagt die Sonne* ("Inook chases the sun"), not much of an improvement.

Beissel's statement is indicative of the fact that every Canadian play "has a distinctive voice," as Yvette Nolan writes,

> whether it comes from the north, an urban centre, the prairies, the west coast or the east. And the Canadian play is not just not American, not only not British, it is Canadian, it is in a voice that speaks to us as Canadians. ... Looking into the

future, we cast a look over a shoulder to see where we came from, how we got here. (Glaap 2003, 131)

Beissel himself prepared an entirely new translation entitled *Inook und das Geheimnis der Sonne* ("Inook and the Secret of the Sun"). As he points out, finding a suitable German title for a translated play is often a difficult task. Should the title be a literal translation? Should it summarize what the play is about? Should it arouse curiosity by being less explicit? Or should the English title be preserved because it is self-explanatory? The following examples illustrate how diversified the approaches are.

Literal translations (original titles are given in square brackets):
- Ann-Marie MacDonald, *Gute Nacht Desdemona (Guten Morgen Julia)* [*Goodnight Desdemona (Good Morning Juliet)*]
- Brad Fraser, *Unidentifizierte Leichenteile & das wahre Wesen der Liebe* [*Unidentified Human Remains and the True Nature of Love*]
- George F. Walker, *Problemkind* [*Problem Child*]

Free translations:
- Morris Panych, *Freudige Erwartung* and *Meine Tante und ich* ("Joyful Expectations" and "My Aunt and I") [*Vigil*]
- Daniel Danis, *Das Lied vom Sag-Sager* [*Le chant du Dire-Dire*]
- Michel Marc Bouchard, *Gefahrenzone* ("Danger Zone") [*Le Chemin des Passes Dangereuses*]

English titles preserved:
- Brad Fraser, *Poor Superman* [*Poor Superman*]
- David Gow, *Cherry Docs* [*Cherry Docs*]

Derivation from English title:
- George F. Walker, *Loretta* [*Featuring Loretta*]
- George F. Walker, *Risiko* ("Risk") [*Risk Everything*]
- George F. Walker, *Nur für Erwachsene* ("For Adults Only") [*Adult Entertainment*]
- Marie Laberge, *Vaterliebe* ("Fatherly Love") [*L'homme gris*]

**TRANSLATORS REFLECTING ON TRANSLATIONS**

Evidently, an essential prerequisite for the production of a Canadian play in a German theatre is an adequate translation of the source script. But how can

German translators cope with the demands of their task? How can they translate a text for the stage, do justice to its distinctive Canadian features, and, at the same time, provide a version that does not sound odd to German ears? The following statements give insights into the working methods of different translators, who were asked to report for this chapter on their specific approaches.

Andreas Jandl, translator of Carole Fréchette's play *Les quatre morts de Marie*, 1991 ("The Four Deaths of Marie"), elaborates:

> In translating the French Canadian text, I was confronted, as obvious as it sounds, with the task of re-creating in German "what the author says," making sure that in word and syntax the things that made a familiar sound to Quebec ears should also sound familiar to German ears and that what sounded striking to Quebec ears should have the same effect on German ears.
>
> Interestingly enough, one foreign language translation of the text was already available. The Canadian dramatist and translator John Murrell had translated Carole Fréchette's text into English. Murrell had entitled his translation *The Four Lives of Mary*. Instead of focusing on her four deaths, Murrell puts the accent on the fact that Marie has four lives. The question arises for the translation into German whether to follow Murrell's interpretation and use "life" instead of "death" in the title. I rejected the idea, not least because Fréchette could easily have called her play "Les quatre vies de Marie" ["The Four Lives of Marie"]. Moreover, on four occasions, the play shows us how Marie's world falls into dust and she meets her death.
>
> In her first life, Marie is a little girl. For the translation, this raises the question of how a ten-year-old child really speaks. In the dialogue with her mother, she must not appear either too adult or too childlike. What would a ten-year-old girl say to her German mother when Marie says "Je t'aime"? "Ich liebe Dich" or "Ich mag Dich" or perhaps "Ich hab' Dich lieb!" No doubt the last. But can you say it just as fluently, as Marie does, three times in a row: "Je t'aime, je t'aime, je t'aime"? Mustn't we take "Ich lieb' Dich, ich lieb' Dich, ich lieb' Dich" to catch the true momentum of the scene?
>
> In every translated text, the question arises of where the play should be set. I wanted to leave Marie in her original world; I wanted a Marie who, though she speaks German, still has her home in Montreal. For this reason, the characters in the German text have kept their French names and hence remain "Pierre" and "Marie" rather than becoming "Peter" and "Maria." With this in mind, should Marie's teacher, called "Mademoiselle Gervais" in the original, also be called "Mademoiselle" in the German text, or should she be "Fräulein" or "Frau," as primary schoolchildren would say in German today? And how should we deal with the name "Gervais"? Can a German actress really pronounce the name without any trouble? And won't a German audience automatically associate

the name Gervais with the yogurt of the same name? Do they have the brand "Gervais" for dairy products in Canada too? To the best of my knowledge, no. So wouldn't it be better if the teacher had a German name? In the end, I kept "Mademoiselle Gervais." Readers and the theatre audience should realize that they are in a French-speaking world, and even if they think of yogurt it doesn't really affect the character.

A man is walking along the Rue St. Laurent, or should it be Sankt-Lorenz-Straße? The Rue St. Laurent is one of the famous main streets in the centre of Montreal, marking a border between the French- and English-speaking parts of the city. What matters is to create the image of a large, busy street, one which underlines the man's loneliness and isolation. Which actual street it is is of no importance. To maintain the internal harmony of the play, I kept the French name, Rue St. Laurent. (letter in German to the author: kindly translated by Neil Johnstone)

Jason Sherman's *Patience* (first production in 1998) was produced at the Freie Kammerspiele in Magdeburg in spring 2005 (eleven performances). It was translated as *Demut* ("Humility") by Ute Scharfenberg. *Patience* is a furiously paced play; the action is almost filmic and poses a great challenge for any stage director. It tells the story of Reuben, a businessman and family man, who is on the brink of the greatest deal in his company's history. He meets with Paul one evening in a Chinese restaurant, and Paul tells him that he has sold his company to finally realize his dream, to gain the freedom to find his true self. Reuben is dubious, but after this meeting things start going wrong for him. The audience sees the events that have led to Reuben's emotional crisis and realizes that it cannot be solved easily. The issues of the protagonist's past are not resolved; instead, they are highlighted. Reuben deemed himself in control of his life and of other people, but he finds that they have dropped him (Glaap 2003, 86–87). Scharfenberg highlights the linguistic problems with which a translator of Sherman's play is confronted:

> All authors, all plays, create their own linguistic space. A particular feature of *Patience* is the rhythmicality of its language. The spoken sequences are given a "beat" by linguistic chops, stops, slight pauses, breaks, and an outpouring of sentences. The author often works with ellipses, that is to say, grammatically incomplete sentences, with repetitions and fillers like "um," "er," "ugh," or "hm." The ups and downs, the rises and falls, create a linguistic dynamic and give the language the feel of a musical composition. The author has also included a number of well-known music titles in his play, showing again that he is particularly interested in the musical aspect of the use of language. In a restaurant scene, the dialogues between two couples and another figure are so precisely slotted into each other that they come across as an open discussion in

which all are involved. For this reason, I tried, when translating the characters' lines, to re-create the original rhythm and to avoid adding any extra "beats."

What is interesting about *Patience* is the use of highly varied literary forms in the play. Slangy dialogues are juxtaposed with monologues containing a high degree of introspection and universality; there are snippets of such varied material as a radio sports-report, an advertising spot, lines from popular songs, a joke being told, the babble of voices in a restaurant with a few audible passages, phone calls, et cetera.

Reading the German text aloud is a good way to test it. If it doesn't fall easily into place of its own accord, there is something wrong, and it needs to be improved. Transposing a play requires research into local references (e.g., the name Svend Robinson, the Canadian Liberal [sic] politician), into quotations (e.g., one from Shakespeare's *Macbeth*), into the historical background, into special aspects of the life of the country in which the original is set (e.g., what is the significance, for a Canadian audience, of a character's moving from Toronto to Vancouver?). And the best thing about translation is of course when the translation begins to come to life on stage. (letter in German to the author; kindly translated by Neil Johnstone)

*The Shape of a Girl* (first produced in 2001), from the pen of Vancouver playwright Joan MacLeod, was staged at the Rheinisches Landestheater in Neuss in 2003. The background of this play is the 1997 murder of Reena Virk, a fourteen-year-old girl in Victoria, BC. Reena was beaten up by a group of girls and one boy, with other girls standing by and watching. When she tried to escape, one of the girls and the boy dragged her back to the waterfront under a bridge and killed her. MacLeod's play, however, is not about this particular murder. What "Braidie, the 15-year-old girl in the play, has in common with the Reena Virk story is that she is a bystander," writes MacLeod: "she is witnessing something terrible happening and eventually coming to action, but the play is about her. Part of Braidie is me from years and years ago, and part of it is made up—sort of a combination" (quoted in Glaap 2004a, 133). *The Shape of a Girl* was written primarily, but not exclusively, for young audiences. These young addressees and the language of the play are at the centre of the comment by Bernd Plöger, who directed and translated the play under the title *Gestrandet* ("Stranded"):

> It was of great importance to me that the language shouldn't talk down to a youthful audience. Of course, the message had to be got across quickly and clearly; the text had to be as concise as Joan MacLeod's original.
> 
> Obviously, place names, like "Whistler," had to be adapted to fit German conditions. Nobody here has ever heard anything about the murder of Reena Virk. On the other hand, as we found in the discussions after the performances,

the subject of mobbing is just as important here and, sad to say, an all too personal experience. The young audiences were also well acquainted with Braidie's personal situation and so could understand the way she behaved.

The title remained a problem for a long time, as a literal German translation wouldn't have worked and in any case would have been too long. All the German equivalents would have been too complicated and would have failed to convey the impact of the English title. So, making a virtue of a necessity, I chose a less interpretable phrase in the hope that in some other place the German language would provide the more appropriate word. Perhaps this was the case with the translation "Buß- und Banntag" for "penalty day." It always seemed right to me, with all due respect to the original, to go for a looser translation of the tricky passages. In any case, handling Canadian English was a great challenge. I really got "hung up" on some passages before I found the right solution. In the end, the essential thing was to preserve the precision of Joan MacLeod's use of language. (letter in German to the author; kindly translated by Neil Johnstone)

*Cherry Docs* by David Gow premiered at the Factory Theatre, Toronto, in April 1998. Given that there are still neo-Nazi groups operating in Germany today, this play is of relevance for audiences and artists alike in this country. Mike Downey is a neo-Nazi skinhead in his twenties who is accused of a racially motivated murder and is defended by Danny Dunkelmann, a liberal, court-appointed Jewish lawyer. The two reluctantly agree to work together but pay a high price for their decision. The title *Cherry Docs*—the German equivalent would be *Springerstiefel*—is preserved in the German translation by Anna Cron. "Docs" refers to the firm (Dr. Martens, pronounced Doc Martens) that produces these particular boots, and "Cherry" refers to their colour. Cron explains how her understanding of the text underlies her translation:

> In the first place, I was fascinated by the conflict in which the young court-appointed defence attorney finds himself. A skinhead, a Jew-hater, has kicked a Pakistani to death, and now it is Danny's professional duty to defend this lout. On the one hand, as a beginner in his profession, he cannot refuse the case; on the other hand, he, as a Jew, is not unbiased toward the defendant. Danny takes his duty very seriously. He tries to grasp the truth, which, for him, goes well beyond the undisputed crime itself. He tries to find the human being behind the criminal, even though he never can, never will, understand what the boy has done. He gets as close to him as he possibly can and risks everything to help the boy take responsibility for his crime and, somehow or other, bring about a change in his pattern of life—a pattern which has been imposed on him by indoctrination.

The play is divided into very simple scenes, which are always associated with Danny's life and involve his religious background. For instance, when he takes out his father's *tallith* and describes the meaning of its fringes, he talks of the history of his people, their suppression and their search for a homeland. And all at once the murdered Pakistani emerges as a martyr and a symbolic figure in this very search for a homeland.

That is what I wanted to get across. The evil Nazi and the poor Jew didn't interest me as clichés. It was rather the way they behave toward each other, and themselves, in the mental anguish of the journey of discovery they both have to make. One wins, the other loses, and in the end both have won and lost.

As I have little contact with comparably brutalized forms of the German language, I had a lot of trouble with the slang used by young Canadians, and in particular that of the neo-Nazis who, like every group, have their own specific language. All the same, despite or perhaps because of these difficulties, I got a lot of pleasure from the work, since I was drawn into the story as if it were a theatrical performance and found myself identifying now with one of the figures, now with the other—something which says a lot about the quality of the original text. (letter in German to the author; kindly translated by Neil Johnstone)

Table 8.1 shows that many German versions of Canadian plays have recently been produced in theatres in Berlin, Neuss, Magdeburg, and Düsseldorf, theatres that have been particularly instrumental in promoting Canadian drama. While most theatres put on full productions of the plays, some texts are presented as staged readings; for example, *Die fünf Lebensalter der Albertine* (*Albertine en cinq temps*; "Albertine in Five Times") by Michel Tremblay was produced at the Gorki Theater Berlin and broadcast by Deutschlandradio in May 2003, *Schafe und Wale* (*Sheeps and Whales*) by Ahmed Ghazali appeared at TiC in Mainz, and *...und viermal stirbt Marie* (*Les quatre morts de Marie*) by Carole Fréchette was produced at the Staatstheater Mainz and subsequently broadcast by several German radio stations.

**REVIEWS BY GERMAN THEATRE CRITICS**

The reception and critical reviews of contemporary Canadian plays in Germany would be a topic for a chapter of its own. One example must suffice here: *Vigil*, a play by Morris Panych, who received the Governor General's Literary Award for Drama in 2004, was first produced at the Rheinisches Landestheater in Neuss in 2003 under the title *Freudige Erwartung* ("Joyful Expectation"; see Glaap 2004b). The titles of a few reviews by German theatre critics must suffice here to give some idea of the varied responses to the subject and tone of Panych's play:

- "Wenn die Tante nicht sterben will" ("When Auntie Refuses to Die"), *Solinger Morgenpost*, 11 January 2003;
- "Ein Jahr auf der falschen Seite gelebt" ("One Year Spent Living on the Wrong Side"), *Solinger Morgenpost*, 16 January 2003;
- "Humor auf dem Rücken des Todes" ("Laughing in the Face of Death"), *Solinger Morgenpost*, 11 January 2003;
- "In 'Freudiger Erwartung' auf das Ableben der Erbtante" ("In Joyful Expectation of Rich Auntie's Death"), *Westdeutsche Zeitung*, 18 January 2003;
- "Glückloser Erbe baut Tantentötungsmaschine" ("Unlucky Heir Builds Aunt-Killing Machine"), *Neuss-Grevenbroicher Zeitung*, 26 January 2003;
- "Packende Neugeburt am Sterbebett" ("An Exciting Birth at the Deathbed"), *Westdeutsche Zeitung*, 20 January 2003;
- "Viel Futter für zwei gute Schauspieler" ("Lots of Food for Two Good Actors"), *Neuss-Grevenbroicher Zeitung*, 18 January 2003.

## IN PLACE OF A SUMMARY

Although plays from Canada have increasingly been gaining ground in German theatres over the past fifteen years, it is still too early to draw general conclusions regarding the criteria used to select Canadian plays for productions. An important question is whether the Canadian aspect or origin of those plays that have been selected was crucial in the decision. So far it seems that the issues they raise, the approaches they use, and the dramaturgical concepts they mobilize have roused the curiosity of German artistic directors. As far as the translation of Canadian plays into German is concerned, there are further questions that cannot yet be answered either. What kind of background information must the translator have about contemporary Canadian culture on the one hand, and how can he or she make the play accessible to a German audience on the other? To put it differently, how can the overall goal of (all) translation, "equivalence in difference," be achieved? The conspicuous success of the productions of works by George F. Walker or Michel Marc Bouchard in a number of German cities provides a promising prospect for the future.

## REFERENCES

Beissel, Henry. *Inook and the Sun*. Toronto: Playwrights Co-op, 1974.
———. *Inuk/Inuk*, transl. Arlette Francière. Toronto: Playwrights Canada Press, 2001.
Gilbert, Reid. "Escaping the 'Savage Slot': Interpellation and Transgression in George F. Walker's *Suburban Motel*." In *Siting the Other: Re-visions of Marginality in Australian*

*and English-Canadian Drama*, ed. Marc Maufort and Franca Bellarsi. Brussels: Peter Lang, 2001. 325–45.

Glaap, Albert-Reiner. "A Canadian Play for Young Audiences: Joan MacLeod's *The Shape of a Girl*." *Zeitschrift für Kanada-Studien* 24.2 (2004): 132–42. (2004a)

———. "The Philosophy, Chemistry and Universality of Morris Panych's Work." *Anglistik* 15.2 (2004): 71–7. (2004b)

———. *Stimmen aus Kanada: 25 kanadische Dramen für deutsche Bühnen*. Trier: WVT, 1997.

———. "Toward a Reception of Canadian Plays in German-Speaking Theatre." *Theatre Research in Canada* 22.2 (2001): 219–28.

———, ed. *Voices from Canada: Focus on Thirty Plays*. Toronto: Playwrights Canada Press, 2003.

Walker, George F. *Risk Everything*. In *Suburban Motel*, ed. George F. Walker. Vancouver: Talonbooks, 1999. 261–311.

# Translated or Traduced? Canadian Literary and Political Theory in a German Context: Northrop Frye, Michael Ignatieff, and Charles Taylor

*Georgiana Banita*
*University of Constance*

When compared to literature, theory may at first glance seem easier to transport into a different language and culture. While this may be true, to some extent, as far as the actual translation of the language is concerned, the assimilation of theory into a foreign culture poses more difficulties than one might expect. Each language contains its own theoretical idiom. Within this system, terms and ideas acquire and develop their significance around points of reference that are specific to one culture alone and can hardly be superimposed onto others. Theory supplies a culture with rationales for what it does, so its procedures are bound to differ radically from one culture to another. Discourses that mark a turning point in one culture will perhaps pass unnoticed in the context of another, if they cannot relate to indigenous discourses, or if translators fail to produce a culturally viable adaptation of the respective texts. Even if translation succeeds from both a linguistic and a cultural point of view, the initial text often undergoes a considerable transformation by absorbing the responses of the receiving culture. The way in which translations reflect back on the original texts can indeed be an enrichment, but in certain situations—or perhaps in most situations—it can also cause an adulteration or even a misinterpretation of the original intent. This is by no means reason enough to contest the transcultural applicability of theory or to dismiss the translation of theory altogether. On the contrary, translating theory facilitates deliberation on issues of general interest, particularly today, in the context of globalization and the effort to forge transnational identities. Cultural exchange goes hand in hand with a globalization of theoretical discourse, which is becoming the locus of debate in increasingly multicultural societies. In the following, I examine some of these ideas in relation to a small selection of

Canadian theoretical texts that have been translated into German, with an eye to revealing the factors at work in their cultural border crossing. Not only have these texts elicited varied responses from German readers, but also the cultural implications of these reactions testify to the works' special status as non-fiction writing, engaging in topical and sometimes controversial discussions.

**TRAVELLING THEORY**

The translation and assimilation of North American and European theory into other, mainly Eastern, cultures is a very topical issue, which is not to suggest that cultural border crossing between North America and Europe presents no problems worth investigating. Within this larger frame, theory travels according to different principles between Canada and Germany. For one thing, Canadian theory is a relatively recent phenomenon that goes back no further than the middle of the past century. It was at this time that Canada shed its formal status as a colony and that nationalist demands for self-determination appeared as a shaping cultural force. Inevitably, Canada's dependence on the United States came under satirical assault. Both literary and political theory appeared in Canada as a result of widespread alienation, out of which grew a self-searching body of theoretical works.[1] The transfer of this material into a German context has cut these texts loose from their moment of origin and only rarely managed to re-enact that moment. While the conceptual and general nature of some theoretical works, such as Marshall McLuhan's, has eased their applicability within the German cultural topography, though with some delay, literary criticism, which is tied to particular literary texts, relies on a certain background knowledge that German readers lacked until the 1960s and 1970s, when the first works of literature by Canadian authors had a real impact on the German book market. But even these books that were selected for translation catered largely to commercial needs and offered only spurious impressions of the state of Canadian literature as a whole. For this reason, important early works of criticism by Northrop Frye, Margaret Atwood, and Linda Hutcheon have never been translated into German. This may be due to the efforts of these theorists to revive precisely that streak of Canadian writing that was most "Canadian" and therefore unfamiliar to German readers.

---

1. Terry Eagleton (1990, 26) describes theory as a particularly virulent form of self-reflexiveness triggered by moments of crisis for which a great expenditure of (self-)analytical energy is needed: "Theory on a dramatic scale happens when it is both possible and necessary for it to do so—when the traditional rationales which have silently underpinned our daily practices stand in danger of being discredited, and need either to be revised or discarded." Although highly variable in its practical application, this statement seems to be very pertinent in relation to Canada in the 1960s.

Similarly, the writings of philosopher George Grant immured themselves by glorifying the very thing that Germany at that time (in the mid-twentieth century) was struggling against, namely a politics of nationalist fervour and distinction from other states (here Canada against the United States) rather than rapprochement. Although texts from various areas of Canadian theory have been translated into German, it is appropriate here to focus only on several authors and titles that have gained attention on an international level—Northrop Frye, Michael Ignatieff, and Charles Taylor—and, when relevant, to mention other translations in the same field. A discussion of Frye may seem less connected with the predominantly political thrust of the other theories that I am dealing with here, but it testifies to the fact that even the transposition of literary theory into a new environment is never completely unimpeded.

## THE "ANATOMY" OF AN UNTRANSLATABLE TITLE: NORTHROP FRYE

Canadian literary theory has always been out of step with its European counterpart. A period of self-doubt and radical revolution in European theory coincided with the formative years of Canadian critical discourse, leading to a rush among Canadian critics to simultaneously borrow and subvert, to skip evolutionary stages and find ways of reinventing CanLit despite and through imitation. The result of this fervour was a "conflicted narrative" (Lecker 1995), which on the one hand searched for Canadianness and paraphrasable, recurrent manifestations thereof (see Davey 1983) and on the other hand denounced its own practices as oblivious of literary form and the new phenomenological discourse of American and European theory. New Criticism never held sway in Canada, partly due to its view of the literary text as object rather than act, unbound to any historical context and implicitly to any cultural environment that would make a text "Canadian." Instead, thematic criticism developed as a response to the European and American zeitgeist of increasingly epistemological and self-thematizing critical discourse. Other critical schools left hardly any imprint on Canadian theory: Marxism, for instance, provided much of European theory of the 1960s and 1970s with a silent interlocutor but gained little if any attention in Canada.

The only major work of Canadian literary theory that has been translated into German is Northrop Frye's *Anatomy of Criticism,* published in English in 1957 and in German as *Analyse der Literaturkritik* in 1964—that is, seven years later. Significantly, by the time the book was available to German readers, Frye had already become the most repudiated critic on the Canadian literary scene, which was moving away from what was structuralist, archetypal, and mythic in Frye in order to subscribe to more fashionable poststructuralist and phenomenological realms of critical discourse. A more unfortunate timing for the translation can hardly be imagined. With *Anatomy of Criticism* practically the only Canadian book of literary criticism translated into German,[2] one can only deplore the extremely reductive view that it offers of Canadian literary theory on the whole and of its more recent developments stimulated by the appropriation of postmodernism. By the time Linda Hutcheon sided with Jean-François Lyotard in his incredulity toward "master narratives" such as those developed by Frye, Canada had learned to prize precisely that "disunity" (Kroetsch 1989) and fragmentation that had earlier triggered its proverbial cultural malaise.

*Anatomy of Criticism* engages in metatheory, and this already puts it at a considerable remove from a literary text. Yet it is precisely this extreme degree of abstraction that opened the door through which Frye's text could be brought out of the enclosed space of Canadian theory of the late 1950s. The prefatory statements confirm that Frye intentionally dispensed with all practical illustrations of his theses, although the book itself originated from a close reading of William Blake and Edmund Spenser's *Faerie Queene* that gradually became entangled in more theoretical structures than the author had anticipated:

> What is here offered is pure critical theory, and the omission of all specific criticism, even, in three of the four essays, of quotation, is deliberate. The present book seems to me, so far as I can judge at present, to need a complementary volume concerned with practical criticism, a sort of morphology of literary symbolism. (Frye 1957, vii)

The words *criticism* and *theory* appear several times in this short excerpt and shade into each other, pointing back to the title of the book and its plurality of meanings, none of which is reflected by its German translation, *Analyse der Literaturkritik*. Whether a case of "mystified misunderstanding" (Hillis Miller 1995, 318) or careless approximation, the naively structuralist German term *Analyse* and the inappropriate *Literaturkritik* seem to corroborate the view that theory is impossible to transfer into another context without the danger of betrayal (see Hillis Miller, 319). I address the second inaccuracy first since it relates to the *content* of the book, and then I return to the cultural *context* of the title.

"Criticism" in Frye refers primarily to New Criticism, which he himself both repudiates and renews. The German word *Literaturkritik* seems highly misleading in view of his introductory disclaimer with regard to *practical* criticism. Several decades before *Anatomy of Criticism*, I. A. Richards's *Principles of Literary Theory*

---

2. The only exception I am aware of is Adams (1988) and a second book by Frye (1966).

was published in English (1924); this work was translated into German only in 1972 under the title *Prinzipien der Literaturkritik*. What Richards purports to achieve with his book is a radical shift from outdated modes of interpretation dealing in speculative aesthetics and idealism to a positivistic view of literature anchored in a scientific perception of interpretation. Richards puts forward a theory of criticism based on behavioural science for which *Literaturwissenschaft* would have offered a much more plausible equivalent, especially since his stance touches on questions of human and social relevance of theory that the German debate around *Literaturwissenschaft* (in the larger context of the *Geisteswissenschaften*— that is, the humanities) has carried to an extreme. That both books should be available in German translation with an almost identical title is confusing insofar as one of them aspires to entrench a qualifying, scientific method of reading and criticism (Richards), while the other operates on the grounds of totalizing, abstract grids (Frye).

The term *Literaturkritik* is also suggestive of how incongruous Frye's study must have seemed on the German critical scene of the mid-1960s, which was indebted to ideas promulgated by Hans-Georg Gadamer and Walter Benjamin. They had called for a stricter focus on literature as the active organ of history, an idea that Hans Robert Jauss helped to introduce in the field of literary studies. This historical perception of literature, however, ran counter to Frye's own methodology. Frye drew largely on English literature in his argumentation but displayed a tendency to totalize and thereby identify overarching modes, archetypes, myths, and genres that structure all literary works, regardless of their historical background. Frye postulated in *Anatomy of Criticism* the four systemic "narrative categories" with the same disregard for specificities that Margaret Atwood later demonstrated in *Survival*. To Frye, literature was an "autonomous verbal structure," a sealed and inward-looking realm, which contains its own history and no other references beyond itself, very much in keeping with the "garrison mentality" that he derived from features of Canadian culture. Frye's idealism and his distaste for history went against the grain of much that German criticism had produced up to 1964, and indeed the book does not seem to have had any immediate impact in Germany. In contrast, French critics such as Paul Ricœur and the Bulgarian Julia Kristeva soon expressed their indebtedness to Frye's work (*Anatomy of Criticism* appeared in French in 1969 as *Anatomie de la critique*). His theory of archetypes and invariant themes could successfully be applied to the comparative study of literature, which, however, did not catch on as early in Germany as it did in France.[3] Only the critic Hans Blumenberg may

---

3. French critics had early shown enthusiasm for comparative studies, to the extent that they imagined them on a global scale, freed from the cultural chauvinism of colonial studies or

have found a kindred spirit in Frye, although he insists more on the conditions that inspire writers to reappropriate a particular myth and their strategies in doing so. Blumenberg brought hermeneutics to bear directly on themes in mythographic theory. His *Arbeit am Mythos* ("Work on Myth," 1979) and the work of a younger theorist, Odo Marquard, turned against the modern appraisal of progress and reason only to become intellectually unfashionable shortly after the authors published their theses and without having founded any major critical schools. Mythographic criticism seems to have taken root more easily in Canadian soil, where Frye was followed by a number of disciples, such as Margaret Atwood (*Survival: A Thematic Guide to Canadian Literature*, 1972), D. G. Jones (*Butterfly on Rock: A Study of Themes and Images in Canadian Literature*, 1970), and John Moss (*Patterns of Isolation*, 1974). Haunted by the lack of a national mythology, Canada absorbed mythic narratives more eagerly than Germany, where national mythology as a path to identity formation collided with the historically and politically grounded tendency to curb superlative national feeling.

That *Anatomy of Criticism* reached Europe so late accounts for its often being regarded as much more antistructuralist than it really is. What this delay also erases is the deep historical Canadian frame which the insistently antihistorian Frye points to. *Anatomy of Criticism* and later *The Critical Path* (1971) are emblematic of a Canadian conservatism that had been at war with the more progressive theory that flourished in Canada after the watermark years of the mid-century. By contrasting conservative myths of concern with liberal myths of freedom, Frye attempts to coin a new critical idiom, in which Canada may define its newly set goals in a tone that can easily be taken for an ersatz religious discourse. Around the same time, George Grant based a new nationalistic stance on similarly religious tones (both Frye and Grant were clergymen).

The German translation of Frye's term "criticism" in the title *Anatomy of Criticism* as *Literaturkritik* clearly dissociates his work from what it purports to be, but alternatives to this term are also fraught with risks and inaccuracies. *Literaturtheorie* would seem to capture the conceptual groundwork of the study and suggest that outermost point of critical discussion that is rendered in English by the perfect equivalent "theory."[4] Upon closer investigation, however, even this possibility is not faultless, since it may lead to the false conclusion that, in theorizing about theory, Frye is doing what Jonathan Culler or Terry Eagleton

---

Eurocentric views on works that they often discussed in terms of "parallelism" and "analogy." See Escarpit (1958) and Etiemble (1963).

4. Eagleton supplies a concise enumeration of the critical stages: "First there is the meta-theory; then the literary theory it takes as its object of inquiry; then literary criticism, which much literary theory reflects on; then literature, the object of critical investigation" (1990, 24).

have done for American criticism. More likely, the "criticism" mentioned in the title is not what Frye investigates but what he himself is doing, "anatomy" being his method. The "aboutness" of Frye's study, however, is not as radical as that which the Frankfurt School termed "critical theory" (*Kritische Theorie* with Adorno and Habermas), which seeks to do away altogether with both critical theory and the literary itself. Frye does not analyze the hidden motives and subtexts of literary works; *Anatomy of Criticism* does not attempt to define, or situate, literary theory in a social context or meditate on its general significance. Strictly speaking, *Literaturtheorie* might even be something of an anachronism: from I. A. Richards to Cleanth Brooks, literary "criticism" was the preferred term to describe what later became literary "theory," after the advent of ideological criticism and its multifarious schools. Also, one should not forget that *Literaturtheorie* is more deeply rooted in a hermeneutical practice than its English equivalent. In the case of Frye, this is significant: whereas modern hermeneutics seeks to work in interdisciplinary ways and expand the act of interpretation to signify a more general, existential mode of access to the world, Frye harbours no such intentions. Instead, he adheres to a strictly structuralist, overarching scheme beyond which he cannot go. Perhaps his work might fit under the title *Literaturwissenschaft,* but his refusal to engage in practical criticism tends to disqualify this translation. So does the complete lack of methodology and the rough-hewn, assertive rather than probing style of his arguments. In fact, what the German term designates in its scientific and systematic connotations had not yet come into being in Canada at the time of the book's publication. Only in the 1970s was Canadian literature first institutionalized within the academic community, and only then were critics encouraged to break with the authoritative discipline of English to revitalize a pre-eminently Canadian critical discourse. *Literaturwissenschaft* is, in fact, a more recent terminological acquisition in the German critical idiom, which still presents English translators with a quandary when faced with texts such as those of Hans Robert Jauss and Wolfgang Iser. The problem is generally avoided by use of the rough approximation "literary theory" (see, e.g., Jauss 1974).

Despite the expectations that a German designation such as *Literaturtheorie* might awaken, Frye's *Anatomy of Criticism* is more accessible than other studies of the same calibre. While his is an abstract approach, it nevertheless proved to be the perfect method for reconstructing the course of Canadian literature in a series of symbols and themes making up a "conscious mythology" (Frye 1971) and was thus favourably received by the Canadian critical community. From the beginning, criticism of English Canadian literature perceived itself as an absent presence and castigated its own ineptitude in tones that are best described by the paper "Why Michel Foucault Does Not Like Canadian Literature," presented at a conference on poststructuralism in Canada as late as 1984 (see Godard 1987, 26). In Canada, literary theory never encountered the same resistance that was found in departments of literary studies in Europe or, for that matter, the United States. The "rise of Canadian," which literary theory went a long way toward promoting, took precedence over the obfuscating "hermeneutics of suspicion" (Krieger 1988, 15) that non-Canadian critics intuited and deplored in the early days of metatheory and metacriticism.

Perhaps the least perilous translation for Frye's ambiguous "criticism" would be the even more ambiguous *Literaturtheorie*, for the simple reason that "theory" and "criticism" are so resistant to definition and malleable to interpretations that an expansion in meaning rather than a limitation would be advisable. As Paul de Man put it, "the main theoretical interest of literary theory consists in the impossibility of its definition" (1986, 3). It is precisely this referential affluence and the haziness of the term "criticism" that the translation of "anatomy" as *Analyse* completely extirpates.

Above all, the link between the title word *anatomy* and the book itself has been lost in the process. One of Frye's four fiction forms along with the novel, the confession, and the romance is the anatomy, a highly digressive and exhaustive form of the Mennipean satire, which Robert Burton's *Anatomy of Melancholy* (1621) serves to illustrate. This form of satire deals with mental attitudes and ideas rather than people and results in such hybrid forms as Huxley's novel of ideas and Sterne's meandering narrative *Tristram Shandy*. Burton's concept of "anatomy" informs Frye's own and reveals by contrast some features of *Anatomy of Criticism* that might otherwise pass unnoticed. While in Burton's text several disciplines intersect to provide a full description of and even cures for melancholy, Frye conducts a similar analysis of symbols and themes, completely ignoring the connections between them. For this reason, his study both is and is not an "anatomy" proper. A later usage by John Milton confirms that "anatomy" is meant to explore the details by particularizing the general ("an Anatomie of the shiest, and tenderest particular truths," 1641), which Frye's generalizing technique practically turns on its head. The critic's own justification for his use of the word sheds some light on his intentions: "The word 'anatomy' in Burton's title means a dissection or analysis, and expresses very accurately the intellectualized approach of this form. We may as well adopt it as a convenient name to replace the cumbersome and in modern times rather misleading 'Menippean satire'" (Frye 1957, 311–312).

In this sense, Frye's own book is a highly conceptual study not of literary texts per se but of the web of connections that ties them together in identifiable patterns and types. The mere concept of dissecting criticism for the purpose of examining its parts (i.e., the links on which its judgments are formed) harks back to the breakthroughs in medicine achieved during Burton's time and points once more to Frye's intention of grounding a systematic, scientific method for the inspection of what has hitherto passed as mysterious, unclassifiable, and immaterial. The Canadian critic indicates that he has a lively awareness of the literal meaning behind the word *anatomy* in its psychopathological connotations as they are expressed in Burton's subtitle ("Philosophically, Medicinally, Historically Opened and Cut Up"). Just as Burton had tried to debunk the attractiveness of a malady associated with genius, so too does Frye target the mannerisms and pretensions of a literary criticism that is restricted to idle value judgment and subjective gossip. Needless to say, *Analyse*, besides being an extremely vague term, reflects Frye's intention only slightly, bringing to mind instead the inflationary use of "anatomy" to describe just about any kind of analysis, from the recently published *Anatomy of Fascism* to the unlikely *Anatomy of the Auschwitz Death Camp*. Strictly speaking, "anatomy" as a trope was already used by Aristotle for logical dissection or analysis, so the German translation is not erroneous as such but ignorant of the title's cultural biography. Significantly, Burton's *Anatomy* was translated into German as *Anatomie der Melancholie*, though not until 1988, too late to have served as a precedent.

As de Man convincingly argues in his discussion of the English translation of Benjamin's "The Task of the Translator" (1986, 73–105), theory relies on complex conceptual words that carry with them a silent history, whose reinterpretation through translation can either illuminate or obfuscate the original text. In the case of Frye's *Anatomy of Criticism*, the German translation prefers to simplify and distort, making the self-irony of the title a mere dry, formalist phrase that the actual reading of the book disproves. This failure of translation is indeed regrettable though, from a hermeneutical perspective, not so surprising. The translation of theory that deals with literary criticism that in turn analyzes literary texts is an act of interpretation in the third degree; in other words, "translations of theory are mistranslations of mistranslations, not mistranslations of some authoritative and perspicuous original" (Hillis Miller 1995, 336–37). This formulation by Hillis Miller can be invoked to excuse some of the inaccuracies discussed above without, however, answering the question of how "fragments of fragments" can be assembled into a translation that might be both "faithful" to the source context[5] and understandable for a new readership.

---

5. The issue of "faithfulness" in translation is currently a major theoretical debate in the discipline of Translation Studies.

## POLITICAL THEORY BEYOND BORDERS: MICHAEL IGNATIEFF

Some topics in theory have reached a high, almost fetishistic, degree of popularity, but Frye's work has not had this resonance, and despite international offers the Canadian professor remained faithful to the University of Toronto. The systematic, inhabitable structure of literary criticism that Frye promised was indeed influential but did not become internationally popular (certainly not in Germany), not only because it went against the zeitgeist but also because his attempt to make the world of criticism more manageable and hospitable draws on the specifically Canadian challenge of mapping and articulating space, where reading is as much a categorizing act as it is the geographical and linguistic colonization of the Canadian landscape.

Canadian political discourse, however, has reached beyond the boundaries of the nation and contributed to the idiom and tendencies that have marked political theory for the past decades. The output of Canadian theory on such diverse topics as multiculturalism (Charles Taylor, Will Kymlicka) and human rights, nationalism, and war (Michael Ignatieff) has heavily influenced the international political discourse. John Ralston Saul (1997, 2000) and Naomi Klein (2001, 2003) have dealt with the economic effects of globalization. My purpose in the following is twofold. First, I examine the Canadianness of political theory in the works of Ignatieff and then review how these works have fared in German political discussions at the time of their publication. The reception of his books seems to have gone through radical swings—from unreserved admiration to cool reticence, with critics demurring at his unmistakably pro-American, at times imperialist, sympathies on the one hand and extolling the merits of his more nuanced, sensitive arguments on human rights issues on the other. Ignatieff's ideas, I argue, have gradually developed toward a minimalist set of beliefs that run against the grain of what the German intelligentsia accepts as valid. Too often Ignatieff, a second-generation Russian Canadian, brings everything down to a very small common denominator or foists values and concepts informed by Western thought upon radically different cultures, thereby making unreasonable demands for universalism and uniformity.[6]

---

6. The danger inherent in his theories is that they risk becoming not a reduction of their original intent but an unwelcome expansion and projection into infinity of what, to all intents and purposes, reflects a concrete historical situation. The reception of Giorgio Agamben's works, particularly in Germany, reveals how theories can be reified into "theoretical overstatements" of a situation that they set out to remedy and end up reducing to the scale of parody. Ignatieff's ideas sometimes verge dangerously on what might be called "formula theory," reducing the issues at hand to a smallest common denominator and proposing programmatic and unilateral solutions. Ignatieff often creates new vocabularies of thought at the risk of great simplification. Consider, for example, his terms "human agency" and "lesser evil."

Ignatieff's works (novels and non-fiction prose) have gained wide international acclaim. When Ignatieff published his first novel, *Asja*, in 1991, he had been working for BBC's Channel 4 and had established himself as a scholar through his work on the English penal system and the Scottish Enlightenment. His works of fiction and his memoir *The Russian Album* contain self-scrutinizing statements on Canadianness and the history of his Russian forefathers, statements that connect with the larger theme of memory and national belonging. Both *Asja* and *Scar Tissue* (1993) were surprisingly successful in Germany, with parts of the latter published by the renowned German national newspaper *Frankfurter Allgemeine Zeitung* (*FAZ*) before the book itself appeared. Other authors, such as the Canadian Janice Kulyk Keefer and the American academic Svetlana Boym (also a Russian expatriate and the author of a celebrated book on nostalgia and the immigrant experience and of a recent novel [see Boym 2003]), have touched on similar themes. However, in contrast to Ignatieff's novels, only one book by Kulyk Keefer and none by Boym have been translated into German. This discrepancy can be explained through the reputation that Ignatieff has built for himself as a historian and media foreman both in England and in the United States, where he headed the Carr Centre for Human Rights Policy at Harvard University until 2005, when he returned to Canada to teach at the University of Toronto and became a Member of Parliament. Ignatieff's books have been translated into several languages. All of his works are available in German, and Ignatieff regularly contributes articles to German newspapers and essay collections (see, e.g., Ignatieff 2001a). His opinions, particularly on the state of international security, are in high demand.

Ignatieff's non-fiction books consist of personal though self-effacing essays in intellectual reportage. Whether Ignatieff carries on conversations with people, recounts childhood memories, or inconspicuously inserts commentaries between the lines, he avoids the arcane terminology and convoluted prose of academia and theory. *Blood and Belonging: Journeys into the New Nationalism* (1993) is the most journalistic of his works to date, partly because it was written in connection with a television series for the BBC. Nationalism seems to be a murky term all through the book, connected with violence but not clearly separated from a healthy national consciousness. In the larger context of his work, nationalism as "the willing suspension of disbelief" (Ignatieff 1998, 38) denotes only that inflated patriotism that aggravates difference into narcissism. The only distinction that Ignatieff makes here is between "ethnic" and "civic" nationalism, the first purportedly German in origin and blameworthy, the second illustrative of his own condition as a cosmopolitan world citizen lacking a national state to which he might feel tied.[7] As a member of the federal Liberal Party, he gives bilingual public speeches that discredit the idea of a "balkanized" Canada, his solution being a revival of federalism and national institutions in place of separatist utopias. Quebec separatism, Ignatieff argues, invites comparison with Isaiah Berlin's view of nationalism as a "bent twig, which, if held down, will snap back with redoubled force once released" (Ignatieff 1998, 115). None of the case studies in the book substantiates this metaphor more convincingly than the discussion of Germany. Far from being melancholic, as in his ruminations on Quebec, Ignatieff ruthlessly lays bare the mystique of "contained" (in the sense of "exclusive") German identities, referring first to the aftermath of the fall of the Berlin Wall and concluding with suggestions for a more democratic reorientation of the new Germany, freed from its myths and utopias. He sketches portraits of people from different parts of Germany, different walks of life and social classes, and allows these people to speak their minds even when their unsettling statements testify to resurgent nationalism, insecurity, or uneasy hypocrisy.

Unease is also what the German reviewer for the *FAZ*, Richard Wagner, displayed in his unfavourable discussion of the book, which appeared in German translation in 1994, one year after the original publication.[8] The journalistic aspect of *Blood and Belonging* with its demand for the negative and the spectacular left a bad impression on the German reader, who must also have reacted to the spectacularly negative portrayal of his own country. In the review, Ignatieff is dismissed as a fanciful jetsetter, with scant understanding of cultural identity formation, who expects people to jettison all national feeling in favour of a world consciousness that only a member of the cosmopolitan elite like Ignatieff himself could in fact afford. The postnational, culturally promiscuous society that Ignatieff describes seems unrealistic and flat to the German reviewer since it neither creates a tension between globalism and provincialism nor describes the energies that this tension might release. Ironically, Ignatieff does point out what forms these "energies" might take: attacks on asylum hostels, torching of Turkish homes, occasional violence among skinhead groups. While he decidedly condemns ethnic nationalism, he does not propose the Europeanization of Germany but calls for a less radical shift to civic nationalism, a shift that would not do away with national feeling altogether but rechannel it toward an identity

---

7. Some passing but revealing remarks in the chapter on Quebec testify to the contrary: "I am as much a child of a federalist Canada as Salman Rushdie is a child of the India created at midnight, 1947" (110); "If federalism can't work in *my* Canada, it probably can't work anywhere" (111; emphasis added).
8. See Richard Wagner, "Schlagfertig, aber atemlos: Michael Ignatieffs Nationalismuskritik," *FAZ*, 14 December 1994, 10.

based on a shared allegiance to the values of democracy. In the eyes of the German reviewer, this is no solution to the quandary of national identity but the sign of a "witty helplessness." Clearly displeased with the suggestion that there would be plenty of room for improvement in what Ignatieff terms "the fragile German democracy" (1993, 61), Wagner asks, "How is that to work? Perhaps by subjecting people to a 'democracy test'? Doesn't Germany already have a democratic constitution?" (my translation). In fact, in 1993, when the English book was published, German citizenship was still being granted on ethnic grounds, and Germany was the only nation (except Israel and its policy toward Jews) that welcomed ethnic Germans to return home, even when their cultural integration posed more problems than that of foreigners who were already integrated citizens in all but name. Wagner's quip on the democracy test is somewhat alarming since it rules out the ability of a nation to create a common, even if "imagined" rather than "tested," identity. Indeed, the concept of a democratic yardstick runs counter to all principles of democracy, which understands itself as a self-regulating system, not as one that brings its adherents into line. Incidentally, Ignatieff's definition of postnational democracy harks back to Habermas's vision of a new, non-alienating form of patriotism as the common factor in adhesion to universal constitutional principles.[9] This is another of the many paradoxes of theory: one idea will pass muster (in this case, the one put forward by Habermas), while a similar suggestion—though written in a more essayistic, critical, and free-spirited formulation—is questioned. Ignatieff levels mild but unsparing criticism at the Frankfurters gathered around placards saying "We Are All Turks" who pay lip service to global, democratic values but betray the falsity of their "moral narcissism" (69) in chauvinistic confessions to the author. Only rarely is the criticism so explicit. At other times, even the terminology that replaces ethnic nationalism with "ethnic essentialism" (73) is criticism enough. Still, in his angry reply, the German reviewer becomes his own worst enemy: while he senses the undertone of resentful accusation, he fends it off by reinforcing the very skepticism toward a democratic, postnational state that

---

9. In his essay "Geschichtsbewusstsein und posttraditionale Identität" ("Historical Conscience and the Postnational Identity") in *Eine Art Schadensabwicklung* (*A Compensation of Sorts*), Habermas speaks of a "constitutional patriotism that only appears after culture and state policy have come further apart than they could within the former national state." It is an abstract form of patriotism, "no longer related to the whole of a concrete nation but based on abstract processes and principles." These principles apply to the "circumstances of coexistence and communication between different, equal members of a community—both in internal and in external relations." Just like Ignatieff, Habermas sees the pendulum swing from nationalism to "the abstract idea of universalizing democracy and human rights, the hard shield that breaks the spears of the national legacy—the language, literature, and history of one's nation" (1987, 173–174).

Ignatieff deplores. In my view, rather than presenting "a coercive organization of shocking close-ups," as this review suggests, *Blood and Belonging* offers that rare insight at "worm's eye level" (Ignatieff 1998, 36) that eschews and successfully debunks theoretical templates in dealing with age-old problems that need new solutions.

One possible reason for the stand-off between the views discussed above may be located in Ignatieff's omission of memory as an important aspect in the discussion of identity formation. His view that nationalism creates a new identity from scratch instead of rescuing an already existing one prevents Ignatieff from acknowledging the transformations that an identity undergoes in time and its connection to the writing of history, with all the conjectural subjectivity and political interest that go with it. Ignatieff's perceptive and involved reports from the field make it possible to grasp Germany's reluctance to assume a location-based national identity if this means giving up the ethnic sense of identity that characterized Germany in the past. However, in the absence of a more thoughtful analysis of a nation's memory, this is rather mystifying. German academia's long-standing interest in the methodology of history and the strategies of collective memory has always lent a unique sharpness to any informed discussion of where Germany is heading and, especially, of where it has come from. Unlike other foreign journalists who have written on Germany in the past decade, such as the American Jane Kramer (1996) for *The New Yorker*, Ignatieff does not seem to be familiar with the academic debates about the meaning of "history" and "historiography" in Germany.

Some of these lacunae—unusual for a historian—disappear in *The Warrior's Honour: Ethnic War and the Modern Conscience* (1998). Here Ignatieff sees history, with James Joyce, as a nightmare from which one tries to awaken. This awakening or recognition takes place only when knowledge of the past has passed through the filter of truth and forgetfulness is not a subterfuge but the natural result of the conscious decision to turn the page. Often the argument circles around Germany and the difference between apportioning individual guilt for the crimes of the past, on the one hand, and collective remorse and atonement, on the other. In this "nightmarish" history, grand narratives have been replaced by two shorter stories, one of globalization, the other of growing anarchy in territories torn by ethnic tensions, famine, and conflict. Ignatieff offers two sets of values that have recently fallen into disgrace as mediators between these apparently unbridgeable dimensions: the doctrine of human rights and a murky, somewhat idealistic, concept of international pity or what Ignatieff calls "the moral imagination." Through television, international disasters have moved into everyone's backyard and have provided Western states with an ideal outlet for human tolerance that they rarely observe at home. Neutral organizations such as the International Red Cross have helped to resuscitate a sense of morality in warfare that had disappeared with the advent of "collateral damage." Considering all these arguments in the book, the German title *Zivilisierung des Krieges* is particularly well chosen: according to Ignatieff, warfare is undergoing a process of emancipation by opening itself to the technology of the media; it is also becoming more refined by adopting the codes of honour once followed by warriors and now revived in human rights doctrines. And, though Ignatieff does not deal with this third item, warfare is turning into a more cultured practice, one that has renounced the older imperial motives in the pursuit of power and is now guided by highly selective rationales for intervention that are more debatable than ever.

Every chapter in this book displays a set of strong moral views and good intentions, which its German reviewers also observed and applauded. Unlike the local (German) political pundits, Ignatieff "does not offend with self-important opinions,"[10] daring instead to stand the Hobbesian morals of the day on their head. What one German reader commends is his clear-headed diagnosis and propensity to relativize all opinions through the accurate rendering of facts, often from the trenches. Ignatieff's arguments are refreshingly non-ideological, in keeping with his doctrine of human rights.

In *Human Rights as Politics and Idolatry*, Ignatieff (2001b) offers an elegant, reasoned account of human rights issues that is as personal as it is universal. Standing apart from controversies that rage over what the right foundation for human rights is, Ignatieff forgoes all traditional notions (dignity, sacredness) and, in the name of moral pluralism, pleads for a pragmatic, non-ideological legitimization of human rights. Instead of a "thick," religiously determined application and interpretation of human rights, he suggests a "thin," self-consciously minimalist doctrine that would have a claim to universalism despite its overt roots in Western values derived from the Enlightenment. The individualist nature of these values implies that personal rights would prevail over collective rights: individualities would be protected irrespective of (and in some cases despite) the acknowledgement of and membership in a larger group. Ignatieff is rather unsympathetic to groups such as the nation-state and only a lukewarm supporter of civil rights associated with location. He himself lacks an authentic group identity that would require its own set of collective rights yet he might be expected to resist his inclination to consider only cosmopolitans like himself and engage with some sympathy with the claims of groups with whom he shares little. By proclaiming all ideology obsolete and obstructive in the

---

10. Katharina Rutschky, "Kritik der zynischen Moral: Michael Ignatieff über 'die Zivilisierung des Krieges,'" *Frankfurter Rundschau*, 8 June 2000, 22–23.

defence of human rights, Ignatieff reveals that his insight is also his blindness: the protection of "human agency," which he defines as the only grounds for human rights, and even his appeal for deliberation on the basis of this bare minimum are more firmly rooted in his Western background than the universal claim of his argument would permit, just as his preference for individual rather than collective rights is the product of a nation with a comparatively short but consistent tradition of individual civil rights. This occurs at the expense of group identity formation, and of a still unresolved conflict over the separation of Quebec, to which Ignatieff predictably offers a devolutionist rather than secessionist solution.

One German reviewer does not, however, shy away from labelling Ignatieff's sympathies as old liberal, meaning thereby a certain leftist leaning.[11] The review from the Swiss newspaper *Neue Zürcher Zeitung* (NZZ) is perhaps the most surprising since it radically questions Ignatieff's reliance on the idea of a "moral imagination" that would allow empathy with victims of conflict and channel in a Golden Rule approach to warfare or to its prevention.[12] Whereas the Swiss reviewer (grudgingly) accepts that ethics may indeed pave the way for humanitarian armed intervention in endangered zones, he maintains that it would also temper the impartiality and roughness that might make the intervention successful. "In the light of reason, Ignatieff's reflections deal with a fiction"— namely, the reviewer argues, the illusion that after the Cold War a dawning era of humanitarian globalism (in the form of volunteer organizations/NGOs) has set in. His skepticism in regard to the ethics of humanitarian aid makes one wonder about his views on the work of the (Swiss-based) International Red Cross. The experience gained from this volunteer work, he laments, connected as it often is with an unwilling, painful partnership in crime, has shattered all illusions about a warless world. The volunteers may hope for a more civilized form of war but cannot expect what Ignatieff praises as a new "war ethic," which is to a large extent the self-serving fiction of "West Point and Sandhurst graduates." According to the *NZZ* reviewer, the upshot of this blindness is the illusion that "nothing is what it may not be"—in other words, a gross overestimation of morals in the politics of war. Despite its less humane purposes and practices, realpolitik poses fewer risks than a supposedly moral approach to warfare. The review ends on this disheartening note.

Ignatieff's latest book on the "morality" of the war against terrorism and the ethics of the "lesser evil" proves exactly how appropriate this reader's skeptical

---

11. See Hans-Peter Kunisch, "Herz in der Dunkelheit: Michael Ignatieff orientiert sich zwischen Zivilisierung und Krieg," *Süddeutsche Zeitung*, 1 July 2000, ROM6.
12. Wolfgang Sofsky, "Moralischer Internationalismus: Michael Ignatieff über die Zivilisierung des Krieges," *Neue Zürcher Zeitung*, 8 June 2000, 65.

diagnosis was. Up to his latest book, Ignatieff had not overtly taken political sides. More often than not, he had argued for "Europe and Canada" against the United States, but with *The Lesser Evil* (2004) he does take some political risks. The book has been widely read in Germany since the publication of the German translation in 2005, partly due to its topicality and applicability to academic debates and seminars on issues of international security and terrorism. Ignatieff attempts to chart a middle course between a moral reading of democratic, constitutional provision and a pragmatic reading thereof, the latter allowing for the suspension of democratic rights for the purpose of their reinforcement and protection. In doing this, he unavoidably rides roughshod over his own previous definition of human rights as the trump: that is, the one law with the highest value that would rule out all others, even in cases of immediate threat. Ignatieff's more recent view is based on a clear distinction between the theoretical and the practical use of principle. While bent on separating the legitimate from the barbarous uses of violence, Ignatieff seems to have resigned himself to the idea that such rules are honoured as much in the breach as in the observance. He takes the position that "exceptions do not destroy the rule, but save it, provided that they are temporary, publicly justified and deployed only as a last resort" (2004, ix). After declaring Islamic terrorism the greatest evil of our days, Ignatieff proceeds to develop his theory of the "lesser evil"—ranging from the temporary suspension of human rights to pre-emptive war—which would gain legitimacy in cases of emergency once it has been given court approval. His is not a Manichean, friend-foe philosophy: he is careful to preface this decision with a series of deliberations in search of a middle way. However, he does not question so much the justification of the "lesser evil" as the ability to keep it under the control of free institutions. In other words, he plainly admits that moral rules may, under certain circumstances, be overridden.

The fact that this argument was used in early-twentieth-century German jurisprudence might cause German readers to shrink from following its logic. Some will be familiar with Carl Schmitt's (and later Walter Benjamin's) apocalyptic skepticism regarding the rule of law in the modern liberal state. Its foundation, they maintain, is very thin and threatens to crack at any moment. Both define the "state of exception," by now a common term in German theoretical discussions, as a ground zero of legislation, a point where the law is suspended (either by a sovereign or by a return to a natural, lawless state) and anarchy takes its place. It is not necessary here to dwell on the variations of this concept in German theory or, for that matter, literature; suffice it to say that these ideas meet with doubt and are discussed with much precaution. Ignatieff briefly touches on Schmitt's theories (2004, 41–42), which defend a view of law not as autonomous but as steered by political power and end up as a project to justify extraconstitutional dictatorship. In trying to winnow out the valuable grains of Schmitt's thought, Ignatieff makes only tentative suggestions whose plausibility is not enhanced by the knowledge that they grow out of an apology for Hitler by Schmitt.

Despite the fact that torture has been legally forbidden since 1948 as part of what Ignatieff welcomes as the "human rights revolution," many cases remain where civilized states break this fragile consensus. Not only the aftermath of 9/11 but also the mere threat of torture by German investigating authorities (as in the case of a Frankfurt kidnapping in 2002) can unleash debates on how far human rights can be disregarded so as to ensure their protection. What German analysts tend to worry about, as Ignatieff himself does, is how this apparently slight, painstakingly teased-out modification will further loosen the prohibition of violence and eventually lead, in keeping with the "slippery slope" effect, to terminal damage in the defence of human rights. Once a single set of rules has been suspended, the exceptional situation sets in, bringing with it a complete slackening of regulations—in other words, the beginning of the end. The categorical answer in the German debate is that using the methods of the aggressors instantly erases the fundamental difference between terrorists and their targets. In May 2004, a televised, apparently off-the-cuff statement by the historian Michael Wolffsohn, to the effect that torture is justified in dealing with suspected terrorists, brought a flurry of complaints and accusations from all political quarters.[13]

Ignatieff does not distinguish between his own theoretical stance on "legal" violence and the actual acts of torture in American prisons. The directness of his statements in favour of the "just war" as a form of pre-emption follows the tone set by North American discourse on "the candour and accountability" of all democratic regimes. *The Lesser Evil* is not a scholarly treatise on condoning violence but a step forward from earlier, casual debates on the "merits" of legitimate violence. Ignatieff has opened a serious deliberation on "just wars" waged in democratic self-defence. The dilemmas that he presents, however, have

---

13. See Severin Weiland, "Bundeswehrprofessor räsoniert über Vorzüge der Folter," *Spiegel Online*, 11 May 2004. Wolffsohn's statement was further complicated by an unfavourable context. First, it was around the same time that the shocking photographs from Abu Ghraib were made public, where American soldiers were shown torturing Iraqi prisoners. Although Wolffsohn markedly rejected torture on prisoners of war, he touched a raw nerve where such distinctions (among prisoners of war, terrorists, suspected terrorists, etc.) do not moderate the gravity of a statement. Second, since he is a professor at the Army Academy in Munich, the acceptability of his opinions becomes a more serious matter. A partial retraction followed, and Wolffsohn insisted that his purely theoretical view is not to be confused with an endorsement of the atrocities committed in Guantanamo and Iraq.

not reached the same degree of urgency in Germany, where questions on the legitimacy of torture are still theoretical puzzles.[14]

Let me now draw some conclusions from the arguments made by Ignatieff and his German supporters and detractors, keeping in mind that he needs to be read for the expertise that flows from his international background. The extrapolation of responses to his work from German reviewers and readers shows how narcissistic the transfer of theory between cultures can be. Although Ignatieff's books are often discussed in a biographical vacuum (except for his being Canadian born and having a peripatetic North American and European career, nothing else is mentioned), some attempt is almost always made to use the foreign theories at hand to illuminate the self-awareness of the receiving culture. Sometimes this is done overtly, while in other cases one sees this in the interpretation of the book and the criticisms levelled at it, as I have shown in the contrast between the German and the Swiss perspectives on *The Warrior's Honour*. We should also note that often the interacting cultures are not so much Canadian and German as they are two different theoretical schools. Unlike literature, theory is more frequently grouped in schools than according to national borders and written first and foremost within a theoretical tradition. Consequently, the reception of Ignatieff's books is less concerned with his Canadian background. Indeed, his own flexible identity clearly plays a role in giving the lie to myths about belonging, which is what Ignatieff does in one form or another in all of his books. Moreover, in trying to understand the separatist claims of ethnic groups, he plays out the Canadian drama of Quebec's struggle for separation that is all the more inexplicable for the lack of a history of conflict—which he understands as "real and recurrent killing" (1998, 101)—between the English and the French populations of Canada. Still, unlike French theorists, for instance, Ignatieff does not argue in a national critical tradition. It is true that he often refers to his compatriots Will Kymlika and Charles Taylor, but like them he aligns his views with a more international discussion. Under the influence of their Oxford years, both Ignatieff and Taylor write in the liberal tradition of Isaiah Berlin, the British thinker of Russian descent, who is also the subject of a biography by Ignatieff published in 1998 (*Isaiah Berlin: A Life*).[15] This is also the reason why earlier Canadian thinkers, who,

---

14. See Lorenz Jäger, "Folter: Schlägerschatten," *FAZ*, 18 June 2004, 35.
15. The book was very well received in Germany and praised by, among others, the German political theorist Axel Honneth, "Fast ein Bildungsroman: Michael Ignatieff erzählt die intellektuelle Biographie Isaiah Berlins," *Frankfurter Rundschau*, 22 March 2000, 13. This is not the place to investigate the exact overlap between the ideas of these three theorists—Berlin, Taylor, and Ignatieff—but I suspect that Ignatieff's use of a political idiom partly inherited from Berlin (e.g., the concepts of negative and positive freedom in his definition of human rights) accounts for the appeal and familiarity of his arguments to German readers.

though robust in their critical standpoint, have not reached German audiences (such as George Grant and Harold Innis), do not profit from the circulation of Ignatieff's works. While some French theorists have acquired a readership in Germany precisely because they are paid homage to in the works of others and not through translations (e.g., Alain Badiou or Jean-Luc Nancy), Canadian political theory seems to have begun only decades ago and to have produced a highly international school interested in globalization issues and a more humane rapport among peoples in a secular world. George Grant, it must nevertheless be said, was a stark defender of nationalism, while Quebec political thinkers and activists such as André Laurendeau and Henri Bourassa also defended what they called "The Canadian Republic" against the traditional British enemy, from which they, as nationalist activists from Quebec, could disentangle more easily than English Canadians.

In 2003, Ignatieff was the first North American recipient of the prestigious Hannah Arendt Prize for Political Thought (sponsored by the Bremen Senate and the Heinrich-Böll Foundation), among other things in recognition of his efforts toward a revival of transatlantic discourse. As Thomas Schmid pointed out in his laudatory speech, his is a liberal internationalist stance that few German political theorists share or can afford to display in the face of accusations that stigmatize their views as neo-imperialist. Ignatieff's trademark genre of "intellectual reportage" offers a lively alternative both to the journalistic reportage and to the overtheorizing analysis that German political authors prefer, which seems to warrant a celebration of his method as refreshingly modest and anti-authoritarian, allowing its judgments to be "colloquial and provisional" and ridding them of ossified grids and jargons.[16] One of the ironies of "travelling theory" is, of course, that Ignatieff is a pupil and biographer of Isaiah Berlin, who was anything but an admirer of Hannah Arendt's work.

In addition to public respect, his theoretical texts have earned Ignatieff increasing popularity with German academia.[17] Moreover, *The Russian Album* has recently been included in comparative literature curricula.[18] On occasion,

---

16. See the laudatory speech by Thomas Schmid in *Festschrift zur Verleihung des Hannah-Arendt-Preises für politisches Denken 2003 an Michael Ignatieff*, www.hannah-arendt.de/cgi-bin/festschriften.pl [consulted 26 February 2007].
17. Even a few seminar titles suffice to show the variety of topics that invite discussions of Ignatieff's theoretical works: "Isaiah Berlin between Philosophy and the History of Ideas" (Marburg), "Terrorism" (Constance), "The History, Idea, and Significance of Human Rights" (Berlin), "Michael Ignatieff—an American [sic] Political Thinker" (Oldenburg), "Introduction to Theories of Citizenship" (Potsdam), and "Atonement: The World Is Coming to Terms with Its Past" (Hannover).
18. Paderborn University, seminar on "New Fiction Forms between Album and Auto-biography."

Ignatieff is still listed as American or "one of the few notable intellectuals in contemporary Britain,"[19] and it would be a fair question to ask what nationality Ignatieff himself subscribes to as an intellectual commuter among four different cultures and a staunch supporter of global citizenship. Theory has to be grasped in the place and time out of which it emerges as a part of that chronotope, working in and for it. At first sight, the internationalism of Ignatieff's work might make it difficult to locate the origins of his standpoint, but his ideas are deeply rooted in Western principles and are often informed by the author's Canadian background. In 2002, when the book *Passages: Welcome Home to Canada* published testimonies by Canadians on the immigrant experience in this country, Ignatieff supplied an introduction in which he once more stressed the significance of becoming (in a civic sense) as opposed to belonging (in an ethnic sense). Two decades earlier Edward Said (1983) had argued along the same lines: a beginning is superior to an origin in that a beginning can be chosen, while the origin can only be acknowledged. It is on this continuous dialectic fluctuation between personal past and communal present, between recognition of private conviction and common morality, that the appeal of Ignatieff's work rests, even for the most distrustful of his critics.

## THE CHALLENGE OF MULTICULTURALISM: CHARLES TAYLOR

The issue of multiculturalism is a major source of political debates on both sides of the Atlantic, and indeed it is hard to find a democratic society today that is not the site of some significant controversy over how individuals and communities should interact so as to better recognize diverse cultural identities. Another Canadian theorist who has tried to offer solutions to this challenge is Charles Taylor. To discuss the impact of his work in Germany, different parameters are needed than the ones that I have employed in my examination of Ignatieff. In fact, in the border-crossing trajectory of Taylor's work, one can discern the four stages that are common to the way that theory travels and that Said identified in his essay "Travelling Theory": the initial context that produces the ideas; the passage through the pressure of further contexts as the ideas develop and take full shape; the conditions of acceptance (or resistance) that confront the transplanted theory; and, finally, the transformed ideas that are accommodated to their new position and seen in a new light (see Said 1983). A full account of how these stages apply to the assimilation of Taylor's work in German translation (almost

---

19. Rüdiger Görner, "Ich bin ein intellektuelles Taxi. Das Leben der Ideen: Michael Ignatieff hat eine Biographie des britischen Gelehrten Isaiah Berlin geschrieben," *Süddeutsche Zeitung*, 22 March 2000, 10.

all of his books have been translated) would be an enormous task. I therefore focus only on a limited aspect: the transfer of Taylor's theses on multiculturalism and the politics of recognition onto German ground.

What I see as the initial context for Taylor's theories is his concept of the formation of the self and of individual identity, which Taylor traces back to the early history of individualism and to the work of Hegel and Herder. I thus preface this part of my discussion with a sketch of those ideas on identity formation that are most relevant to the present analysis. Taylor's political discourse is centred on the idea of a community precisely because it is grounded upon a notion of the self as "situated" and involving a particular understanding of agency and responsibility. This self is not only authentic—that is, "inwardly derived, personal, original" (Taylor 1992, 34)—but also aware of its motivations and able to reflect on them in a "vocabulary of worth." Although most fundamental for the constitution of the subject, the articulation of this deep, genuine self is highly unstructured. The self is not transparent to itself but dependent on a context that informs its constitution, be it through interactions with particular individuals or with more abstract social determinants making up a public area where privilege and recognition are negotiated. This dialogical self will thus give precedence to collective over individual rights, so as to ensure the survival of a community that is in itself a sine qua non for the individual's constitution. Two consequences of this view are relevant for Taylor's political discourse. First, the social context of tradition becomes the moral starting point for each individual in that it provides narratives about what the "good life" might mean, along with the linguistic idiom without which the self cannot be articulated at all (language, in this case French, is essential to Taylor). Second, what makes identity possible as a relational phenomenon is precisely this notion of a context that not only allows a centripetal self-exploration but also stages a process of alterity that sets the self apart from some other. Imagining this other becomes crucial in positing individual identity, an argument developed in Hegel's dialectic of master and slave, on which Taylor premises his discussion of the politics of recognition.[20]

Seen in the light of the Canadian situation and the demands for recognition by Quebec and by Canada's Native populations, respect for distinct identities within a liberal society gains in political urgency. The main thrust of Taylor's position on this issue is established in his *Multiculturalism and the Politics of Recognition* (1992). In the following, I look at this next stage before moving on to a discussion of what Taylor's views gain or lose from their transplantation into Germany.

---

20. On Hegel's construction of recognition and its adaptation by Taylor, see Siemerling (1999).

Taylor derives many of his arguments from the Canadian (specifically French Canadian) context, but the challenge of multiculturalism and recognition is endemic to liberal democracies: the recognition of diverse identities within a society entails, beyond constitutional representation, a public acknowledgement of citizens' identities as men or women, African Americans, Christians, Jews, English or French Canadians, and so on. Taylor's argument hinges on the link between recognition and identity. Identity is partly shaped by recognition or by its absence. The denial of recognition is therefore not only a breach of courtesy but also the withholding of a vital human need. This hinges, in turn, on the premise that self-perception is not a monological process, since the human mind is generated dialogically, through interaction with "significant others" (George Herbert Mead, cited in Taylor 1992, 32). According to Taylor, the politics of recognition as a modern phenomenon encompasses two main strands. The first is a politics of universalism that emphasizes the equal dignity of all individuals, which emerged after the collapse of former social hierarchies based on "honour" and inequality. The second is a politics of difference that recognizes everyone for his or her unique identity. This is connected with the understanding of individual identity as it developed at the end of the eighteenth century, especially with Rousseau and Herder. Together with this notion came a sense of authenticity and truthfulness to oneself, derived from the concept that every human being possesses an intuitive moral feeling and that our moral salvation depends on an authentic moral contact with ourselves. While the first strand (of universalism) demands the recognition of a universal human potential by focusing on what all human beings share, the second strand (of difference) acknowledges the forms in which this potential has materialized in the case of each individual. Universalism is associated by Taylor with a special reading of liberalism (referred to as "procedural"), in which individual freedoms are ensured and no collective views on the "good life" are prescribed. Within these perspectives, individuals are considered able to decide for themselves what the right purposes are, thereby proclaiming their complete autonomy. In contrast, the politics of difference ascribes to each individual a unique identity, the preservation of which might imply the enforcement of "substantive"—as opposed to procedural—aims on a whole group of human beings, thereby restricting, to a certain extent, their freedom. The ambiguities of this distinction are dealt with in more detail in my discussion of Jürgen Habermas's response to Taylor's essay. At any rate, Taylor maintains that the two versions of politics come into conflict, an idea that he illustrates by referring to the Canadian situation. The examination of constitutional legitimacy for laws protecting the French language in Quebec brings Taylor to the heart of the question of how universalistic liberalism interacts with diversity. While a liberal society such as English Canada, moulded after the American model, would not espouse collective notions of the "good," Quebec governments have maintained that the survival of French culture is a common purpose that all members of the community should subscribe to. With all the historical implications for French Canadians, *la survivance* of French culture and the laws that promote it go beyond making this culture accessible to the current population; it aims instead at *creating* new members by ensuring that future generations will continue to identify as French speakers. By taking this position, Quebec has opted for a different (according to Taylor), "more hospitable" (1992, 61), variant of liberalism that is more sensitive to difference and diversity. The distinct culture of Quebec is preserved through consistent language legislation that obliges parents to send their children to French-language schools only, outlaws commercial signage in any language other than French, and forces mid-size and large businesses to be run in French.[21] Of course, minimal human rights such as the negative liberties defined by Ignatieff are closely observed, which takes the sting out of revoking or restricting certain privileges for reasons of public policy.

Taylor's argument marks a new stage in the long-standing debate over liberalism versus communitarianism. Liberalists subscribe to the Kantian view that individual rights are the only acceptable legitimation for government, while any form of *volonté générale* would undesirably limit personal freedoms. The communitarian perspective, informed by a Hegelian, dialectical formation of consciousness, stresses the contribution of collective goals to the development of personal identities. Taylor's approach departs from the minimal universalism of the liberal view and threatens thereby to gloss over the inevitable multiplicity of any society, but Taylor does so with an eye to reaching a compromise between the two solutions: he gives a green light to collective goals, provided that they do not infringe on human rights. Reasonable as this proposal is, its significance lies not in the compromise that it has reached but in the skill with which Taylor makes the two positions almost indistinguishable. In both cases, human rights are the final trumps; in both cases, human beings are accorded a fair degree of freedom to pursue their authentic identities and demand their recognition. Thus considered, the opposition between liberal and communitarian is hardly an opposition at all but more of a range of possibilities.

---

21. See Taylor (1992, 52–53). One year after the publication of *Multiculturalism and the Politics of Recognition*, some of these regulations were modified. An amendment was added to the Charter of the French Language in 1993, extending the right to English-language education to all Canadian citizens and introducing the current regulations on the "marked predominance" (but not exclusivity) of French on outdoor commercial signs.

While Taylor leans toward collective, substantive goals, a German respondent to his essay, the philosopher Jürgen Habermas (1993), sides more with the liberal tenet of personal autonomy. As he argues, an awareness of personal liberties is, in fact, the necessary premise for an overarching idea of the common good. This only proves once more how spurious the contrast actually is between the two positions. I do not have space here to address Habermas's reply in detail, though some points must be made in order to understand his view as being informed by a cultural background different from Taylor's. Taylor simplifies the politics of equal dignity and proposes instead a difference-sensitive liberalism that, in fact, lacks the basic liberal principle of personal autonomy. What Habermas brings to the discussion is a host of distinctions, some of which can only be inferred from the way in which he applies terms that he has formulated and reformulated in previous books (see Habermas 1981, 1988, 1991, 1992). One such concept is that of autonomy. Habermas sees a difference between private and public autonomy, where the first refers to the individual's capacity to pursue a personal conception of the good life, while the second, based on the first, extends to a sense of obedience to self-imposed laws. In this light, Taylor's purportedly communitarian common goal presupposes a stronger measure of individual autonomy than Taylor had envisaged. To complicate matters, the enforcement of substantive goals on a diverse community and maintaining respect for its members are two different matters for Habermas but not for Taylor. While state justice must remain neutral with regard to substantive notions of the good life, Habermas argues, these notions must be respected as the result of a rational accountability of all human beings for the moral choices that they make. Any restriction of this autonomy, such as that defended by Taylor and which passes, confusingly enough, as a form of respect, is nothing less than oppression. That someone should speak on behalf of all French Canadians and force on them the protection of their language and culture would translate for Habermas as an encroachment on human rights. Rights liberalism, one can conclude, does not suppress difference, as Taylor seems to imply, although it does not prioritize it either. But the neutrality that Habermas's notion of liberalism professes is also a hidden form of commitment that is not neutral at all and will marginalize those conceptions of the good life that prefer to assert themselves on a collective level, just as liberal English Canada tends to dismiss separatist leanings in Quebec as unreasonable.[22] Taylor's own view of liberalism as a "fighting creed" that will have to draw the line at some point, beyond which its creeds are questioned,

---

22. In the previous section, I explained how Ignatieff tries to come to terms with this struggle but fails to do so since his only argument is the lack of violent cohabitation, when in fact the French Canadian collective national feeling would imply far more than that.

corroborates this line of reasoning, although the line has been drawn much closer than Taylor assumed it actually would be. Indeed, the "hospitable" variant of liberalism that he espouses is ready to make substantive distinctions that *must* be made in a world of intermingling cultural identities, but to accept this one must make a substantive distinction that liberalism, in whatever variant, cannot afford. What is of more interest here is Habermas's relaxation of his strong concept of autonomy and his acknowledgement of an unavoidably common, ethical content in any constitutional form of government. One particular group of citizens that forms a nation shares a context of traditions and experiences that can only be unique and thereby expressive of a particular life form irreplaceable by another. For this reason, a nation's historical experience will impose a certain pattern of interpretation on the constitutional principles of that nation, even when they prescribe universalist human rights. Specific collective needs in Germany account for the institutional guarantees enjoyed by the Christian churches and the Jewish community in this country or the constitutional privileges accorded to the family as distinct from other types of lifelong companionship. This, however, does not preclude the fact that such common experiences may be divergent and as such in need of public deliberation. But despite these concessions to difference, state neutrality must be maintained, and any privilege for any one "way of life" at the expense of others must be withheld—a statement that would also find agreement with Taylor.[23]

The specific Canadian and German backgrounds or "ways of life" on which Taylor's and Habermas's views respectively are founded therefore make up a part of their thinking. Canada faces a different set of challenges with regard to multiculturalism than Germany. Here I would like to take a step back in order to look at how this discourse on recognition and identity can be understood in a German context. Surely the question of Quebec and the concept of a "distinct society" are part of an international debate that affects other regions as well: Catalonia as an autonomous region in Spain and Scotland as a nation recognized by the United Kingdom come to mind. However, the relevance of Quebec for German debates on multiculturalism and the sensitivity to difference displayed by the Canadian liberal state are limited. Taylor's inspiring collection of articles *Reconciling the Solitudes* (1993), which deals exhaustively with the issue of Quebec, is the only one of his books not to have been translated into

---

23. "Governing a contemporary society is continually recreating a balance between requirements that tend to undercut each other, constantly finding creative new solutions as the old equilibria become stultifying. There can never be in the nature of the case a definitive solution" (cited in Laforest 1994, 195).

German.[24] It is thanks to the merits of his monographs on Hegel and William James and his extensive preoccupation with German philosophy that Taylor has been canonized within German academia to an extent as yet unmatched by any other Canadian theorist, with the exception perhaps of Marshall McLuhan. In recognition of his contribution to philosophy and political thought, he was honoured with the Hegel Prize of the City of Stuttgart in 1997, previously awarded (among others) to the philosophers Hans-Georg Gadamer, Paul Ricœur, and Jürgen Habermas and to the sociologist Niklas Luhmann. Habermas has also been a member on the selection board of Suhrkamp, the publishing house that is mainly responsible for the dissemination of Taylor's texts and of other books that engage in the debates on identity and recognition. Suhrkamp published, for instance, the work of Axel Honneth, whose *Kampf um Anerkennung* strikes similar notes to those of Taylor's and Habermas's statements on struggles for recognition (see Honneth 1992). The difference, Taylor maintains, has to do with methodology and perspective:

> These different approaches are of course not opposed to each other, but focus on different sides of the phenomenon. ... So what I am doing on a more general level is trying to find a vocabulary to understand this development and how it came about, and I think that Axel Honneth is rather looking for the normative grid to tell us what to do in this situation. (2002b, 175)

This is true to the extent that both Taylor and Habermas begin by giving empirical diagnoses on the state of the liberalism that they adopt or reject, but they go on to offer normative solutions along the lines of enhancing sensitivity to identity by allowing it to extend from individual to group identity in the case of Taylor, and by steering an imperfect state neutrality toward a more deliberate negotiation of privileges in the case of Habermas. The question is whether their analyses of how recognition of identities came to play such an important role and how far the limits of recognition can be stretched without going beyond the borders of the liberal state still maintain their legitimacy when they cross national borders. From the foregoing, it is clear that Taylor and Habermas not only meet on common ground but also seem to reject the same thing: namely, the "fundamentalist" notion that refutes an individual's capacity to pursue his or her own idea of the good life by refusing to tolerate competing ideas. This "negative agreement" goes a long way toward showing how competing theories converge to nuance a debate (liberalism versus communitarianism) that is hardly

---

24. From 1975 to 2002, eight books by Taylor were published in German (see Taylor 1975, 1978, 1988, 1993, 1994, 1995, 2002a, 2002c).

a debate at all but more of a "hospitable" neutrality mediating between distinct life forms such as, in this case, the Canadian and the German. Two solitudes are thereby, even if only temporarily, reconciled.

## CONCLUSION

In dealing with these texts and the reactions that they have elicited in Germany, I have tried to offer a comparative analysis in which various cultural strata have become entangled. As Clifford Geertz once wrote, "cultural analysis is guessing at meaning, assessing the guesses, and drawing explanatory conclusions from the better guesses" (1973, 5). While the field is far from being fully mapped out, some guesses have proven to be more fruitful and helpful than others. Not only political theory but also theory in general deals with and creates communities that do not set their boundaries according to national borders. Yet there is doubtless some trace of locale in every theoretical stance: the case of Northrop Frye in German, for example, presents the perils of an untimely translation whose ground in terms of the cultural genealogy of the text was poorly prepared. Ignatieff's and Taylor's texts, on the other hand, are more transparent due to the strands of German theory that surface in them and their apt articulation of events and debates that are current in most liberal cultures. This threefold case study of the works of two intellectuals born in Quebec (Taylor and Frye) and one English Canadian (Ignatieff) who grew up near Quebec may seem to imply that German interest in Canadian theory has graduated over the past four decades from marginal curiosity to involved awareness. There is something valid in this assumption, but it is by no means unproblematic. While it seems to imply that Canadian theoretical books have *created* their own German readership over the years, as Canadian works of fiction have done, I tend to endorse the less spectacular view that instead it was the gradual opening of Canadian theory to international issues that triggered German readers' interest, whether or not these works are identified as Canadian in origin. My analysis has shown that Canadian literary and political theory is only partly concerned with Canada and is open to many other topics. This openness should be seen in the context of the mobility that theory enjoys in the era of its infinite reproduction: both Taylor and Ignatieff have ventured beyond Canada (unlike Frye), received prizes and held professorships in Germany (Taylor), and consequently raised the stakes for their work from national to global considerations. Since many of their works have been assimilated and canonized in Germany, recent translations of Canadian fiction are likely to meet with a German readership that is better informed on current Canadian issues: to give only a recent example, David Bezmogis's debut short-story collection *Natasha* (London, 2004; Cologne, 2005)—which retells the experiences of a Russian émigré settling in Toronto in the 1980s—poses questions of ethnic integration and cultural identity in the Canadian immigrant milieu for which the theoretical views discussed above could offer a useful vocabulary of deliberation.

**REFERENCES**

Adams, Howard. *Prousts Figuren und ihre Vorbilder* [*A Proust Souvenir*], Frankfurt: Suhrkamp, 1988 / Frankfurt: Insel, 2000.

Boym, Svetlana. *Ninochka*, Albany: State University of New York Press, 2003.

Davey, Frank. *Surviving the Paraphrase: Eleven Essays on Canadian Literature*. Winnipeg: Turnstone, 1983.

de Man, Paul. *Resistance to Theory*. Minneapolis: University of Minnesota Press, 1986.

Eagleton, Terry. *The Significance of Theory*. Oxford: Basil Blackwell, 1990.

Escarpit, Robert. *Sociologie de la littérature*. Paris: Presses de l'Université de France, 1958.

Etiemble, René. *Comparaison n'est pas raison. La crise de la littérature comparée*. Paris: Gallimard, 1963.

Frye, Northrop. *Anatomy of Criticism: Four Essays*. Princeton: Princeton University Press, 1957.

———. *Shakespeares Vollendung: Eine Einführung in die Welt seiner Komödien* [*A Natural Perspective: The Development of Shakespearean Comedy and Romance*]. Munich: Nymphenburger Verlagshandlung, 1966.

———. *The Bush Garden: Essays on the Canadian Imagination*. Toronto: Anansi, 1971.

Geertz, Clifford. *Interpretation of Cultures*. New York: Basic Books, 1973.

Godard, Barbara. "Structuralism / Post-Structuralism: Language, Reality and Canadian Literature." In *Future Indicative: Literary Theory and Canadian Literature*, ed. and introd. John Moss. Ottawa: University of Ottawa Press, 1987. 25–51.

Habermas, Jürgen. *Theorie des kommunikativen Handelns*. Frankfurt: Suhrkamp, 1981 [*The Theory of Communicative Action*, Boston 1984].

———. *Eine Art Schadensabwicklung*. Frankfurt: Suhrkamp, 1987.

———. *Nachmetaphysisches Denken*. Frankfurt: Suhrkamp, 1988 [*Postmetaphysical Thinking*, Cambridge, Mass. 1992].

———. *Erläuterungen zur Diskursethik*. Frankfurt: Suhrkamp, 1991 [*Justification and Application: Remarks on Discourse Ethics*, Cambridge, Mass. 1993].

———. *Faktizität und Geltung*. Frankfurt: Suhrkamp, 1992 [*Between Facts and Norms*, Cambridge, Mass. 1995].

———. "Anerkennungskämpfe im demokratischen Rechtsstaat," Commentary on Charles Taylor, *Multikulturalismus und die Politik der Anerkennung*. Frankfurt: Suhrkamp, 1993, 147–96.

Hillis Miller, J. *Topographies*. Stanford: Stanford University Press, 1995.

Honneth, Axel. *Kampf um Anerkennung: Zur moralischen Grammatik sozialer Konflikte*. Frankfurt: Suhrkamp, 1992.

Ignatieff, Michael. *Blood and Belonging: Journeys into the New Nationalism*. London: Chatto & Windus, 1993.

———. *The Warrior's Honour: Ethnic War and the Modern Conscience*. London: Chatto & Windus, 1998.

———. "Das Fernsehen und die humanitäre Hilfe," in Hans Magnus Enzensberger (ed.), *Krieger ohne Waffen: Das Internationale Komitee vom Roten Kreuz*, Frankfurt: Eichborn, 2001a. 281–302.

———. *Human Rights as Politics and Idolatry*. Princeton: Princeton University Press, 2001b.

———. *The Lesser Evil: Political Ethics in an Age of Terror*. Edinburgh: Edinburgh University Press, 2004.

———. *Das kleinere Übel: Politische Moral in einem Zeitalter des Terrors*, Berlin: Philo, 2005.

Jauss, Hans Robert. "Literary History as a Challenge to Literary Theory" ["Literaturgeschichte als Provokation der Literaturwissenschaft"], in Ralph Cohen (ed.), *New Directions in Literary History*, London: Routledge & Kegan Paul, 1974.

Klein, Naomi. *No Logo!* [*No Logo*], Munich: Riemann, 2001.

———. *Über Zäune und Mauern* [*Dispatches from the Front Lines of the Globalization Debate*], Frankfurt: Campus, 2003.

Kramer, Jane. *The Politics of Memory: Looking for Germany in the New Germany*. New York: Random House, 1996.

Krieger, Murray. *Words about Words about Words: Theory, Criticism and the Literary Text*. Baltimore: The Johns Hopkins University Press, 1988.

Kroetsch, Robert. *The Lovely Treachery of Words: Essays Selected and New*. Toronto: Oxford University Press, 1989.

Laforest, Guy. "Philosophy and Political Judgment in a Multinational Federation," in James Tully (ed.), *Philosophy in an Age of Pluralism: The Philosophy of Charles Taylor in Question*, Cambridge: Cambridge University Press, 1994.

Lecker, Robert. *Making It Real: The Canonization of English Canadian Literature*. Concord, Ont.: Anansi, 1995.

Said, Edward W. *The World, the Text, the Critic*. Cambridge, Mass.: Harvard University Press, 1983.

Saul, John Ralston. *Der Markt frisst seine Kinder* [*The Unconscious Civilisation*], Frankfurt: Campus, 1997.

———. *Von Erdbeeren, Wirtschaftsgipfeln und anderen Zumutungen des 21. Jahrhunderts* [*The Doubter's Companion*], Frankfurt: Campus, 2000.

Siemerling, Winfried. "Alterity and Recognition: Charles Taylor and the Limits of Self-Certainty." *Texte: Revue de critique et de théorie littéraire* 23.24, 1999: 63–82.

Taylor, Charles. *Erklärung und Interpretation in den Wissenschaften vom Menschen* [*Selection of Essays*], Vorwort Garbis Kortian, Frankfurt: Suhrkamp, 1975.

———. *Hegel* [*Hegel*], Frankfurt: Suhrkamp, 1978.

———. *Negative Freiheit? Zur Kritik des neuzeitlichen Individualismus* [*Selection of Essays*], Nachwort Axel Honneth, Frankfurt: Suhrkamp, 1988.

———. *Multiculturalism and the Politics of Recognition*. Princeton: Princeton University Press, 1992.

———. *Multikulturalismus und die Politik der Anerkennung* [*Multiculturalism and the Politics of Recognition*], Frankfurt: Fischer, 1993.

———. *Quellen des Selbst: Die Entstehung der neuzeitlichen Identität* [*Sources of the Self: The Making of Modern Identity*], Frankfurt: Suhrkamp, 1994.

———. *Das Unbehagen der Moderne* [*The Malaise of Modernity*], Frankfurt: Suhrkamp, 1995.

———. *Die Formen des Religiösen in der Gegenwart* [*Varieties of Religion Today: William James Revisited*], Frankfurt: Suhrkamp, 2002a.

———. "On Identity, Alienation and the Consequences of September 11th." Interview with Hartmut Rosa and Arto Laitinen. In *Perspectives on the Philosophy of Charles Taylor*, ed. Arto Laitinen and Nicholas H. Smith. Acta Philosophica Fennica. Vol. 71. Helsinki: Societas Philosophica Fennica, 2002b. 165–95.

———. *Wieviel Gemeinschaft braucht Demokratie? Aufsätze zur politischen Philosophie* [Selection of Essays], Frankfurt: Suhrkamp, 2002c.

# Selecting Canadiana for the Young: The German Translation of English Canadian Children's Literature

*Martina Seifert*
*Queen's University, Belfast*

Children's literature, much more than literature for adults, "provides an x-ray vision into the perceptual frameworks held by those who produce it" (Rubio 1994, 229). This "x-ray vision" becomes even more incisive when we look at children's literature in translation, as "translational norms expose more clearly the constraints imposed on a text that enters the children's system" (Shavit 1986, 112). Thus, surveying a body of translated children's literature over a considerable period of time, one soon discovers significant patterns and trends and gains invaluable insights into prevalent cultural concepts and frameworks. The patterns that emerge from such longitudinal studies, however, convey much more insight into the importing culture than into the imported one. The following analytical overview of the twentieth century shows that the highly successful translation of English-language Canadian children's literature into German has been structured fundamentally by the target culture's changing needs and concepts within its children's literature system.[1] This chapter reveals that the importation, translation, marketing, and reception of English Canadian children's literature in Germany have been governed by two major principles: first, up to the 1980s, pre-existing hetero-images of Canada not only influenced but also determined the transfer; second, translation strategies have since undergone radical changes, departing from image-bound preferences and moving toward an ignorance of, or even obliteration of, distinctive cultural traces.

The translation of English-language Canadian children's literature in Germany has a tradition dating back to the early twentieth century, which marks the historical

---

1. On children's literature as part of the literary polysystem, see Shavit (1986).

beginnings and the first success stories of Canadian literature translated into German. Canadian children's literature, or what has been perceived, published, and marketed as such in the target system, was celebrated in Germany long before its "adult" counterpart. While almost no attention was paid to Canadian fiction in Germany until the 1980s, imports from Canada's children's literature had been common for more than eight decades before the avalanche of translation started within the general literary polysystem.[2] More than 400 titles by over 150 different Canadian children's authors have appeared in German translation to date, and that number does not yet include the large second and third editions of some of the most prominent authors, such as Ernest Thompson Seton, Farley Mowat, and James Houston. Given these numbers, children's literature makes up a remarkably large part of the body of Canadian writing in German translation—a phenomenon that distinguishes Canadian texts from other national literatures in translation. Moreover, this presence is not just quantitative; it also concerns the dissemination and popularity of these texts. Imports from Canada, regardless of the time period, seem to have served the needs of the target culture, providing and perpetuating exotic images on the one hand and compensating for underrepresented genres in the target system (not focused on place or culture) on the other.

While the latter preferences have become prominent only since the early 1980s, a time of radical change within both the Canadian and the German children's literature systems, the more popular exotic images of Canada determined translation practices until that time. Until the 1980s, literary imports for children and young adults from Canada could be grouped into three major categories: adventure and outdoor survival stories, stories about Canada's Native peoples, and realistic animal stories. In Germany, all of these categories either belonged to children's or youth literature from the outset or moved into this realm in the early twentieth century, when the reception of Canadian literature began. Among the first writers to be translated were Egerton Ryerson Young and Ernest Thompson Seton, both as early as 1899, followed by Charles G. D. Roberts, Vilhjalmur Stefansson, Jack O'Brien, Rutherford George Montgomery, Grey Owl, and Chief Buffalo Child Long Lance, all of whom were translated before World War II and remained popular long after that period. After 1945, new editions of their books were joined by the works of authors such as Jack Hambleton, John D. Craig, John

---

2. Surprisingly, these striking aspects of intercultural transfer have not yet triggered academic interest, neither within German or Canadian children's literature research nor within the otherwise very active Canadian Studies community in the German-speaking countries. Comparative research on Canadian children's literature remains a desideratum. For a first introduction to Canadian children's literature in German translation, see Seifert (2005). For a comprehensive exploration of the topic, see Seifert (2006, 933–1005).

Francis Hayes, Farley Mowat, and James Houston. All of these (male) authors cater to either one or more of the three categories mentioned above. Nature and Natives, the "two most obvious potential phenomena for an exploration of the other" (Groß 1995, 27), were the prime features in the translated texts. The fact that these texts were imported in such numbers and should prove to be so immensely popular can be understood only in the context of imagological[3] research. As images of Canada in German children's and youth literature seem to have determined the translation and reception of Canadian texts for more than eight decades, they need to be delineated briefly here.

## TRADITIONAL IMAGES OF CANADA

Images of Canada have been remarkably uniform in Germany. As the country of endless wilderness, ice-glittering romance, and grim backwoods reality, Canada has featured prominently in literature for the young since the late nineteenth century. Its most important imagined features are its emptiness, virginity, and nordicity, its vastness and distance from civilization, its harsh climate, its wild animals (contact with at least one bear seems to be obligatory in German juvenile novels), and its masculinity. German authors have celebrated Canada as a country of men and for men only; the protagonists are almost exclusively male, the authors are almost exclusively male, and even the women writers call it "a country of men" in their books. We read, for example, that "this country needs only real men, men who have the courage to fight snow, ice, frost, starving Natives, voracious wolves, and frantic dogs" (Kraus 1935, 10).[4] The depiction of Canada in German literature provides an impressive example of how strongly such images can be gendered. The "men-in-the-wilderness" concept has been so dear to the German reading public that it has resulted in a denial of Canada's urbanization and industrialization. Canada essentially remains premodern in German children's and youth literature, a destination for male adolescents who refuse the monotony of grey cities. It thus serves as a counterimage to the German self-image; it is imagined as Germany's "other," spacious to the point of being almost unpopulated, full of freedom and adventure, a place where one can live free from the constraints of culture.

These images have not changed substantially over the past 100 years; only their interpretation has altered, ranging from an adventure playground and training ground for male protagonists in the 1920s, a "survival-of-the-fittest" arena for

---

3. The analysis of intercultural imagery, of ethnic stereotyping, and of the discursive construct of national identity is known in French, German, and Dutch as *Imagologie*. It originated in comparative literature and social psychology. In English, the term "Image Studies" is often used alongside that of "imagology."
4. Translated from German. All translations of German quotations are my own.

Aryan heroes during the Nazi regime (1933–1945), and a tabula rasa escape fantasy for the German postwar imagination to a place of spiritual healing and self-discovery, which today seems to qualify easily as an ecological paradise. Juvenile novels were especially powerful in cementing these perceptions of Canada in Germany, as the vast majority of German texts featuring the country are adventure stories.

The powerful effects that such prevailing national images have had on the translation of foreign-language literature have not yet been thoroughly investigated, neither within the field of comparative image studies nor within translation theory. Although Translation Studies has examined how dominant norms of a target culture not only influence but in fact govern the production and reception of translations, one of the most crucial questions seems to have been largely ignored to date: that is, the question of how existing images of a particular country have influenced the reception, distribution, and evaluation of literary texts from this country on an international scale. It is especially interesting to investigate which books have been translated and which have not as well as which ones have been translated only long after their initial publication dates. Comparatists Hugo Dyserinck (1991, 128–29) and Peter Soenen (1995, 1997) have pointed out that, in selecting works for translation, preference is usually given to those books that match the existing images and expectations of foreign readers and that works by authors whose work is not in line with the fixed images of their country are translated either less often or not at all. Text selection occurs through a filter of culturally determined, image-bound patterns of perception that eliminates everything that does not fit the image grid. These moments of interaction between image and translation can take place at three different levels: the level of selection (the strategies and decisions of publishers catering to the expectations of the reading public), the level of translation (the role played by individual translators and their image-bound interpretations of texts), and the level of reception (including marketing, reviews, awards, recommendation lists, and so on). In the following, I focus primarily on the levels of selection and reception. The examples will show how translations of English Canadian children's and youth literature became instrumental in the representation of popular images of Canada and how prefaces and paratexts were used to fix these images of otherness.

## WILD ANIMALS, REAL MEN, AND NATIVES

Both Ernest Thompson Seton's and Charles G. D. Roberts's realistic animal stories, with their Canadian wilderness settings and their harsh Darwinian principles, had high levels of circulation in Germany. They received rave reviews, appeared on the major recommendation lists for the young, and have remained popular to this day. When Roberts's first translations appeared in the 1920s and 1930s, the "Father of Canadian Poetry" and "Dean of Canadian Letters" was praised by German reviewers as a "hunter, backwoodsman, animal lover and nature worshipper," "a poet from the boondocks and the prairies" (see paratext in Roberts 1927). Of Roberts's impressive oeuvre—more than 1,000 separate pieces exist, including poems, novels, short stories, romances, travel guides, histories, and essays—only his animal stories (and a few scattered poems) were translated into German. In her 1935 PhD dissertation, Helene von Kieseritzky stressed Roberts's "Nordic roots and blood heritage," which for her "keep him connected to the northern Germanic people" (50). This reading mirrors the ideology that the image of Canada was subjected to by the mid-1930s, when the Nordic landscape was idealized in Germany as a breeding ground for a tough, virile, and ruthless Aryan race. While Roberts's fame in the Soviet Union (Black and Black 1995, 7) had already led to his enthusiastic reception during the Weimar Republic, with some of his animal stories actually being translated from Russian into German, it also helped his publication in East Germany. The GDR censorship files contain favourable appraisals of his animal stories, not least by the prominent writer Arnold Zweig.

Roberts's enduring popularity was surpassed only by that of Seton, who remains the Canadian author with the highest number of published titles. His *Wild Animals I Have Known*, 1898 (*Bingo und andere Tierhelden*, 1899), was translated just one year after its initial publication and went through numerous editions, as did his other books. The Franckh'sche Verlagsbuchhandlung, his German publisher, called him its most famous and best-selling author. By 1923, over a million books by Seton had been sold, and by 1950, fifty-two different titles had been published. All German reception documents praise the authenticity of his fiction and emphasize his personal hunting and trapping experience "in the Canadian virgin forests." The priority given to this wilderness context resulted in a curious image-bound marketing of the author as a "real man," who "even in his old age" was still "over 1.80 metres tall, lean, wiry, and strong" and "could be a match for men twenty years younger than himself."[5] Seton also received a good deal of attention in German academic circles in the 1930s and was warmly received at Bonn University in December 1936 with his wife, Julia. He and his wife took turns demonstrating various aspects of Native culture, with Julia singing medicine songs in different costumes.[6] Given the selectivity of translation and the general denigration of English-language literature during the time of National

---

5. Culled from publisher's materials from the 1950s.
6. For a detailed exploration, see Allen (2004).

Socialism,[7] Seton's eager reception reveals the popularity and power as well as the flexibility applied in interpreting prevailing images of Canada. His woodcraft and outdoor survival books, *Rolf in the Woods*, 1911 (*Rolf, der Trapper*, 1920),[8] and *Two Little Savages: Being the Adventures of Two Boys Who Lived as Indians and What They Learned*, 1903 (*Zwei kleine Wilde: Ein Buch von Jan und Sam und ihrem Treiben in ihrem Reich und auf der Farm in Sanger*, 1923),[9] were on all the Nazi lists of "Approved Literature." After 1945, the enthusiastic reception of Seton continued unbroken. In 1960, in honour of the 100th anniversary of his birthday, Kosmos published two high-quality jubilee editions, *Die schönsten Tiergeschichten von Ernest Thompson Seton* and *Bingo und andere Tierhelden*, the latter short-listed for the prestigious German Youth Literature Prize (Deutscher Jugendliteraturpreis). As with Roberts, several of Seton's animal stories were also published in the Soviet-occupied zone and the GDR,[10] with Soviet approval.[11]

Other Canadian authors who had already been recommended for the young in the 1920s and 1930s were self-constructed Natives such as Sylvester Long, alias Chief Buffalo Child Long Lance, and Archibald Stansfeld Belaney, alias Grey Owl or Wa-Sha-Quon-Asin. Long Lance and Grey Owl "gave German readers two popular Indian images, that of the gorgeously mounted Plains warrior, advocating honesty and fearlessness, and that of the quaint (Woodland) environmentalist, preaching harmony with mother earth" (Lutz 2000, 42). Texts by both authors have remained extremely popular, speaking for both the endurance of the image and its changing interpretations. Politically functionalized during National Socialism (see Haible 1998, Lutz 2000, 40–44), their texts were later celebrated in postwar Germany for their escapist potential and were subsequently often read as ecological and spiritual manifestos. A postwar example is Walter Bauer's book on Grey Owl, *Der weisse Indianer*, 1960 ("The White Indian"), which evokes the Canadian wilderness as a place where freedom from civilization, in particular from recent German history, can be found. The discovery that both "Natives" were imposters did not affect the German book market—editions published

---

7. Although translation was not simply suppressed—commercially successful translated genres such as adventure fiction continued to be published en masse despite official denigration—it was certainly restricted (see Sturge 1981, 203).
8. Also published as *Rolf und sein roter Freund* (1937) and as *Mit den letzten Trappern in Prairie und Urwald* (after World War II).
9. Also published as "Jan und Sam im Walde" (after World War II).
10. For the ridiculous censorship discussion surrounding Seton's animal story "Tito," published in 1949 by the GDR Kinderbuchverlag, see Lokatis et al. (1997, 25–26).
11. Seton has been translated into Russian more frequently than any other Canadian author. "In 1983 alone Russian translations of Seton totalled nearly half a million" (Black and Black 1995, 7–8).

during the late 1990s still refer to them as "Indians," many decades after they were exposed as frauds. Grey Owl's evocation of Canada's "great Northland," his environmental mission, the protection of Natives, wild animals, and nature—all corresponded perfectly to the expectations of the German audience. Grey Owl was also known in the GDR through a translation from Russian.[12] All of his books, especially the children's story *The Adventures of Sajo and Her Beaver People*, were published in Germany in high print runs, went through many editions, and remain popular to this day.

The translation of *Sajo* also provides some interesting insights into what Johan Soenen refers to as an "image-bound way of translating the text."[13] Drawing heavily on popular images of Canada, as well as on German literary conventions, Käte Freinthal translated some of the descriptions of Canadian nature on the first pages of Grey Owl's novel as follows: "the great land" becomes "the immeasurably great land," "far away" from the towns is turned into "the farthest away from the towns," and "in the woods" becomes "in the harsh, grim woodland," a canonical phrase used by German authors to describe Canada. In addition, the past tense of the original text is transformed into the present tense: Grey Owl's "I, who once was one of them [the Ojibway people]" becomes "I, who am one of them," and "this tale of Long Ago" becomes merely "this tale," thus projecting the idea of a current Canadian reality in place of nostalgic memories of a Canada gone by. While the vast majority of adventure stories by German authors written after 1945 are historical novels or at least carry a feel of the past, those set in Canada still evoke the present.[14] Freinthal's translation of *Sajo* is a striking example of how a translation can be adapted to conform to existing models in the target system. That this 1938 translation of *Sajo* was used again for the 1998 edition, and that this reuse of old translations is common practice, exemplify the fixed, invariable image of Canada in this domain.

---

12. Michael Prišvin's novel *Seraja Sova* ("Grey Owl") was published in 1954 and starts with the inscription "The journey to a country where animals can still live in peace."
13. On the role of the individual translators and their interpretations of the original texts, Soenen points out that "the image of a nation ... can be so dominant in the translator's mind, that it cannot but influence the translator's approach and the ultimate result of his own linguistic reproduction of the original message. Mitigations or intensifications in content, omissions or additions of words and notions ..., grammatical and stylistic modulations and modifications, and other sorts of changes ... are often caused by image-bound interpretation" (1995, 20).
14. See, for instance, Fred Larsen, *Männer im roten Rock*, 1955 ("Men in Red Coats"), Heinz Hartmann, *Pelztierjäger in Kanada*, 1955 ("Trapper in Canada"), Fritz Helke, *Wo alle Straßen enden*, 1957 ("Where All Streets End"), Kurt Ritter, *Mit Pferd und Kanu durch Kanada*, 1957 ("With Horse and Canoe through Canada"), Franz Schnell, *3 x P und rotes Kanu*, 1968 ("3 x P and Red Canoe"), Werner Egli, *Bis ans Ende der Fährte*, 1984 ("To the End of the Trail"), or the adventure novels of Wolfgang Bittner, written in the 1990s.

The German infatuation with "Indians," their "Indianthusiasm" (Lutz 2000, 37), has kept alive the interest in stories featuring Canada's First Nations in the German children's literature system. Edith Sharp's *Nkwalla*, 1958 (*Nikwalla der Indianer-Junge*, 1958), which won a Governor General's Literary Award and a place on the Hans Christian Andersen Honour List, was translated into German in the same year of its original publication and appeared in different editions. Doris Anderson's *Slave of the Haida*, 1974 (*Kim-ta, der Sohn des Häuptlings*, 1978), was published by Benzinger in 1978 in a translation by the well-known Austrian author Käthe Recheis, whose own work deals with North American Native peoples and shows astounding parallels to Anderson's text. Both stories are moral maturation tales for children and have very similar narrative constellations—a young boy has to pass a test of initiation in an exotic Canadian setting in order to save his people.

During the 1980s, more books by women authors exploiting this genre started to appear in German translation, such as Brenda Bellingham's *Stormchild*, 1985 (*Sturmkind*, 1989), Anne Cameron's *Dreamspeaker*, 1978 (*Dreamspeaker*, 1996), Mary-Ellen Collura's *Winners*, 1984 (*Siksika*, 1987), Jan Hudson's *Sweetgrass*, 1984 (*Süßes Gras*, 1987), and *Dawn Rider*, 1992 (*Schnell wie der Wind*, 1992). It comes as no surprise that the first Canadian book to win the prestigious German Youth Literature Prize in 2000 also deals with Native issues: Richard Van Camp, a member of the Dogrib Nation from the Northwest Territories, won the prize for his intense novel about adolescence, *The Lesser Blessed*, 1996 (*Die ohne Segen sind*, 2000). The vivid translation by the well-known German author Ulrich Plenzdorf—his first translation—certainly contributed to the novel's success on the German market. The original was promoted as fiction for adults in Canada and not as young adult literature, so the German version of *The Lesser Blessed* demonstrates how texts can address different audiences, and even move systems, depending on the norms and conventions established in the target culture.[15] Indeed, Van Camp is one of the few voices from inside Native communities that have found their way into German children's and youth literature.

## ADVENTURE AND SURVIVAL

Exoticism was also provided by Canadian authors of adventure fiction translated in the 1950s and 1960s. Unlike the European tradition, Canadian adventure fiction is set almost exclusively in exotic places in its own country. Thus, historical adventure tales by John Francis Haynes or Jack Hambleton's bush pilot and

---

15. To pave the novel's way into the young adult book market, Plenzdorf's translation has smoothed out some scenes considered too violent or obscene.

ranger stories set in northern Ontario were highly compatible with the image-bound German reception. The paratexts stress the Canadian wilderness settings, underlining that in this "hard, beautiful country" "only real men and robust guys can survive."[16] Hambleton is also the only Canadian author to have had two of his books nominated for the German Youth Literature Prize—recognition the likes of which he never received in Canada. Some authors, such as Hambleton and Fred Bodsworth,[17] have been far more popular in Germany than in their home country since they wrote within the prevailing hetero-images of Canada in Germany.

Another outstandingly popular type of narrative imported from Canada between the 1950s and the mid-1980s was the outdoor survival story, especially when it featured a pair of young teenagers, one white and one Native or Inuit, stranded in a northern Canadian wilderness. James Houston's *Frozen Fire*, 1977 (*Feuer unter dem Eis*, 1979), *Black Diamonds*, 1982 (*Das schwarze Gold der Arktis*, 1984), and *Ice Swords*, 1985 (*Elfenbeinjäger im ewigen Eis*, 1987), belong to this category, as does Farley Mowat's *Lost in the Barrens*, 1956 (*Das Geheimnis im Norden*, 1961). In these stories, the survival of the white boy usually depends on the "traditional" knowledge and wisdom of the Native or Inuit protagonist. Apart from their wilderness settings and traditional adventure action, these texts advocate tolerance and intercultural understanding and thus serve multiple needs of the target culture: German postwar notions about re-education against xenophobia and hostility powerfully conjoined with constructed exotic images. Mowat and Houston are extremely popular in Germany, where their books are distributed by book clubs and have sold tens of thousands of copies. Both have enjoyed a wide audience, perhaps wider than they might have wished: Mowat's *The Dog Who Wouldn't Be*, 1957 (*Der Hund, der mehr sein wollte*, 1959), for example, was enthusiastically received as a "dog-manual" by magazines such as *The German Hunter*, *St. Hubertus*, and *The Swiss Hunting Journal* and praised as fascinating and stimulating, particularly for the hunter. Mowat's environmental stories, with their evocation of the great Canadian wilderness and its noble Natives and animals set against corrupted white civilization, were readily welcomed by image-bound German audiences. In 1980, his story "The Snow Walker," which depicts the struggle of an Inuit community, was also published for children in East Germany. Mowat's critique of imperialism and materialism certainly increased imports, and the censorship files stress his focus on cultural

---

16. See the blurb in Hambleton (1955).
17. Bodsworth's novel *The Sparrow's Fall* was also picked up by the Bertelsmann book club, where it sold 155,000 copies as opposed to 29,000 in Canada. See William French, "CanLit: Gathering Groupies All over the World," *Globe and Mail*, 15 April 1980, 15.

conflicts, underlining the fact that Canada faces a cultural and political crisis typical of capitalist societies. A similar discourse accompanied the reception of John D. Craig. While the market in West Germany was merely interested in Craig's adventure stories, his young adult novel *No Word for Good-Bye* (1969), in which a group of Ojibway people have to give up their native land to a huge capitalist company, was published in the Soviet Union and subsequently came out in the GDR (*Sommer am Kinniwabi*, 1981).

In summary, it can be said that until the 1980s virtually no text that presented Canada as anything other than a vast northern wilderness inhabited by animals, Natives, and a few white male adolescents qualified for translation, and the titles selected for translation in the context of existing hetero-images helped to perpetuate such conceptual constructs. This should not suggest that the translations are not at all representative of Canadian children's literature; the wilderness does, of course, feature prominently, and "stories of survival in a harsh and mysterious land are abundant" (McGillis 1996, 335). It is striking, however, how clearly the selection of texts operated according to the German image of Canada as a wilderness for boys only; books with a non-wilderness setting, books by female authors,[18] or books with female protagonists were generally not translated until the 1980s.[19] Neither Catharine Parr Traill's *Canadian Crusoes* (1852), which would have fit the wilderness image perfectly, nor Margaret Marshall Saunders's enormously popular dog story *Beautiful Joe* (1894) made it into German translation, nor did Canadian fantasy authors such as Catherine Anthony Clark and Ruth Nichols. Out of the 102 female authors listed in the catalogue *Canadian Children's Books 1799–1939*, only four were discovered for the German book market, a mere two of them were published as children's literature, and only one novel, Constance Lindsay Skinner's *The White Leader*, 1926 (*Der weiße Häuptling*, 1930), was translated soon after its publication in Canada. Although a classic tale of wilderness survival, Jan Truss's *Jasmine* (1982), with its female protagonist, did not qualify for German translation, nor did earlier Muriel Denison's *Susannah: A Little Girl with the Mounties* (1936), even though the Royal Canadian Mounted Police are a stock ingredient in German adventure stories. Sheila Egoff and Judith Saltman (1990) point out that an author such as Nellie McClung, who sets her

---

18. Interestingly, the boom of Canadian "adult" fiction on the German market in the 1980s began with and has been sustained by female authors, with many more titles published by female than male writers. This accounts for the changing reception patterns since the 1980s. See the chapter by Brita Oeding and Luise von Flotow in this volume.
19. The few exceptions are confined to the rule of a non-urban setting. The only real exceptions to these translation principles are Eva Lis Wuorio's *The Canadian Twins*, 1956 (*Die kanadischen Zwillinge*, 1961), set in different towns across Canada, and Lyn Cook's early multicultural story *The Bells on Finland Street*, 1950 (*Morgen läuft Du für Kanada*, 1956), set in Sudbury, Ontario.

stories in small Canadian towns, provides her readers with an opportunity "to see Canada as something more than a wilderness" and that she—together with Lucy Maud Montgomery and Ralph Connor—has "crossed international borders to an extent that has probably not been matched since" (12), but for her too the German border has remained impenetrable.

## ANNE OF GREEN GABLES

The most striking example of "non-reception" or extremely delayed reception in Germany, which unites all these image criteria—a female author, female protagonists, and a non-wilderness setting—is Canada's most famous and enduringly popular celebrity author, Lucy Maud Montgomery. Montgomery, a "foundation of Canadian identity" (Fiamengo 2002, 226) and chosen by *Maclean's* as one of twenty-five "Canadians who inspired the world" (see Granatstein and Hillmer 2000), has been one of the best-known ambassadors for Canada, and her famous red-haired heroine, Anne, is popular in countries such as Poland, Portugal, Taiwan, and Japan. Rosemary Ross Johnston has remarked that, "to most Australian girls, Canadian literature would mean Anne" (1997, 24), and Gabriella Åhmansson writes, "I yet have to meet a Swede who isn't at least vaguely familiar with *Anne of Green Gables*. ... [F]or almost 90 years it simply has not been possible to grow up female in Sweden and not at least hear of Montgomery's books" (1994, 14). Written in 1908, *Anne of Green Gables* was translated into Swedish in 1909, into Dutch in 1910, and into Polish in 1912. Six years later Norwegian and Danish translations followed, then a Finnish version appeared, and subsequently it was translated into French, Japanese, Portuguese, Icelandic, Hebrew, Spanish, Korean, Turkish, and Italian. However, it did not find its way to Germany until 1986, almost eighty years after its initial publication. It was not even translated after World War II, when there was a tremendous demand for international children's literature, nor was it translated in the wake of the astounding success of Astrid Lindgren, who proclaimed not only that *Anne of Green Gables* is one of her favourite books but also that her immortal heroine Pippi Longstocking owes her red hair, braids, freckles, and other characteristics to Anne. Although a huge number of girls' stories were imported from the United States, Britain, France, and Sweden, according to the records of Montgomery's heirs in Toronto, no inquiry was made about a possible translation of *Anne* into German before the mid-1980s.

Although the reasons for this late reception cannot be fully explored here, it is apparent that *Anne of Green Gables* simply did not represent what German publishers were looking for when importing Canadian literature. At least three aspects are of central relevance: the novel's setting; its focus on family, community life, and domesticity; and its matriarchal, female social arrangement, all of which collided with traditional German images of Canada. As for the setting, the novel is set among the green, untroubled pastures, still waters, and rolling farmlands of Prince Edward Island (see Fiamengo 2002, 237). It depicts small-town life with well-defined borders, an idealized image of peace and seclusion. The landscape is mild, gentle, tame, and sunny, and the land has been lovingly cultivated into a park or garden. Canada is presented as a pastoral, picturesque, idyllic, and "feminized" place where old-fashioned values reign. While Johnston argues that Montgomery's depiction of Prince Edward Island represents Canada in the world, that it is the one place which, from the perspective of other nations, is "significantly Canada" (1997, 24), this certainly cannot be claimed for the German reception. Images of Canada as a wilderness for men did not allow for this version of a female garden or enchanted park. As a 1999 travel guide to eastern Canada warns its readers, "German fans of Canada will not find the 'great freedom' here, as Prince Edward Island is too small and too rural" (Helmhausen 1999, 149).

That *Anne of Green Gables* was finally translated in 1986 was due only to the German screening of Kevin Sullivan's world-famous film adaptation. Loewe, the publisher, counted on good sales following the TV screening. It instructed the translator, Irmela Erckenbrecht, to abridge the original by twenty percent and to let her translation be guided by the film, actually putting the German synchronization scripts at her disposal (personal correspondence, 16 May 2003). The translation fate of this Canadian classic attests to the decisive influence that other media can have on literary translations as well as to the extreme liberties taken when translating for children.[20] What was shown on TV had to appear in the book; everything else was superfluous. Hence, not only are three chapters missing in the only German version of *Anne,* but also, with the focus on the action, most of the descriptions of nature and landscape are left out; the sights, sounds, smells, and textures of Prince Edward Island are expunged; the sense of place, which for many is the soul of this book, is diminished. In addition, national identifiers such as Marilla's famous "Give me a native born at least ... a born Canadian" were simply cut out. Small wonder that the novel was never perceived as Canadian, and although 800,000 copies were sold in Germany Montgomery is still not well known there. In the publisher's promotional material, the Canadian setting is hardly mentioned; some reviews claim that Anne is from the United States, and there is even some gender confusion surrounding the author in literary encyclopedias that state, "L. M. Montgomery became famous for his

---

20. For an elaboration on the peripheral position of children's literature within the literary polysystem, which allows the translator of children's literature great liberties, see Shavit (1986, 111–32).

*Anne of Green Gables"* (Bravo-Villasante 1977, 121). This ignorance or deliberate erasure of distinctive cultural markers may well reflect the changed translation and marketing strategies in the mid-1980s.

## THE 1980s: CHANGES IN SOURCE AND TARGET CULTURES

By the time L. M. Montgomery was finally published in Germany, the strategies and selection principles determining the translation of Canadian children's literature were undergoing radical changes due to developments in both source and target cultures. The mid-1970s had seen the emergence of a distinctly Canadian children's literature, following the rise of Canadian nationalism and the maturing of the country into a postcolonial phase. In a manner similar to the development of Australian children's literature in the 1950s or Irish children's literature in the 1980s, Canada experienced a sudden explosion in publishing for children due to institutional and economic improvements and, most importantly, government support of the arts, which saw children's books as an integral and significant part of the overall cultural enterprise. As publishing grants and financial assistance fostered the establishment of small presses and specifically children's book publishers, there was an unprecedented surge in production that was now profitable even for a comparatively small population and despite vast distances. Furthermore, an "infrastructure" for children's literature developed, with the opening of the Children's Book Centre in Toronto, the appointment of a children's literature librarian at the National Library in 1976, and the establishment of various prizes, including the Governor General's Literary Award for Children's Literature in 1975. The same year saw the launching of the major literary journal *Canadian Children's Literature / Littérature canadienne pour la jeunesse,* attesting to growing academic interest in the field. The participation of Canadian publishers, editors, writers, and illustrators in international book fairs soon earned Canadian children's literature "a high level of recognition and respect in the international world of publishing" (Jobe 1987, 7). Invaluable personal contacts developed between publishers at the international book fairs held in Frankfurt and, most importantly, in Bologna, which the first sizable Canadian contingent attended in 1978, assisted by the Department of External Affairs. Prior to that point, only "a couple of insightful publishers—May Cutler from Tundra Books and Anne Millyard of Annick Press—had realized the importance of having their books represented" (Jobe 1987, 7). In 1986, forty-seven Canadian publishers participated in the Fiera del Libro per Ragazzi (Bologna Children's Book Fair).

As a result of these developments, the number of translations from Canada has increased rapidly over the past two decades. More than half of the 150 Canadian authors translated into German were translated in the 1990s. According to Astrid Holzamer at the Canadian Embassy in Berlin, the publication of Canadian literature in Germany increased by 760 percent over the past ten years, with children's books being one of the most productive sectors. Canadian children's literature is now received within the general context of English-language children's literature imported from Britain or the United States, whose dominant feature is that everything that sells is imported,[21] provided that it is not too culture specific. The latter point is of central relevance since the functions attributed to foreign-language children's literature imports have undergone serious revision since the mid-1970s. Didactic postwar ambitions and concepts of re-education have been abandoned, and imported children's literature is no longer instrumentalized as a vehicle for the transmission and promotion of positive hetero-images. With these ambitions becoming secondary or insignificant, the translation politics of German publishers have experienced a dramatic reorientation; while previously imported children's literature was generally of interest as a carrier of ethnocultural information, publishers now privilege stories with few or no cultural markers. Canadian authors whose work is considered too regional or culture-bound have almost no chance of entering the German children's book market. Only one of Kevin Major's excellent young adult novels (*Hold Fast*, 1978) was published in German (*Lass nicht locker*, 1982), because Newfoundland was considered too regionally specific. This fate is shared by other Newfoundland authors or books with Newfoundland settings, such as Sharon McKay's award-winning *Charlie Wilcox* or Mary C. Sheppard's wonderful coming-of-age novel *Seven for a Secret* (2001). Although eleven of Monica Hughes's science fiction and adventure stories have been translated into German, her book *My Name Is Paula Popowich!* (1983), which traces a young girl's move from Toronto to the Prairies and the subsequent discovery of her Ukrainian heritage, was not imported. Furthermore, a representative from the Oetinger publishing house, which has published five of Brian Doyle's brilliant novels in congenial translations by Sylke Hachmeister, told me that Oetinger was reluctant to publish his other novels, *Up to Low* (1982), *Easy Avenue* (1988), *Covered Bridge* (1990), and *Uncle Ronald* (1996), because the level of Canadiana in them made it too much of a "peculiar microcosm."[22] At a time when Canadian children's literature has finally become

---

21. Sixty to seventy percent of all imported children's books on the German market are translations from English.
22. For the same reason, Doyle's *Mary Ann Alice* (2001) was not imported by Oetinger. It was published, however, by Sauerländer-Verlag in 2004, translated by the renowned translator Cornelia Krutz-Arnold. Supported by a publishing grant from the Canada Council for the Arts and against the background of Doyle's success on the German market, the publication was not much of a

a vital "forum for exchange and communication regarding Canadian questions about identity" (Hoogland 1997, 41), offering insights into the complexity and heterogeneity of Canadian cultural identities, as well as sharp regional loyalties and urban experiences, the German market is no longer interested in importing and promoting such culture-specific images. Almost no historical novels (e.g., work by Suzanne Martel, Barbara Greenwood, Geoffrey Bilson, Marsha Hewitt, Bernice Thurman-Hunter, Ken Roberts, and Paul Yee), so central to the postcolonial goal of rewriting and redefining national identity, have been translated. Likewise, none of the numerous Canadian time-travel stories explicitly involved with questions of national identity—such as Janet Lunn's much acclaimed *Root Cellar* (1981), Margaret Buffie's *Who Is Francis Rain?* (1983), or Kit Pearson's *A Handful of Time* (1987)—has found its way into Germany. Of the thirty novels selected by Joyce Bainbridge and her teacher's group in 2002 for the purpose of "national identity formation" in the Canadian classroom, a mere eight have been translated into German, and of the forty-three picture books that were listed only one has crossed the cultural border.

Moreover, even if these books do find their way into Germany, their distinctive cultural markers are bleached out or simply ignored. The Canadian origin is concealed by generalized language indications, such as "translated from English" or, worse, "American English," a habit that has only recently been changed by a small number of publishers. Unlike the authors published before the 1980s, almost none of the Canadian writers of children's or teen fiction has been marketed as Canadian. There are few references to Canada in the publishers' promotional materials or the paratexts, least of all in the reviews. Although the translation of Sarah Withrow's *Bat Summer*, 1998 (*Fledermaussommer*, 1999), was funded by the Canada Council, neither the book's cover nor the fourteen reviews that I found disclose the Canadian setting, let alone that of Toronto. Only one reviewer mentions that the author is Canadian, while two identify her home as the United States and England respectively. Although setting is absolutely central to all of Brian Doyle's books, reviewers often do not refer to it, and if they do they dwell on traditional images with exotic attributes, emphasizing, for instance, Ottawa's harsh climate and placing it in "northern Canada" (Wenke 1999, 20). Obviously, images of Canada that depart from the traditional stereotypes are being ignored in the reception process, while those that cater to the long-accepted hetero-images are underlined and intensified. The case of Tim Wynne-Jones clearly demonstrates these ambiguities. The marketing and reviews of his books alternately employ exoticizing and levelling-out strategies. The Canadian settings

---

risk. In 2003, Oetinger finally dared to put out Doyle's *Hey Dad* (*Der Sommer als ich dreizehn war*), twenty-five years after the original was published.

of his young adult novels *Stephen Fair*, 1998 (*Ausgeträumt*, 2001), and *The Boy in the Burning House*, 2000 (*Brandspuren*, 2001), are hardly mentioned in the reviews. On the other hand, the reviews of his teen novel *The Maestro*, 1995 (*Flucht in die Wälder*, 1999), indulge in stereotypical diction and imagery, emphasizing the "loneliness and seclusion" of the "very exotic Canadian setting," "the adventurous quest," and the author's own residence "in the woods." In her critique in the prominent German children's literature journal *Eselsohr*, Annette Kliewer is so seduced by popular images of Canada that she misinterprets the nature of the novel: "The Canadian woods—pure adventure still exists here: only those who have learned to cope in the wilderness can survive"; she recommends the book for boys "in civilized Germany" (2001, 22). This might well have been written seven or eight decades ago. The translation of *The Maestro* as *Flucht in die Wälder* ("Flight into the Woods") also illustrates that there is still a reliance on manifest images to help in the promotion and contextualization of Canadian literature in Germany. Wynne-Jones's picture books, like the wonderful cooperations with artist Ken Nutt in *Zoom at Sea* and *Zoom Away*, have not been translated despite the author's popularity.

## PICTURE BOOKS

Picture books present a case in point for the changing importation strategies over the years. In the 1970s, at a time when literary imports were still considered mediators of cultural information, three picture books by William Kurelek, *A Prairie Boy's Winter*, *A Prairie Boy's Summer*,[23] and *Lumberjack*, were published in German. In 1976, Jungbrunnen, an Austrian publishing house that has been very active in importing Canadian titles, published Ann Blades's *Mary of Mile Eighteen*, 1971 (*Mary von km 18*, 1976), and in the early 1980s Carlsen imported Blades and Betty Waterton's *Petranella*, 1980 (*Petranella*, 1982), and *A Salmon for Simon*, 1978 (*Ein Lachs für Simon*, 1984). All these picture books cater to the stereotypical German images of Canada as an exotic, vast, rural, even premodern place: the rugged, untamed northern wilderness and extreme climate of *Mary of Mile Eighteen*, Simon's remote island on the Canadian West Coast, and the isolation of the lumber camps in Kurelek's *Lumberjack* support this reading. In *Petranella*, a little girl and her parents leave an ugly, unnamed industrial city in Eastern Europe to emigrate to Canada, where they camp in the woods, listen to the owls and

---

23. *A Prairie Boy's Winter* and *A Prairie Boy's Summer*, phenomenal publishing successes for Tundra, came out with a preface by well-known German author Peter Härtling in one abridged volume, entitled *Die Krähen nehmen den Sommer mit* ("The Crows Are Taking the Summer with Them"; see Kurelek 1979). For the translation, the norms and child images of the target culture came into play, and scenes considered unsuitable for children were cut out. As a consequence, the work's capacity to address both children and adults was lost.

wolves at night, admire the northern lights, and finally settle the virgin land. As a result of the fact that in the German imagination these images are applied to the entire country, Waterton's original phrase "a country road in Manitoba" was translated as "somewhere in Canada." The potential alterity of these texts, however, was of little interest: references to the Ukrainian heritage of Kurelek's William (translated as "Wilhelm" in German) and to the Mennonite heritage of Blades's Mary were deleted in the translations.

Since the mid-1980s, a time when the Canadian picture book scene began to develop[24] and gradually to reflect national and regional identity, cultural diversity, and contemporary experience, picture books with Canadian settings or themes have no longer been imported into Germany. Brian Deines, Don Kilby, and Murray Kimber, who "deliver the soul of the Prairies" (Polidori 2002, 6), are not known in Germany, nor are Ron Lightburn or Dianna Bonder, who picture the splendour of the Rockies, let alone an artist such as Geoff Butler, who portrays rural Newfoundland. There is not a single Canadian city setting on the German picture book market, such as Jan Thornhill's *Wild in the City* (1995) or Ian Wallace's *Mr. Kneebone's New Digs* (1991)—a challenging text about urban poverty. Neither has the quintessentially Canadian view in picture books by Julie Lawson, Sue Ann Alderson, Jan Andrews, Peter Eyvindson, Phoebe Gilman, Jim McGuhan, or Sharon Jenning attracted the attention of the German market. No picture books are imported that portray the lives of contemporary Canadian children or deal with immigration or multiculturalism; there is nothing by Paul Yee or Ian Wallace, and although Indian Canadian Rachna Gilmore's novel *A Friend like Zilla*, which features a developmentally delayed child and is set on Prince Edward Island (again a setting never mentioned in the German reviews), was published by both Erika Klopp Verlag (1997) and Beltz und Gelberg (2001), her award-winning and much acclaimed picture books *Lights for Gita*, *Roses for Gita*, and *A Gift for Gita* (all illustrated by Alice Priestley), which deal with the adjustment of an Indian immigrant child to life in Canada, have not been translated. Neither have picture books by Native authors such as Michael Arvaarluk Kusugak, Thomas King, or Tomson Highway been imported, nor have Richard Van Camp's and George Littlechild's picture books (*A Man Called Raven*, 1997, *What's the Most Beautiful Thing You Know about Horses?*, 1998), even though Van Camp was awarded the German Youth Literature Prize. Visible alterity seems to be acceptable only in

---

24. Picture books have been the slowest genre to develop, with low production values, few authors and illustrators, little editing, art direction, or design, and prohibitive costs of production and printing (see Judith Saltman, "Final Thoughts: A Speech Given at the Elizabeth Mrazik-Cleaver Picture Book Award Ceremony, June 2003," www.ibby-canada.org/saltman.html [consulted December 2004]).

allegorical, universal form: Melanie Watt's *Leon the Chameleon* made it into German translation under the telling title *Leon ist anders*, 2001 ("Leon Is Different").

Furthermore, severe differences in the style of illustration have proven a real hindrance to the importation of Canadian picture books. In particular, the photographic realism of artists such as Ron Lightburn, Ian Wallace, Georgia Graham, and Les Tait has been deemed too North American for German publishers. Other styles have also been rejected, sometimes resulting in re-illustrations. Although the licences for Robert Munsch's world-famous *The Paper Bag Princess*, 1980 (*Die Tüten-Prinzessin*, 1987), and his more sentimental *Love You Forever*, 1986 (*Ich werde dich immer lieben*, 2000), were bought by the German publisher Lappan, the entire artwork was replaced.[25] Sheila McGraw's illustrations in *Love You Forever* were exchanged for work by Steffen Butz,[26] while the popular pictures of Michael Martchenko for *The Paper Bag Princess* were replaced with the funky artwork of Helge Nyncke, which attracts a much older audience. Asked about the reason for this unusual decision, the publisher stated in a personal communication that Martchenko's pictures were "too cartoon-like," making the book look "cheap," "like 'shopping mall literature.'" Other titles by the team Munsch and Martchenko had also been discussed, but the publisher determined that all the artwork would have to be replaced and thus decided against them. Ravensburger, however, published one of the team's collaborations, the ingenious *Jonathan Cleaned Up—Then He Heard a Sound*, 1981 (*Endstation! Alles Aussteigen!*, 1983). Picture books by Stéphane Poulin, Pierre Pratt, Gilles Tibo, Kady MacDonald Denton, Michelle Lemieux, and Marie-Louise Gay—whose *Stella* series (in German *Sophie*) is extremely popular, with more than 30,000 copies sold—have been imported on a larger scale. Many of these artists are French Canadian, and their style is considered more "European" by German publishers.

**PROMOTION/FUNDING**

Several institutions of cultural transfer have been active in promoting Canadian children's literature in German-speaking countries; however, it is doubtful whether their engagement has really made a difference to market mechanisms. Between 1989 and 2003, the Canada Council for the Arts funded twenty-one children's literature translations with its International Translation Program

---

25. Although re-illustration is common practice with fiction (including book covers), it is very unusual for the picture book genre. It is difficult to understand why someone would want to import a picture book if the artwork is of no interest.

26. The book's reputation in Canada is rather low, and the original illustrations were classified by Egoff and Saltman as "insignificant" and "as banal as the text" (1990, 151). It is, however, very popular in Germany.

Grant, almost exclusively in the field of young adult fiction.[27] While funding from the Canada Council for the Arts does make a difference in many countries, it seems to play no significant role in Germany, according to Catherine Mitchell of Tundra Books and Diane Vanderkooy of Scholastic Canada. Susan Shipton, sales and rights manager of Annick Press, states in a personal communication of 12 November 2004 that "We always make foreign publishers aware of this opportunity, but as they must apply only after the contract is signed and there is no guarantee they will receive funding, it cannot be a large factor in the decision-making process." In this context, it seems less surprising that some titles received funding that were not in need of additional promotion, titles such as *The Boy in the Burning House*, 2000 (*Brandspuren*, 2001), by Tim Wynne-Jones; *The Only Outcast*, 1998 (*Flucht nach vorn*, 2001), and *Inspite of Killerbees*, 2002 (*Zickenzoff und Killerbienen*, 2003), by Julie Johnston; and *Angel Square*, 1984 (*Der Mann mit der Maske*, 2000), *Hey Dad*, 1978 (*Der Sommer als ich dreizehn war*, 2003), and *Mary Ann Alice*, 2002 (*Mary Ann Alice*, 2004), by Brian Doyle. All of these titles were bound to sell well, with one or two other books by their authors already very successful on the German market.

Although the Canadian Embassy in Germany has focused many efforts on importing, promoting, and disseminating Canadian writing, children's literature has only recently become a central issue. In 2003, the award-winning author Kathy Kacer, supported by the Embassy, went on a reading tour in Germany to present her book *Clara's War* (2001), published in German by Ravensburger under the more explicit title *Die Kinder aus Theresienstadt*, 2003 ("The Children from Terezin"). In cooperation with the Embassy, the International Youth Library (IYL) in Munich organized a travelling exhibition in 2001, which presented a selection of 100 recent Canadian titles and was accompanied by an introductory catalogue. The IYL, which holds more than 8,000 Canadian children's books in its archival collection, has been active in the promotion of foreign children's literature for decades: "I came, saw, heard and was conquered by the excellence and many-sidedness of Canadian children's literature," said Hamish Fotheringham of the IYL in 1976 after attending the Loughborough International Summer Seminar in Toronto. Fotheringham had hoped to have Dennis Lee's poetry translated into

---

27. Among them are Anne Cameron's *Dreamspeaker*, 1978 (*Der Traumdeuter*, 1999), Mary Blakeslee's *Will to Win*, 1988 (*Ich werd' es schaffen!*, 1992), Welwyn Wilton Katz's *Whalesinger*, 1990 (*Wenn Wale singen*, 1995), Kit Pearson's *The Sky Is Falling*, 1989 (*Unter anderen Sternen*, 1997), Deborah Ellis's *The Breadwinner*, 2000 (*Die Sonne im Gesicht*, 2001), and William Bell's *Zack*, 1998 (*South on 61*, 2000), and *Speak to the Earth*, 1994 (*Sprich mit der Erde*, 2001), both published by Urachhaus in Stuttgart, a publisher that has also introduced Julie Johnston to the German market and has generally been very active in the translation of Canadian young adult fiction.

German by James Krüss[28] and had initially planned a larger exhibition of Canadian children's literature in Germany, but the first project was never realized, and the second had to wait another twenty-five years. In 1991, the IYL published a sixty-page "Guide to Canadian Children's and Youth Literature" (*Wegweiser durch die kanadische Kinder- und Jugendliteratur*), with introductory essays, bibliographies, contact addresses, secondary sources, and other relevant information. In 2002, the library hosted an international illustrators' forum, with Marie-Louise Gay and Anishinabe author Myrelene Ranville among the speakers. In addition, the IYL's annual exhibition and catalogue *The White Ravens* regularly recommends Canadian titles (more than sixty between 1997 and 2000) but has triggered hardly any translations as a result.

The motivation for translating English-language Canadian children's literature is complex, with market considerations being the governing factor. According to Canadian publishers of children's literature, fiction for middle readers and teens appears to be the primary category of interest for the German market, with a clear dominance of young adult fiction, represented by authors such as Tim Wynne-Jones, Julie Johnston, Diana Wieler, Martha Brooks, Deborah Ellis,[29] and more recently Susan Coyne, Karen Levine, and Bill Richardson. Following the triumphal march of the *Harry Potter* series, fantasy has become highly popular, with Kenneth Oppel's *Silverwing, Sunwing,* and *Firewing* trilogy featuring among the best-selling titles. Some books have been translated because their authors have proven very successful outside the field of children's literature: two children's books by Margaret Atwood (*Up in the Tree*, 1978, and *Princess Prunella and the Purple Peanut*, 1995) and Mordecai Richler's *Jacob Two-Two* series (1975, 1987) were imported for this reason, generally long after their original publication dates. The translation of other titles was motivated by the target culture's need to cover certain topics as compensation for underrepresented or missing themes and genres. Ronald Lee's *Goddam Gypsy*, 1971 (*Verdammter Zigeuner*, 1980), Marlene Nourbese Philip's *Harriet's Daughter*, 1988 (*Harriet und schwarz wie ich*, 1993), and William Bell's *Zack*, 1998 (*South on 61*, 2000), are good examples. All

---

28. "I plan as soon as the opportunity presents itself to bring these poems to the notice of James Kruss [sic], the author of *My Great-Grandfather and I*. Kruss [sic] is the only German poet I know who shares the same wavelength as Dennis Lee and would be his ideal translator" (Fotheringham 1976, 5). However, except for Sheree Fitch's *If You Could Wear My Sneakers: A Book about Children's Rights* (*Wärst du mal ich und ich mal du*, 1999), no English Canadian children's poetry has been translated.

29. While Jungbrunnen has recently published two of Deborah Ellis's teen novels, *The Breadwinner*, 2000 (*Die Sonne im Gesicht*, 2001), and its follow-up, *Parvana's Journey*, 2002 (*Allein nach Mazar-e Sharif*, 2003), both set in war-shattered Afghanistan, her award-winning novel *Looking for X* (1999), set in downtown Toronto, did not make it into German translation.

these young adult novels focus on intercultural conflicts—a topic long lacking in quality on the German market and thus covered by imports from North America and Britain. Such texts, however, are perceived as universal treatments of their themes; whether they are set in New York, London, or Toronto has been utterly irrelevant to their reception in Germany.

## CONCLUSION

Authors such as Monica Hughes, Jean Little, Julie Johnston, William Bell, Kenneth Oppel, Brian Doyle, Iain Lawrence, Polly Horvath, and many others have done very well on the German market. They and their books, however, are not perceived as originating in a Canadian context—neither are they marketed as Canadian, nor do most reviews mention their Canadian origin, and most of the publishers that I talked to did not even recall that the authors they publish are actually Canadian. Consequently, Canada now belongs both to the familiar and to the exotic realms in the German children's book market. While Canadian children's literature is currently perceived as culturally similar to its German counterpart, the image of Canada is still firmly rooted in the context of exotic wilderness.

Although there is much Canadian children's literature in German translation today, the image of Canada in German children's literature does not derive from these recent imports. Distinctive cultural features are erased, ignored, or overlooked. Most young readers in Germany have no idea that some of their favourite books, particularly those that focus on modern urban themes or fantasy scenarios, have been written by Canadians. Although Catherine Mitchell of Tundra Books says that it might well be "the grand compliment" that these authors have such a universal appeal and are not perceived as Canadian, this ignorance of a country's postcolonial endeavours is symptomatic of the mechanisms of a global village dominated by the mass market. Enriching as the translations are for the German book market, they have neither deepened cross-cultural knowledge nor challenged the perennial images of Canada or promoted new images. Thus, the image of Canada remains basically unaltered, still dominated by the "freedom and adventure" ideology of certain German authors, who never fail to explicitly mark their territory as Canadian. Young male protagonists still roam the Canadian wilderness in German juvenile novels, for example in Wolfgang Bittner's *Die Fährte des grauen Bären*, 1991 ("The Trail of the Grey Bear"), or in *Wo die Berge namenlos sind*, 1989 ("Where the Mountains Have No Names"), and although Canada now features in genres other than adventure novels these, too, perpetuate the old images. In a recent picture book called *Gute Reise, kleiner Bär*, 1999 ("Farewell Little Bear"), a teddy bear travels to the place "where all bears live happily"—that is, Canada—but finds it too wild, too cold, and too dangerous for his taste. The picture book *Der Geburtstagsbär,* 1996 ("The Birthday Bear"), begins with the sentence "This story is set in Canada. In Canada, there are mountains, rivers, Indians and bears." Numerous other examples could be cited to confirm that this discourse of exoticism did not undergo any serious changes in the twentieth century. While Canadian writers for children are involved in "a lengthy mapping process" (Wynne-Jones 1997, 20), while "change" is the single most common phenomenon in Canadian culture (Jobe 1997, 29), and while the "country is constantly inventing itself as it goes along" (Ellis 1997, 21), this dynamic nature contrasts sharply with the largely static German images of Canada. None of the German children's authors writing today presents a modern or urban version of Canada; none presents the complexity and diversity of Canadian culture, its distinct regionalism, multiculturalism, or diverse ethnic landscapes. Where recent Canadian children's authors who have made it into German translation could present alternative images of Canada, their Canadian setting and content largely go unrecognized, and the German hetero-images remain the same—a demonstration of the degree to which the popular concept of intercultural understanding through translations remains an idealistic construct.

**REFERENCES**

Åhmansson, Gabriella. "Mayflowers Grow in Sweden too: L. M. Montgomery, Astrid Lindgren and the Swedish Literary Consciousness." In *Harvesting Thistles: The Textual Garden of L. M. Montgomery,* ed. Mary Henley Rubio. Guelph: Canadian Children's Press, 1994. 14–22.

Allen, Deborah A. "The Reception and Perception of North America's Indigenous Peoples in Germany, 1871–1945: A Study with Specific Reference to the North American Indian Image" (PhD diss., University of Constance, 2004).

Bainbridge, Joyce M. "The Role of Canadian Children's Literature in National Identity Formation." *English Quarterly* 34.3/4 (2002): 66–74.

Belaney, Archibald Stansfeld. *The Adventures of Sajo and Her Beaver People.* Toronto: Macmillan, 1935.

———. *Sajo und ihre Biber,* transl. K. Freinthal. Stuttgart: Franckh, 1938.

Black, Joseph, and J. L. Black. "Canada in the Soviet Mirror: English-Canadian Literature in Soviet Translation." *Journal of Canadian Studies* 30.2 (1995): 5–18.

Bravo-Villasante, Carmen. *Weltgeschichte der Kinder- und Jugendliteratur: Versuch einer Gesamtdarstellung,* transl. Hiltrud Minwegen. Hannover: Schroedel, 1977.

Dyserinck, Hugo. *Komparatistik: Eine Einführung.* 3rd ed. Bonn: Bouvier, 1991.

Egoff, Sheila, and Judith Saltman. *The New Republic of Childhood: A Critical Guide to Canadian Children's Literature in English.* Toronto: Oxford University Press, 1990.

Ellis, Sarah. Statement in "What's Canadian about Canadian Children's Literature? A Compendium of Answers to the Question." *Canadian Children's Literature* 87 (1997): 21.

Fiamengo, Janice. "Towards a Theory of the Popular Landscape in *Anne of Green Gables*." In *Making Avonlea: L. M. Montgomery and Popular Culture*, ed. Irene Gammel. Toronto: University of Toronto Press, 2002. 225–37.
Fotheringham, Hamish. "Canadian Literature Seen Through an International Eye." In *Review* (Winter 1976): 5–7.
Granatstein, J., and N. Hillmer. "Canadians Who Inspired the World." *Maclean's*, 4 September 2000, 30–31.
Groß, Konrad. "North of Canada—Northern Canada: The North in 19th Century Juvenile Fiction." *Zeitschrift für Kanada-Studien* 28 (1995): 19–32.
Haible, Barbara. *Indianer im Dienste der NS-Ideologie: Untersuchungen zur Funktion von Jugendbüchern über nordamerikanische Indianer im Nationalsozialismus*. Hamburg: Kovac, 1998.
Hambleton, Jack. *Flieger überm Busch* [*Forest Ranger*]. Stuttgart: Thienemann, 1955.
Helmhausen, Ole. *Ostkanada entdecken & erleben*. Ostfildern: Mairs Geographischer Verlag, 1999.
Hoogland, Cornelia. "Constellations of Identity in Canadian Young Adult Novels." *Canadian Children's Literature* 86 (1997): 27–42.
Jobe, Ron. "The Effect of the International Children's Book Industry on Canadian Publishing Endeavours for Children and Young People." *Canadian Children's Literature* 47 (1987): 7–11.
———. Statement in "What's Canadian about Canadian Children's Literature? A Compendium of Answers to the Question." *Canadian Children's Literature* 87 (1997): 29.
Johnston, Rosemary Ross. Statement in "What's Canadian about Canadian Children's Literature? A Compendium of Answers to the Question." *Canadian Children's Literature* 87 (1997): 24.
Kliewer, Anette. "Sohn kämpft gegen Vater." *Eselsohr* 3 (2001): 22.
Kraus, Robert. *Freibeuter unter dem Nordlicht*. Bremen: Burmester, 1935.
Kurelek, William. *Die Krähen nehmen den Sommer mit* ["The Crows are Taking the Summer with Them"], trans. Fritz Deppert. Ravensburg: Maier, 1979.
Lokatis, Siegfried, et al. *Jedes Buch ein Abenteuer: Zensur-System und literarische Öffentlichkeiten in der DDR bis Ende der sechziger Jahre*. Berlin: Akademie-Verlag, 1997.
Lutz, Hartmut. "Receptions of Indigenous Canadian Literature in Germany." In *Reflections of Canada: The Reception of Canadian Literature in Germany*, ed. Martin Kuester and Andrea Wolff. Marburg: Universitätsbibliothek, 2000. 36–63.
McGillis, Rod. "Canada." In *International Companion Encyclopedia of Children's Literature*, ed. Peter Hunt. London: Routledge, 1996. 333–43.
Polidori, Josiane. "Canadian Children's Literature: Multi-faceted Landscape." In *Children's Books from Canada: A Recent Selection*. Munich: International Youth Library, 2002. 5–6.
Prišvin, Michael. *Seraja Sova*. 1954.
Rubio, Mary. "Children's Literature (Overview)." In *Encyclopedia of Post-colonial Literatures in English*, ed. Eugene Benson. Vol. 1. London: Routledge, 1994. 228–30.
Seifert, Martina. *Ent-Fernungen: Fremdwahrnehmung und Kulturtransfer in der deutsch-sprachigen Kinder- und Jugendliteratur seit 1945*. Vol. 2, *Kulturtransfer: Studien zur Repräsentanz einzelner Herkunftsliteraturen*, with Gina Weinkauff. Munich: iudicium, 2006.
———. "The Image Trap: The Translation of English-Canadian Children's Literature into German." In *Children's Literature Global and Local: Social and Aesthetic Perspectives*,

ed. Emer O'Sullivan, Kimberley Reynolds, and Rolf Romøren. Oslo: Novus Press, 2005. 227–39.

Shavit, Zohar. *Poetics of Children's Literature.* Athens, Georgia: University of Georgia Press, 1986.

Soenen, Johan. "Imagology and Translation." In *Multiculturalism: Identity and Otherness,* ed. Nedret Kuran Burçoglu. Istanbul: Bogaziçi University Press, 1997. 125–38.

———. "Imagology in the Framework of Translation Studies." In *Bella: Essays on Translation, Imagology and Literature,* ed. Johan Soenen. Antwerp: Linguistica Antverpiensia, 1995. 17–22.

Sturge, Kate. *"The Alien Within": Translation into German During the Nazi Regime.* Munich: iudicium, 2004.

von Kieseritzky, Helene. *Englische Tierdichtung: Eine Untersuchung über Rudyard Kipling, Charles G. D. Roberts und Ernest Thompson Seton.* (University Diss., Jena, 1935).

Wenke, Gabriela. "Ein toter Gangster in Ottawa: 'Halbblut' Chip wird Zeuge eines Mordes." *Eselsohr* 11 (1999): 20.

Wynne-Jones, Tim. Statement in "What's Canadian about Canadian Children's Literature? A Compendium of Answers to the Question." *Canadian Children's Literature* 87 (1997): 19–20.

# French, Female, and Foreign: French Canadian Children's Literature in German Translation

*Nikola von Merveldt*
*Université de Montréal*

## A PROMISING START

Once upon a time, German translations of French Canadian children's literature were off to a promising start: between 1947 and the late 1950s, more than twenty little books featuring gingerbread men, magic cauldrons, strawberry fairies, and noble savages were translated from French into German and illustrated with naive, brightly coloured pictures. Lucille Desparois, lovingly called "Tante Lucille" by her admiring audience, was the author of these modern fairy tales that blend literary techniques from the moral tale with oral storytelling traditions of French Canadian folklore (Lepage 2000, 220–25). Tante Lucille told her stories on Radio-Canada, the French-language national radio station created in 1936 to give French Canadian culture a voice. But there were no publishers of children's books in Quebec until the 1970s (Lepage 2000, 284–85), so the stories went into print in French and Dutch in the Netherlands (published by Mulder and Zoon in the 1940s and 1950s). From there, they eventually reached the German market as well. In 1947, when Germany was a war-torn country in which a whole generation of children had grown up under Nazi dictatorship, the desire for edifying children's literature was considerable. With their mix of morals and adventure, Tante Lucille's stories perfectly fit this demand, and Mulder, a German branch of Mulder and Zoon located in Emmerich am Rhein on the German-Dutch border, brought out a whole series. Since the books were published anonymously, however, German children never knew that they were reading stories by a French Canadian author. Specific references to Quebec culture had acquired universal or exotic qualities: the local idiom had disappeared, specific place names had lost their reference, and the Iroquois Indian simply became the stereotype of the good savage. In German translation, Tante Lucille's specifically French Canadian tales turned into archetypal narratives transporting Christian moral values.

This first rendezvous manqué between French Canadian and German children's literature set the tone for further encounters. They can be summarized under a number of points: first, encounters usually take place through an intermediary—in the case mentioned above, it was a Dutch publisher, and later it was English-speaking Canada and the international book fairs of Frankfurt and Bologna; second, encounters are shaped by both Quebec's and the importing country's historical and literary situations, with the German translations showing much less interest in specifically French Canadian culture or setting than in universal themes such as first love, friendship, and coming of age; third, most French Canadian authors and illustrators published in German are female—as are most of the protagonists whom they create; and fourth, the Quebec origins of the artists are not always evident.

## QUÉBÉCITÉ

Since the days of Tante Lucille, at least one thing has changed: from the late 1980s onward, Quebec children's literature stopped being imported into Germany for its Christian moral values. By that time, French Canadian literature had in fact gained a reputation for being daringly open and sincere—especially concerning sexual matters. The first French Canadian book to be translated after Tante Lucille's moral tales—some thirty years later—was thus *Venir au monde* (*Welcome to the World*; see Hébert and Labrosse 1987), a non-fiction sex education bestseller for children. The publisher, Les éditions de la courte échelle,[1] continues to sell the greatest number of titles to German publishers, all of them young adult novels featuring strong female heroines who face the difficulties of coming of age. Louise Mongeau, foreign rights director at Les éditions de la courte échelle, says that German publishers of young adult fiction appreciate the clear style of Quebec writers and their frank, non-moralizing approach to issues such as suicide, anorexia, and teenage sexuality.[2]

While the realist approach of French Canadian young adult novels seems to be their main selling point, picture books created for young children by Quebec artists are translated into German (and many other languages) mainly for their vivid illustrations and rich imagination (Sarrazin 1991). Marie-Louise Gay, Pierre Pratt,

---

1. Founded by Bertrand Gauthier as Éditions du tamanoir in 1974, the publishing house adopted its present name in 1978.
2. Thanks to Louise Mongeau for a telephone interview in April 2005.

Stéphane Poulin, and Rémy Simard are all well known in Germany and around the globe—but not necessarily as Quebec artists. The *québécité* of their work falls victim to the harsh reality of the publishing business: to make their livings as illustrators, these artists publish most of their books with Anglo-Canadian publishing houses such as Annick Press and Groundwood, both located in Toronto.[3] Whereas the Quebec market is fairly restricted—especially since the budget of school libraries has been cut—the Anglo-Canadian publishing houses offer a gateway to the huge U.S. market. Financial considerations thus play a major role in choosing to publish outside Quebec. But this strategic choice has consequences for the outside perception of these books: even though many of the texts by Gay, Pratt, Poulin, and Simard were originally written in French and published simultaneously in both French and English, German translations are generally based on the English translation, which is often an adaptation of the French original.[4]

In the case of Pratt's widely popular picture books, published in Germany by Middelhauve, a great part of the success must be attributed to the superb translations by Mirjam Pressler—again translations from the English adaptation and not from the French original. Pressler is a well-known translator of more than 200 Hebrew, Dutch, and English children's books and an author in her own right. She has been awarded numerous prizes, including the Deutsche Jugendbuchpreis, the Carl-Zuckmayer-Medal for her services to the German language, and a special award for translation. Her name functions as a seal of quality, guaranteeing the quality of both plot and tone. Thanks to her, many Hebrew and Dutch books have found their way onto German bookshelves. Whereas the Dutch and Hebrew publications are always clearly identified as to an author's nationality, this is not the case for the French Canadian picture books by Pratt. Since Pressler does not

---

3. Groundwood is part of the Douglas and McIntyre publishing group and publishes in Canada, the United States, and Latin America.
4. Marie-Louise Gay started her career as an illustrator with Quebec publisher Les éditions la courte échelle but soon moved on to publish her books simultaneously in both French (mostly with Dominique et Compagnie) and English (mostly with Stoddard and Groundwood/Douglas and McIntyre). The German translations of the successful Stella series published by Carlsen are all based on her English texts (Gay translates her English texts into French herself): *Stella, Star of the Sea* (Toronto: Groundwood, 1999), *Stella, étoile de la mer* (Saint-Lambert: Dominique et Compagnie, 1999), *Sophie und das weite Meer*, trans. Sophie Birkenstädt (Hamburg: Carlsen, 2000); *Stella, Queen of Snow* (Toronto: Douglas and McIntyre, 1999), *Stella, reine des neiges* (Saint-Lambert: Dominique et Compagnie, 2000), *Sophie und der erste Schnee*, trans. Sophie Birkenstädt (Hamburg: Carlsen, 2002); *Stella the Forest Fairy* (Toronto: Groundwood, 1999), *Stella, fée des forêts* (Saint-Lambert: Dominique et Compagnie, 2002), *Sophie und die Waldfee*, trans. Sophie Birkenstädt (Hamburg: Carlsen, 2002); *Good Night Sam* (Toronto: Groundwood, 2003), *Bonne Nuit Sacha* (Saint-Lambert: Dominique et Compagnie, 2003), *Gute Nacht, Theo*, trans. Sophie Birkenstädt (Hamburg: Carlsen, 2003).

translate from French, the German text is based on the English adaptation by David Homel. The phrase "translated from English" printed on the title page of *Dem Hut nach!, Mein Hund ist ein Elefant!*, or *Was für ein Besuch!*[5] thus inevitably situates the book within the English-speaking world despite the French spelling of the artist's name. The desire for a good German translation and marketing considerations completely erase the French Canadian origin of Pratt's books.

Yet the example of Pressler shows that a prominent public figure from the literary world (publisher, author, or translator) is often the best intermediary for otherwise neglected literature—especially if this intermediary is capable of capturing the original text's tone.[6] Harry Rowohlt's brilliant and hugely successful German translations of Philip Ardagh's Eddi-Dickens trilogy is another case in point.[7] A similar advocate for French Canadian children's literature could put this *terra incognita* on the map for young German readers and the publishing industry.

**DETOURS**

For the time being, however, the position that some French Canadian creators of children's books hold within the Anglo-Canadian publishing industry may ironically be the key to their international success. But their success is also due to the fact that images travel more easily than texts, that picture book texts are shorter and translation costs thus lower. For German publishers, English also presents less of a language barrier than French. However, the main reason for the relatively high number of sold rights may be due to the greater outreach of Anglo-Canadian publishers who are part of the international, English-speaking systems of distribution and usually have a good network of agents familiar with the various national markets.

Quebec publishers of children's literature, in contrast, have long been less concerned with exporting than with nation building. Until the late 1980s, they

---

5. Pierre Pratt, *Léon sans son chapeau / Follow That Hat!*, English adaptation by David Homel (Toronto: Annick Press, 1992), *Dem Hut nach!*, trans. (from English) Mirjam Pressler (Cologne: Middelhauve, 1994); Rémy Simard (text) and Pierre Pratt (ill.), *Mon chien est un éléphant! / My Dog Is an Elephant*, English adaptation by David Homel (Toronto: Annick Press, 1994), *Mein Hund ist ein Elefant!*, trans. (from English) Mirjam Pressler (Cologne: Middelhauve, 1995); Bénédicte Froissart (text) and Pierre Pratt (ill.), *Les fantaisies de l'oncle Henri / Uncle Henry's Dinner Guests*, English adaptation by David Homel (Toronto: Annick Press, 1990), *Was für ein Besuch!*, trans. (from English) Mirjam Pressler (Cologne: Middlehauve, 2001).
6. That is also the opinion of Hartung and Müssener (1991).
7. Philip Ardagh, *Awful End* (London: Faber, 2000), *Schlimmes Ende*, trans. Harry Rowohlt (Munich: Bertelsmann, 2003; awarded the Deutsche Jugendliteraturpreis for both text and translation); *Dreadful Acts* (London: Faber, 2001), *Furcht erregende Darbietungen*, trans. Harry Rowohlt (Munich: Bertelsmann, 2003); *Terrible Times* (London: Faber, 2002), *Schlechte Nachrichten*, trans. Harry Rowohlt (Munich: Bertelsmann, 2004).

concentrated on the project of establishing a French Canadian tradition of children's literature. Considering that generations of francophone children grew up in Canada without a literature of their own and used imported books from France, this was doubtless necessary.[8] Furthermore, provincial funding put Quebec publishers in the fortunate position of not being dependent on foreign rights sales. This independence allowed them to target the relatively small Quebec market, but it may also have isolated them to some extent—even within Canada (Poulin 2003, 99–102).

This may explain why many Quebec publications for children and young adults have reached the German market via one or more detours—and why there are comparatively few. Silke Weniger, a literary agent in Munich who represents a number of North American children's publishers and distributors, has described the "failed reception" of one such book.[9] Michèle Marineau's *La Route de Chlifa*, a young adult novel interweaving plot lines set in Lebanon during the civil war and in Quebec, found its way into her agency in English translation and via the English Canadian publisher and distributor Raincoast Books.[10] When Weniger offered this novel, winner of the prestigious Governor General's Literary Award, to German publishers, they all declined with the argument that German readers would not want to take the detour via Canada to learn about the civil war in Lebanon. A narrative technique that had served reader identification in the Canadian context thus became an obstacle to greater international distribution. Danish and Dutch readers, in contrast, seemed to have no problem with this cultural triangle.[11] But this specific case of "failed reception" reflects the more general conflict between culture-specific literature for young readers and the demands of the global market.

The detours caused by the global market can also change the character of a book so completely that original publishers hardly recognize their own products. This was the case with the German translation of *Yeux noirs* by Gilles Tibo, Quebec's most prolific children's book author, who won the 2000 Mr. Christie's Book Award for this book.[12] It is the story of a blind boy that was first published by Quebec publisher Robert Soulières with exquisite design, Braille elements, and poetic white-on-black illustrations by Jean Bernèche. The international publishing group North-South acquired the rights for the text, transformed the black-and-white paperback

---

8. See the roundtable discussion by Marie-Louise Gay, Robert Soulières, and Christiane Duchesne, as transcribed by Landreville (2004).
9. I wish to thank Silke Weniger for this interview in July 2004.
10. Michèle Marineau, *Route de Chlifa* (Montréal: Les éditions Québec/Amérique, 1992). The English translation by Susan Ouriou, *Road to Chlifa*, was published by Red Deer Press in 1992.
11. Dutch edition: Michèle Marineau, *De weg naar Chlifa* (Haarlem: Gottmer, 1998), trans. from the French original. Danish edition: Michèle Marineau, *Vejen til Schlifa* (Århus: Modtryk, 1996), trans. from the English translation.
12. Gilles Tibo (text) and Jean Bernèche (ill.), *Yeux noirs* (Saint-Lambert: Éditions Soulières, 1999).

novel for beginning readers into a picture book with colourful illustrations by French artist Zaü, and launched the book on the French and German market.[13] This cultural transfer resulted in a very different product. The subtlety and magic of the mini-novel gave way to a far more marketable picture book.

**GOING INTERNATIONAL**

Changes such as the globalization of children's literature, a steadily increasing number of French Canadian titles,[14] and a growing desire in Quebec to open up to the world have changed the situation over the past twenty years. Quebec publishing houses have developed foreign rights sections, started to attend the international book fairs in Frankfurt and Bologna in increasing numbers,[15] and begun to establish international networks. Federal and provincial government funding plays a major role in this growing globalization and reflects a certain institutionalization of cultural exports. Several agencies, programs, and committees have been set up to support publishers in their global enterprise. Québec Édition is a committee of the Association nationale des éditeurs de livre (ANEL), dedicated to the export and promotion of French Canadian literature abroad. It organizes trade missions and collective booths at major book fairs to stimulate international exchange. These activities are made possible through the support of the Société de développement des entreprises culturelles (SODEC), the Association pour l'exportation du livre canadien (AELC), and le Conseil des arts du Canada/the Canada Council for the Arts.

In 1999, SODEC started a program with an annual budget of CDN $100,000 to fund translations of Quebec literature. Many publishers use these funds to translate excerpts of works that they wish to present to foreign publishers at international fairs and elsewhere. These provincial programs as well as the Canada Council for the Arts translation grants are major selling points since they assist the publishing houses in acquiring foreign rights by financing the translation. With government funding, publishers are more willing to take the risk of publishing a translation. National awards such as the Governor General's Literary Award or Mr. Christie's Book Award are also being recognized by international publishers who use them to promote the translations.

---

13. Gilles Tibo (text) and Zaü (ill.), *Schwarze Augen,* trans. Geraldine Elschner and Gerda Wurzenberger (Gassau: Nord-Süd, 2005). In her online review, German critic Martina Meier notes that Tibo is one of the most widely read "Canadian" authors. See http://rezensionen.literaturwelt.de/content/buch/t/t_tibo_gilles_schwarze_augen_mame_15382.html [consulted 19 August 2005].

14. In 2000, 678 titles for children and young adults were published in Quebec; see Léger and Fournier (2002, 4).

15. Thanks to Pierre Lévesque of Québec Édition for having supplied statistics of participation in book fairs for 2002–2004.

In general, however, Quebec publishers of children's books have not been the most active players on the international scene, although there are, as always, notable exceptions. Les éditions des 400 coups, a publishing house that produces picture books, comics, and coffee table books and was founded in Montreal in 1994, bridged the ocean by establishing itself in France. It opened an office in Ivry-sur-Seine in 1996, and its books are now distributed in France by Le Seuil, which is also the gateway to the German publishing market. This is how two books written by French author Thierry Lenain and illustrated by Quebec artist Stéphane Poulin found their way onto German bookshelves as titles from France: *Kein Kuss für Tante Marotte!* and *Kleiner Zizi*.[16] Two previous picture books by Poulin had been translated from English into German thanks to the efforts of Annick Press and its literary agent: *Benjamin und die Wunderkissen* and *Mutters Lieblinge*.[17] In Germany, Poulin is thus marketed as Anglo-Canadian or as French but never as the French Canadian he really is.

In 2004, Les éditions de la courte échelle, the first publishing house for children in Quebec and the first to go international, received the SODEC excellence award for exportation.[18] Foreign rights sales make up fifteen to twenty percent of its total sales. But out of the 240 books translated into eighteen different languages, only six have been translated into German (all with funding from the Canada Council for the Arts and the mention "translated from Canadian French"), and some of them are already out of print.[19] La courte échelle sells many more titles to Spain or Korea than to Germany, for example.

---

16. Thierry Lenain, *Touche pas à mon corps, Tatie Jacotte!* (Laval: Les 400 coups, 1999), *Kein Kuss für Tante Marotte!*, trans. Michaela Kolodziejcok (Berlin: Altberliner Verlag, 2000); *Petit Zizi* (Laval: Les 400 coups, 1997), *Kleiner Zizi*, trans. Michaela Kolodziejcok (Berlin: Altberliner, 1999/2000).

17. Stéphane Poulin, *Benjamin et la saga des oreillers* (Toronto: Annick Press, 1989), *Benjamin and the Pillow Saga* (Toronto: Annick Press, 1989), *Benjamin und die Wunderkissen*, trans. Hildegard Krahé (Oldenburg: Lappan, 1990); Stéphane Poulin, *Les amours de ma mère: Contes et mensonges de mon enfance* (Toronto: Annick Press, 1990), *My Mother's Loves: Stories and Lies from my Childhood* (Toronto: Annick Press, 1990), *Mutters Lieblinge: Geschichten und Lügen aus meiner Kindheit*, trans. Hildegard Krahé (Oldenburg: Lappan, 1991).

18. "Prix d'excellence à l'exportation de la SODEC," *Le Devoir*, 20–21 November 2004, H4.

19. Out of print are Marie-Francine Hébert, *Venir au monde* (see footnote 1); Carole Fréchette, *Do pour Dolores* (Montréal: Les éditions de la courte échelle, 1999), *Do wie Dolores*, trans. Rosemarie Griebel-Kruip (Düsseldorf: Patmos, 2000); Charlotte Gingras, *Été avec Jade* (Montréal: Les éditions de la courte échelle, 1999), *Ein Sommer mit Jade*, trans. Sabine Demmerle-Conté (Stuttgart: Urachhaus, 2003); Charlotte Gingras, *La liberté? Connais pas* (Montréal: Les éditions de la courte échelle, 1998), *Freiheit nimmt man sich*, trans. Rosemarie Griebel-Kruip (Düsseldorf: Patmos, 2001). The mediocre German translations of the young adult novels surely have added to their lack of success. The only teenage novel to be successful on the German market is Sylvie Desrosiers, *Le long silence* (Montréal: Les éditions de la courte échelle, 1996), *Das lange Schweigen*, trans. Brigitte Uppenbrink (Düsseldorf: Patmos, 1999; paperback edition Munich: Bertelsmann, 2002).

What could be the reasons for this limited number of German translations? One reason is certainly that the German market for children's literature is already quite satiated. German publishers have commitments to their own authors before they begin to acquire foreign rights. There is a strong German-language production, and books for children or young adults are translated largely from English and Scandinavian languages. Furthermore, within the context of EU enlargement and the construction of a new European identity, the trend is to look east rather than west. Another factor may well be a lack of French-language skills on the German side and a lack of interest in the francophone world in general. Finally, there is a marked difference in publishing conventions in Quebec and German-speaking countries: whereas series of forty- or sixty-page paperback mini-novels with very short chapters aimed at young readers sell well in Quebec, novels in Germany, Switzerland, and Austria tend to be longer, hardback, and of higher production value. Narrative structures also tend to be more complex in German children's literature.[20]

The German edition of Yves Beauchemin's *Antoine et Alfred,* a novel for young readers, serves to illustrate the different publishing conventions (Beauchemin 1992). The original French text was published by Les éditions Québec / Amérique in the conventional small paperback format with a cartoon-like cover illustration of a boy and an anthropomorphic rat protagonist. The German edition, published by Erika Klopp Verlag, comes in a larger hardcover format with an elaborate cover illustration spreading all the way across the back cover. It shows a boy and a rather lifelike rat standing on the branch of a tree and looking down at the street life of a distinctly European town. Despite this visual change in setting, the Canadian origin of the text is not denied. In a translator's note on the opening page of the book, Tilde Michels mentions that Beauchemin, "an author from Canada," wrote this story for a little boy who was very ill. But the editor and translator adapt Beauchemin's text to German publishing and reading conventions: the chapter division is changed to create a slower rhythm, the typeface is slightly smaller than the beginner's reading font of the French original, and the margins are somewhat larger. Most notably, the tone is gently altered, and Beauchemin's slapstick humour is reduced. This change in tone may be due to the rat's sex change. Whereas the rat is called Alfred in Beauchemin's original text (in accordance with the male gender of the word *rat* in French), the German translator apparently thought that the feminine gender of German *Ratte* called for a female name, Albertine.

Basic knowledge of the German children's book market as well as of German culture in general is an important factor in selling foreign rights to German-

---

20. See the comparison of Franco- and Anglo-Canadian literature by Marineau (2002).

speaking publishers. Agents know the major trends and each publisher's profile and can specifically target potential buyers. Michèle Lemieux's success on the German market, for instance, can be largely attributed to her intimate knowledge of the German publishing scene. Born and trained in Quebec, Lemieux went to Germany to study illustration. She then decided to become her own agent and present her work to selected publishers at the book fairs in Bologna and Frankfurt. This is how her award-winning international bestseller *Gewitternacht* (*Stormy Night*) first went into print in Germany, published by Beltz and Gelberg in 1996.[21] Her German-language skills also allow her to go on promotional tours in Germany and to participate in events such as the Berlin Children's Festival at the 2004 Berlinale, where she was awarded the Gläserner Bär ("Glass Bear") for her animated version of *Stormy Night* (Zerpner 2004). But her case remains an exception.

It must also be noted that Lemieux's work is not only popular in Germany but also enjoys general international success. Lemieux is celebrated as an artist from Canada but not as a typically Canadian one. Her work is universal in its outlook; it does not try to promote *québécité,* nor is it specifically geared to a Quebec audience. This does not mean that cultural translation is no longer necessary. Lemieux remembers offering her book proposal *Was hört der Bär (What's That Noise?)* to the publishing house Otto Maier in Ravensburg. The German publisher liked the idea of the friendly bear asking various animals what that strange noise could be, but there was one problematic detail: Lemieux had chosen an imposing eagle as one of the bear's interlocutors. To German eyes, this eagle was an uncomfortable reference to their heraldic animal, which did not seem to fit into a picture book for young children. The eagle was changed into an owl, and the book, originally published in 1984, is still selling in Germany after more than twenty years.[22]

Cultural boundaries or stereotypes play an important role in the export and import of children's and young adult books. In fact, a further reason for the limited success of French Canadian children's literature in German may simply be that Quebec writing for children does not fit the mould of the German image

---

21. Michèle Lemieux, *Gewitternacht* (Weinheim: Beltz Verlag, 1996). The French edition, *Nuit d'orage,* was published by the French publisher Seuil jeunesse in 1998, the English edition by Kids Can Press, Toronto, in 1999.

22. Michèle Lemieux (text and ill.), *What's That Noise?* (Toronto: Kids Can Press, 1989), *Was hört der Bär?,* trans. Cris Baisch (Ravensburg: Otto Maier, 1984); Michèle Lemieux (text and ill.), *Quel est ce bruit?,* trans. Christiane Duchesne (Richmond Hill, ON: Scholastic Canada, 1990). A previous French translation by Jenny Ladoix was published by Gallimard in 1986. Lemieux shared this information at the roundtable discussion "L'audace des créateurs en littérature pour la jeunesse" at the Goethe-Institute, Montreal, 17 May 2005.

of Canada. In this volume, Martina Seifert shows that Germans seem to have a very clear-cut image of what Canada ought to be:

> [I]t can be said that until the 1980s virtually no text that presented Canada as anything other than a vast northern wilderness inhabited by animals, Natives, and a few white male adolescents qualified for translation, and the titles selected for translation in the context of existing hetero-images helped to perpetuate such conceptual constructs. (228)

This image has largely determined the choice of Anglo-Canadian works for children to be translated into German. Contemporary Quebec literature, in contrast, is largely "feminine," urban, and resolutely modern.

Take, for instance, Cassiopée, the heroine of Michèle Marineau's *Cassiopée: L'été polonais* ("Cassiopée: The Polish Summer"), who runs away from her home in Montreal to stay with Polish friends in New York (Marineau 1988). In the sequel, *L'été des baleines* ("The Summer of the Whales"), the romantic landscape of the Quebec coastline is transformed into an ironic backdrop to a disillusioning break-up with her first love, and Cassiopée is happy to return to her urban surroundings and leftist boyfriend (Marineau 1988). Marie-Louise Gay's red-haired picture book character Stella (or "Sophie" in the German translation) overpowers her little brother Sam (alias "Theo" in German and "Sacha" in French), and the landscape she moves in is more fantastic than "Canadian"—except for the snow, of course.[23] And even if Dominique Demers's quaint character Mademoiselle Charlotte, with her pebble friend Gertrude, may seem old-fashioned, she misses no opportunity to undermine the patriarchal system in her roles as mysterious librarian, teacher, postwoman, et cetera.[24] These Quebec heroines are strikingly at odds with the German image of "Canadianness," and, not surprisingly, only Gay's picture books have been translated into German.

It is surely no coincidence that nature features prominently in three of the five young adult novels sold by Les éditions de la courte échelle to German publishers, who are still haunted by the Canadian wildlife stereotype. Charlotte Gingras's *Été avec Jade* ("Summer with Jade") is set on a lonely island far north in the rough wilderness; in her novel *La liberté? Connais pas* ("Freedom? Don't Know That"), the encounter with a moose is a key moment in the life of the young girl protagonist;[25] and in *Do pour Dolores* ("Do for Dolores"), Carole Fréchette takes

---

23. See footnote 5.
24. Dominique Demers, *Une bien curieuse factrice* (Montréal: Les éditions Québec/Amérique, 1999); *La mystérieuse bibliothécaire* (Montréal: Les éditions Québec/Amérique, 1997); *La nouvelle maîtresse* (Boucherville: Québec/Amérique jeunesse, 1994).
25. Charlotte Gingras, *Été avec Jade* (Montréal: Les éditions de la courte échelle, 1999), *Ein Sommer*

the reader on a scenic tour of Quebec, from the Jacques-Cartier bridge across the St. Lawrence River all the way to Abitibi in the Far North (Fréchette 1999). Themes rather than literary quality seem to have determined the decision to translate these works. But since little contemporary French Canadian literature conforms to the image of masculinity and wildlife adventure, it may be perceived as non-Canadian and therefore not importable as "Canadian."

Finally, French Canadian literature is simply not French—it is French with a difference, just as it is Canadian with a difference. It is neither and both at the same time. It is a young literature full of ideas, sincerity, and vitality, ready to reach out to the world. It may be time to put Quebec on the map for German child readers—at the welcome risk of moving some mental boundaries and altering the imaginary landscape.

**OUTLOOK: "100% AUDACE"**

In 2005, UNESCO nominated Montreal the world capital of books. To celebrate this event, Communication Jeunesse, the French Canadian counterpart to the Canadian Children's Book Centre, decided to mount an exhibition of contemporary illustrations of children's literature from Quebec. To reflect the new desire of French Canadian authors, illustrators, and publishers to enter into dialogue with foreign publishers, Communication Jeunesse decided to invite one international partner to share the floor. Its choice was Germany. Communication Jeunesse collaborated with the International Youth Library in Munich, a UNESCO project, and the Goethe-Institute in Montreal, and the project was generously funded by the Quebec Ministry of Culture and Communication and the State of Bavaria Quebec Office.

The exhibition, "100% Audace—100% Audacity," showcased original artworks by twenty-six Quebec and twenty-six German illustrators and opened up interesting intercultural perspectives. It was first shown at the Musée du Château Dufresne from 2 April to 31 July 2005. Instead of reinforcing cultural stereotypes, it worked with an open concept playing on imaginative and artistic affinities as well as contrasts between the two national literatures. From Montreal, the exhibition moved to the Bibliothèque Gabrielle Roy in Quebec City (1–29 October 2005). A series of activities and visits accompanied the event.[26] Barbara Scharioth,

---

mit Jade, trans. Sabine Demmerle-Conté (Stuttgart: Urachhaus, 2003); Charlotte Gingras, La liberté? Connais pas (Montréal: Les éditions de la courte échelle, 1998), Freiheit nimmt man sich, trans. Rosemarie Griebel-Kruip (Düsseldorf: Patmos, 2001).

26. The events were also covered in the German press by Annette Zerpner. See her article "Elefant im Trollkochtopf. Früher lesen: Ein internationales Treffen von Kinderbuchautoren in Montréal," FAZ, 8 June 2005.

the director of the International Youth Library, came to Montreal in April 2005 to share her vision of international understanding through children's literature, and authors and illustrators crossed the ocean to participate in public events and professional encounters. Both the Bibliothèque Gabrielle Roy in Quebec City and the International Youth Library in Munich offer bursaries for writers, illustrators, and scholars of children's literature, and the governments of Quebec and Bavaria plan to set up an exchange program for translators.

This kind of exchange based on cultural affinities, reciprocal curiosity, personal contacts, and a strong institutional network is most promising. Quebec author and translator Michèle Marineau makes similar observations concerning the cultural transfer between French and English Canada, stating that the translation of her novels, or the Anglo-Canadian novels that she translated herself, depended more on personal contacts or chance than on official translation programs. The building of personal networks at book fairs and through exchange programs seems to be a key to success (Marineau 2004, 74–76).

It is therefore possible to close this account of the German reception of the "other" Canadian children's literature on a positive note. Even though there is only a limited record of French Canadian titles translated into German to this time, the situation may be about to change.

**REFERENCES**

Beauchemin, Yves. *Antoine et Alfred*. Montreal: Les éditions Québec/Amérique, 1992; *Andi und Albertine*, transl. Tilde Michels. Hamburg: Erika Klopp Verlag, 1995.

Fréchette, Carole. *Do pour Dolores*. Montreal: Les éditions la courte échelle, 1999; *Do wie Dolores*, transl. Rosemarie Griebel-Kruip. Düsseldorf: Patmos, 2000.

Hartung, Harald, and Helmut Müssener. "Diffusion et traduction. La littérature canadienne, *terra incognita* sur la carte littéraire. Table ronde avec Marie-Claire Blais, Paul Chamberland, Monique Daviau, Harald Hartung, Bodo Morshäuser, Michael Mundhenk, Karin Reschke, Herbert Wiesner." In *Berlin à Montréal. Littérature et métropole*, ed. Friedhelm Lach and Hans-Herbert Räkel. Montreal: VLB, 1991. 233–43.

Hébert, Marie-Francine (text), and Darcia Labrosse (ill.). *Venir au monde*. Montreal: Les éditions de la courte échelle, 1987; *Auf die Welt kommen*, transl. Peter Baumann. Oldenburg: Lappan, 1989.

Landreville, Ginette. "La Table Ronde des créateurs." *Lurelu* 26/3 (2004): 5–11.

Léger, Danielle, and Claude Fournier. *Les statistiques de l'édition au Québec 2001: Publications reçues en dépôt légal*, Quebec: Bibliothèque nationale, 2002.

Lepage, Françoise. *Histoire de la littérature pour la jeunesse. Québec et francophonies du Canada*. Orleans: Éditions David, 2000.

Marineau, Michèle. *Cassiopée: L'été polonais*. Montreal: Les éditions Québec/Amérique, 1988.

———. "Littérature québécoise et littérature candienne-anglaise. Deux mondes, deux styles." *Lurelu* 25.2 (2002): 9.

———. "Suis-je une auteure canadienne?" *Lurelu* 26.3 (2004): 74–76.

Poulin, Andrée. "La traduction des livres jeunesse: deux solitudes." *Lurelu* 25.3 (2003): 99–102.

Sarrazin, Francine. *La griffe québécoise dans l'illustration du livre pour enfants.* Montreal/Quebec: Communication-Jeunesse/Musée de la civilisation, 1991.

Zerpner, Annette. "Elefantös: Berliner Kinderliteraturfestival." *Frankfurter Allgemeine Zeitung*, 8 June 2005.

# Northern Lights in German Theatres: How Quebec Plays Come to Germany

*Andreas Jandl*
*Berlin*

This chapter[1] explores the different ways in which theatre texts from francophone Canada travel to Germany. It examines the support available from European and Canadian institutions and the roles played by agencies and publishers. A case study of the way Daniel Danis's *Le chant du Dire-Dire* travelled to Germany provides a real-life example.

## NO DIRECT CONTACT

There is no direct route to Germany for French Canadian dramatists, a situation quite unlike that of Anglo-American authors. German publishers seldom look for new authors beyond the offers made by North American agencies. The Anglo-American agencies[2] that handle promising pieces, however, usually cover the United States and English-speaking Canada; they do not deal with French Canada. In New York and Hollywood, dramatic work from Quebec is relatively unknown and therefore hardly ever offered by these agencies.

German publishers' automatic interest in work from the United States does not apply to French Canada; hardly any German publishers maintain regular contacts in Montreal, let alone a literary scout. Thus, if you are a successful writer in Montreal, you are definitely not going to be noticed by German publishing houses. Montreal has one of the most productive and most innovative theatre landscapes of the world, yet, when Daniel Danis's *Le chant du Dire-Dire* premiered at Espace Go in Montreal in 1998, very few people in Germany took note of

---

1. This chapter was translated from German by Luise von Flotow.
2. Large North American agencies such as the William Morris Agency, International Creative Management, and Creative Artists Agency as well as smaller ones such as Brett Adams, Writers and Artists, the Gerch Agency, Abram's Artists, the Joyce Ketay Agency, and the Artists Agency represent dramatic authors as well as actors, singers, set designers, et cetera.

it. This "gaze past Quebec" can undoubtedly be linked to the fact that German publishers and editors who have an interest in francophone material from beyond the boundaries of France are rare.

**ACCESS VIA FRANCE**

Because Quebec and France share the same language, the most likely route for French Canadian works to enter Germany is via France. But even within the French-German exchange, there is no "high road" for Quebec authors; Canadian authors have to share the attention of the French-speaking theatre world with their colleagues from France. Moreover, the types of plays that are successful in France do not necessarily correspond to the taste of the German public. Generally, German audiences are closer to the British in their theatre aesthetics, and British dramatists are staged much more often in Germany than their French counterparts. The Quebec texts imported to France, however, are more likely to correspond specifically to French tastes. This is why certain Quebec pieces that might be of interest to German audiences never even arrive in France and thus do not make it to Germany either.

Quebec theatre people, for their part, do not make contact with Germany a first priority either: Quebec agencies[3] maintain close contact with England and France, but Germany is not in their line of vision. Frankfurt, Munich, and Berlin seem to be much farther away than Paris or London. And few if any Quebec agents speak German.

Table 12.1 shows some of the ways that a play from Quebec might reach a German theatre publisher or land straight in the hands of a German producer, each column suggesting a different country as a possible point of departure.

**TABLE 12.1**

*Quebec Plays: Routes to Germany*

|  | CANADA | FRANCE/BELGIUM | GERMANY | GERMAN THEATRE |
|---|---|---|---|---|
| PRODUCTIONS | CEAD via newsletter, website, *Week of Dramaturgy*, international translators' seminars | SACD via *Actes de theatre*, website, contacts with German publishers, awards |  |  |

---

3. The most important are Agence Goodwin, Agence Duchesne, Première Scène, and Act'Art.

|  | CANADA | FRANCE/BELGIUM | GERMANY | GERMAN THEATRE |
|---|---|---|---|---|
| AGENCIES | Canadian agents: Agence Goodwin, Agence Duchesne | French theatre: Théâtre de la Colline, Théâtre Ouvert | German radio productions: DLR, WDR, SR | |
| PUBLISHERS | Canadian publishers: Leméac, Dramaturges éditeurs, Les herbes rouges, Duchesne éditeur | French publishers: Actes Sud Papier, Arche éditeur, Éditions Lansmann (Belgium) | German publishers: Rowohlt, S. Fischer, Desch, Pegasus, Korn-Wimmer, Per Lauke | Dramatic advisers, freelance directors, and groups |
| THEATRE FESTIVALS | Canadian festivals: Festival des Amériques, Carrefour international du théâtre | French festivals: Festival d'Avignon, Festival de Maubeuge, Mousson d'été, Pont-à-Mousson | German festivals: Spielart Munich, Berliner Festspiele, Euroscene Leipzig, Perspectives Saarbrücken | |
| THEATRE PRODUCTIONS | Canadian productions on international tours such as W. Mouawad or Robert Lepage | Writers' residencies such as La Chartreuse (Avignon) | | |

Although texts by Quebec authors make their way to Germany only with considerable difficulty, this has recently begun to change. Since the late 1990s, three or four French Canadian pieces per year have been arriving at German theatre publishing houses, but from the beginnings of Quebec drama in the 1960s up to that point plays from French Canada had generally passed unnoticed. Indeed, as recently as 1999, Hanspeter Plocher expressed his regret that so few plays from Quebec can expect to be translated or staged in Germany.[4]

---

4. His production of Tremblay's *Schwesterherzchen* [Les belles soeurs] at the university theatre in Augsburg in 1987 was one of the spectacular exceptions to this rule.

## THEATRE PUBLISHERS

Publication in the catalogue of a theatre publisher is a major step toward the dissemination of a theatre text in Germany. Unlike in North America and France, theatre publishers in Germany function both as publishers who make a text available as a stage script and as agents for their authors. In their role as agents, they propose suitable plays to dramatic advisers, their potential clients, and play an important part in the planning of a season's productions in the 250 different state, city, and private theatres in Germany. Editors often know what type of work might interest individual dramatic advisers.

I turn now to Danis's text to trace the path that it took before arriving on German stages. *Le chant du Dire-Dire* ("The Song of the Say-Say") was written in 1996, and Danis immediately transferred the management of all the rights (performance, translation, et cetera) to Agence Goodwin in Montreal. Goodwin and the smaller, more recent Agence Duchesne are the most important agencies for French Canadian theatre authors. Since the beginning of Danis's career, Natalie Goodwin has represented him in all legal and financial matters, negotiated contracts with theatres, collected royalties, and dealt with taxes, thus leaving him free to focus on his work.

The first step in the journey to Europe was not due to Goodwin, however; it occurred when Danis became a member of CEAD, the Centre d'auteurs dramatiques, in Montreal. This centre is financially supported by the city, the Province of Quebec, and the federal government; its objective is to develop and disseminate Quebec drama in Quebec and abroad. It was founded in 1965 and today takes care of 600 authors. A jury decides if an author should become a member. Full-time dramatic advisers who work at the centre counsel these authors on artistic issues: for example, they may collaborate in the revision of a text or workshop it with actors to test its effectiveness on stage. Beyond artistic support, CEAD also does public relations work for its authors. When an author becomes a member, his or her work is filed in the CEAD archive, thus becoming accessible to the public. CEAD also publishes an electronic newsletter that lists new works and is sent out several times a year. It presents each piece by means of a short summary and a text excerpt. Furthermore, the CEAD website (www.cead.gc.ca) provides details on about 300 authors. These details include short descriptions of the individual and his or her work, information on productions, translations, actors involved, and reviews. A search engine on the site facilitates searches by author's name, title, actors, and themes.

Every year since 1985, CEAD has organized a Semaine de la dramaturgie ("Week of Dramaturgy"), during which fifteen new plays from Quebec are presented to an international audience. Since 2003, a parallel event, a biennial meeting of translators, has taken place: ten translators from different countries meet to discuss selected pieces and work on sample translations. A further important aspect of the work of CEAD is its exchange programs with non-French-speaking countries, during which plays from Quebec are translated by the partnered country: exchange programs have already taken place with Mexico (1999), Belgium (2001), Scotland (2002–2004), and Ireland (2005). With regard to Germany, CEAD has a limited program of dissemination. None of the projects planned with German theatres has yet been carried out, nor is there any direct contact with German theatre publishing houses.

Nonetheless, CEAD took the first steps in getting Danis's work to Europe. It sent one of his texts to the international competition held at the theatre festival in Maubeuge, in northern France. *Cendres de cailloux* (*Stone and Ashes* in English, *Kieselasche* in German) won first prize and drew the attention of French theatre people, most importantly from Théâtre Ouvert (which later published one of Danis's texts) and from Alain Françon, future director of the Théâtre de la Colline. In April 1998, Danis's next piece, *Le chant du Dire-Dire,* followed, only five months after its Montreal premiere, and was directed by Françon at the Théâtre de la Colline in Paris.

Subsequently, the French publisher Arche éditeur, which has close ties to the Théâtre de la Colline, took an interest in the piece and bought the European rights from Agence Goodwin, from which point on the European distribution of the play lay in the hands of this Paris publisher. Unlike most Belgian or French publishers, and much like its German counterparts, Arche éditeur is not only a publisher but also an agent.

Usually, in France, another important actor takes part as an agent in the international transfer of theatre texts: the Société des auteurs et compositeurs dramatiques (SACD; Association of Drama Writers and Composers; see www.sacd.fr). If a dramatist gains recognition and is staged in France, the SACD usually gets involved. The organization manages the rights of almost all French dramatists. Authors who are represented by individual publishers such as Arche éditeur are the exception. Together with the Fondation Beaumarchais and Entr'Actes, the SACD plays a decisive role in the dissemination of theatre texts within France and abroad. It administers performance and translation rights for virtually all French-speaking dramatists in France, supports authors and directors financially via the Fondation Beaumarchais, and promotes distribution of the works of its authors via the Entr'Actes agency. It works with theatre authors from all francophone countries—from France, Belgium, Africa, and Quebec.

The Fondation Beaumarchais awards a number of bursaries to dramatists, while Entr'Actes published a journal twice a year, *Les actes du théâtre*,[5] edited by Sabine Bossan. The journal provided summaries of selected works, short portraits of authors, and excerpts. It was published in English and French and had a print run of 2,500. *Les actes du théâtre* was sent out to selected German theatres and publishing houses by the SACD section that deals with foreign promotion and licences. Francophile theatre publishers in German-speaking countries such as Desch, Rowohlt, Pegler, Pegasus, Merlin, Hartmann and Stauffacher, and Felix-Bloch-Erben were regular recipients of the journal. Other important partners of the SACD that supply information on developments in francophone theatre to German theatre people are the Bureau du théâtre et de la danse in Berlin, the Instituts français, a number of individual dramatic advisers, and a handful of private persons, usually translators. Like CEAD in Montreal, the SACD in Paris uses independent juries to decide on writers' bursaries and the pieces that it will accept in its repertoire. If an author is accepted as member of the SACD, the association takes care of rights, royalties, and promotion.

None of this applies, however, to *Le chant du Dire-Dire* since the rights were with the publisher. Moreover, the promotion work of the SACD is separate from that of CEAD: the two organizations do not cooperate. So, to recapitulate, Danis's *Le chant du Dire-Dire* was sent out by CEAD to the theatre festival at Maubeuge, moved to the Théâtre de la Colline in Paris, and from there sent to the catalogue of Arche éditeur, which bought the European rights from the Canadian Agence Goodwin. But how did the piece move on to Germany? In 1998, the directors of five European theatres known for their interest in contemporary drama met to discuss the international exchange of theatre works. France and Germany were represented by the Théâtre de la Colline and the Berliner Schaubühne respectively. The French contingent recommended Danis's piece to their German colleagues. After a skeptical reaction to Danis's verbose and highly figurative style, the Schaubühne decided to produce the piece in Berlin. At the same time, Katharina von Bismarck, an editor at Arche éditeur, mobilized her German connections to find a German publisher for Danis. She thought S. Fischer in Frankfurt to be the most likely partner and sent a copy of the text with her personal recommendation. The S. Fischer editors liked the piece, and when the decision of the Schaubühne was announced and a production seemed imminent

---

5. *Les Actes du théâtre* 22 (2006), a special issue on humour, was the last publication of this kind. Since December 2006, the information has been published on the Internet. Useful sites include the following: www.cead.qc.ca, www.sacd.fr, www.theatertexte.de, www.theaterparadies-deutschland.de, www.theater-translation.net, www.kanada-info.de, www.quebec-info.de, www.theatre-contemporain.net, www.aqad.qc.ca.

Arche éditeur and S. Fischer were able to reach an agreement. Fischer bought the rights for the German-speaking countries.

Translator Uta Ackermann created *Das Lied vom Sag-Sager* out of *Le chant du Dire-Dire*, and on 30 March 2000 the German version premiered in Berlin. *Theater Heute* ("Theatre Today"), a German theatre journal, published the text in May 2000, and it was sent out to theatres. Besides the production at the Berliner Schaubühne, there have been five additional stagings in Germany. With a combination of luck and mobility, *Das Lied vom Sag-Sager* thus arrived in Germany, joining the (few) other Quebec pieces that have made it this far (see Table 12.2). Since spring 2005, the cultural office of Quebec in Berlin has been offering an overview of Quebec plays published in German.[6]

TABLE 12.2

*Quebec Plays Performed and/or Published in Germany*

| YEAR OF TRANSLATION | PUBLISHER | AUTHOR | GERMAN TITLE | PERFORMANCES |
|---|---|---|---|---|
| 1981 | Vlb | Michel Garneau | *Emily wird nie wieder von der Anemone gepflückt werden* (*Emilie ne sera plus jamais cueillie par l'anémone*) | — |
| 1987 | Niemeyer Verlag | Michel Tremblay | *Schwesterherzchen* (*Les belles-sœurs*) | Premiere: Feb. 1987, Romanistentheater, University of Augsburg; Director: Hanspeter Plocher |
| 1989 | Theaterverlag Desch | Marie Laberge | *Vaterliebe* (*L'homme gris*) | Premiere: 1989, Württembergische Landesbühne Esslingen; five other productions |

---

6. See www.mri.gouv/qc.ca/munich/de/delegation/culture/theatre_quebecois.asp.

| YEAR OF TRANSLATION | PUBLISHER | AUTHOR | GERMAN TITLE | PERFORMANCES |
|---|---|---|---|---|
| 1996 | Korn-Wimmer Theaterstückverlag | Larry Tremblay | Anatomiestunde (Leçon d'anatomie) | — |
| 1996 | Pegasus Verlag | Michel-Marc Bouchard | Die Geschichte von Teeka (L'histoire de l'oie) | Premiere: June 1996, Carrousel, Theater in der Parkaue Berlin; seven other productions |
| 1997 | Theaterverlag Desch | Robert Lepage / Marie Brassard | Polygraph (Le polygraphe) | Premiere: Oct. 1997, Bühnen der Stadt Köln; one other production |
| 1997 | Theaterverlag Desch | Marie Laberge | Aurélie, meine Schwester (Aurélie, ma sœur) | Swiss premiere: 1999/2000, Kellertheater Winterthur |
| 1997 | Theaterverlag Desch | Marie Laberge | Der Falke (Le faucon) | Premiere: 1997/1998, Südthüringsches Staatstheater Meiningen; five other productions |
| 1999 | S. Fischer | Daniel Danis | Das Lied vom Sag-Sager (Le chant du Dire-Dire) | Premiere: March 2000, Schaubühne Berlin; five other productions |
| 1999 | Rowohlt Theaterverlag | Michel-Marc Bouchard | Gefahrenzone (Le chemin des Passes-dangereuses) | Premiere: Nov. 2000, Rheinisches Landestheater Neuss; Swiss premiere: 2004, Theater Neumarkt Zurich |

| YEAR OF TRANSLATION | PUBLISHER | AUTHOR | GERMAN TITLE | PERFORMANCES |
|---|---|---|---|---|
| 2000 | Rowohlt Theaterverlag | Michel-Marc Bouchard | Die verlassenen Musen (Les muses orphelines) | Premiere: March 1998, Rheinisches Landestheater Neuss; Austrian premiere: Oct. 2003, Dietheater Vienna; two other productions |
| 2001 | Theaterverlag Desch | Marie Laberge | Vergessen (Oublier) | Premiere: Jan. 2003, Vereinigte Bühnen Krefeld-Mönchengladbach; Swiss premiere: Oct. 2003, Theater Effingerstrasse Bern |
| 2001 | Suhrkamp Theaterverlag | Normand Chaurette | Der kleine Köchel (Le petit Köchel) | Premiere: Oct. 2001, Hamburger Schauspielhaus |
| 2001 | S. Fischer | Daniel Danis | Celle-là (Celle-là) | — |
| 2001 | S. Fischer | Daniel Danis | Kieselasche (Cendres de cailloux) | Swiss premiere: Jan. 2002, Theater Neumarkt Zurich; German premiere: Oct. 2003, Inteata Cologne |
| 2002 | Per H. Lauke Verlag | Éveline de la Chenelière | Erdbeeren im Januar (Des fraises en janvier) | Premiere: 2003 Stadt-Theater Elmshorn; one other production |

| YEAR OF TRANSLATION | PUBLISHER | AUTHOR | GERMAN TITLE | PERFORMANCES |
|---|---|---|---|---|
| 2002 | S. Fischer | Michael Mackenzie | *Die Baronin und die Sau* (*La baronne et la truie*) | Tryout: Oct. 2001, Theater Tri-bühne Stuttgart; Premiere: May 2005, Theater am Wallgraben Freiburg; one other production |
| 2002 | Verlag der Autoren | Sébastien Harrison | *Titanica* (*Titanica*) | — |
| 2002 | Korn-Wimmer Theaterstückverlag | Marie Brassard | *Jimmy, Traumgeschöpf* (*Jimmy, créature de rêve*) | Premiere: Oct. 2002, Bremer Theater |
| 2003 | S. Fischer | Daniel Danis | *Zungenspiel der Felsenhunde* (*Le langue-à-langue des chiens de roche*) | — |
| 2003 | Pegasus Verlag | Larry Tremblay | *Der Bauchredner* (*Le ventriloque*) | — |
| 2003 | Per H. Lauke Verlag | François Archambault | *15 Sekunden* (*15 secondes*) | Premiere: Oct. 2004, Schauspiel Essen |
| 2003 | Per H. Lauke Verlag | Stéphane Hogue | *Spass muss sein* (*Ceci n'est pas une pipe*) | — |
| 2004 | Pegasus Verlag | Frédérik Blanchette | *Der Sicherheitsabstand* (*Le périmètre*) | Swiss premiere: Sept. 2005, Stadttheater Bern; German premiere: Sept. 2006 |

| YEAR OF TRANSLATION | PUBLISHER | AUTHOR | GERMAN TITLE | PERFORMANCES |
|---|---|---|---|---|
| 2004 | Pegasus Verlag | Nathalie Boisvert | *Das Marstraining* (*L'été des Martiens*) | Premiere: March 2006, Rheinisches Landestheater Neuss; one other production |
| 2004 | Rowohlt Theaterverlag | François Letourneau | *Cheech* (*Cheech*) | Premiere: June 2006, Staatsschauspiel Dresden; one other production |
| 2005 | Theaterverlag Desch | Michel Tremblay | *Imperativ Präsens* (*Impératif présent*) | — |
| 2005 | Felix-Bloch-Erben | Carole Fréchette | *Die sieben Tage des Simon Labrosse* (*Les sept jours de Simon Labrosse*) | Premiere: Oct. 2005, Maxim Gorki Theater Berlin; four other productions |
| 2005 | — | Suzanne Lebeau | *Der kleine Oger* (*L'ogrelet*) | Premiere: Sept. 2006, Werkstatt der Kulturen, Berlin |
| 2005 | Verlag der Autoren | Wajdi Mouawad | *Verbrennungen* (*Incendies*) | Premiere: Oct. 2006, Staatstheater Nürnberg as well as at Deutsches Theater Göttingen; one other production |
| 2005 | Korn-Wimmer Theaterstückverlag | Marie Brassard | *Peepshow* (*Peepshow*) | Premiere: May 2007, Schauspiel Bonn |
| 2006 | Korn-Wimmer Theaterstückverlag | Marie Brassard | *Die Dunkelheit* (*The Darkness*) | Premiere: Nov. 2006, Bremer Theater (Brauhauskeller) |
| 2006 | Felix-Bloch-Erben | Carole Fréchette | *Yann und Beatrix* (*Jean et Béatrice*) | — |

Obviously, not every French Canadian theatre text can become a success in Germany, nor can every French Canadian author attract an audience. This applies to Quebec authors just as it does to authors from New York, London, or Helsinki. But time and again some of the "stars" from the great North do speak to German theatre audiences. This is where mediators are necessary, people who pave the way for theatre texts that might appeal to a German public to cross the Atlantic and reach the publishing houses. And, of course, this journey requires curious and open-minded publishers who work through intuition and are ready to take risks. For the past few years, the number of theatre publishing houses taking up Canadian francophone authors has been increasing. At the same time, the number of productions of Quebec pieces has grown as well. It seems that German-speaking audiences are slowly but surely discovering a long-neglected enclave in North America, an enclave whose drama is convincing in its diversity and innovation and does not have to fear international competition.

**REFERENCE**

Plocher, Hanspeter. "Äquivalenzprobleme bei der Übersetzung von Michel Tremblay, *Les Belles-Sœurs.*" *Zeitschrift für Kanada-Studien* 35.1 (1999): 117–31.

# Low Motility: Transferring Montreal Playwright Stephen Orlov's *Sperm Count* to Germany

*Brita Oeding*
*Toronto*

## INTRODUCTION

Translators never work on a translation alone. Although for a large part of their working time they may sit by themselves doing the groundwork, every translation is the result of collaborative efforts. Sometimes, these collaborations work out well; at other times, the translator faces certain adversities along the way. They may take many forms, among them personal or culture-based misunderstandings, rights and contract issues that are different from country to country, and diverse other obstacles. This chapter describes one such "adventure," the translation and transfer of Stephen Orlov's play *Sperm Count,* which premiered in London in 2001, into German. The chapter sheds light on some of the problems that transatlantic, transcultural translation projects can face. It is meant to provide an impulse for other translators and translation scholars to engage with questions about Canadian cultural exports involving translation, both from a practical and from a theoretical point of view. Yet it is also meant to raise awareness of literary translation as an essential aspect of any cultural export, a fact that every translator is aware of but that government discourse on cultural exports—in Canada and elsewhere—often, if not always, fails to mention.

Recent debates attest to this neglect just as they confirm the ongoing government interest in cultural export as a diplomatic tool. The Canadian government has referred to "public" or "soft" diplomacy, which consists to a large extent of the export of cultural products, as the "third pillar" of diplomacy. Soft diplomacy is anchored in soft power, "the ability to achieve desired outcomes in international affairs *through attraction rather than coercion*" (Gilboa 2002, 84; emphasis added), a counterbalance to the use of military and economic power. Like other types of diplomatic effort, it is meant to make a nation's causes attractive to people around the world, and this ideally results in selling the country's goods. Thus, instead of being swallowed up by globalization and increasing homogenization, individual countries seek to differentiate themselves through soft or cultural power—that is, through the export of their most attractive cultural products—in order to follow up with the export of their goods (von Flotow and Oeding 2004). The question that arises in this context is whether the foundation of this particular "pillar" of Canadian diplomacy is secured by adequate funding.

Not only has the Canadian Department of Foreign Affairs and International Trade (DFAIT) expressed its intent to export culture, but also federal funding has been allocated for this purpose to DFAIT itself, to Heritage Canada, to the Canadian Council for the Arts, and to provincial arts councils. In 2001, for example, according to the Canada Conference for the Arts (a watchdog and lobby group), CDN $56 million was awarded to the Canada Council for the Arts "to ensure ... and to project a strong and original Canadian voice [abroad]."[1] Of this amount, $32 million was to be used to encourage the export of cultural products and services in partnership with DFAIT and to explore new markets for Canadian artists. Cultural products are used to "brand" Canada around the world as a diverse and innovative country. A new "export readiness program" at the Department of Canadian Heritage will enable Canadian cultural businesses and organizations to take advantage of rapidly expanding opportunities.[2]

While these amounts make only small dents in the federal budget, the announcements signal a desire for growing cultural recognition in the world and the hope that this recognition will subsequently support enhanced communications and economic relations, appealing to public perceptions abroad, according to Evan Potter (2003). Fairly recently, an e-discussion, "Showcasting Canadian Culture and Know-How Abroad," was initiated by DFAIT, one of the objectives being the improvement of government assistance to cultural exports.[3]

Oddly, however, translation is rarely mentioned as one of the most important tools for this transfer. Yet it is precisely that—a vital instrument of export—particularly in the realm of verbal culture; both the message and its effectiveness depend upon adequate translations.

THE PLAY *SPERM COUNT*

Stephen Orlov, the author of the play *Sperm Count*, is a highly productive and successful playwright living in Montreal. He has served as president of Canada's

---

1. Canada Conference for the Arts bulletin "Funding Influx," 14/01 (a–c).
2. Ibid.
3. www.dfait-maeci.gc.ca/cip-pic/library/culturesummary-en.asp [consulted April 2005].

national drama development centre, Playwrights' Workshop Montreal, as vice president of the Playwrights Guild of Canada, and as playwright-in-residence at Montreal's major theatre, the Centaur. Born in Boston, Orlov began his writing career as an academic and freelance journalist, covering war and social upheaval in Cambodia, China, and the Philippines. He came to Canada in 1972 for graduate studies at McGill University. His first play, *Isolated Incident*, a parody of a tumultuous incident in Montreal, won the Special Juror's Prize at the 1989 Quebec Drama Festival; it was shown in English and Hindi in Montreal in 1988–1989. Subsequent plays have been showcased in theatre centres such as London, Toronto, Chicago, and New York. Orlov's comedy *Freeze* was a major success in Montreal in 2001–2002, where it was sold out for six weeks. The play is written in English with a peppering of French. It captures the increasingly common Montreal practice of interweaving both languages within the same conversation, even within the same sentence. A political allegory of Quebec at the turn of the century, the play uses the impact of the ice storm catastrophe of 1998 as a "natural equalizer" to show more direct interaction between "the two solitudes" of the English and French communities. The storm stands as a metaphor for "cooler," more tolerant times compared to the heat of the separatist movement of the 1960s, 1970s, and 1980s.

When Orlov came to the University of Ottawa in 2002 to give a talk about his work, *Sperm Count* in particular, I immediately realized that this play, which he had discussed at some length, would be an excellent piece to translate into German. A short synopsis will help explain why.

*Sperm Count*, a comedy in two acts, follows the emotional roller-coaster ride of a Jewish writer and his Palestinian urologist into the bizarre world of reproductive technology. Set in Boston shortly after the 1991 Persian Gulf War, this diasporic tale unfolds when David Stein discovers his infertility and consults the best specialist in town, Dr. Said Hamid. David's dilemma soon drives a wedge into his family as the protagonists embark on a harried journey full of detours and dead ends. David's resentful bride, Lena, puts her body and their marriage on the line through hormone shots and in-vitro failures. His estranged father, Jacob, a Holocaust survivor with the sharp tongue of a bigot, is furious that his liberal son should entrust the family lineage to a Palestinian immigrant. A sperm character, a figure in David's imagination, appears upon ejaculation as an adolescent with an attitude. It rekindles David's childhood nightmares and fuels his fears about fatherhood. Infertility becomes a multilayered metaphor as cultures, generations, and genders clash. The plot, interweaving laughter and pathos, builds toward an emotional climax with an unexpected twist.

What Orlov told me about his play in our first conversation made me think that the play could be adapted for a German audience in several ways. His critical and metaphorical yet humorous approach to tense Jewish-Palestinian relations would, in my view, touch several nerves in Germany. The ongoing aftermath of the Holocaust and Germany's contemporary sociopolitical situation, riddled by immigration, intercultural relations, and historical repercussions, have highly sensitized German culture to issues raised by the play. In fact, Orlov's work addresses several contemporary challenges that are by no means restricted to Anglo-American or German societies and reach beyond the Jewish-Palestinian context. These challenges include close living and working arrangements of people of different ethnicities who may, in other parts of the world, fight bitter battles. The play addresses artificial insemination and genetic technologies and, related to them, the evolving patterns of late childbirth and the emancipation of both women and men in relationships. It also revolves around the clash of generations shaped by drastically different personal histories and memories. Whereas the play's oldest protagonist, Jacob, for instance, barely survived the Holocaust and came to live in North America, his son and daughter-in-law grew up there—that is, in peace, safety, and economic stability, albeit haunted by Jacob's memories.

As for Canada, it is portrayed as a multicultural, peaceful country with political stability and an openness that allows immigrants to raise their children safely, even close to other ethnic groups who would be considered "the enemy" in other parts of the world. The play deals with the implications that such (almost too close) proximity has in a humorous way—none of it is life threatening. These circumstances are part of the objectives of Canada's Constitution and hence worth projecting as the country's image in Europe.

During our first meeting, Orlov and I discussed a potential German audience and its possible response to this multilayered play. In a recent interview, Orlov returned to the question of reception:

> I think it is important, whether it is in Germany or any other country, that a forum is created for the Jewish diaspora to express itself on all issues about Jewish identity, including our relationship to the Israeli-Palestinian conflict. I have tried to do that with my play. I use fertility as a multilayered metaphor of culture, generation, and gender, with all three conflicts "pinballing" off each other, hopefully with hits of pathos and comedy. In that sense, the Jewish-Palestinian conflict, how it plays itself out over here, not over there, is one of the three distinct yet interrelated subplots of the play. So much of the identity of Jews all over the world has appropriately been moulded by the horrendous experience of the Holocaust. Other factors like class [and] cultural and political status have had a big impact in our evolving identity during the postwar era. But especially in the last thirty years or so, Israel has had an enormous influence in

the sculpting of a new Jewish identity for the diaspora. And I think it is important for non-Israeli Jews to address this fact. North American Jews are not Israelis; we are different from Israelis in so many ways, yet we cannot escape the impact of Israeli government policies on our identity. Whether it is Likud or Labour in power, there is little room for indifference, especially when it comes to the Israeli-Palestinian conflict. Despite a lot of denial, that conflict influences our identity not merely as Jews but as citizens of the world.

And I believe the issues raised in the play have a deep relevance for Germany, partly because of the impact the Holocaust has had on German identity today. They have had to deal with the horrendous legacy of Nazi Germany. We lost millions; Germans lost their humanity. And they have been trying to reclaim it ever since. It is about time that Germans see and hear something else about Jewish identity beyond the Holocaust, something that is having a huge impact on Jewish identity today, a conflict that is playing itself out among Jews in every part of the world. And that is our stand on Israel's policies toward the Palestinians. We are not just people with angst about the Holocaust repeating itself. Unfortunately, the Holocaust has been used to justify repressive Israeli government policies toward Palestinians, policies that deprive them of a homeland, of a state of their own. When that happens, we must remove those ideological blinders of history. We cannot ever forget the Holocaust, but neither should it be used to repress other people. In *Sperm Count*, I address this issue, most overtly in a surreal nightmare scene.[4]

Orlov was excited about the idea of a translation for the German stage, not only, as he states above, because he finds it important to present the diasporic view on current Jewish-Palestinian issues—a view that necessarily differs from perspectives originating in Israel and Palestine—but also because of Germany's role in creating contemporary Jewish identity. The play shows a possible world of communication between Jews and Palestinians who happen to be in contact while living outside Israel but who nonetheless remain closely attached to their native communities through personal and cultural memories. This play would provide German audiences with a different view of contemporary Jewish life in the form of a metaphor that does not directly refer to Nazi Germany's devastating impact on Jewish life (as so many globally distributed films and plays do). Instead, the play examines pressing issues of today that both Jews and Palestinians struggle with and reconnects them to historical, identity-shaping traumas that reveal the suffering on all sides.

We agreed to pursue the possible translation and sale of the play to German

---

4. This and the following quotations are excerpts from an interview that I conducted in June 2005.

theatres. But how to proceed? Orlov had briefly mentioned that a German publisher had already expressed some interest in a publication, but so far no theatre agent or theatre had come forward. At that point, we already encountered, albeit unknowingly, a first obstacle in the form of a misunderstanding that was to slow down the transfer of the play to Germany considerably. This problem is discussed in more detail below.

## THE DEVELOPMENT AND RECEPTION OF THE PLAY

The fairly explosive content of *Sperm Count* caused different reactions in the theatre world. The Bronfman Centre for the Arts in Montreal invited Orlov to showcase a scene of the play at the annual conference of the Association of Jewish Theatre of North America, which the centre hosted in Montreal in 2001. Orlov and some actors read a scene from the play. After hearing the reading, director Julia Pascal from England approached Orlov and told him that she was interested in producing the play. Pascal, the first woman to direct at the National Theatre in London, is the artistic director of one of the main Jewish theatre companies in Great Britain. Her company has produced many plays with Holocaust themes. *Sperm Count* was also one of the plays featured in the Festival of Jewish Arts and Culture in London in 2001, which many international theatre companies and playwrights attended. The festival took place in the anxiety-ridden atmosphere immediately after 9/11, when many people were not even boarding airplanes. Orlov went to England in October 2001 to attend the rehearsals. He described the atmosphere to me as follows:

> It was a very militant time in London; the Muslim community was highly mobilized because of the US-American invasion in Afghanistan. Huge antiwar demonstrations took place. All this right around the time of the production. The festival received bomb threats, jeopardizing the play's production, but we just went ahead, and fortunately nothing happened.

*Sperm Count* received mostly positive reviews. On 30 November 2001, the *Jewish Chronicle*, the major Jewish newspaper in England, wrote that "Orlov has spun a web of political and emotional anxieties. The fascinating quirk of the play is the trust between a Palestinian doctor and a Jewish patient, but the author gets a lot of comic mileage out of the emasculating effect of a low sperm count." *Jewish Renaissance* commented in the winter of 2002, "The issues ... Israeli politics, medical research, medical ethics, and both marital and filial relations are filled with both humour and insight. A highly intelligent script with unexpected cliffs and interesting observations. ... The ultimate praise must go to Stephen Orlov and Julia Pascal, the director."

The mixed reaction from *The Guardian* on 4 December 2001 also had a positive spin for Orlov since it addressed something that he had intended with his work: "Orlov writes rather well. ... *Sperm Count* tackles a lot of issues, perhaps it tackled too many. ... In the end, the head is spinning." Orlov commented to me that

> this was exactly what I wanted the audience to feel, this roller-coaster ride of emotions ..., the pinballing effect knocking people around. ... In times like this, every difference between the couple gets magnified, and they all crash head-on, one after the other, spinning the couple around, knocking them off their feet. They end up taking it out on each other. And in the world of the new millennium, we cannot escape the fact that so often cultures, genders, and generations all collide at the same time in the same place in so many ways.

Audience reactions were terrific; the play received standing ovations, a lot of attention, and an invitation to a week-long international conference on Jewish theatre and Jewish playwrights in Tel Aviv, which Orlov attended midway through the run. About a dozen Israeli directors and artistic directors expressed interest in *Sperm Count* and asked to read it for production consideration. But no production or contract has come out of it yet. Orlov responded to my question about Israeli reluctance to take on the play as follows:

> The situation was very difficult, politically, at the time in Israel. The suicide bombings had just begun; we stopped by a spot in Haifa where hours before a Palestinian blew himself up. And then Sharon responded with the first aerial bombing of Ramallah. There was a lot of tension and confusion, especially for Israeli progressives. I think the play was too provocative for the time ... maybe it still is.

As we know, that situation has not yet changed significantly.

On the same note, Orlov finds his role as a diasporic playwright a difficult one:

> Some great Israeli playwrights criticize their government's treatment of Palestinians in their plays, and they get produced often in Israel, occasionally in North America. But it is different for a Jew living outside of Israel to write about the conflict. I set my plays in North America because that is the world I know. I am not Israeli, I do not speak Hebrew. But even that, writing about how Palestinians and Jews of the diaspora deal with the conflict, is somehow considered "unkosher." And we have a tough time getting produced. My own experience tells me that most artistic directors of Jewish theatres in North America and non-Jewish artistic directors of mainstream theatres with a large

Jewish subscription base shy away from plays that are critical toward Israel. The few that are produced by them are usually by Israeli playwrights. For example, Israeli playwright Joshua Sobol is produced often outside Israel, but the reverse direction is uncommon. Yes, we are not experiencing a dangerous life shaped by threats, pitched battles, suicide bombings on buses around the corner that you find in Israel, and we do not experience the loss of loved ones from those incidents, but that does not mean we do not have something to say about it all. Something important. And we can offer a different perspective; there is much to be learned from the entangled relationship of Jews and Palestinians living outside of Israel.

## MISUNDERSTANDINGS AND CONTRACT DISCUSSIONS

The arguments discussed above may have spurred German Jewish playwright Johannes Kaetzler, who attended the performance of *Sperm Count* in London, to recommend the play to Whalesong Verlag in Germany. Orlov was contacted, but a series of misunderstandings ensued that significantly delayed the sale of the play. Whalesong presented itself as a *Verlag*, a "publisher." In North America, a publisher takes care of the publication and distribution of a dramatic work, while a theatre agency looks after the sale, production, and adaptation of the play. Hence, Orlov assumed that Whalesong was interested in translating and publishing the play. But the rights that it wanted to acquire, such as stage production, DVD, CD, film, and others, were those normally handled in North America by an agent/producer. It was confusing, and Orlov was understandably reluctant to enter any negotiations. Besides, he was "more interested in translating and staging the play than in reducing it to a book on a shelf." In retrospect, it seems that it would have been easy to clarify the matter between the two parties, but at the time Orlov did not probe any further, and neither did I as the prospective translator. I realized what the misunderstanding was all about only when I spoke to the manager of Whalesong Verlag directly. The company indeed acts as an agency and was not intending to publish the play at all. It does the usual work of a German theatre agent: translate and print scripts, sell the plays to theatres in Germany, and then negotiate postproduction adaptations.

It took several months to clear up this initial misunderstanding. Orlov recalls that

> all of this was a huge misunderstanding. It took almost nine months for me to realize that they were really an agency. Even when we got into negotiations, I said, "Look, you know in our contracts here [in Canada] we only give publishers publishing and distribution rights, not everything that you want." And then they

said, "We do this and this and that. ..." But there was no clarification that they are not a publishing house but an agency.

Further delays were due to numerous details of the contract. At that point, as the prospective translator, I had taken the role of mediator between the German agency and the playwright in Canada, also linking Orlov to contacts of my own in the German union IG Druck und Papier, which represents the publishing industry, writers, and translators. Together with these experts, we studied the small print of the contract that was eventually offered to Orlov and discussed possible modifications. We also got information on the status and reputation of the agency, which, at that point, made a good impression. One of Orlov's main points of discontent with the contract was the fact that, while in Canada the artist receives a share of the gross revenue, such as the seat sales in the theatre, the sales of the publication, and so on, the German contract offered a percentage of the net income only. The clause reads as follows: "The publisher shall pay the author 60% of all net receipts which the publisher collected from the exploitation of the work." Orlov commented, "They offered a percentage of net—that is, of the profits. And for the playwright, there is no way to know what kind of unexpected expenses they will deduct from gross sales before you come to net." In the end, Whalesong agreed to change the contract to a percentage of gross.

Another item in the contract that we thought should be changed was the question of advance payment, as discussed in the following excerpt from an e-mail that I wrote to Orlov after talking to my union contact in Germany:

> On the topic of advances: If you want an advance, there are two options: if the play is a success, the publisher/agent crossbreed will take this amount out of the gains. If the play—however unlikely!—is not a success, they may want that advance back from you. You should protect yourself against that by putting in the contract that you do not have to pay back advances even if the amount made by production/publication does not cover the advances.

We were able to change this in the contract as well, so that no advance would have to be paid back to Whalesong. In general, Whalesong was very cooperative and forthcoming. In these two particular cases, the problems hinged not on a misunderstanding as before but on different contract conditions in each country. The delays, Orlov concluded, were mostly due to the fact that he "did not quickly get the answers [he] wanted or needed" to proceed confidently with the contract negotiations. Matters were undoubtedly complicated by the fact that *Sperm Count* was only the second of Orlov's plays to be translated into a foreign language and sold to an agency in another country.[5] In our discussions about the agreements, the misunderstandings, and the incongruities with Canadian contracts, we often regretted not having someone with experience on both the Canadian and the German sides to assist us in simplifying the process.

Orlov presented the problem at the Canadian Playwrights' Guild Annual General Meeting (2001). The guild acknowledged that it knows very little about international contracts and would have to work on it, a statement that sheds more light on the export situation for Canadian plays. In fact, many playwrights at the meeting expressed the wish for plays and productions to find a smoother passage between Canada and foreign countries. In this case, there was a flurry of e-mails and phone calls between Germany and Canada, between Orlov, Whalesong, our union contacts in Germany, and me, seeking clarification on legal terms and regulations. Mobility and motility were, indeed, very low. The lack of support structures could very well have prevented any transfer at all. Considering that the Canadian government has repeatedly stressed its interest in exporting Canadian culture, this is a weak point that needs substantial improvement. Orlov also remarked that the government's first priority is not the creator or translator but the producer. Artists receive travel grants and promotional support for readings and conferences, but this aid is minor compared to what artistic directors receive for touring countries and pitching plays that they have already produced. The distribution of funds reveals the government's expectations about what might become a successful cultural export. Instead of relying merely on artistic directors' choices, support for the translation and distribution of plays would enhance the number and diversity of exported plays. In addition, there is the fact that government funds pay only for translations of plays (on a per word basis) that are already commissioned for production by a foreign theatre. This stipulation makes it impossible for an agency to tap into those funds unless it can sell the play to a company before the translation is completed. This is a difficult situation, especially at a time when Canadian plays have not yet established as solid a reputation abroad as, for example, Canadian fiction has in Germany.

## THE TRANSLATION

With the contract negotiations in progress, Orlov recommended me as a translator to the agency, arguing that, living only 200 kilometres apart, we would be able to meet and work closely together. This soon turned out to be a real benefit for the translation, because Orlov's reading and acting out his characters' voices helped me tremendously in the interpretation and translation process.

However, before the translation was complete, other problems surfaced. I

---

5. Orlov's aforementioned play *Isolated Incidents* was translated into Hindi in 1987–1988.

had begun to work on the text while the contracts were still being negotiated between Orlov, Whalesong, and me, and I had already advanced to Act II by the time we finally agreed on all the terms. With respect to the translator's contract, Whalesong agreed to all the changes I asked for; we extended the time frames for changes potentially necessary after the translation's completion from three to five weeks. I asked for clarification regarding the translation copyrights and for mention of this in the contract, which Whalesong immediately agreed to. Upon my request, they also included a clause stating that in any publication or other German-language distribution of the play my name as translator would appear on the same page as the play's title and author—I had looked in vain for the translator's name in both works of fiction and plays too often.

At this point, the contract looked good to us, and we thought that it was only a matter of time until the play would be sold to a German theatre, as Whalesong intended to do. They were already negotiating with the prestigious Maxim Gorki Theater in Berlin. But suddenly an unanticipated problem materialized and delayed the process for at least another four to five months. After having sent a much revised translation draft to Whalesong, I received an e-mail from the head of the company, with the contact of the dramatist who would be reading the translation and approving it. When I finally got his feedback, I learned that he considered my translation of the speech of Jacob, the father, problematic.

The character, Jacob Stein, seventy-five years old, is a Polish Holocaust survivor and the father of David, the main protagonist. Jacob is prone to prejudices and has a sharp tongue. He has always trusted his hard-headedness more than any emotional openness in dealing with his family. Jacob came to the United States as an adult, a traumatized survivor. His English is not that of a native speaker, and this shows in emotional or stressful situations, of which the play has many. While this is not overly obvious, it is noticeable in the word order of several passages where Jacob falls back into a slightly patchy "immigrant" version of English. It also manifests itself subtly as a slight lack of fluency or an awkward expression. There is, however, no consistent or obvious linguistic pattern. His idiom is in fact not the result of a linguistic study but the result of Orlov's experience and imagination. Orlov and I had agreed that his deviant word order is a distinct trait.

In a drama translation, the focus is usually on the stage production. Hence, the translation is tailored for an oral production, and the translated text often undergoes many further changes during rehearsals. We saw Jacob's resorting to a Yiddish/Polish word order in emotional or distressful situations as an important feature of his character, for it revealed his origins and the gap between him and his son. Thus, it seemed vital to show this linguistic variety in the translation, and the question was how to do this. One source I consulted was the German version of Art Spiegelman's *Maus I* and *Maus II* and the language used for the protagonist's father, also a Polish immigrant to the United States and a Holocaust survivor. The sentence structure of this character, however, is consistently deviant from the English word order, following a pattern. It is thus very different from Jacob's irregular variations in *Sperm Count*. Interviews with Polish immigrants in Germany, conducted by a colleague for a research project, yielded the same findings and did not provide much help. When Orlov focused on Jacob's voice in one of our meetings, it also became clear that, apart from an idiosyncratic word order, he gave Jacob a strong accent, which emphasized the linguistic gap between the play's characters even more than the written text did. While on the level of text and translation it is very challenging to render phonetic components, such as accent, the distinction on the semantic level became even more meaningful as one of Jacob's significant characteristics.

After sending the first draft, in which I had rendered the irregularities in Jacob's speech on the grammatical level, several further misunderstandings surfaced. Whalesong's dramatist had by then become involved and told me that Jacob's "accent" sounded merely "awkward" or "like a bad translation" and that I should translate his utterances so that they comply with "normal"—that is, Standard—German. I explained that I had not produced an "accent" since that is a phonetic phenomenon and could be decided on by the future director of *Sperm Count* and the actor who would play the role of Jacob. More importantly, I also pointed out that the English original, too, revealed Jacob's Polish origins at the grammatical level. Finally, Orlov clarified his position in an e-mail on 15 November 2004 to Whalesong's artistic director:

> What is most important about Jacob's character is that as a Holocaust survivor, he is an immigrant in America and he must speak as an immigrant, and that would apply to the German translation as well—he should speak as an immigrant in Germany, which I'm sure is your intention. Accents needn't be written into the text; good actors can deliver that on their own. ... But Jacob's grammatical structure is far more important for the text. In my English text, I wrote Jacob's character using the grammar that a Yiddish immigrant of his background would use in America. That not only ensures authenticity of his character to the audience but it also helps deliver his wit with a correct rhythm and timing. Just as his English grammar was influenced by Yiddish, so it seems to me that his spoken German grammar should be influenced by Yiddish—the way a Polish-Jewish immigrant of his generation would speak today in Germany.

And in an e-mail to the dramatist on 15 December 2004, Orlov confirmed this again: "If Jacob's sentence structure is too refined, he would sound more like a German intellectual than a Jewish immigrant from Poland of his age."

Whalesong, however, did not comply with our view, and it became very difficult to communicate about these aspects of the text. After further attempts to explain our position, Whalesong told me that they would ask another translator of English-language plays into German for an opinion on Jacob's original voice. We never received the results of that translator's reading. The dramatist, however, made several suggestions for changes in the translation that would "correct" Jacob's German. After having spoken to Orlov again, I agreed to make a few changes to Jacob's sentence structure, trying to maintain significant elements that would distinguish his idiolect from that of the others, and in the end we compromised. I still feel, just as Orlov does, that something essential regarding the understanding of the play was lost here and that there should have been more of an attempt to work Jacob's slightly aberrant word order into the text. In our interview Orlov expressed this view as follows:

> It is a play about immigrants, and the children of immigrants. ... They have to speak like immigrants, they cannot speak like highbrow university professors. ... I think there has not been enough sensitivity to that, especially in the creation of one of the immigrant characters; in the original English play, he speaks with Yiddish grammar. ... It is about sentence structure, and the Old World has to be stamped on the delivery and the timing, so that is reflected grammatically. ... Jacob has to be seen as an immigrant character in Germany.

Of course, the mix-up regarding the "accent" was also a source of amusement. Orlov took to calling the dramatist "Secret TranslAgent Man," and I wondered whether a beginner's course on a German's love of Standard German might be offered in linguistics. On another note, and further complicating the matter, Whalesong also criticized Jacob's character delivery: it had expected it to have more "Jüdischen Mutterwitz." The literal translation of this would be "Jewish mother wit," a metaphor that refers to quick-wittedness, handed down from Jewish elders. While I was familiar with the expression, applied to my own work it felt very strange. Jacob certainly has a way of making dry, sarcastic commentaries that question any preconceived notions of "how things should be" and undermine his son's already crumbling self-confidence. But is this really a genetically predetermined feature, a "typical Jewish trait," passed on from generation to generation and therefore to appear in the translation of a drama in which all but one of the protagonists are Jewish? Thus, in the eyes of the German theatre agency, my translation partly failed: not only did it distort Standard

German (in order to render Jacob's immigrant's voice), but it also failed to adorn it with the "typical" Jewish witticisms. While Orlov had already suggested that Jacob's sentence structure was important to "ensure authenticity of his character to the audience," and that it was crucial to deliver "his wit with a correct rhythm and timing," no further attempts were made by the agency to respond to this. Instead, it requested that I "smooth out" Jacob's language and bring in more of his "Jüdischen Mutterwitz." Whalesong apparently never considered that "smoothing out" Jacob's language might also negate the idiomatic qualities of his humour.

Humour, Jewish or other, was definitely what was needed here. We returned from these linguistic and cultural dead-ends to finalize the sale and ensure that the play would be sold for the fall season in 2005. This date had ruled the translation deadline and influenced our willingness to compromise. The amount of time that the whole process had already taken had shortened our breath. In retrospect, I would say that the artistic components suffered due to the inordinate attention we had to pay to contacts, contracts, and communication issues between Germany and Canada.

At the time of writing this chapter, we are waiting for the commitment of a theatre to produce the play. Whalesong is negotiating with Maxim Gorki Theater in Berlin. The interest of the Canadian government, represented by the Canadian Embassy in Berlin, in disseminating Canadian cultural products in Germany has raised hopes at Whalesong and at Maxim Gorki Theater with regard to funding for the advertising and promotion of the play. Monies allocated for the cultural work done by the Canadian Embassy in Berlin may facilitate the production of *Sperm Count* in Germany. Stephen Orlov is currently working on *Birthmarks*, the sequel to *Sperm Count*, for which he received a grant by the Canada Council for the Arts and which he also hopes to have translated into German, this time with fewer difficulties.

**REFERENCES**

Gilboa, Eyton. "Real-Time Diplomacy: Myth and Reality." In *Cyber-Diplomacy: Managing Foreign Policy in the 21st Century*, ed. Evan Potter. Kingston: McGill-Queen's University Press, 2002. 83–109.

Potter, Evan. "Canada and the New Public Diplomacy." Unpublished manuscript, 2003.

von Flotow, Luise, and Brita Isabel Oeding. "Soft Diplomacy, Nation Branding, and Translation: Telling Canada's 'Story' Globally." In *Translation: Reflections, Refractions, Transformations*, ed. Paul St. Pierre and Prafulla C. Karr. New Delhi: Pencroft International, 2004. 173–93.

# Antonine Maillet in German: A Case Study

*Klaus-Dieter Ertler*
*University of Graz*

In 1979, the Paris publisher Grasset & Fasquelle brought out an Acadian novel that became instrumental in moving Acadian French / French Canadian literatures via various institutions from the periphery into the centre of attention of critics and the reading public.[1] The book was entitled *Pélagie-la-charrette,* a rather strange title for French ears, and was written by Antonine Maillet, who had become the foremost Canadian representative of Acadian French writers with her earlier work *La Sagouine* (1971), the monologue of a seventy-two-year-old cleaning lady. All her subsequent novels had similar regional themes and were written in a style that, in its almost epic form, could be described as the literary version of orality.

Maillet's particular narrative form seemed to correspond to the requirements of Parisian literary specialists in the late 1970s. In 1977, her novel *Les cordes-de-bois* was nominated for the Goncourt Prize. Two years later *Pélagie-la-charrette* finally won the prize. Among the reasons why a francophone work not originating in France was selected to join the ranks of the winners of this prestigious prize are the highly innovative literary style of this particular work and, more importantly, the fact that Maillet had previously published literary criticism and theory that used François Rabelais and Mikhail Bakhtin to examine the particularities of Acadian French. Furthermore, 1979 was the 375th anniversary of the founding of the French settlement of Acadie, and this provided an additional reason for awarding the prize to Maillet.

The Goncourt Prize always ensures international interest. In German-speaking countries, this particular award did not, however, garner much interest, nor did it lead to a German translation of the book. This lack of interest may have been due to the difficulty of the book's language, the style of the writing, or the provincial theme. It is very likely that translators would have recognized the enormous difficulties involved in transferring the countless Acadian regionalisms and

---

1. This chapter was translated from German by Luise von Flotow.

expressions into German. Indeed, it took three years for the English translation to appear, after Philip Stratford, former professor of literature at the Université de Montréal, undertook the risky project and finally published the book in Garden City, New York, in 1982 as *Pélagie*. It required yet another combination of academic and publishing interests for the first German translation of Maillet's book, which appeared in 2002 under the alienating title *Mit der Hälfte des Herzens* ("With Half a Heart").[2] In what follows, I first retrace the path that led to the publication of the translation and then examine the German version.

## PERSUADING THE PUBLISHERS

Since the middle of the 1990s, a number of interdisciplinary centres for Canadian Studies have been established at universities in German-speaking countries, giving rise to strong synergies and bringing into contact a series of different disciplines all focused on Canada. One such centre was set up at the Karl-Franzens-Universität in Graz, Austria, which, in collaboration with the university's Institute for Translation Studies, developed a project to translate French Canadian works. The first publication that it produced was the collection of texts entitled *Relations des Jésuites* (*Von Schwarzröcken und Hexenmeistern. Robes noires et sorciers: Jesuitenberichte aus Neu-Frankreich*; Ertler 1997), a publication supported by Austrian government funding[3] that appeared as a bilingual edition with the publishing house Reimer. The reception was notable but limited to academic circles and (literary) journals.

As a second project, two Quebec novels, *L'avalée des avalés* by Réjean Ducharme and *Les lettres chinoises* by Ying Chen, were selected for translation into German, and translation samples as well as justifications for the planned publications were sent off to the most likely German publishers. Simultaneously, an academic study entitled *Kleine Geschichte des frankokanadischen Romans* ("A Brief History of the French Canadian Novel"; Ertler 2000) and introductory academic articles (Ertler 2003) were published to sensitize the reading public to these works.

The reception of these materials was rather ambivalent. While the "Brief History" was well received, publishers' reactions to the two translation projects were far from enthusiastic. Their negative responses usually evoked the full publishing program, but now and then there was direct criticism of the texts, as the following excerpts show:

---

2. The German editor did not accept the translator's proposal, which was the literal translation "Pélagie, die Karrenfrau." Economic factors might have been the reason for this change, as *Mit der Hälfte des Herzens* might correspond more to the German romantic tradition.
3. Fonds zur Förderung wissenschaftlicher Forschung ("Fund for the Support of Academic Research").

Dear Professor Ertler,

... The novel is rather weak. Boring. It sticks to the surface of what we already know, and what it tries to sell as poetry strikes me as kitsch. Its most interesting aspect is the use of the old-fashioned epistolary form, which I like very much (especially after seeing what Natalia Ginzburg does with it). I am aware that you read and responded to this novel differently than I did; otherwise you would not have taken the trouble to prepare a translation sample. It may also be a question of age: a younger reader may be more easily persuaded that *Les lettres chinoises* has literary qualities (after all, literary sensitivities also depend on such demographic banalities).[4]

I read about the writer Ducharme, whom I didn't know at all, ... with great interest; he clearly represents a different calibre of writer than the rather lightweight Ying Chen. Still, the excerpt from *Die Verschlungenen der Verschlungenen*[5] (a title that must be avoided at all costs) did not really appeal to me. The text is typical of the experimental 1960s and like many such texts has acquired a certain patina. It may be that my reservations have more to do with the translation than the original (are you the translator?) since I found its language rather stiff.[6]

These comments show that, while Ducharme's text was read with more interest than Ying Chen's novel, no translation was planned. More generally, English Canadian texts were thought to be of higher literary quality than French Canadian works since, as one academic colleague informed me, Quebec does not have a writer like Margaret Atwood.

The labour involved in sending proposals to numerous German-language publishers was not entirely unsuccessful, however. A few months later the Deutscher Taschenbuch Verlag (dtv) expressed interest in the project of the Graz Centre for Canadian Studies. But this publisher wanted neither Réjean Ducharme nor Ying Chen in translation; instead, in the vague words of one of the editors, it was after a "pretty little novel" from French Canada. It was a surprise to discover that the publisher meant Antonine Maillet's highly formalistic novel, which was full of translation challenges. Andrea Maria Humpl, a translator versed in Acadian culture,[7] took on the job.

---

4. Excerpt from correspondence with Droschl Publishers, 3 January 2001, here and in the following translated into English.
5. This is the translation of the French title *L'avalée des avalés* ("The Devoured of the Devoured").
6. Excerpt from correspondence with Droschl Publishers, 29 January 2001.
7. Andrea Maria Humpl studied Romance and German philology at the University of Graz. She wrote her PhD dissertation about Italian writer and journalist Guido Piovene and his American diaries and articles. Humpl did her research on "migration literature" at the Université de Montréal and visited Acadie many times.

## ON THE TRANSLATION OF MAILLET'S *PÉLAGIE-LA-CHARRETTE*

The following synopsis of the novel will clarify to what extent the work is based on the cultural intricacies of the Acadian region, which the translation had to accommodate; these intricacies include the oral aspects of Acadian French and its stylistic particularities—regional expressions, proverbs, and special terms—and the literary parameters that are part of the communicational and cultural history of Acadia and serve as vectors of identity and nationality. The book's themes are closely linked to agriculture, everyday life, celebrations, and customs, and the narrative is carried by stories and history, elements that are a part of Acadian identity.

### The Story Line

*Pélagie-la-charrette* tells the story of the Acadian people, who generally consider themselves the direct descendants of the colonists of Port-Royal on the East Coast of Canada and whose domains, unlike those of Quebec and Montreal, appear on maps at the beginning of the seventeenth century. With the British conquest in 1755, the Acadians fell victim to ethnic cleansing and were forced off their properties on the Baie française, now Bay of Fundy. After the "Grand Dérangement," as the event came to be called later, there was a general exodus toward the south, toward Louisiana, the other French colony in North America, where numerous settlers hoped to establish a new life. In later years, many of the exiles returned to their original lands, establishing the basis for a new Acadia, one that has gained in self-confidence over the past decades and the current revaluation of regional cultures.

The story of *Pélagie-la-charrette* starts about fifteen years after the Grand Dérangement with Pélagie Bourg, also known as LeBlanc, who at the age of twenty had to leave the area of Grand'Pré and whose odyssey took her to the symbolic Île d'espoir ("Isle of Hope") in Georgia, United States. She suffers from the general poverty there, is homesick, and decides to invest her last remaining funds in a cart and six oxen in order to undertake the journey back to Acadia—with her four children and a number of others who join the expedition homeward along the way. After many trials and adventures, and a journey on foot via South Carolina, Virginia, Maryland, Pennsylvania, and Massachusetts, the group actually reach their Canadian East Coast homeland, and Pélagie can look back with pride on her accomplishment until she is suddenly struck down by illness and dies. The sacrosanct project of bringing the dispersed Acadians home, however, has been fulfilled.

## The German Version and Its Paratexts

The presentation of the German version (see Maillet 2002) reveals how the publisher used paratexts to create transcultural connections for German readers. The cover displays a naturalistic northern landscape painting by Frederick Edwin Church (1826–1900), a member of the American Hudson River School, that bears the title *Twilight in the Wilderness* (1860). The painting has a heroic aura to it and can be taken to symbolize the search for the Promised Land. The spectacular panorama may well tune the European reader in to the ideal of the "unspoiled landscape" of the northeastern United States, while the idealized twilight atmosphere evokes a mood that is presumably appreciated by German readers.[8]

The upper third of the cover announces the publisher's new series "dtv Premium," within which this novel is being presented; dtv Premium consists of a selection of "important" books and authors and currently has 240 titles. A characteristic of the series is the carefully constructed cover and flap design that makes the reader's experience, as the publisher announces, a "haptic event." In the lower part of the cover, dtv notes the novel's institutional position in large letters: "winner of the Goncourt Prize"; German readers also learn that this is the "first German edition."

On the back of the volume are three citations from the French press that judge the book "valuable" as well as a summary of the content: "a great Canadian novel[9] of destiny about the yearning for homeland." The isotopy of pathos and empathy could hardly be more explicit; it conjoins the two cultural areas of production and reception: destiny, yearning, and the notion of *Heimat* ("homeland")—a widely used term in German culture—come together and are evocative well beyond the translated text.

A further summary of the content and a short biographical notice on the author appear in a note on the blurb. These texts have evidently been produced by someone not versed in French since the biography contains two serious errors: it claims that Maillet was born in "Buctouche" and published a work entitled "La sanguine" (actually *La Sagouine*). The summary on the blurb provides a clear historical account of the events, emphasizing the tension between exile and homeland and working with the positive and negative actants that recall fairy-tale figures. The biblical reference is noteworthy: the chosen people congregate after their experience of the diaspora and begin their journey homeward. Finally,

---

8. It should be mentioned here that Humpl, the translator, produced and submitted for the cover a number of watercolours suitable to the novel's themes. However, the publisher's cover designers took no notice and preferred nineteenth-century landscape painting.
9. In most German-language readers' minds, this means English Canadian and not French Canadian.

there is a theoretical introduction that subscribes to current discussions about memory and the new historical novel, "an epic that takes up the tradition of orally transmitted myths and legends and mixes these with actual events; a text that can be read as the 'memory of an entire people'."

The publisher's cover design thus offers a series of aids to orient the German reader in this complex text. They consist of a very limited but clear framework in which the text is embedded and construct a basis for reception that permits members of the other (i.e., German) culture to participate. References to the "memory of an entire people" may well provide an easy interpretive bridge for German readers who recognize the concept from their own national history.

I should note at this point that the Graz Centre for Canadian Studies offered to write a foreword and an afterword, as it seemed unwise to publish such a complex and difficult book without accompanying materials. The publisher rejected this offer with the comment that the book was being designed for a wide public that would be put off by the academic nature of such paratexts.

## *The Translation*

Translator Andrea Maria Humpl masterfully met the challenges of transferring the cultural patterns of the text. On the one hand, she was able to turn the oral narrative recounted in pronounced Acadian French into a German version that does not entirely depend on one specific regional version of the language. On the other hand, she maintained a certain regional colouring by using elements from the oral discourse of Bavaria and Austria. (It should be noticed that the editor's lector adapted some of these regionalisms and vernacular phrases to Standard German.) The translation carefully follows the often intricate dialogues and uses techniques of modulation that facilitate the text's readability in German. For instance, the longer names of the members of the troupe are shortened. Although from a philological point of view this is a debatable technique, the rather ponderous name of Charles à Charles, for instance, is occasionally reduced to Charles. Sometimes such reductions "wipe out" entire families; the families travelling on the ship *Nightingale,* for example "les LeBlanc, les Richard, les Roy, les Belliveau, les Bourg et les morceaux de familles Babin et Babineau" (Maillet 1979, 52), are not mentioned. The reduction of family names was proposed by the editor's lector, who tried to create a more reader-oriented and accessible version.

The greatest problems facing the translator were the Acadian regionalisms, the proverbs, and the song texts. The typical Acadian recurrent song of the travelling troupe cannot be rendered since that particular French song is not known in

German: "Et j'ai du grain de mil, et j'ai du grain de paille, et j'ai de l'oranger, et j'ai du tri, et j'ai du tricoli, et j'ai des allumettes, et j'ai des ananas, j'ai de beaux, j'ai de beaux, j'ai de beaux oiseaux ..." (Maillet 1979, 52). The translation reads, literally, "Ich habe Hirsekorn, ich habe Strohkorn, ich habe etwas vom Orangenbaum, ich habe Tri, ich habe Tricoli, ich habe Streichhölzer, ich habe Ananas, ich habe schöne, schöne, schöne Vögel" (Maillet 2002, 41).

On the other hand, the relatively well-known song "Alouette" is left untranslated (Maillet 2002, 237–238). This, together with the rendering of names of people and places, provides one of the few occasions where the translation stays close to the original text. Local terms for herbs and plants such as "ramenelle" often remain untranslated (Maillet 2002, 140), though adaptations are found occasionally: "tétines-de-souris," for instance, becomes "Glaskraut" (Maillet 1979, 219; Maillet 2002, 191).

The Acadian regionalisms and expressions that recur constantly—"ça s'adoune" ("klar doch"), "astheure" ("jetzt"), and "jongler" ("träumen")—present certain problems for translation, and though they are translatable in theory they lose all Acadian connotation in practice. The translator sought solutions in adaptations and more or less equivalent expressions but was not able to fully reproduce the power of these semantic elements.

As the examples above demonstrate, the transfer of a text from one cultural system to another is not easy. Clearly, the German version in its smart market-oriented packaging is based on parameters that are different from those of Maillet's novel. Following the proposal of the publisher, about ten to fifteen percent of the source-text meaning was cut in translation. The reason for this decision might have been the intention to create a more readable text and to avoid the barrier of the complex, entangled family relations. Instead of using the Grand Dérangement (1755) as the historical reference for the forced removal of the Acadians by British troops, the German translation puts its focus on Pélagie, who is enslaved in Georgia and whose goal is to return home to the northeast. Collective memory, with its national symbols and customs, recedes into the background; instead, we are presented with the story of a "small people" who are striving in a "homeward" direction, a cluster of concepts that undoubtedly carries significant connotations in German.

## PRESENTING A GENERIC "BOOK ABOUT WOMEN"

Another look at the dtv Premium series reveals that books focused on women protagonists are an important part of the publisher's program; the "nice" story of an energetic woman such as Pélagie presumably corresponds perfectly with the readership envisaged for this series.

What is lost in the German paratext, however, is the historical aspect that leads back to the Grand Dérangement. The frame of the novel is obscured, and much like the case of the myth around Évangeline this shifts the reader's attention away from the historical aspect to the personal story of Pélagie and her activities. German-speaking readers are more likely to recognize historical moments such as the American War of Independence or the slave trade in Georgia than the more peripheral, francophone story of the ethnic cleansing of the Acadians in 1755.

Indeed, the title and the image on the cover lead the reader in this direction. Only the name of the author and the mention of the "Prix Goncourt" make reference to the French origins of the book. The focus is on the romanticizing, American aspect, as the enormous gap between the two titles epitomizes: *Pélagie-la-charrette* ("Pélagie, the Cart Woman") becomes *Mit der Hälfte des Herzens* ("With Half a Heart"), a significant change that supports the change in the reception focus. At the least, Pélagie's name could have been maintained in the title, and an image of the Acadian landscape on the cover would have been more appropriate given the fact that there is no immediate historical link between Acadia and the Hudson River. At least in these respects, the translator's proposals might have been accepted. Finally, the novel lacks a proper introduction that would grant readers a meaningful reading experience and free it of its current fate as a dramatic *Heimatgeschichte* ("story about the 'homeland'").

The reception of the translated novel in Germany and Austria was not very intense. The translator was invited to some reading tours at German cultural centres (among others, Munich), but there was no critical feedback in the press. So it is clear that the book did not have the same impact in Germany as it had in France in the 1970s and 1980s.

The most important paratextual elements that influence a novel's reception by readers were thus produced without help from the translator or a fully informed editor in the publishing house. Unfortunately, this approach has subverted the intercultural dimension of the book and undermined the authentic transfer of cultural communication and cultural memory.

### REFERENCES

Chen, Ying. *Les lettres chinoises*. Montreal: Leméac, 1993.
Ducharme, Réjean. *L'avalée des avalés*. Paris: Gallimard, 1966.
Ertler, Klaus-Dieter. "Der frankokanadische Roman von der 'Révolution tranquille' bis zur Gegenwart—vom Plurikulturalismus zum Transkulturalismus." *Zeitschrift für Kanada-Studien* 42.1 (2003): 7–28.

———. *Eine kleine Geschichte des frankokanadischen Romans.* Tübingen: Narr, 2000.

———, ed. and transl. *Von Schwarzröcken und Hexenmeistern. Robes noires et sorciers/ Jesuitenberichte aus Neu-Frankreich. Relations des Jésuites de la Nouvelle-France (1616– 1649).* Berlin: Reimer, 1997.

Maillet, Antonine. *Mit der Hälfte des Herzens*, transl. Andrea Maria Humpl. Munich: dtv, 2002.

———. *Pélagie*, transl. Philip Stratford. Garden City, N.Y.: Doubleday, 1982.

———. *Pélagie-la-Charrette.* Paris: Grasset & Fasquelle, 1979.

# CONTRIBUTORS

**Georgiana Banita** is a PhD student in North American literature at the University of Constance. She studied English and American literature and German literature at the Universities of Jassy (Romania) and Constance. At the University of Constance, she was the recipient of the DAAD (German Academic Exchange Service) prize for foreign students in 2003 and of the VEUK prize for the best exam results at the School of Literature for the year 2005–2006. Her publications include an article on Janice Kulyk Keefer in *The Canadian Short Story: Interpretations,* ed. Reingard M. Nischik (2007). Among her articles accepted to be published in Europe and the U.S.A. are contributions on Sylvia Plath, Arthur Miller, Philip Roth, and Raymond Williams.

**Klaus-Dieter Ertler** is a professor of Romance languages and literatures at the University of Graz, Austria. His main research interests include the francophone novel, the *Jesuit Relations* of New France, and systems theory as an epistemological model. His recent publications include *Der frankokanadische Roman der dreißiger Jahre: Eine ideologiekritische Darstellung* (Tübingen: Niemeyer, 2000); *Kleine Geschichte des frankokanadischen Romans* (Tübingen: Narr, 2000); *Canada 2000: Identity and Transformation/Identité et transformation* (ed. with Martin Löschnigg; Frankfurt: Peter Lang, 2000); *Canada in the Sign of Migration and Trans-Culturalism/Le Canada sous le signe de la migration et du transculturalisme* (ed. with Martin Löschnigg; Frankfurt: Peter Lang, 2004); *Ave Maris Stella: Eine kulturwissenschaftliche Einführung in die Acadie* (ed. with Andrea Maria Humpl and Daniela Maly; Frankfurt: Peter Lang, 2005); and *Migration und Schreiben in der Romania* (ed.; Münster: LIT, 2006).

**Stefan Ferguson** is a high school teacher in Markdorf, Germany. He studied at the University of Nottingham, England, before taking an MA degree in English and

French and a PhD in North American literature at the University of Constance, Germany. His doctoral dissertation (available on microfiche) is on the topic of translating Margaret Atwood into German.

**Luise von Flotow** is a professor of Translation Studies at the University of Ottawa. She has taught at the Universities of Freiburg, Strasbourg, and Vienna and as a visiting professor in Chile, Turkey, Iran, and Ecuador. Her research is focused on cultural and political differences between cultures and eras and their expression in translation; she has published extensively in this area: *Translation and Gender: Translating in the "Era of Feminism"* (1997), also available in Chinese and Czech translation; *The Politics of Translation in the Middle Ages and the Renaissance* (co-edited with Daniel Russell and Renate Blumenfeld-Kosinski, 2001); "How Simone de Beauvoir Talks Sex in English" (2002), "Julia Evelina Smith, Traductrice de la Bible: Doing More than Any Man Has Ever Done" (2002); "Sacrificing Sense to Sound: Mimetic Translation and Feminist Writing" (2004); "Self-Translation and Exile: Nancy Huston, 'Passing' in Paris" (2006); "La traducción a principios del siglo XXI: El fin de la equivalencia" (2006); "Frenching the Feature Film Twice" (2006). She is also a translator of literary texts from German and French and is currently translating a selection of texts by Ulrike Meinhof as well as *La langue et le nombril* (1998), a history of Quebec's obsession with language. *The Third Shore*, an anthology of East-Central European women writers (post-1989), which she co-edited and translated with Agata Schwartz, has just come out with Northwestern University Press (2006).

**Albert-Reiner Glaap** is a professor emeritus at Heinrich-Heine-University, Düsseldorf. He was awarded an OBE by H.M. Queen Elizabeth II in 1991 and was made an Honorary Member of the Playwrights Guild of Canada in 2006. His special fields of research are contemporary Canadian and British drama, the teaching of English as a Foreign Language, and the translation of literary texts from English into German. Recent publications include *Performing National Identities: International Perspectives on Contemporary Canadian Theatre* (co-edited with Sherrill Grace, 2003); *Voices from Canada: Focus on Thirty Plays* (2003); *A Guided Tour through Ayckbourn Country* (co-edited with Nicholas Quaintmere, 2nd rev. ed., 2004); and *Contemporary Canadian Plays: Overviews and Close Encounters* (co-edited with Michael Heinze, 2005); as well as numerous articles in various scholarly journals, book publications, and theatre programs.

**Eva Gruber** is an assistant professor in the Department of American Studies, University of Constance, and has been teaching there since 2004. Her PhD dissertation on humour in Native North American literature, for which she conducted research at the University of Arizona in Tucson, will be published in the U.S.A. in 2008. Her research interests include Native North American writing, conceptualizations of "race" in twentieth-century American literature, and intersections of historiography, autobiography, and fiction in contemporary North American novels. She has published on Thomas King's short fiction and on humour and other aspects of Native North American writing.

**Andreas Jandl,** Berlin, works as a literary translator specializing in Canadian fiction and drama. He studied theatre, English Studies, and French Studies, obtaining his master's degree in *art dramatique* from UQAM, Montreal, and has worked as a dramaturge and festival organizer for several theatres and international theatre festivals. He has translated, among others, texts by Daniel Danis, Xavier Durringer, Carole Fréchette, Stéphane Hogue, Donal McLaughlin, John Murrell, Michael Mackenzie, Gaétan Soucy, and Michel Tremblay.

**Barbara Korte** is a professor of English literature at the University of Freiburg, Germany. She received her degrees from the University of Cologne and taught at the Universities of Reading (GB), Chemnitz, and Tübingen. She has worked on Canadian pioneer women, Margaret Atwood, and landscape poetry. Recent publications include studies of travel writing (*English Travel Writing: From Pilgrimages to Postcolonial Explorations,* 2000) and black and Asian British culture (*Bidding for the Mainstream? Black and Asian Film in Britain since the 1990s,* 2004). A major current interest is the cultural memory of World War I in Britain. She is editor of *The Penguin Book of First World War Stories* (2007).

**Nikola von Merveldt** is an assistant professor in the Department of Modern Languages of the Université de Montréal. She has an MA in European literature (Cambridge University) and a PhD in comparative literature (Munich University). Her research in children's literature focuses on text-image relations. She is a member of the interdisciplinary research group Interacting with Print: Cultural Practices of Intermediality (1750–1850) and works mainly on eighteenth-century French and German juvenile literature. She is also a regular contributor to the International Youth Library in Munich.

**Klaus Peter Müller** is a professor of English at the Johannes Gutenberg University in Mainz, Germany. His published works include articles on British, Canadian, and Irish literatures, literary theory, Translation Studies, Cultural Studies, and the relationships between literature and epistemology, constructionism, anthropology, and culture. He has also published various books on these topics, among them *Epiphanie: Begriff und Gestaltungsprinzip im Frühwerk von James Joyce* (Frankfurt, 1984); (ed.) *Contemporary Canadian Short Stories* (Stuttgart, 1990, reprinted with additions 2002); (ed.) *Englisches Theater der Gegenwart: Geschichte(n) und Strukturen* (Tübingen, 1993); (with Barbara Korte and Josef Schmied) *Einführung in die Anglistik* (Stuttgart/Weimar, 1997, 2nd ed. 2004); (ed., with Barbara Korte) *Unity in Diversity Revisited? British Literature and Culture in the 1990s* (Tübingen, 1998); and *Wertstrukturen und Wertewandel im englischen Drama der Gegenwart* (Trier, 2000). He is currently working on a book about translations of British short stories into German.

**Reingard M. Nischik** is a professor of American literature at the University of Constance, Germany. She belongs among the pioneers of Canadian literature studies in Germany and Europe at large, with her first article on CanLit published in 1981. Since then, among her numerous publications, there have been more than thirty articles and fifteen books exclusively or partly devoted to Canadian literature. To these publications belongs the trailblazing volume that she co-edited with Robert Kroetsch, *Gaining Ground: European Critics on Canadian Literature* (1985). More recent books that she has edited and co-authored include *The Canadian Short Story: Interpretations* (Rochester, NY: Camden House, 2007), with contributors deriving mainly from Germany, and *Margaret Atwood: Works and Impact*, with international contributors (Rochester, NY: Camden House; Toronto: Anansi, 2000/2002), for which she received the Best Book Award of the Margaret Atwood Society. Nischik has for decades contributed to cultural transfer between Canada and Germany in many different ways, including her managing editorship of the German interdisciplinary journal *Zeitschrift für Kanada-Studien*, which she co-edited from 1992 to 2005. Central interests of her research are Canadian fiction and Margaret Atwood's œuvre as well as a comparative approach to American and Canadian literature and the interstices between literature and the visual media. She is currently co-authoring and editing "History of Canadian Literature: English-Canadian and French-Canadian," the first history of Canadian literature prepared for an American publisher (2008–09), with mainly Canadian and German contributors.

**Brita Isabel Oeding** was a PhD student at the University of Ottawa and works as a translator and teacher. Her recent publications include "Literary Trailblazers: Canadian Women Writers in German Translation" (2003); "Vermittlung von kanadischer Literatur: Selektions- und Finanzierungsprozesse im Transfer von kanadischer Literatur" (with Luise von Flotow, 2005); "Soft Diplomacy, Nation Branding, and Translation: Telling Canada's Story 'Globally'" (with Luise von Flotow, 2004).

**Fabienne Quennet** is an academic assistant in the Sprachenzentrum at the University of Marburg. She studied American Studies, English literature, and Media Studies in Germany and the United States, and her dissertation on Louise Erdrich was published in 2001. More recently, she has also worked and published in the field of Jewish Canadian literature, producing essays that include "The Workings of Memory in Anne Michaels's *Fugitive Pieces*" (2000), "Mordecai Richler, Montreal, and the War: Reading *The Street*" (2005), "Jewish Canadian Literature: A Short Introduction" (2005), and "Mordecai Richler, 'Benny, the War in Europe and Myerson's Daughter Bella'" (2007). She has taught courses on Jewish Canadian literature and lectured on the history of Jewish Canada. Forthcoming is an essay on the shtetl in the work of Jewish Canadian women writers Lilian Nattal and Nancy Richler.

**Martina Seifert** is currently working as a DAAD lecturer at Queen's University, Belfast, while completing her PhD dissertation on images of Canada in German children's and youth literature. She graduated from the University of Leipzig, Germany, in English, German, and German as a Foreign Language. Her publications include book chapters and articles on postmodernism and fantasy in children's literature, on Canadian time-travel stories, on the animal stories of Charles G. D. Roberts, and on contemporary Newfoundland literature. Her book *Rewriting Newfoundland Mythology* (2002) deals with the changing approaches to the regional in contemporary Newfoundland literature, taking as an example the works of Tom Dawe. She is also the co-author of *Ent-Fernungen* (2006), a two-volume study on interculturality in German children's literature after 1945.

# NAME AND TITLE INDEX

*"transl." refers to translator; "illustr." refers to illustrator, and "t" refers to table.*

## A
Acco, Anne, 119
Achimoona (Campbell), 121
Ackermann, Uta, 170t8.1, 263, 264t12.2
*The Acrobats* (*Die Akrobaten*) (Richler), 69n16, 144, 153, 163
*Across the Bridge* (*Die Lage der Dinge*) (Gallant), 69
Adams, Howard, 117–18
Adorno, T. W., 157, 193
*Adult Entertainment* (*Nur für Erwachsene*) (Walker), 173t8.1, 179
*The Adventures of Sajo and Her Beaver People* (*Sajo und ihre Biber*) (Belaney), 58, 225, 240
Agamben, Giorgio, 196n6
*Ahornblätter* (Kloss), 56, 77
*Alberta Rebound: Thirty More Stories by Alberta Writers* (van Herk), 62
*Albertine en cinq temps* (*Die fünf Lebensalter der Albertine*) (Tremblay), 184
Alderson, Sue Ann, 235
Alexie, Sherman, 114
Alford, Edna, 42t2.1, 47n2.2
*Alias Grace* (Atwood), 87
"Alice Munro Reading Box" (*Alice Munro Lesebox*) (Munro), 72
*All My Relations: An Anthology of Contemporary Canadian Native Fiction* (King), 60, 121

*All Quiet on the Western Front* (*Im Westen nichts Neues*) (Remarque), 154
Allen, Deborah A., 223n6, 240
*Almighty Voice and His Wife* (Moses), 120
"The Almost Meeting" (Kreisel), 147, 147n10–11
*AlterNatives* (Taylor), 111n1, 121
"Among the Swiss in Canada: Short Stories" (*Unter Schweizern in Kanada: Kurzgeschichten*) (Böschenstein), 56
*Les amours de ma mère: Contes et mensonges de mon enfance* (*Mutters Lieblinge: Geschichten und Lügen aus meiner Kindheit*) (Poulin - illustr.), 249n17
*Les amours de ma mère: Contes et mensonges de mon enfance* (*My Mother's Loves: Stories and Lies from my Childhood*) (Poulin - illustr.), 249n17
*Anatomy of Criticism* (*Analyse der Literaturkritik*) (Frye), 189, 195
*Anatomy of Criticism* (*Anatomie de la critique*) (Frye), 191
*Anatomy of Criticism* (Frye), 6, 189–94
*Anatomy of Melancholy* (*Anatomie der Melancholie*) (Burton), 194–95
*Anders schreibendes Amerika: Literatur aus Quebec 1945–2000* (Baier and Filion), 10, 25, 79
Anderson, Benedict, 61, 76

Anderson, Doris, 226
Anderson-Dargatz, Gail, 91
Andrews, Jan, 235
Andrews, Lynn, 114n4, 116
"The Angel of the Tar Sands" ("Der Engel des Teersandes") (Wiebe), 64
*Angel Square (Der Mann mit der Maske)* (Doyle), 237
*Angel Wing Splash Pattern* (Van Camp), 121
*Animal Heroes* (Seton), 55
*Anne of Green Gables* (Montgomery), 229–31
Annharte Baker, Marie, 119, 131, 139
*Another Time* (Mandel), 61, 77
*Anthology of Canadian Native Literature in English* (Moses and Goldie), 121
*Anthology of German-Mennonite Writing in Canada* (Epp and Wiebe), 77
Anthony Clark, Catherine, 228
*Antoine et Alfred* (Beauchemin), 250, 254
Appadurai, Arjun, 14, 25
*Arcadian Adventures with the Idle Rich (Die Abenteuer der armen Reichen)* (Leacock), 32n11, 36, 65
Archambault, François, 266t12.2
Archer, Keith, 61n11, 78
Ardagh, Philip, 246, 246n7
Arendt, Hannah, 206, 206n16
Arima, Eugene, 60
Armstrong, Jeannette, 119
  "I Study Rocks/Ich betrachte Steine," 140
  *Looking at the Words of Our People: First Nations Analysis of Literature*, 60
  *Native Poetry in Canada: A Contemporary Anthology*, 118
  *Slash*, 124, 125n11, 126–27, 131, 140
  *Whispering in the Shadows*, 124
Arnold, Armin
  Canadian short stories, 45

*Kanadische Erzähler der Gegenwart*, 40, 41n24–25, 44, 55–57, 59, 64–65, 81
"Preisgekrönte kanadische Autorin: Eiskalt in Quebec," 85n16
Arvaarluk Kusugak, Michael, 235
*As Birds Bring Forth the Sun* (MacLeod), 72
Asham Fedorick, Joy, 119
*Asja* (Ignatieff), 197
Atwood, Margaret, 4, 10, 19, 21, 53, 66
  *Alias Grace*, 87
  American writers, outselling, 81n6
  anthologies, recent and older writers, 47n2.2
  *Bluebeard's Egg*, 67
  *Bluebeard's Egg (Der Salzgarten)*, 67
  *Bodily Harm (Verletzungen)*, 82n8
  *Cat's Eye (Katzenauge)*, 87
  *Dancing Girls and Other Stories*, 66–67, 82n8
  *The Edible Woman (Die essbare Frau)*, 82n8
  feminist/women's rights, 40, 85–91
  Germany writers, comparison to, 84
  *Good Bones (Gute Knochen)*, 67
  "Guerrilla in the Wilderness" ("Guerilla in der Wildnis"), 85
  *The Handmaid's Tale (Der Report der Magd)*, 39, 82, 87
  *The Handmaid's Tale (Die Geschichte der Dienerin)* (film), 82
  "Happy-Ends," 67
  *Lady Oracle (Lady Orakel)*, 82n8, 83n11
  *Life before Man (Die Unmöglichkeit der Nähe)*, 82
  *Moral Disorder*, 67
  *Murder in the Dark (Die Giftmischer: Horror-Trips und Happy-Ends)*, 66–67, 82n8
  *The Oxford Book of Canadian Short Stories in English*, 41n25, 75

NAME AND TITLE INDEX  301

*Princess Prunella and the Purple Peanut*, 238
reviews and reviewers, 85, 85n18, 86–91
*The Robber Bride (Die Räuberbraut)*, 87
short story anthologies, 42t2.1
*Surfacing*, 4, 32, 33n13, 36, 39, 48, 81–82, 82n8, 94, 98–109
*Surfacing (Der lange Traum)*, 33, 81, 99, 109
*Surfacing (Strömung)*, 32, 32n11–12, 33, 39, 81, 99, 102, 105–9
*Survival: A Thematic Guide to Canadian Literature*, 191–92
*The Tent (Das Zelt)*, 67
*True Stories (Wahre Geschichten)*, 82n8, 94
"Under Glass" ("Unter Glas"), 66–67, 82n8
*Up in the Tree*, 238
"When It Happens" ("Wenn es passiert"), 45, 67
*Wilderness Tips (Tips für die Wildnis)*, 66
*Auf der Suche nach April Raintree* (May), 126n12
*Augen im Busch* (Roberts), 55
*Aurélie, ma soeur (Aurélie, meine Schwester)* (Laberge), 264t12.2
*L'avalée des avalés* (Ducharme), 284
*Awful End (Schlimmes Ende)* (Ardagh), 246n7
"The Awful Fate of Melpomenus Jones" ("Das fürchterliche Schicksal des Melpomenus Jones") (Leacock), 65
*The Axe's Edge* (Gunnars), 57n8

**B**
*Babes of the Wild (Gestalten der Wildnis)* (Roberts), 55n4
Bäcker, Paul, 171t8.1

Badiou, Alain, 206
Baier, Lothar, 10, 25, 79, 154
Bailey, Don, 42t2.1, 47n2.2
Bainbridge, Joyce, 233
Baisch, Cris, 251n22
Bakhtin, Mikhail, 283
"Bambinger" (Richler), 153n17, 163
Banauch, Eugen, 147n10
*Bärenmann und Büffelgeist: Indianermärchen aus Nord- und Südamerika* (Diederichs), 122n10, 142
Barfoot, Joan, 36, 91
*Barney's Version (Wie Barney es sieht)* (Richler), 69n16, 153, 155
*La baronne et la truie (Die Baronin und die Sau)* (Mackenzie), 266
Bartsch, Ernest
  *Die weite Reise: Kanadische Erzählungen und Kurzgeschichten*, 40, 41n24, 45, 45n26, 46, 54, 56, 59, 63, 63n13, 64, 68–70, 72, 81, 153n17
*Bat Summer (Fledermaussommer)* (Withrow), 233
Bauer, Walter, 224
Baum, Peter, 126, 128
Baumann, Peter, 121–22n9, 137
Beauchemin, Yves, 250, 254
*Beautiful Joe* (Marshall Saunders), 228
*Beautiful Losers (Schöne Verlierer)* (Cohen), 148–50
Begamudré, Ven, 57n8
*The Beggar Maid (Das Bettelmädchen: Geschichten von Flo und Rose)* (Munro), 71–72
*The Beggar Maid (Das Bettelmädchen)* (Munro), 66, 88
*The Beggar Maid* (Munro), 71, 88
Beissel, Henry, 165, 169t8.1, 176–79, 185
Belaney, Archibald Stansfeld, 58, 224, 240
  *See also* Grey Owl
Bell, William, 237n27, 239

*Les belles-soeurs* (*Schwesterherzchen*) (Tremblay), 259n4, 263t12.2
Bellingham, Brenda, 226
Bellow, Saul, 94, 154–55
*The Bells on Finland Street* (*Morgen läufst Du für Kanada*) (Cook), 228n19
Benjamin, Walter, 191, 195, 203
*Benjamin and the Pillow Saga* (Poulin - illustr.), 249n17
*Benjamin et la saga des oreillers* (*Benjamin and the Pillow Saga*) (Poulin - illustr.), 249n17
*Benjamin et la saga des oreillers* (*Benjamin und die Wunderkissen*) (Poulin - illustr.), 249, 249n17
*Benjamin und die Wunderkissen* (Lenain), 249
*Benjamin und die Wunderkissen* (Poulin - illustr.), 249
Berkenhopp, Donald, 170t8.1
Berlin, Isaiah, 205–6, 206n17
*Berliner Tagesspiegel*, 20
"Bernadette" (Gallant), 70
Bernèche, Jean, 247, 247n12
*Best Maritime Short Stories* (Peabody), 61
*The Betrayal* (Kreisel), 147
Bezmogis, David, 159, 214
Biegert, Claus, 126, 142
Bilson, Geoffrey, 233
*A Bird in the House* (*Ein Vogel im Haus: Eine Kindheit in der kanadischen Prärie*) (Laurence), 68
"A Bird in the House" ("Ein Vogel im Haus") (Laurence), 68tent
Birdsell, Sandra, 61
Birkenstädt, Sophie, 245n4
*Birthmarks* (Orlov), 282
*Bis ans Ende der Fährte* ("To the End of the Trail") (Egli), 225n14
Bishop, Elizabeth, 24, 42t2.1, 47n2.2
Bissoondath, Neil, 57
Bittner, Wolfgang, 225n14, 239–40

*Black Diamonds* (*Das schwarze Gold der Arktis*) (Houston), 227
Blades, Ann, 234
Blais, Marie Claire, 20, 80
Blaise, Clark, 41n25, 42t2.1, 45n26, 47n2.2
Blake, William, 190
Blakeslee, Mary, 237n27
Blanchette, Frédérik, 266n12.2
*Blood and Belonging: Journeys into the New Nationalism* (Ignatieff), 197–98, 200, 216
Blue Cloud, Peter, 118–19, 124, 130, 133, 137, 139, 141
*The Blue Mountains of China* (*Wie Pappeln im Wind*) (Wiebe), 64n14
*Bluebeard's Egg* (Atwood), 67
*Bluebeard's Egg* (*Der Salzgarten*) (Atwood), 67
Blumenberg, Hans, 191–92
Boas, Franz, 122n10
"The Boat" ("Das Boot") (MacLeod), 73
*Bobbi Lee: Struggles of a Native Canadian Woman* (*Bobbi Lee, Indian Rebel*) *Das Leben einer Stadtindianerin aus Kanada*) (Maracle), 117, 139
*Bobbi Lee* (Maracle), 125
Bock, Gabriele, 27n2, 33, 100–104, 105n14, 109, 146n4
*Bodily Harm* (*Verletzungen*) (Atwood), 82n8
Bodsworth, Fred
 German popularity, 227
 Indians, fictionalized accounts of, 112
 *The Sparrow's Fall*, 136n22, 227n17
 *The Sparrow's Fall* (*Läuft, Füße, Läuft*), 32n11, 33n13, 38, 48, 136n22
 *The Strange One of Barra* (*Der Fremde von Barra*), 32n11, 38, 48
 *The Strange One of Barra* (*Kanina*), 38, 48
 writer, "middle-brow," 36

Böhnke, Reinhild
East German translator, 27, 99, 104, 106–7
"The Long Dream" (*Der lange Traum*), 33, 99, 105, 109
"The Long Dream" (*Strömung*), 99–101, 105, 107, 109
*Surfacing* (*Der lange Traum*), 33, 99, 105, 109
*Surfacing* (*Strömung*), 33
Boisvert, Nathalie, 267t12.2
Böll, Annemarie and Heinrich, 68
"A Canadian Youth" ("Eine kanadische Jugend"), 145
*In Lower Town*, 146n4
*One Way Ticket: I Don't Want to Know Anyone Well* (*Ein kleines Stückchen Blau: Erzählungen*), 39, 50, 145
"A Small Piece of Blue," 145
Bonder, Dianna, 235
*A Book of Canadian Stories* (Pacey), 41n25
*The Book of Grey Owl: Selected Wildlife Stories* (*Im Land der Nordwinde: Wäschakwonnesin erzählt*) (Belaney), 58
*The Book of Jessica* (Campbell), 128
*The Book of Mercy* (*Wem sonst als Dir*) (Cohen), 148, 151
"Born Indian" ("Von Geburt Indianer") (Kinsella), 59, 68, 112
Böschenstein, Hermann, 56
Boschmann, Hella, 87n24
Bosco, Monique, 159
Bossan, Sabine, 262
Bouchard, Michel Marc, 5, 9, 17n14, 79n1, 165, 185
*Le chemin des Passes-Dangereuses* (*Gefahrenzone*), 169t8.1, 179, 264t12.2
*L'histoire de l'oie* (*Die Geschichte von Teeka*), 169t8.1, 264t12.2

*Les muses orphelines* (*Die verlassenen Musen*), 170t8.1, 265t12.2
Bourassa, Henri, 206
Bowering, George, 42t2.1, 47n2.2
Bowie, Douglas, 42t2.1
*The Boy in the Burning House* (*Brandspuren*) (Wynne-Jones), 234, 237
Boyle, T. C., 154
Boym, Svetlana, 197, 215
"Boys and Girls" ("Jungen und Mädchen") (Munro), 72
Brand, Dionne
"No Rinsed Blue Sky, No Red Flower Fences" ("Kein klarblauer Himmel, kein Zaun aus roten Blumen"), 57
Brant, Beth, 59–60, 121–23, 140
Brassard, Marie, 170–71t8.1, 264t12.2, 266–67t12.2
Bravo-Villasante, Carmen, 231, 240
*The Breadwinner* (*Die Sonne im Gesicht*) (Ellis), 237n27, 238n29
*Breathing Water* (Crate), 124
"A Brief History of the French Canadian Novel" (*Kleine Geschichte des frankokanadischen Romans*) (Ertler), 19, 284
"The Broken Globe" ("Der verbeulte Globus") (Kreisel), 57, 162
Brooks, Martha, 62, 238
*Brothers in Arms* (Wheeler), 121
*Büffel und Beeren: Die Küche der Blackfoot-Indianer* (Hungry Wolf), 141
Buffie, Margaret, 233
Burnard, Bonnie, 84
Burton, Robert, 194–95
Butler, Geoff, 235
*Butterfly on Rock: A Study of Themes and Images in Canadian Literature* (Jones), 192
Butz, Steffen, 236, 236n26

## C

Callaghan, Morley, 42t2.1, 63, 63n13, 64
Cameron, Anne, 59, 112
  *Daughters of Copper Woman* (*Töchter der Kupferfrau: Mythen der Nootka-Indianerinnen und andere Frauengeschichten*), 58, 114n4
  *Dreamspeaker* (*Dreamspeaker*), 226
  *Dreamspeaker* (*Traumdeuter*), 114n4, 226, 237n27
Cameron, Eric, 41n24, 42t2.1, 45, 59
Campbell, Maria, 118
  *Achimoona*, 121
  *The Book of Jessica*, 128
  *Halfbreed* (*Cheechum's Enkelin: Autobiographie einer kanadischen Halbindianerin*), 58, 117, 128, 139
  *Jessica*, 120
  *Stories from the Road Allowance People*, 124
Campbell Scott, D., 46, 47n2.2, 65, 112
*Canada in the World* (Government of Canada), 12, 25
*Canada Made Me* (*Kanada hat mich gemacht*) (Levine), 68, 145, 162
"Canadian Authors in German Translation" ("Kanadische Autoren in deutscher Übersetzung") (Holzamer), 22n20, 36n20, 53, 66, 77, 97, 99, 232
*Canadian Children's Books 1799–1939*, 228
*Canadian Children's Literature / Littérature canadienne pour la jeunesse*, 231
*Canadian Crusoes* (Parr Traill), 228
"A Canadian Play for Young Audiences: Joan MacLeod's *The Shape of a Girl*" (Glaap), 182, 186
*Canadian Short Stories* (Knister), 41n25
*Canadian Short Stories* (Weaver), 41n25
*The Canadian Short Story: Interpretations* (Nischik), 19, 26
*The Canadian Twins* (*Die kanadischen Zwillinge*) (Wuorio), 228

"A Canadian Youth" ("Eine kanadische Jugend") (Böll transl.), 145
"A Canadian Youth" ("Eine kanadische Jugend") (Levine), 145
*Capital Tales* (Fawcett), 76
Cardinal, Harold, 117–18
Cariou, Warren, 124
Carr, Emily, 42t2.1, 47n2.2, 59
Carter, Dyson, 37, 49
*Cassiopée: L'été polonais* ("Cassiopée: The Polish Summer") (Marineau), 252, 254
*The Catcher in the Rye* (Salinger), 146n6
*Cat's Eye* (*Katzenauge*) (Atwood), 87
*Ceci n'est pas une pipe* (*Spass muss sein*) (Hogue), 266t12.2
*Celle-là* (*Celle-là*) (Danis), 265ft12.2
*Cendres de cailloux* (*Steinasche Kieselasche*) (Danis), 170t8.1, 261, 265t12.2
Chandler Haliburton, T., 46, 47n2.2, 65
*Le chant du Dire-Dire* (*Das Lied vom Sag-Sager*) (Danis), 170t8.1, 179, 257–58, 260–62, 264ft12.2
*Le chant du Dire-Dire* (*Das Lied vom Sag-Sager*) (Ackermann - transl.), 263, 264t12.2
*Charlie Wilcox* (McKay), 232
"Chassidic Song" ("Chassidische Weise") (Kreisel), 57, 162
Chaurette, Normand, 17n14, 170t8.1, 265t12.2
*Cheech* (*Cheech*) (Letourneau), 267t12.2
Cheecho, Shirley, 120
Chen, Ying, 24, 284–85
Chenelière, Éveline de la, 265t12.2
*Cherry Docs* (*Cherry Docs*) (Gow), 5–6, 171t8.1, 179, 183–84
*Chiefly Indian* (Pennier), 118
Chislett, Anne, 168
*A Choice of Enemies* (*Der Boden trägt mich nicht mehr*) (Richler), 69n16, 144, 153–54

*Clara's War (Die Kinder aus Theresienstadt)* (Kacer), 237
*The Clockmaker: Or, The Sayings and Doings of Samuel Slick, of Slickville (Sam Slicks Reden und Thun)* (Haliburton), 65
Clutesi, George
  "Ko-ishin-mit and Son of Eagle" ("Ko-ishin-Mit und der Adler"), 59
  "Ko-ishin-Mit und die Schattenwesen," 59
  native mythology, 127n13, 130–31
  short story anthologies, 42t2.1
  *Son of Raven, Son of Deer: Fables of the Tse-shat People (Sohn des Raben, Sohn des Rehs)*, 59, 115, 122–23, 141
Cohen, Leonard, 36, 80, 143n1, 144, 148–52, 159
  *Beautiful Losers (Schöne Verlierer)*, 148–50
  *The Book of Mercy (Wem sonst als Dir)*, 148, 151
  *Death of a Lady's Man (Letzte Prüfung)*, 149
  *Energy of Slaves (Die Energie von Sklaven)*, 149, 151
  *The Favorite Game (Das Lieblingsspiel)*, 148–51
  *Flowers for Hitler (Blumen für Hitler)*, 148–49, 151, 160
  *Let Us Compare Mythologies*, 148
  *Parasites of Heaven*, 149
  *Parasites of Heaven (Parasiten des Himmels: Gedichte aus zehn Jahren)*, 148, 151
  *The Spice-Box of the Earth*, 148–49
Cohen, Matt, 42t2.1, 47n2.2, 143n1, 144, 147, 147n8, 159
*Collected Stories* (Gallant), 69
*The Collected Works of Billy the Kid (Die gesammelten Werke von Billy the Kid)* (Ondaatje), 172t8.1
Collura, Mary-Ellen, 226
"The Colonized Halfbreed" ("Das kolonisierte Halbblut") (Adams), 117
*Coming through Slaughter (Buddy Bolden's Blues)* (Ondaatje), 172t8.1
"Compatriots" (Lee Warrior), 113
Connor, Ralph, 229
Conradi, Arnulf, 66, 94, 96–97, 97n8, 99, 99n11, 109
*Contemporary Canadian Short Stories* (Müller), 73, 77
Cook, Lyn, 228n19
Copeland, Ann, 42t2.1, 47n2.2
*Les cordes-de-bois* (Maillet), 283
"Cornet at Night" ("Ein Kornett in der Nacht") (Ross), 64
*Covered Bridge* (Doyle), 232
Coyne, Susan, 238
Craig, John D., 220, 228
Crate, Joan, 119, 124
Crawford, Isabella Valancy, 64–65
*Criminal Genius (Genie und Verbrechen)* (Walker), 172t8.1
*The Critical Path* (Frye), 192
Cron, Anna, 171t8.1, 183–84
Cronin, Michael, 4, 7
"The Crows are Taking the Summer with Them" (*Die Krähen nehmen den Sommer mit*) (Kurelek), 241
Culler, Jonathan, 192
Culleton, Beatrice, 117, 124–25, 125n11, 127, 139
"Culture and Foreign Policy" (Saul), 14–15, 17
Cuthand, Beth, 119

**D**

Damm, Kateri, 119
*Dance of the Happy Shades* (Munro), 70, 72
*Dancing Girls and Other Stories* (Atwood), 66–67, 82n8

"Danger Zone" (*Gefahrenzone*) (Bouchard), 179
Daniels, Greg, 119
Danis, Daniel, 5, 17n14
   *Le langue-à-langue des chiens de roche* (*Zungenspiel der Felsenhunde*), 266t12.2
   *Celle-là* (*Celle-là*), 265ft12.2
   *Cendres de cailloux* (*Steinasche Kieselasche*), 170t8.1, 261, 265t12.2
   *Le chant du Dire-Dire* (*Das Lied vom Sag-Sager*), 170t8.1, 179, 257–58, 260–62, 264ft12.2
   *The Darkness* (*Die Dunkelheit*) (Brassard), 267t12.2
"Das alte Leben" (Herrmann), 60
"Das alte Leben" (Pitseolak), 60
"Das Fernsehen und die humanitäre Hilfe" (Ignatieff), 216
*Das kleinere Übel: Politische Moral in einem Zeitalter des Terrors* (Ignatieff), 216
"Das letzte Hindernis" ("The Last Barrier") (Roberts), 55
*Das Tipi am Rand der großen Wälder: Eine Schwarzfuß-Indianerin schildert das Leben der Indianer, wie es wirklich war* (Hungry Wolf), 141
*Das Zelt* (Atwood), 67
*Daughters of Copper Woman* (*Töchter der Kupferfrau: Mythen der Nootka-Indianerinnen und andere Frauengeschichten*) (Cameron), 58, 114n4
Davey, Frank, 189, 215
Davies, R., 20, 36, 42t2.1, 47n2.2, 53, 66
*Dawn Rider* (*Schnell wie der Wind*) (Hudson), 226
De la Roche, Mazo, 36, 80, 80n2
de Man, Paul, 194–95, 215
*De weg naar Chlifa* (Marineau), 247n11

"A Death in the Family" ("Ein Todesfall in der Familie") (Brant), 59, 122, 140
*Death of a Lady's Man* (*Letzte Prüfung*) (Cohen), 149
Deines, Brian, 235
*Dem Hut nach!* (Pratt), 246n5
Demers, Dominique, 252, 252n24
Demmerle-Conté, Sabine, 249n19, 253n25
Denison, Muriel, 228
*Der Erde eine Stimme geben* ("To Give Voice to the Earth") (Biegert), 126, 142
*Der Geburtstagsbär* ("The Birthday Bear") (Bittner), 240
*Der gefleckte Fremdling* (Roberts), 55n4
*Der Mann mit dem Notizbuch: Erzählungen* (El-Hassan editor), 147
*Der Mann mit dem Notizbuch: Erzählungen* (Levine), 39, 147
*Der Mond über der Eisbahn: Liebesgeschichten* (Munro), 72
*Der steinerne Engel* (*The Stone Angel*) (Schlüter - transl.), 39
"Der Tod, die andere Seite des Mondes: Kanada auf der Suche nach sich selbst" (Schwarzkopf), 89n31
*Der Traum meiner Mutter: Erzählungen* (Munro), 71
*Der weisse Indianer* ("The White Indian") (Bauer), 224
*Der Wolf von Winnipeg und andere Tiergeschichten* (Seton), 55
*Des fraises en janvier* (*Erdbeeren im Januar*) (Chenelière), 265t12.2
Desparois, Lucille. *See* Lucille, Tante
*The Desperate People* (*Chronik der Verzweifelten*) (Mowat), 32n11, 38, 50
Desrosiers, Sylvie, 249n19
*The Diary of Anne Frank* (Salinger), 146n6
Dickenson, Don, 42t2.1, 47n2.2

*Die Fährte des grauen Bären* ("The Trail of the Grey Bear") (Bittner), 239
*Die Geschichte der Dienerin* (*The Handmaid's Tale*) (film) (Schlöndorff), 82
*Die Hintergründe zu den Helsinki Roccamatios* (Martel), 63
*Die Jupitermonde* (Munro), 72
*Die Krähen nehmen den Sommer mit* ("The Crows Are Taking the Summer with Them") (Härtling), 234n23
*Die Liebe einer Frau: Drei Erzählungen und ein kurzer Roman* (Munro), 71
*Die schönsten Sagen aus der Neuen Welt* (Dreecken and Schneider), 122n10, 142
*Die schönsten Tiergeschichten von Ernest Thompson Seton and Bingo und andere Tierhelde* (Seton), 55, 224
"Die Stätte des Unrats" (Laurence), 68
"Die Stimme Kanadas" ("Canada's Voice") (Schneider), 154
*Die Verschlungenen der Verschlungenen* (Ducharme), 285
*Die weite Reise: Kanadische Erzählungen und Kurzgeschichten* (Bartsch), 40, 41n24, 45, 45n26, 46, 54, 56, 59, 63, 63n13, 64, 68–70, 72, 81, 146n4, 153n17
*Die Zeit*, 19, 45
Diederichs, Ulf, 122n10, 128, 142
*Digging Up the Mountains* (Bissoondath), 57
*Dinner along the Amazon* ("Dinner entlang des Amazonas") (Findley), 68
*A Discovery of Strangers* (*Land jenseits der Stimmen*) (Wiebe), 64n14
"Disneyland" (Gowdy), 73
*The Diviners* (Laurence), 68
*Django, Karfunkelstein, and Roses* (*Django, Karfunkelstein & Rosen: Erzählungen*) (Levine), 68, 146, 162
"Do You Know that the Trees Talk? Indian Wisdom" (*Weißt du dass die Bäume reden: Weisheit der Indianer*) (Recheis), 121–22n9, 138, 141
*Dog Sleeps: Irritated Texts* (Reid), 76
*The Dog Who Wouldn't Be* (*Der Hund, der mehr sein wollte*) (Mowat), 227
Dormagen, Adelheid, 172t8.1
*The Doubter's Companion* (*Wirtschaftsgipfeln und anderen Zumutungen des 21. Jahrhunderts*) (Saul), 196, 216
Doyle, Brian, 232, 232n22, 233, 233n22, 237, 239
*Dreadful Acts* (*Furcht erregende Darbietungen*) (Ardagh), 246n7
*Dreamspeaker* (*Dreamspeaker*) (Cameron), 226
*Dreamspeaker* (*Traumdeuter*) (Cameron), 114n4, 226, 237n27
Dreecken, Inge, 122n10, 142
Drew, Wayland, 42t2.1, 47n2.2
"The Drummer of All the World" ("Der Weltentrommler") (Laurence), 68
"Drummer" ("Schlagzeuger") (Vanderhaeghe), 69
Ducharme, Réjean, 284–85, 285n5
Duchesne, Christiane, 251n22
*Duddy Kravitz* (Richler), 154
Duhm-Heitzmann, Jutta, 85n15, 86n20, 154
Dumont, Marilyn, 119, 131
Dyserinck, Hugo, 222, 240

E

Eagleton, Terry, 188n1, 192, 192n4, 215
*Easy Avenue* (Doyle), 232
Eddi-Dickens trilogy, 246
*The Edible Woman* (*Die essbare Frau*) (Atwood), 82n8
Egli, Werner, 225n14
Egoff, Sheila, 228, 236n26, 240
"Eine kanadische Jugend" (Levine), 68, 162
El-Hassan, Karla

anthologies of Canadian literature, 35, 35n19
*Der Mann mit dem Notizbuch: Erzählungen*, 147
*Erkundungen: 26 kanadische Erzähler* ("Explorations"), 29, 32n11, 40–41, 44, 46, 49, 67–68
*Kolumbus und die Riesendame: Kurzgeschichten aus Kanada*, 41, 44, 48–49, 59, 68–69, 73, 92, 122
review/afterwords for GDR editions, 35, 39, 45n26
women writers, 82n9
Ellis, Deborah, 237n27, 238, 238n29
Elschner, Geraldine, 248n13
*Emilie ne sera plus jamais cueillie par l'anémone (Emily wird nie wieder von der Anemone gepflückt werden)* (Garneau), 263t12.2
*The End of Civilization (Das Ende der Zivilisation)* (Walker), 172t8.1
*Energy of Slaves (Die Energie von Sklaven)* (Cohen), 149, 151
Engel, Howard, 42t2.1, 144, 147, 147n8, 159, 161
Engel, Marian, 36
*Englische Literatur im Überblick* (Findeise and Seehase), 35n18, 37, 49, 51
*The English Patient* (Ondaatje), 86
Enzensberger, Hans Magnus, 69, 216
Epp, Georg, 56, 56n5, 77
*Erkundungen: 26 kanadische Erzähler* ("Explorations") (El-Hassan and Militz editors), 29, 32n11, 40–41, 44, 46, 49, 66–68
*Erkundungen* ("Explorations") (Volk und Welt), 32n11, 46
Ertler, Klaus Dieter, 19, 284, 290
"Es gibt eine kanadische Literatur" ("There Is Such a Thing as Canadian Literature") (Pache), 19, 81

*Eskimo Stories from Povungnituk, Québec* (Arima and Nungak), 60
*Été avec Jade (Ein Sommer mit Jade)* (Gingras), 249n19, 252–53n25
*Été avec Jade* ("Summer with Jade") (Gingras), 252
*L'été des baleines* ("The Summer of the Whales") (Marineau), 252
*L'été des Martiens (Das Marstraining)* (Boisvert), 267t12.2
Etienne, Gérard, 24
Evans, Allen Roy, 38n22
"Extradited" ("Ausgeliefert") (Crawford), 64
Eyvindson, Peter, 235

**F**
*The Faber Book of Contemporary Canadian Short Stories* (Ondaatje), 75
*The Facts behind the Helsinki Roccamatios (Aller Irrsinn dieses Seins: Vier Erzählungen)* (Martel), 63
*Faerie Queene* (Spenser), 190
*Falling Angels (Fallende Engel)* (Gowdy), 73
*The Falling Woman, (Die fallende Frau: Kurzgeschichten)* (Lambert), 62
*Les fantaisies de l'oncle Henri/Uncle Henry's Dinner Guests (Was für ein Besuch!)* (Pratt), 236, 246n5
*Le faucon (Der Falke)* (Laberge), 171t8.1, 264t12.2
*The Favorite Game (Das Lieblingsspiel)* (Cohen), 148–51
Fawcett, Brian, 76
*Fearless Warriors* (Taylor), 121
*Featuring Loretta (Loretta)* (Walker), 173t8.1, 179
*The Feet of the Furtive (Elen, Wolf und Bär)* (Roberts), 55n4
*The Feet of the Furtive (Jäger und Gejagte)* (Roberts), 55n4

Fenimore Cooper, James, 112
*Fenster zur Welt* ("Window to the World"), 29
Fiamengo, Janice, 229–30, 241
Fife, Connie, 119
*15 secondes (15 Sekunden)* (Archambault), 266t12.2
*Figures in Paper Time* (Truhlar), 76
Filion, Pierre, 10, 25, 79
Findeisen, Helmut, 35n18, 37, 49, 51
Findley, Timothy, 36, 42t2.1, 47n2.2, 68
*A Fine Balance* (Mistry), 22
*Firebird (Feuervogel)* (Scollard), 172t8.1
*Firewing* (Oppel), 238
"First We Take Turtle Island, Then We Take Berlin" (Taylor), 113, 138
Fischer, Elisabeth, 90, 90n36
Fitch, Sheree, 238n28
Flater, Leah, 62
*Flippin' In* (Chislett), 168
*Flowers for Hitler (Blumen für Hitler)* (Cohen), 148–49, 151, 160
*Flüstere zu dem Felsen* ("Whisper to the Rock") (Ludwig), 126, 142
"Flying a Red Kite" ("Der rote Drachen") (Hood), 68
"Flying a Red Kite" ("Einen roten Drachen steigen lassen") (Hood), 68–69
Foley, James, 61n11, 77
*Food and Spirits* (Brant), 59, 122
*Forbidden Voice: Reflections of a Mohawk Indian* (Greene), 117n6
Ford, Richard, 94
*Forms of Devotion: Stories and Pictures (Formen der Zuneigung: Geschichten und Bilder)* (Schoemperlen), 73, 77
Fortner Keay, Arden, 47n2.2
Fotheringham, Hamish, 237–38
*Four Feathers* (Lutz), 117, 119, 121, 123, 131n18, 138, 140, 142
Françon, Alain, 261
*Frankfurter Allgemeine Zeitung*, 19

Fraser, Brad, 168, 170t8.1, 179
*Frauen in Canada: Erzählungen und Gedicht* (Herrmann), 54, 57, 59, 63, 65, 67–68, 70, 72, 77, 122
Fréchette, Carole, 17n14
*Do pour Dolores*, 249n19, 254
*Do pour Dolores* ("Do for Dolores"), 252–53
*Jean et Béatrice (Yann und Beatrix)*, 267t12.2
*Les quatre morts de Marie (*The Four Deaths of Marie)*, 180–81
*Les quatre morts de Marie (und viermal stirbt Marie)*, 184
*Les sept jours de Simon Labrosse (Die sieben Tage des Simon Labrosse)*, 267t12.2
Freeman, Minnie Aodla, 58
*Freeze* (Orlov), 271
"Freezing Cold in Quebec" ("Eiskalt in Quebec") (Hébert), 85
Freinthal, Käte, 225, 240
*Fresh Girls and Other Stories (Fetisch und andere Stories)* (Lau), 62
Freund, René, 169t8.1
Freund, Wieland, 129n16, 137
Friedrich, Gottfried
*Gute Wanderschaft, mein Bruder: Eine kanadische Anthologie*, 32n11, 33n14, 40–41, 44, 49, 55, 57, 59, 63–64, 66, 68, 82n9, 122
*A Friend like Zilla* (Gilmore), 235
*Friend of My Youth (Glaubst Du es war Liebe?)* (Munro), 71, 89
Friesé, Maria, 90n34
"From the Fifteenth District" ("Aus dem fünfzehnten Bezirk") (Gallant), 70
*From the Fifteenth District (Späte Heimkehr: Eine Novelle und acht Erzählungen)* (Gallant), 69
Fröschle, Hartmut, 56, 77

*Frozen Fire (Feuer unter dem Eis)* (Houston), 227
Frye, Northrop, 6, 188–95
*Funny, You Don't Look like One: Observations from a Blue-Eyed Ojibway* ("Ich bin ein Ojibway") (Taylor), 113, 138
*Further Adventures of a Blue-Eyed Ojibway* (Taylor), 113

## G

Gadamer, Hans-Georg, 191, 213
Gallant, Mavis, 36, 81
   *Across the Bridge (Die Lage der Dinge)*, 69
   "Bernadette," 70
   *Collected Stories*, 69
   *From the Fifteenth District (Späte Heimkehr: Eine Novelle und acht Erzählungen)*, 69
   "From the Fifteenth District" ("Aus dem fünfzehnten Bezirk"), 70
   German and European history, 69–70
   *Green Water, Green Sky (Grünes Wasser, grüner Himmel)*, 69
   *Home Truths*, 70
   "Orphans' Progress" ("Der Waisenkinder Reise"), 36, 70
   *The Pegnitz Junction (Blockstelle Pegnitz)*, 69
   short story anthologies, 42t2.1
Gardner, Ethel B., 123
Garneau, Michel, 263t12.2
Garner, Hugh, 41n24, 42t2.1, 59
Garnet Ruffo, Armand, 119
Gass, Ken, 165
Gauthier, Bertrand, 244n1
Gay, Marie-Louise, 236, 238, 244–45, 245n4, 247n8, 252
*Gedichte-Lieder-Geschichten / Poems-Songs-Stories* (Blue Cloud), 119
Geertz, Clifford, 214–15
"Gelegenheitskauf im Dezember" (Valgardson), 66

Genette, Gérard, 33, 49
*Geniesh: An Indian Girlhood* (Willis), 117n6
*A Gentle Earthquake (Ein sanftes Erdbeben)* (Blue Cloud), 141
*Geometry of Miracles (Geometry of Miracles)* (Lepage), 171t8.1
George, Chief Dan, 118
German Youth Literature Prize (Deutscher Jugendliteraturpreis), 224
Gerson, Carole, 62
Ghazali, Ahmed, 184
*A Gift for Gita* (Gilmore), 235
Gilboa, Eytan, 13, 25, 269, 282
Gilman, Phoebe, 235
Gilmore, Rachna, 235
Gingras, Charlotte, 249n19, 252–53n25
Ginzburg, Natalia, 285
Glaap, Albert-Reiner, 165–67
   "A Canadian Play for Young Audiences: Joan MacLeod's *The Shape of a Girl*", 182, 186
   "The Philosophy, Chemistry and Universality of Morris Panych's Work," 184, 186
   *Toronto at Dreamer's Rock*, 120
   "Voices from Canada: 25 Canadian Dramas for German Stages" (*Stimmen aus Kanada: 25 kanadische Dramen für deutsche Bühnen*), 120, 168
   *Voices from Canada: Focus on Thirty Plays*, 168, 179, 181
"God Is Not a Fish Inspector" ("Gott ist kein Fischereiinspektor") (Valgardson), 66
*Goddam Gypsy (Verdammter Zigeuner)* (Lee), 238
Godfrey, Dave, 42t2.1, 47n2.2
Goldie, Terry
   *Anthology of Canadian Native Literature in English*, 121
*Good Bones (Gute Knochen)* (Atwood), 67

*Good Night Sam* (*Bonne Nuit Sacha*) (Gay), 245n4
*Good Night Sam* (*Gute Nacht, Theo*) (Gay), 245n4
*Goodnight Desdemona* (*Good Morning Juliet*) (*Gute Nacht Desdemona*) (*Guten Morgen Julia*) (MacDonald), 179
Görner, Rüdiger, 207n19
"Gott ist kein Fischereiinspektor" (Valgardson), 66
Gottfried, Friedrich, 82n9, 92
Government of Canada, 12, 16, 25
Gow, David, 5–6, 171t8.1, 179, 183
Gowdy, Barbara, 10, 73–75, 80, 91, 97
Grady, Wayne, 41n25
Graf, Christof, 148, 151–52
Graham, Georgia, 236
Grant, George, 189, 192, 206
Grauer, Lally, 118
*Great Leader of the Ojibway: Mis-Quona-Queb* (Redsky), 117n6
*Green Grass, Running Water* (*Wenn Coyote Tanzt*) (King), 59, 124, 125n11, 126, 128n15, 129n16–129n17, 130–31, 133, 133n19, 134, 134n20–134n21, 135, 140
*Green Water, Green Sky* (*Grünes Wasser, grüner Himmel*) (Gallant), 69
Greene, Alma, 117n6
Greenstein, M., 143, 143n1, 150–51, 160
Greenwood, Barbara, 233
Greer, Germaine, 89
Greffrath, Mathias, 158
Greif, Hans-Jürgen, 19
Greve, F. P. *See* Grove, Frederick Philip
Grey Owl, 36, 58, 116, 220, 224–25. *See also* Belaney, Archibald Stansfeld
Griebel-Kruip, Rosemarie, 249n19, 253n25, 254
Groß, Konrad, 19, 221, 241
Grove, Frederick Philip, 42t2.1, 56

"Guerilla in der Wildnis" (Zauneck), 85n17
"Guerrilla in the Wildnerness" ("Guerilla in der Wildnis") (Atwood), 85
*Guests Never Leave Hungry* (Sewid), 117n6
"Guide to Canadian Children's and Youth Literature" (*Wegweiser durch die kanadische Kinder- und Jugendliteratur*), 238
Gunnars, Kristjana, 57n8
"Gursky Was Here" (Baier), 154
*Gute Reise, kleiner Bär* ("Farewell Little Bear") (Bittner), 240
*Gute Wanderschaft, mein Bruder: Eine kanadische Anthologie* (Friedrich and Riedel), 32n11, 33n14, 40–41, 44, 49, 55, 57, 59, 63–64, 66, 68, 82n9, 122

**H**
Habermas, Jürgen, 193, 199, 199n9, 209, 211–13, 215
Hailey, Arthur, 36, 80, 80n3
*Halbblut* (May), 125–26n12
"Halfblood: The Girl April Raintree" (*Halbblut: Das Mädchen April Raintree*) (Culleton), 125
*Halfbreed* (*Cheechum's Enkelin: Autobiographie einer kanadischen Halbindianerin*) (Campbell), 58, 117, 128, 139
Halfe, Louise, 119, 131–32
Haliburton, T. C., 42t2.1, 46, 47t2.2, 65
"Halloween" ("Das Halloween-Fest") (Waddington), 163
Hambleton, J., 220, 226–27, 227n16, 241
*A Handful of Time* (Pearson), 233
*The Handmaid's Tale* (*Der Report der Magd*) (Atwood), 39, 82, 87
*The Handmaid's Tale* (*Die Geschichte der Dienerin*) (Atwood), 82
"Happy-Ends" (Atwood), 67
Hardy, Frank, 37

*Harpoon of the Hunter* (*Die Harpune des Eskimos*) (Markoosie), 60n10
*Harriet's Daughter* (*Harriet und schwarz wie ich*) (Nourbese Phillip), 238
Harrison, Sébastien, 266
Härtling, Peter, 234n23
Hartmann, Heinz, 225n14
Hasselmann, Kristine, 171t8.1
*Hateship, Friendship, Courtship, Loveship, Marriage* (*Himmel und Hölle*) (Munro), 71
Hayes, John Francis, 228–29
Haynes, John Francis, 226
*Heaven* (*Heaven*) (Walker), 173t8.1
Hébert, Anne, 20, 80, 85
Hébert, M.-F., 244, 249, 249n19, 254
Heibert, Frank, 169–70t8.1, 172–73t8.1, 174, 176
Heide, Christopher, 165
Hekkanen, Ernest, 76
Helke, Fritz, 225n14
Helwig, David, 43t2.1, 47n2.2
*Here and Now* (Blaise and Mecalf), 41n25
Herrmann, Birigit
  "Das alte Leben," 60
  *Frauen in Canada: Erzählungen und Gedicht*, 54, 57, 59, 63, 65, 67–68, 70, 72, 77, 122
Herzog, Werner, 172t8.1
Hettmann, Fredrick, 122n10
Hewitt, Marsha, 233
*Hey Dad* (*Der Sommer als ich dreizehn war*) (Doyle), 233n22, 237
Highway, Tomson, 131, 165, 235
  *Kiss of the Fur Queen* (*Der Kuss der Pelzkönigin: Ein indianischer Lebensweg von heute*), 117, 125, 139
  *The Rez Sisters*, 120–21
Hillis Miller, J, 195, 215
Hodgins, Jack, 20, 43t2.1, 47n2.2, 68
Hogue, Stéphane, 266t12.2
*The Hohenzollerns in America: With the Bolsheviks in Berlin and Other Impossibilities* (*Die Hohenzollern in Amerika und andere Satiren*) (Leacock), 65
*Hold Fast* (*Lass nicht locker*) (Major), 232
Hollingshead, Greg, 76
Holzamer, Astrid H.
  "Canadian Authors in German Translation" ("Kanadische Autoren in deutscher Übersetzung"), 22n20, 36n20, 53, 66, 77, 97, 99, 232
*Home Truths* (Gallant), 70
Homel, David, 246, 246n5
*L'homme gris* (*Vaterliebe*) (Laberge), 171t8.1, 179, 263t12.2
Honneth, Axel, 205, 213, 215
*Honour the Sun* (Slipperjack), 124, 136n22
Hood, Hugh, 43t2.1, 45n26, 47n2.2, 68–69
*Hoof and Claw* (Roberts), 55
Horstmann, Ute, 172t8.1
Horvath, Polly, 239
*The House in the Water: A Book of Animal Stories* (Roberts), 55
*House Made of Dawn* (Momaday), 115
Houston, James, 220–21, 227
Hudson, Jan, 226
Hughes, Monica, 232, 239
*Human Rights as Politics and Idolatry* (Ignatieff), 201–3, 216
Humpl, A. Maria, 285, 285n7, 287n8, 288, 291
Hungry Wolf, Adolph, 114n4
Hungry Wolf, Beverly, 124–25, 141

I

*I Don't Know Anyone Too Well, and Other Stories* (*Der Mann mit dem Notizbuch: Erzählungen*) (Levine), 68
"I Study Rocks / Ich betrachte Steine" (Armstrong) 140
*Ice Swords* (*Elfenbeinjäger im ewigen Eis*) (Houston), 227
*Ich bin Schildkröte / I Am Turtle* (Blue Cloud), 118–19, 137, 139

*Ich kenne deine Träume: Songs und Gedichte mit Illustrationen von Jürgen Jaensch* (Graf), 151
*If You Could Wear My Sneakers: A Book about Children's Rights (Wärst du mal ich und ich mal du)* (Fitch), 238n28
Ignatieff, Michael, 6, 189, 196–207, 196n6, 198n7–8, 199n9, 201n10, 202n11–12, 205n15, 210, 210n22, 214
  *Asja*, 197
  *Blood and Belonging: Journeys into the New Nationalism*, 197–98, 200, 216
  "Das Fernsehen und die humanitäre Hilfe," 216
  *Das kleinere Übel: Politische Moral in einem Zeitalter des Terrors*, 216
  *Human Rights as Politics and Idolatry*, 201–3, 216
  *Isaiah Berlin: A Life*, 205
  *The Lesser Evil: Political Ethics in an Age of Terror*, 203–4, 216
  *The Russian Album*, 197, 206
  *Scar Tissue*, 197
  *The Warrior's Honour: Ethnic War and the Modern Conscience (Zivilisierung des Krieges)*, 201, 205, 216
*Illustrated Guide to North American Mythology (Mythen der Indianer)* (Spence), 122n10, 142
*Imagined Communities* (Anderson), 61, 76
*Impératif présent (Imperativ Präsens)* (Tremblay), 267t12.2
*In Lower Town* (Böll - transl.), 146n4
*In Lower Town* (Levine), 146n4
*In Search of April Raintree (Halbblut! Die Geschichte der April Raintree)* (Culleton), 117, 124–25, 125n11, 127, 139
*In the Language of Love (In der Sprache der Liebe)* (Schoemperlen), 77
"In the Midst of My Fever" ("In der Mitte meines Fiebers") (Layton), 144, 160

*In the Shadow of Evil* (Culleton), 124
*In the Skin of a Lion* (Ondaatje), 157
*In the Village of Viger* (Scott), 65
*Incendies (Verbrennungen)* (Mouawad), 267t12.2
*Indianermärchen aus Kanada* (Hettmann), 122n10
*Indians Don't Cry* (Kenny), 121
Innis, Harold, 206
*Inook and the Sun (Inuk und das Geheimnis der Sonne)* (Beissel), 169t8.1, 177–79, 185
*Inside Out: An Autobiography by a Native Canadian* (Tyman), 117n6
*Inspite of Killerbees (Zickenzoff und Killerbienen)* (Johnston), 237
*Inuit: Vom Mut der Eskimo* (Mowat), 77
*Inuit Stories: Povungnituk* (Nungak), 60
*Is This a Man* (Levi), 156
*Isaiah Berlin: A Life* (Ignatieff), 205
Iser, Wolfgang, 193
*Island: Collected Stories (Die Insel: Erzählungen)* (MacLeod), 72–73
*Isolated Incident* (Orlov), 271

**J**
*Jacob Two-Two and the Dinosaur (Ein Geschenk für Jacob Zweizwei)* (Richler), 153, 238
*Jacob Two-Two Meets the Hooded Fang (Jacob Zweizwei in Gefahr)* (Richler), 153, 238
Jäger, Lorenz, 205n14
*Jaguar Woman and the Wisdom of the Butterfly Tree (Die Jaguarfrau und die Lehren des Schmetterlingbaumes)* (Andrews), 114n4
"Jalna" series (De la Roche), 80n2
Jandl, A., 5, 10, 165n1, 170t8.1, 180–81
*Jasmine* (Truss), 228
Jauss, Hans Robert, 191, 193, 216
Jelinek, Elfriede, 83
Jenning, Sharon, 235

*Jessica* (Campbell), 120
"Jewish Writers of the Prairies: A Postmodern Reading of the Canadian Diaspora" (Klooß), 147n9, 160
"Jim Munroes Werbung" (Haliburton), 65
*Jimmy, créature de rêve (Jimmy, Traumgeschöpf)* (Brassard), 170t8.1, 266t12.2
Joe, Rita, 119, 140
Johnson, E. Pauline, 115
Johnston, Basil H., 58, 123–24, 141
Johnston, Julie, 237, 237n27, 238–39, 241
"Jokemaker" ("Spaßvogel") (Kinsella), 68
*Jonathan Cleaned Up—Then He Heard a Sound (Endstation! Alles Aussteigen!)* (Munsch), 236
Jones, D. G., 192
*Joshua Then and Now (Joshua damals und jetzt)* (Richler), 69n16, 144–45, 152–53

**K**
"Ka-ims's Gift: A Sto:lo Legend / Ka-ims Geschenk: Eine Legende der Sto: lo" (Gardner), 123
Kacer, Kathy, 159, 237
Kaetzler, Johannes, 276
Kaey, Arden, 43t2.1
Kagerer, Marion, 171t8.1
Kaiser, E., 88, 88n29, 89, 89n30, 146
*Kamouraska* (Hébert), 80, 85
*Kampf um Anerkennung* (Honneth), 213, 215
*Kanada: Photo-Impressionen aus der letzten Wildnis* (Patterson), 55
*Kanada erzählt: 17 Erzählungen* (Sabin), 41, 41n24, 48, 50, 54, 63n13, 64, 67–70, 78, 82n9, 122, 145, 153n17, 154
*Kanadische Erzähler der Gegenwart* (Arnold and Riedel), 40, 41n24–25, 44, 55–57, 59, 64–65
*Kanadische Literaturgeschichte* (Groß et al.), 19, 221, 241
Kane, Margo, 120

Kapurta, Dora, 171t8.1
Kattan, Naïm, 159
*Keeper 'n Me (Hüter der Trommel)* (Wagamese), 59, 124, 125n11, 131–32, 139
Keeshig-Tobias, Lenore, 117, 119, 134, 140
*Kein Kuss für Tante Marotte!* (Lenain), 249, 249n16
*Kein Kuss für Tante Marotte!* (Poulin - illustr.), 249, 249n16
Kennedy, Dan, 117, 117n6
Kennedy, Leo, 43t2.1, 47n2.2
Kenny, George, 120–21, 123
Kilby, Don, 235
Kimber, Murray, 235
*The Kindred of the Wild (Tiermütter)* (Roberts), 55n4
King, Thomas, 123, 131, 133, 136, 235
  *All My Relations: An Anthology of Contemporary Canadian Native Fiction*, 60, 121
  *Green Grass, Running Water (Wenn Coyote Tanzt)*, 59, 124, 125n11, 126, 128n15, 129n16–129n17, 130–31, 133, 133n19, 134, 134n20–134n21, 135, 140
  *Medicine River*, 124
  "Native Literature of Canada," 112, 115, 119–20
  *One Good Story, That One*, 121
  *A Short History of Indians in Canada*, 121
  *Truth and Bright Water*, 113, 124
Kinsella, W. P., 112
  anthologies, recent and older writers, 47n2.2
  "Born Indian" ("Von Geburt Indianer"), 59, 68, 122
  "Jokemaker" ("Spaßvogel"), 68
  short story anthologies, 43t2.1
Kirchner, Gerhard, 88, 88n27, 153
*Kiss of the Fur Queen (Der Kuss der Pelzkönigin:*

*Ein indianischer Lebensweg von heute)* (Highway), 117, 125, 139
"Kitwancool" ("Kitwancool") (Carr), 59
Klein, A. M., 143, 143n1, 152, 159, 159n25–26
Klein, Naomi, 144
  *No Logo!* (*No Logo*), 157–59, 161, 196, 216
  *Über Zäune und Mauern* (*Dispatches from the Front Lines of the Globalization Debate*), 196, 216
*Kleine Geschichte des frankokanadischen Romans* ("A Brief History of the French Canadian Novel") (Ertler), 19, 284
*Kleiner Zizi* (Lenain), 249, 249n16
*Kleiner Zizi* (Poulin - illustr.), 249, 249n16
Kliewer, Annette, 234
Klooß, Konrad, 19, 147n9, 160
Klooß, Wolfgang, 19, 147n9, 160
Kloss, Heinz, 56, 77
Knister, Raymond, 41n25
Knowles, Ric, 120n7
"Ko-ishin-mit and Son of Eagle" ("Ko-ishin-Mit und der Adler") (Clutesi), 59
"Ko-ishin-Mit und die Schattenwesen" (Clutesi), 59
Kogawa, Joy, 22
Kolodziejcok, Michaela, 249n16
*Kolumbus und die Riesendame: Kurzgeschichten aus Kanada* (El-Hassan editor), 41, 44, 48–49, 59, 68–69, 73, 92, 122
Kotzwinkle, William, 149
Krahé, Hildegard, 249n17
Kramer, Jane, 200
Kraus, Robert, 221, 241
Kreisel, Henry, 43t2.1, 56–57, 77, 147, 147n10–11, 162
Krekeler, Elmar, 90–91, 91n37
Kristeva, Julia, 191
Krüss, James, 238, 238n28
Kulyk Keefer, Janice, 197

Küng, Max, 153n18
Kunisch, Hans-Peter, 202n11
Kunstmann, Antje, 73, 97
Kurelek, William, 234, 234n23, 235, 241
Kyburz, Walter, 145n2
Kymlicka, Will, 196, 205

**L**

Laberge, Marie, 5
  *Aurélie, ma soeur* (*Aurélie, meine Schwester*), 264t12.2
  *Le faucon* (*Der Falke*), 171t8.1, 264t12.2
  *L'homme gris* (*Vaterliebe*), 171t8.1, 179, 263t12.2
  *Oublier* (*Vergessen*), 171t8.1, 265t12.2
"Labrie's Wife" ("Labries Frau") (Scott), 65
Labrosse, Darcia, 244, 254
Ladoix, Jenny, 251n22
*Lady Oracle* (*Lady Orakel*) (Atwood), 82n8, 83n11
Laferrière, Dany, 24
Laforest, Guy, 212n23, 216
*Lake of the Prairies* (Cariou), 124
Lambert, Shaena, 62
"The Lamp at Noon" ("Die Lampe am Mittag") (Ross), 64
Landreville, Ginette, 247, 254
Langspeer, Büffelkind, 127n13
*Le langue-à-langue des chiens de roche* (*Zungenspiel der Felsenhunde*) (Danis), 266t12.2
LaRocque, Emma, 119
Larouche, Michel, 19
*Larry's Party* (*Alles über Larry*) (Shields), 90
*Larry's Party* (Shields), 90
Larsen, Fred, 225n14
"Last Spring They Came Over" ("Im letzten Frühling kamen sie herüber") (Callaghan), 63n13
*Laterna Magika: Stories* (Begamudré), 57n8

Lau, Evelyn, 62
Laurence, Margaret, 17, 36, 61, 80–81, 84
  African short stories, 67
  "A Bird in the House" ("Ein Vogel im Haus"), 68
  A Bird in the House (Ein Vogel im Haus: Eine Kindheit in der kanadischen Prärie), 68
  "Die Stätte des Unrats," 68
  The Diviners, 68
  "The Drummer of All the World" ("Der Weltentrommler"), 68
  "The Loons" ("Die Seetaucher"), 68
  "The Nuisance Grounds," 68
  "Pferde der Nacht," 68
  short story anthologies, 43t2.1
  The Stone Angel (Der steinerne Engel), 28, 32n11, 39, 49
  The Tomorrow-Tamer (Die Stimmen von Adamo: 10 Erzählungen), 67
  women's movement, 39
Laurendeau, André, 206
L'avalée des avalés ("The Devoured of the Devoured") (Ducharme), 285n5
Lawrence, Iain, 239
Lawson, Julie, 235
Layton, Irving, 43t2.1, 47n2.2, 144, 147, 160, 162
Le chemin des Passes-Dangereuses (Gefahrenzone) (Bouchard), 169t8.1, 264t12.2
Le polygraphe (Polygraph) (Lepage and Brassard), 171t8.1, 264t12.2
Leacock, Stephen, 37n21
  anthologies, recent and older writers, 46, 47n2.2
  Arcadian Adventures with the Idle Rich (Die Abenteuer der armen Reichen), 32n11, 36, 65
  "The Awful Fate of Melpomenus Jones" ("Das fürchterliche Schicksal des Melpomenus Jones"), 65
  The Hohenzollerns in America: With the Bolsheviks in Berlin and Other Impossibilities (Die Hohenzollern in Amerika und andere Satiren), 65
  Literary Lapses: A Book of Sketches, 65
  "The Marine Excursion of the Knights of Pythias" ("Die Wasserfahrt der Pythia-Ritter"), 65
  Nonsense Novels (Der Asbestmann und andere Nonsens-Novellen), 65
  short story anthologies, 43t2.1
  Sunshine Sketches of a Little Town, 65
  Winsome Winnie and Other New Nonsense Novels (Die liebreizende Winnie: Neue Nonsens-Novellen), 65
Leatherstocking Tales (Fenimore Cooper), 112
Lebeau, Suzanne, 267t12.2
Lecker, Robert, 189, 216
Leçon d'anatomie (Anatomiestunde) (Tremblay), 264t12.2
Lee, Dennis, 238, 238n28
Lee, Ronald, 238
Lee Warrior, Emma, 113
Legenden der kanadischen Indianer (Regehr-Mirau), 123n10, 142
Lemieux, Michèle, 251, 251n21-22
Lemieux, Michelle, 236
Lenain, Thierry, 249, 249n16
Léon sans son chapeau / Follow That Hat! (Dem Hut nach!) (Pratt), 246n5
Léon sans son chapeau / Follow That Hat! (Pratt), 246n5
Leon the Chameleon (Leon ist anders) (Watt), 236
Leonard Cohen: Partisan der Liebe Cohen (Graf), 151
Leonard Cohen: Partisan der Liebe (Papst), 152
Leonard Cohen: Songs of a Life (Graf), 151
Lepage, Françoise, 243, 254
Lepage, Robert, 171t8.1, 259t12.1, 264t12.2
Les actes du théâtre (Bossan), 262, 262n5
Les fantaisies de l'oncle Henri / Uncle Henry's Dinner Guests (Pratt), 246n5

*Les muses orphelines* (*Die verlassenen Musen*) (Bouchard), 170t8.1, 265t12.2
*The Lesser Blessed* (*Die ohne Segen sind*) (Van Camp), 124, 141, 226
*The Lesser Blessed* (Van Camp), 125n11
*The Lesser Evil: Political Ethics in an Age of Terror* (Ignatieff), 203–4, 216
*Let Us Compare Mythologies* (Cohen), 148
Letourneau, François, 267t12.2
*Les lettres chinoises* (Chen), 284
Leube, Anna, 153, 153n19
Lévesque, Pierre, 248n15
Levi, Primo, 156
Levine, Karen, 159, 238
Levine, Norman, 36, 45n26, 143–44, 159
   *Canada Made Me* (*Kanada hat mich gemacht*), 68, 145, 162
   "A Canadian Youth" ("Eine kanadische Jugend"), 145
   *Der Mann mit dem Notizbuch*, 39
   *Der Mann mit dem Notizbuch: Erzählungen*, 147
   *Django, Karfunkelstein, and Roses* (*Django, Karfunkelstein & Rosen: Erzählungen*), 68, 146, 162
   "Eine kanadische Jugend," 68, 162
   in German, 145–47
   *I Don't Know Anyone Too Well, and Other Stories* (*Der Mann mit dem Notizbuch: Erzählungen*), 68
   *In Lower Town*, 146n4
   *One Way Ticket*, 68, 145
   *One Way Ticket: I Don't Want to Know Anyone Well* (*Ein kleines Stückchen Blau: Erzählungen*), 39, 50, 68, 145, 146n4, 162
   short story anthologies, 43t2.1
   "A Small Piece of Blue" ("Ein kleines Stückchen Blau"), 68, 145
*L'histoire de l'oie* (*Die Geschichte von Teeka*) (Bouchard), 169t8.1, 264t12.2
*La liberté? Connais pas* ("Freedom? Don't Know That") (Gingras), 252
Lieske, Tanya, 87, 87n26
*Life among the Qallunaat* (Freeman), 58
*Life before Man* (*Die Unmöglichkeit der Nähe*) (Atwood), 82
*Life in Harmony with Nature* (*Vater Sonne, Mutter Erde: Zeugnisse indianischen Lebens im Einklang mit der Natur*) (Hungry Wolf), 114n4
"Light Satiric Pieces from German Canadian Literature: John Adam Rittinger, Walter Roome, Ernst Loeb, Rolf Max Kully" (*Heiteres und Satirisches aus der deutschkanadischen Literatur: John Adam Rittinger, Walter Roome, Ernst Loeb, Rolf Max Kully*) (Böschenstein), 56
Lightburn, Ron, 235–36
*Lights for Gita* (Gilmore), 235
Lindsay Skinner, Constance, 228
*Literary Lapses: A Book of Sketches* (Leacock), 65
*Literatur in Quebec: Eine Anthologie* (Greif and Ouellette), 19
Little, Jean, 239
*Little Voice* (Slipperjack), 124
Littlechild, George, 235
*Lives of Girls and Women* (*Kleine Aussichten: Ein Roman von Mädchen und Frauen*) (Munro), 70–71
*L'ogrelet* (*Der kleine Oger*) (Lebeau), 267t12.2
Long, Sylvester, 224
   *See also* Long Lance, Chief Buffalo Child
"The Long Dream" (*Der lange Traum*) (Böhnke - transl.), 99, 105, 109
"The Long Dream" (*Strömung*) (Böhnke - transl.), 99–101, 105, 107, 109
Long Lance, Chief Buffalo Child, 116, 220, 224. *See also* Long, Sylvester
*Le long silence* (*Das lange Schweigen*) (Desrosiers), 249n19
*Looking at the Words of Our People: First

*Nations Analysis of Literature* (Armstrong), 60
"The Loons" ("Die Seetaucher") (Laurence), 68
*Lost in the Barrens* (*Das Geheimnis im Norden*) (Mowat), 227
*The Love of a Good Woman* (Munro), 71
*Love You Forever* (*Ich werde dich immer lieben*) (Munsch), 236
Lowry, Malcolm, 34n16, 80, 80n3
   anthologies, recent/older writers, 47n2.2
   short story anthologies, 43t2.1
   *Under the Volcano*, 24, 34
   *Under the Volcano* (*Unter dem Vulkan*), 32n11, 34, 50
Lucille, Tante, 243–44
   *Venir au monde* (*Welcome to the World*), 244
Ludwig, J., 43t2.1, 47n2.2, 126, 147, 162
Ludwig, Klemens, 126, 142
Luhmann, Niklas, 213
*Lumberjack* (Kurelek), 234
Lunn, Janet, 233
Lutz, Hartmut, 4, 30n22, 112, 112n3, 113, 115–20, 124–25, 125n12, 126–27, 127n13, 130, 131n18, 134–35, 138, 224, 226

**M**
MacDonald, Ann-Marie, 91, 179
MacDonald Denton, Kady, 236
MacEwan, Grant, 43t2.1, 47n2.2
MacEwen, Gwendolyn, 43t2.1
Mackenzie, Michael, 266
MacLennan, Hugh, 36, 38, 50
MacLeod, A., 43t2.1, 47n2.2, 61, 72–73
MacLeod, Joan, 165, 182–83
*The Maestro* (*Flucht in die Wälder*) (Wynne-Jones), 234
*The Magic Mountain* (Mann), 157
Mailer, Norman, 146n6
Maillet, Antonine, 285
   *Les cordes-de-bois*, 283
   *Pélagie-la-Charrette*, 6, 283–84, 286–90
   *La Sagouine*, 283, 287
   "With Half a Heart" (*Mit der Hälfte des Herzens*), 284, 284n2, 290
Major, Kevin, 232
*Making It New* (Metcalf), 41n25
*A Man Called Raven* (Littlechild), 235
*Man Descending* (Vanderhaeghe), 69
Mandel, Eli, 61, 77, 159n26
Manguel, Alberto, 24
Mann, Thomas, 157
Maracle, Lee, 118–19
   *Bobbi Lee: Struggles of a Native Canadian Woman*, 125
   *Bobbi Lee: Struggles of a Native Canadian Woman* (*Bobbi Lee, Indian Rebel: Das Leben einer Stadtindianerin aus Kanada*), 117, 139
   *Ravensong*, 124, 136n22
   *Sojourner's Truth and Other Stories*, 59, 121–22
   *Sundogs*, 124
   "Who's Political Here? " ("Wer ist hier eigentlich politisch?"), 59, 122, 140
"Margaret Atwood, Power Politics" (Nischik), 110
*Margaret Atwood: Works and Impact* (Nischik), 19, 26, 93, 95
"The Marine Excursion of the Knights of Pythias" ("Die Wasserfahrt der Pythia-Ritter") (Leacock), 65
Marineau, Michèle, 247, 247n10–247n11, 250n20, 252, 254
Markoosie, Germaine A., 59–60, 60n10
Marquard, Odo, 192
Marriott, Ann, 43t2.1, 47n2.2, 81
Marshall Saunders, Margaret, 228
Martchenko, Michael, 236
Martel, Émile, 9, 11, 79n1
Martel, Suzanne, 233

Martel, Yann, 63
*Mary Ann Alice* (Doyle), 232n22
*Mary Ann Alice* (*Mary Ann Alice*) (Doyle), 237
*Mary of Mile Eighteen* (*Mary von km 18*) (Blades), 234
"A Matter of Balance" ("Gleichgewicht") (Valgardson), 66
*Maus I* (Spiegelman), 280
*Maus II* (Spiegelman), 280
May, Karl, 112, 126n12, 128
McCarthy, Cormac, 154
McClung, Nellie, 228
McCourt, Edward, 43t2.1, 47n2.2
McGillis, Rod, 228, 241
McGraw, Sheila, 236
McGuhan, Jim, 235
McKay, Sharon, 232
McLuhan, Marshall, 188, 213
McNamara, Eugene, 43t2.1, 47n2.2
Mead, George Herbert, 209
*Medicine River* (King), 124
*Medicine Woman* (*Die Medizinfrau: Der Einweihungsweg einer weißen Schamanin*) (Andrews), 114n4
*Medieval Hour in the Author's Mind* (Hekkanen), 76
Meier, Martina, 248n13
*Mein Hund ist ein Elefant!* (Pratt), 246n5
Melynk, George, 61n1, 77
*Memoir* (*Memoiren*) (Murrell), 172t8.1
"Men in Red Coats" (*Männer im roten Rock*) (Larsen), 225n14
Messer, Leah, 119
Metayer, Maurice, 60
Metcalf, John, 41n25, 43t2.1
Meyer, Hans-Werner, 170t8.1, 171t8.1
Michaels, Anne, 134n1, 144, 155–57, 159
  *Fugitive Pieces* (*Fluchtstücke*), 143, 155–56, 162
  *Miner's Pond*, 155
  "Singing for the Dead" ("Singen für die Toten"), 157

  *Skin Divers*, 155
  *The Weight of Oranges*, 155
Michels, Tilde, 250
Militz, H., 30n7, 41, 44, 46, 49, 66–68, 77
Miller, Hillis, 195, 215
Millet, Kate, 89
Milne, A. A., 149
Milton, John, 194
*Miner's Pond* (Michaels), 155
Mistry, Rohinton, 22, 57
*Mit Pferd und Kanu durch Kanada* ("With Horse and Canoe through Canada") (Ritter), 225n14
Mitchell, W. O., 43t2.1, 47n2.2
*Modern Canadian Stories* (Rimanelli and Ruberto), 41n25
*Moderne Erzähler der Welt: Kanada*, 44
*Moderne Erzähler der Welt* (Riedel), 40–41, 45, 45n26, 49–50, 122
*Modernity at Large: Cultural Dimensions of Globalization* (Appadurai), 14, 25
*Mohawk Trail* (Brant), 121
Mojica, Monique, 120, 120n7, 121, 131
Momaday, N. Scott, 115
*Mon chien est un éléphant!/My Dog Is an Elephant* (*Mein Hund ist ein Elefant!*) (Pratt), 246n5
*Mon chien est un éléphant!/My Dog Is an Elephant* (Pratt), 246n5
Mongeau, Louise, 244n2
*Monkey Beach* (*Strand der Geister*) (Robinson), 124, 125n11, 141
Montgomery, Lucy Maud, 229–31
Montgomery, Rutherford George, 220, 231
*The Moons of Jupiter* (*Die Jupitermonde*) (Munro), 71
"The Moons of Jupiter" (Munro), 33n14
Moore, Brian, 36
*Moose Meat and Wild Rice* (Johnston), 58, 124
*Moral Disorder* (Atwood), 67

Morency, Pierre, 9, 79n1
Morf, Marie-Elisabeth, 169t8.1
Morgan, Bernice, 61
*Morley Callaghan's Stories* (Callaghan), 63
Moses, Daniel David, 119–21, 140, 165
Moss, John, 192
Mouawad, Wajdi, 267t12.2
Mowat, Farley, 38n22, 112, 220–21
   *The Desperate People* (*Chronik der Verzweifelten*), 32n11, 38, 50
   *The Dog Who Wouldn't Be* (*Der Hund, der mehr sein wollte*), 227
   *Inuit: Vom Mut der Eskimo*, 77
   *Lost in the Barrens* (*Das Geheimnis im Norden*), 227
   *People of the Deer*, 28n4
   *People of the Deer* (*Gefährten der Rentiere*), 38
   short story anthologies, 43t2.1, 54
   *Snow Walker* (*Der Schneewanderer*), 60, 227
   *Snow Walker* (*Inuit: Vom Mut der Eskimo*), 60
   "Walk Well, My Brother," 63
*Mr. Kneebone's New Digs* (Wallace), 235
Müller, Jürgen E., 4, 19, 73, 77
Müller, Marianne, 32n12, 35–36, 39, 50
*Multiculturalism and the Politics of Recognition* (Taylor), 208, 210n21
Munro, Alice, 4, 21, 36, 45n26, 61, 66, 81
   "Alice Munro Reading Box" (*Alice Munro Lesebox*), 72
   anthologies, recent/older writers, 47n2.2
   *The Beggar Maid*, 71, 88
   *The Beggar Maid* (*Das Bettlermädchen*), 66, 88
   *The Beggar Maid* (*Das Bettlermädchen: Geschichten von Flo und Rose*), 71–72
   "Boys and Girls" ("Jungen und Mädchen"), 72
   *Dance of the Happy Shades*, 70, 72
   *Der Mond über der Eisbahn: Liebesgeschichten*, 72
   *Der Traum meiner Mutter: Erzählungen*, 71
   *Die Jupitermonde*, 72
   *Die Liebe einer Frau: Drei Erzählungen und ein kurzer Roman*, 71
   *Friend of My Youth* (*Glaubst Du, es war Liebe?*), 71, 89
   German reviews on, 88–91, 97, 154n20
   *Hateship, Friendship, Courtship, Loveship, Marriage* (*Himmel und Hölle*), 71
   *Lives of Girls and Women* (*Kleine Aussichten: Ein Roman von Mädchen und Frauen*), 70–71
   *The Love of a Good Woman*, 71
   "The Moons of Jupiter," 33n14
   *The Moons of Jupiter* (*Die Jupitermonde*), 71
   *Open Secrets* (*Offene Geheimnisse*), 71
   *The Progress of Love* (*Der Mond über der Eisbahn: Liebesgeschichten*), 71, 89
   *Runaway* (*Tricks: Acht Erzählungen*), 71–72
   *Selected Stories*, 72
   short story anthologies, 43t2.1
   *The View from Castle Rock* (*Himmel und Hölle*), 72
   *Who Do You Think You Are?*, 66, 71–72, 77, 88
   *Who Do You Think You Are?* (*Das Bettlermädchen*), 88
   "Who Do You Think You Are? ("Was glaubst du, wer du bist?"), 72
   "Wild Swans" ("Wilde Schwäne"), 72
Munsch, Robert, 236
*Murder in the Dark* (*Die Giftmischer: Horror-Trips und Happy-Ends*) (Atwood), 66–67, 82n8
Murrell, John, 172t8.1, 180
"Mütter des Nordens" ("Mothers of the North") (Roberts), 55

*Mutters Lieblinge: Geschichten und Lügen aus meiner Kindheit* (Poulin - illustr.), 249, 249n17
*Mutters Lieblinge* (Lenain), 249
*My Great-Grandfather and I*. Kruss (Krüss), 238n28
*My Heart Soars* (*Und es jubelt mein Herz*) (George), 118
*My Mother's Loves: Stories and Lies from my Childhood* (Poulin - illustr.), 249n17
*My Name Is Paula Popowich!* (Hughes), 232
*My Name Is Seepeetza* (Stirling), 117n6
*My Spirit Soars* (*Und es jubelt mein Geist*) (George), 118
*La mystérieuse bibliothécaire* (Demers), 252n24
*Myths of the North American Indians* (*Die Mythen der nordamerikanischen Indianer*) (Taylor), 122n10, 142

**N**
*Nachrichten aus Ontario: Deutschsprachige Literatur in Kanada* ("News from Ontario: German-Language Literature in Canada") (Fröschle), 56, 77
Nadel, Ira B., 152, 162
*The Naked and the Dead* (Mailer), 146n6
Nancy, Jean-Luc, 206
*Natasha* (Bezmogis), 214
"Native Literature of Canada" (King), 112, 115, 119–20
*Native Poetry in Canada: A Contemporary Anthology* (Armstrong and Grauer), 118
*Nature Power* (Robinson), 124
Naumann-Maerten, Gabriele, 165–67
*Never Judge a Book by Its Cover* (*Verlegtes Glück*) (Seymour), 169t8.1
*New Oxford Book of Canadian Short Stories* (Atwood and Weaver), 75

Nichols, Ruth, 228
*Nieve Immaculada*, 11
Nischik, Reingard M.
  *The Canadian Short Story: Interpretations*, 19, 26
  *Kanadische Literaturgeschichte*, 19, 221, 241
  "Margaret Atwood, Power Politics", 110
  *Margaret Atwood: Works and Impact*, 19, 26, 93, 95
  "Zur Behandlung anglo-kanadischer Kurzgeschichten: Tendenzen, Materialien und Hilfsmittel.", 147, 160, 162
*Nkwalla* (*Nikwalla der Indianer-Junge*) (Sharp), 226
*No Foreign Land: The Biography of a North American Indian* (*Frei wie ein Baum: Ein Indianer erzählt sein Leben*) (Poole and Pelletier), 117, 125, 139
*No Great Mischief* (*Land der Bäume*) (MacLeod), 72
*No Logo!* (*No Logo*) (Klein), 157–59, 161, 196, 216
"No Rinsed Blue Sky, No Red Flower Fences" ("Kein klarblauer Himmel, kein Zaun aus roten Blumen") (Brand), 57
*No Word for Good-Bye* (*Sommer am Kinniwabi*) (Craig), 228
Nolan, Yvette, 113, 165, 178
*Nonsense Novels* (*Der Asbestmann und andere Nonsens-Novellen*) (Leacock), 65
Norman, Howard, 60
*Northern Tales: Traditional Stories of Eskimo and Indian Peoples* (Norman), 60
Nourbese Phillip, Marlene, 24, 238
*La nouvelle maîtresse* (Demers), 252n24
Nowlan, Alden, 43t2.1
"The Nuisance Grounds" (Laurence), 68
Nungak, Zebedee, 60

## 322 TRANSLATING CANADA

Nutt, Ken, 234
Nyncke, Helge, 236

## O

O'Brien, Flann, 149
O'Brien, Jack, 220
*October Stranger* (Kenny), 120
Oeding, Brita Isabel, 270, 282
O'Hagan, Howard, 43t2.1
*Ojibway Ceremonies* (*Großer Weißer Falke: Der Lebenskreis eines Ojibwa*) (Johnston), 58, 141
*Ojibway Heritage* (*Und Manitu erschuf die Welt: Mythen und Visionen der Ojibwa*) (Johnston), 58, 141
"Oka/Oka" (Joe), 140
*On the Eve of Uncertain Tomorrows* (Bissoondath), 57
Ondaatje, Michael, 10, 22, 73, 81n6, 97
    Canadian plays produed in Germany, 172t8.1
    *The Collected Works of Billy the Kid* (*Die gesammelten Werke von Billy the Kid*), 172t8.1
    *Coming through Slaughter* (*Buddy Bolden's Blues*), 172t8.1
    *The English Patient*, 86
    *The Faber Book of Contemporary Canadian Short Stories*, 75
    *Running in the Family*, 69
    *In the Skin of a Lion*, 157
    "Tanten," 69
*One Good Story, That One* (King), 121
"One School Day Afternoon" ("Eines Schulnachmittags") (Keeshig-Tobias), 117
"One-Two-Three Little Indians" ("Ein, zwei, drei kleine Indianer") (Garner), 59
"One-Two-Three Little Indians" (Garner), 41n24
*One Way Ticket: I Don't Want to Know Anyone Well* (*Ein kleines Stückchen Blau: Erzählungen*) (Böll and Wagner - transl.), 39, 50, 145
*One Way Ticket: I Don't Want to Know Anyone Well* (*Ein kleines Stückchen Blau: Erzählungen*) (Levine), 39, 50, 68, 145, 146n4, 162
*One Way Ticket* (Levine), 68, 145
*The Only Outcast* (*Flucht nach vorn*) (Johnston), 237
*Open Secrets* (*Offene Geheimnisse*) (Munro), 71
Oppel, Kenneth, 238–39
Orlov, Steven
    *Birthmarks*, 282
    *Freeze*, 271
    *Isolated Incidents*, 271, 278n5
    *Sperm Count*, 6, 269–82
"Orphans' Progress" ("Der Waisenkinder Reise") (Gallant), 36, 70
*The Other Side of Nowhere: Contemporary Coyote Tales* (*Die andere Seite von Nirgendwo: Zeitgenössische Coyote Geschichten*) (Blue Cloud), 119, 141
Otto, Maria, 121–22n9, 136, 140
*Oublier* (*Vergessen*) (Laberge), 171t8.1, 265t12.2
Ouellette, François, 19
Ouriou, Susan, 247n10
*The Oxford Book of Canadian Short Stories in English* (Atwood and Weaver), 41n25, 75
*The Oxford Companion to Canadian Literature*, 37

## P

Pacey, Desmond, 41n25
Pache, Walter, 19, 24, 45n26, 81, 98
Page, P. K., 44t2.1, 47n2.2
"The Painted Door" ("Die frisch gestrichene Tür") (Ross), 64
*Painting the Dog: The Best Stories of Leon Rooke* (Rooke), 76

Panych, Morris, 165, 172t8.1, 179, 184–85
*The Paper Bag Princess (Die Tüten-Prinzessin)* (Munsch), 236
"Paper Eclipse/Papierfinsternis" (Moses), 140
*Parasiten des Himmels: Gedichte aus zehn Jahren* (Cohen), 148, 151
*Parasites of Heaven* (Cohen), 149
Parr Traill, Catharine, 228
*Parvana's Journey (Allein nach Mazar-e Sharif)* (Ellis), 238n29
Pascal, Julia, 274
*Patience (Demut)* (Sherman), 181–82
*Patterns of Isolation* (Moss), 192
Patterson, Freeman, 55
Peabody, George, 61
Pearson, Kit, 233, 237n27
*Peepshow (Peepshow)* (Brassard), 267t12.2
*The Pegnitz Junction (Blockstelle Pegnitz)* (Gallant), 69
*Pélagie-la-Charrette* (Maillet), 6, 283–84, 286–90
Pelletier, Wilfred, 117, 125, 139
*Pelztierjäger in Kanada* ("Trapper in Canada") (Hartmann), 225n14
*Penguin Book of Canadian Short Stories* (Grady), 41n25
Pennier, Henry, 118
*People of the Deer (Gefährten der Rentiere)* (Mowat), 38
*People of the Deer* (Mowat), 28n4
*Le périmètre (Der Sicherheitsabstand)* (Blanchette), 266n12.2
*Le petit Köchel (Der kleine Köchel)* (Chaurette), 170t8.1, 265t12.2
*Petranella (Petranella)* (Waterton), 234
Pettinger, Christine, 170t8.1
"Pferde der Nacht" (Laurence), 68
"The Philosophy, Chemistry and Universality of Morris Panych's Work" (Glaap), 184, 186
"Piety" ("Frömmigkeit") (Layton), 162
*Pilgrims of the Wild (Kleiner Bruder: Grau-*

*Eule erzählt von Indianern, Bibern und Kanufahrern)* (Belaney), 58
Piovene, Guido, 285n7
Pitseolak, Ashoona, 60
*Pitseolak: Pictures out of My Life* (Pitseolak), 60
*A Planet of Eccentrics* (Begamudré), 57n8
Plenzdorf, Ulrich, 226, 226n15
Plocher, Hanspeter, 259, 268
Poliquin, Daniel, 9, 79n1
Pollock, Sharon, 165
*Le polygraphe (Polygraph)* (Lepage and Brassard), 171t8.1, 264t12.2
Poole, Ted, 117, 139
*Poor Superman (Poor Superman)* (Fraser), 179
Potter, Evan, 12–13, 26, 270, 282
Poulin, Andrée, 255
Poulin, Stéphane, 236, 245, 247, 249, 249n17
"The Prairie: A State of Mind" (Kreisel), 56, 77
*A Prairie Boy's Summer* (Kurelek), 234, 234n23
*A Prairie Boy's Winter* (Kurelek), 234, 234n23
Pratt, E. J., 53, 66, 112
Pratt, Pierre, 236, 244–46, 246n5
"Preisgekrönte kanadische Autorin: Eiskalt in Quebec" (Arnold), 85n16
Pressler, Mirjam, 245–46, 246n5
Prichard, Katharine, 37
Priestley, Alice, 235
*Princess Pocahontas and the Blue Spots* (Mojica), 121
*Princess Prunella and the Purple Peanut* (Atwood), 238
*Principles of Literary Theory (Prinzipien der Literaturkritik)* (Richards), 190–91, 193
*Prison of Grass: Canada from the Native Point of View* (Adams), 118
Prišvin, Michael, 225n12
*Problem Child (Problemkind)* (Walker), 179

*The Progress of Love (Der Mond über der Eisbahn: Liebesgeschichten)* (Munro), 71, 89

**Q**
*A Quality of Light* (Wagamese), 124
*Quebec und Kino: Die Entwicklung eines Abenteuers* (Larouche and Müller), 19
*Quel est ce bruit?* (Lemieux), 251n22

**R**
Rabelais, François, 283
Raddall, Thomas H., 44t2.1, 47n2.2
Rand, Silas, 122n10
Ranville, Myrelene, 238
*Ravensong* (Maracle), 124, 136n22
*The Rebirth of Canada's Indians* (Cardinal), 117–18
Recheis, Käthe, 121–22n9, 121n9, 138, 141, 226
*Recollections of an Assiniboine Chief* (Kennedy), 117, 117n6
*Reconciling the Solitudes* (Taylor), 212
*Red Dust* (Valgardson), 66
*Red Fox (Der rote Fuchs)* (Roberts), 55n4
*Red Plaid Shirt* (Schoemperlen), 77
Redbird, Duke, 119, 127n13, 139
Redsky, James, 117n6
Regehr-Mirau, Meta, 123n10, 142
Reichart, Manuela, 88, 88m28, 89, 89n33
Reid, Gilbert, 185
Reid, Monty, 76
*Relations des Jésuites (Von Schwarzröcken und Hexenmeistern. Robes noires et sorciers: Jesuitenberichte aus Neu-Frankreich)* (Ertler), 284
Remarque, Erich Maria, 154
"The Return" (MacLeod), 73
*The Revenge of Ishtar (Die Rache der Ischtar)* (Zeman), 55
*The Rez Sisters* (Highway), 120–21

*The Rich Man* (Kreisel), 147
Richards, I. A., 190–91, 193
Richardson, Bill, 238
Richler, Mordecai, 5, 36, 143–44, 159
*The Acrobats (Die Akrobaten)*, 144, 153, 163
"Bambinger," 153n17, 163
*Barney's Version (Wie Barney es sieht)*, 69n16, 153, 155
*A Choice of Enemies (Der Boden trägt mich nicht mehr)*, 69n16, 144, 153–54
*Duddy Kravitz*, 154
*Jacob Two-Two and the Dinosaur (Ein Geschenk für Jacob Zweizwei)*, 153, 238
*Jacob Two-Two Meets the Hooded Fang (Jacob Zweizwei in Gefahr)*, 153, 238
*Joshua Then and Now (Joshua damals und jetzt)*, 69n16, 144–45, 152–53
short story anthologies, 44t2.1
*Solomon Gursky Was Here (Solomon Gursky war hier)*, 69n16, 153, 153n18, 154, 154n20, 163
"Some Grist for Mervyn's Mill," 41n24
"Some Grist for Mervyn's Mill" ("Wasser auf Mervyns Mühle"), 69
*Son of a Smaller Hero (Sohn eines kleineren Helden)*, 69n16, 144, 153
*St. Urbain's Horseman (Der Traum des Jakob Hersch)*, 69n16, 144, 152–53
*The Street*, 153
"Wasser auf Mervyn's Mühle," 153n17
Richler, Nancy, 159
Ricoeur, Paul, 191, 213
Riedel, Walter
Canadian literature in Germany, 27n1, 29, 36, 36n20, 38n22
Canadian short stories, 45
*Gute Wanderschaft, mein Bruder: Eine kanadische Anthologie*, 32n11,

33n14, 40–41, 44, 49, 55, 57, 59, 63–64, 66, 68, 82n9, 122
*Kanadische Erzähler der Gegenwart*, 40, 41n24–25, 44, 48, 55–57, 59, 64–65
*Moderne Erzähler der Welt*, 40–41, 44–45, 45n26, 49–50, 122
Rimanelli, Giose, 41n25
*Risk Everything* (Walker), 174–76, 174n2, 179, 186
Ritter, Kurt, 225n14
*Road to Chlifa* (Ouriou), 247n10
*The Roaring Girl* (Hollingshead), 76
*The Robber Bride (Die Räuberbraut)* (Atwood), 87
Roberts, Charles G. D., 36, 44t2.1, 55, 55n4, 220, 222–23
Roberts, Ken, 233
Robinson, Eden, 58–59, 121, 124, 125n11, 136, 141
Robinson, Harry, 124, 133
*Rolf in the Woods (Mit den letzten Trappern in Prairie und Urwald)* (Seton), 224n8
*Rolf in the Woods (Rolf, der Trapper)* (Seton), 224
*Rolf in the Woods (Rolf und sein roter Freund)* (Seton), 224n8
Rooke, Leon, 68, 76
*Root Cellar* (Lunn), 233
Rosenthal, Caroline, 95, 110
*Roses for Gita* (Gilmore), 235
Ross, Sinclair, 44t2.1, 64
Rotchin, Glen, 152
Roth, Philip, 94, 154–55
*La Route de Chlifa* (Marineau), 247, 247n10
Rowohlt, Harry, 149, 246, 246n7
Roy, Gabrielle, 20, 80
Ruberto, Roberto, 41n25
Rumpf, Frank, 87, 87n25
*Runaway (Tricks: Acht Erzählungen)* (Munro), 71–72
*Running in the Family* (Ondaatje), 69

"Running on the March Wind" (Rennen auf dem Märzwind") (Keeshig-Tobias), 140
*The Russian Album* (Ignatieff), 197, 206
Rutschky, Katharina, 90–91, 90n35, 201n10
Ryerson Young, Egerton, 220

**S**
Sabin, Stefana
*Kanada erzählt: 17 Erzählungen*, 41, 41n24, 48, 50, 54, 63n13, 64, 67–70, 78, 82n9, 122, 145, 153n17, 154
*La Sagouine* (Maillet), 283, 287
Said, Edward, 207, 216
*Une saison dans la vie d'Emmanuel* (Blais), 80
Salinger, J. D., 146n6, 150
*A Salmon for Simon (Ein Lachs für Simon)* (Waterton), 234
Saltman, Judith, 228, 235n24, 236n26, 240
Salutin, Rick, 165
Sarrazin, Francine, 244
Saul, John Ralston, 9, 13n7
"Culture and Foreign Policy," 14–15, 17
*The Doubter's Companion (Wirtschaftsgipfeln und anderen Zumutungen des 21. Jahrhunderts)*, 196, 216
*The Unconscious Civilisation (Der Markt frisst seine Kinder)*, 196, 216
*Scar Tissue* (Ignatieff), 197
Schanko, Ulrike, 172t8.1
Scharfenberg, Ute, 172t8.1, 181–82
"Schlagfertig, aber atemlos: Michael Ignatieffs Nationalismus-kritik" (Wagner), 198n8
Schlöndorff, Volker, 82
Schloz, Günther, 84n13, 87
Schlüter, Herbert, 39, 49
Schmid, Thomas, 206, 206n16
Schmidt-Henkel, Hinrich, 170t8.1

Schmitt, Carl, 203
"Schnee" ("Snow") (Grove), 56
"Schnee" (Valgardson), 66
Schneider, Richard C., 154
Schneider, Walter, 122n10, 142
Schnell, Franz, 225n14
   *3 x P und rotes Kanu* ("3 x P and Red Canoe"), 225n14
Schoemperlen, Diane, 73, 75, 77
Schostak, Renate, 89, 89n32–33
Schröder, Jörg, 148, 148n14
Schütte, Wolfgang, 157
*Schwarze Augen* (Tibo), 248n13
Schwarzkopf, Margarete von, 85n18, 89, 89n31
Scofield, Gregory, 117n6, 119
Scollard, Rose, 172t8.1
Scott, Duncan Campbell, 44t2.1, 46, 47t2.2, 65, 112
*The Second Scroll* (Klein), 143
*The Secret Journal of Alexander Mackenzie* (Fawcett), 76
*The Secret Trail* (Roberts), 55
Seehase, Georg, 35n18, 37, 49, 51
Seifert, Martina, 252
*Selected Stories* (Munro), 72
*Seraja Sova* ("Grey Owl") (Prišvin), 225n12
Seton, Ernest Thompson, 36–37, 220
   *The Adventures of Sajo and Her Beaver People*, 225
   *Animal Heroes*, 55
   animal stories, 55, 222, 224
   Canadian author, most published, 223
   *Der Wolf von Winnipeg und andere Tiergeschichten*, 55
   *Die schönsten Tiergeschichten*, 55
   *Die schönsten Tiergeschichten von Ernest Thompson Seton* and *Bingo und andere Tierhelde*, 224
   German Youth Literature Prize (Deutscher Jugendliteraturpreis), 224

*Rolf in the Woods* (*Mit den letzten Trappern in Prairie und Urwald*), 224n8
*Rolf in the Woods* (*Rolf, der Trapper*), 224
*Rolf in the Woods* (*Rolf und sein roter Freund*), 224n8
Russian translations, 224n11
"Tito," 224n10
*Two Little Savages: Being the Adventures of Two Boys Who Lived as Indians and What They Learned* (*Zwei kleine Wilde: Ein Buch von Jan und Sam und ihrem Treiben in ihrem Reich und auf der Farm in Sanger*), 224, 224n9
*Wild Animals I Have Known* (*Bingo und andere Tierhelden*), 223
*Zottelohr und andere Geschichten*, 55
*Seuils* (Genette), 33, 49
*Seven for a Secret* (Sheppard), 232
*The Seven Streams of the River Ota* (*Die sieben Ströme des Flusses Ota*) (Lepage), 171t8.1
Sewid, James, 117n6
Seymour, Blicker, 169t8.1
*Shape of a Girl*, 5
*The Shape of a Girl* (MacLeod), 182–83
Sharp, Edith, 226
*Sheeps and Whales* (*Schafe und Wale*) (Ghazali), 184
Sheppard, Mary C., 232
Sherman, Jason, 165, 181–82
Shields, Carol, 4, 17, 88–91
*A Short History of Indians in Canada* (King), 121
"A Sick Call" ("Ein Krankenbesuch") (Callaghan), 63n13
*Silent Words* (Slipperjack), 124
*Silverwing* (Oppel), 238
Simard, Rémy, 245, 246n5
Simon, Lorne, 124
Simpson, Leo, 44t2.1, 47n2.2

"Singing for the Dead" ("Singen für die Toten") (Michaels), 157
*Skin Divers* (Michaels), 155
*The Sky Is Falling* (*Unter anderen Sternen*) (Pearson), 237n27
*Slash* (Armstrong), 124, 125n11, 126–27, 131, 140
*Slave of the Haida* (*Kim-ta, der Sohn des Häuptlings*) (Anderson), 226
Slipperjack, Ruby, 124, 136n22
"A Small Piece of Blue" (Böll and Wagner - transl.), 145
"A Small Piece of Blue" ("Ein kleines Stückchen Blau") (Levine), 68, 145
Smiley, Jane, 154
Smith, Ray, 44t2.1, 45n26, 47n2.2
*Snow Walker* (*Der Schneewanderer*) (Mowat), 60, 227
*Snow Walker* (*Inuit: Vom Mut der Eskimo*) (Mowat), 60
*So Long, Leonard: Leben und Lieder von Leonard Cohen* (Graf), 151
Soenen, Johan, 225, 225n13, 242
Soenen, Peter, 222
Sofsky, Wolfgang, 202n12
*Sojourner's Truth and Other Stories* (Maracle), 59, 121–22
*Solomon Gursky Was Here* (*Solomon Gursky war hier*) (Richler), 69n16, 153, 153n18, 154, 154n20, 163
"Some Grist for Mervyn's Mill" (Richler), 41n24
"Some Grist for Mervyn's Mill" ("Wasser auf Mervyns Mühle") (Richler), 69
*Someday* (Taylor), 120
*Son of a Smaller Hero* (*Sohn eines kleineren Helden*) (Richler), 69n16, 144, 153
*Son of Raven, Son of Deer: Fables of the Tse-shat People* (*Sohn des Raben, Sohn des Rehs*) (Clutesi), 59, 115, 122–23, 141
"Song of Bear's Breakfast" (Moses), 140

Sontheimer, Michael, 158
"Sophie" ("Sophie: Mutter der Gräber") (Carr), 59
Soulières, Robert, 247, 247n8
*The Sparrow's Fall* (Bodsworth), 136n22, 227n17
*The Sparrow's Fall* (*Lauft, Füße, lauft*) (Bodsworth), 32n11, 33n13, 38, 48, 136n22
*Speak to the Earth* (*Sprich mit der Erde*) (Bell), 237n27
Spence, Lewis, 122n10, 142
Spenser, Edmund, 190
*Sperm Count* (Orlov), 6, 269–82
Spettigue, Douglas, 44t2.1
*The Spice-Box of the Earth* (Cohen), 148–49
Spiegelman, Art, 280
*The Spirit at Hidden Valley: A Good Medicine Story* (*Das Geheimnis des verborgenen Tales: Eine Mutter-Erde-Geschichte*) (Hungry Wolf), 114n4
*St. Urbain's Horseman* (*Der Traum des Jakob Hersch*) (Richler), 69n16, 144, 152–53
*Staging Coyote's Dream: An Anthology of First Nations Drama in English* (Mojica), 120n7
Staudacher, Cornelia, 146
Stefan, Verena, 83, 92
Stefansson, Vilhjalmur, 220
Stein, David L., 44t2.1, 47n2.2, 271
*Stella, Queen of Snow* (*Sophie und der erste Schnee*) (Gay), 245n4
*Stella, Queen of Snow* (*Stella, reine des neiges*) (Gay), 245n4
*Stella, Star of the Sea* (*Sophie und das weite Meer*) (Gay), 245n4
*Stella, Star of the Sea* (*Stella, étoile de la mer*) (Gay), 245n4, 247n8, 252
*Stella* (*Sophie*) (Gay), 236
*Stella the Forest Fairy* (*Sophie und die Waldfee*) (Gay), 245n4

*Stella the Forest Fairy* (*Stella, fée des forêts*) (Gay), 245n4
*Stephen Fair* (*Ausgeträumt*) (Wynne-Jones), 234
Sterne, Lawrence
   *Tristram Shandy*, 194
Steuben, Fritz, 112, 128
Stirling, Shirley, 117n6
*The Stone Angel* (*Der steinerne Engel*) (Laurence), 28, 32n11, 36, 39, 49
*The Stone Angel* (*Der steinerne Engel*) (Schlüter - transl.), 39, 49
*The Stone Diaries* (*Das Tagebuch der Daisy Goodwill*) (Shields), 90
*The Stone Diaries* (Shields), 90
*Stones and Switches* (Simon), 124
*Stories by Canadian Women* (Sullivan), 65
*Stories from Canada* (*Erzählungen aus Kanada*) (Uthe-Spencker), 41n24–25, 44, 51, 59, 63n13, 65
*Stories from Canada* (*Erzählungen aus Kanada*) (Weaver), 81, 92
*Stories from the Canadian North* (Whitaker), 62
*Stories from the Road Allowance People* (Campbell), 124
*Stormchild* (*Sturmkind*) (Bellingham), 226
*Stormy Night* (*Gewitternacht*) (Lemieux), 251n21
*Stormy Night* (Lemieux), 251
*Stormy Night* (*Nuit d'orage*) (Lemieux), 251n21
"Stranded" (*Gestrandet*) (MacLeod), 182–83
*The Strange One of Barra* (*Der Fremde von Barra*) (Bodsworth), 32n11, 38, 48
*The Strange One of Barra* (*Kanina*) (Bodsworth), 38, 48
Stratford, Philip, 284
*The Street* (Richler), 153
Stromberg, Kyra, 85n14, 85n18, 86, 86n21, 87, 87n23
Struck, Karin, 83

*Stuttgarter Zeitung*, 20
*Suburban Motel* (Walker), 166, 174n2, 186
*Süddeutsche Zeitung* (Pache), 19
Sullivan, Rosemary, 65
*Sundogs* (Maracle), 124
*Sunshine Sketches of a Little Town* (Leacock), 65
*Sunwing* (Oppel), 238
*Surfacing* (Atwood), 4, 32, 33n13, 36, 39, 48, 81–82, 82n8, 94, 98–109
*Surfacing* (*Der lange Traum*) (Atwood), 33, 81, 99, 109
*Surfacing* (*Der lange Traum*) (Böhnke - transl.), 33, 99, 105, 109
*Surfacing* (*Strömung*) (Atwood), 32, 32n11–12, 33, 39, 81, 99, 102, 105–9
*Surfacing* (*Strömung*) (Böhnke - transl.), 33
*Survival: A Thematic Guide to Canadian Literature* (Atwood), 191–92
*Susannah: A Little Girl with the Mounties* (Denison), 228
*Swann: A Mystery* (*Mary Swann*) (Shields), 90
*Sweetgrass* (*Süßes Gras*) (Hudson), 226

T
Tait, Les, 236
*Tales from Firozsha Baag* (*Das Kaleidoskop des Lebens*) (Mistry), 57
*Tales from the Igloo* (*Geschichten der Eskimos*) (Metayer), 60
*Tales from the Margin* (Grove), 56
*Tales of an Empty Cabin* (*Ihre Mokassins hinterließen keine Spuren: Grau-Eule erzählt, aufgeschrieben im Jahre*) (Belaney), 58
*Tales the Elders Told* (*Nanabusch und Großer Geist: Geschichten der Odschibwä-Indianer*) (Johnston), 58, 141
"Tanten" (Ondaatje), 69
"The Task of the Translator" (Benjamin), 195
Taylor, Charles, 6, 189, 196, 205, 205n15

multiculturalism, challenge of, 207–14
*Multiculturalism and the Politics of Recognition*, 208, 210n21
*Reconciling the Solitudes*, 212
Taylor, Colin C., 122n10, 142
Taylor, Drew Hayden, 120, 120n8, 165
  *AlterNatives*, 111n1, 121
  *Fearless Warriors*, 121
  "First We Take Turtle Island, Then We Take Berlin," 113, 138
  *Funny, You Don't Look like One: Observations from a Blue-Eyed Ojibway* ("Ich bin ein Ojibway"), 113, 138
  *Further Adventures of a Blue-Eyed Ojibway*, 113
  *Someday*, 120
  *Toronto at Dreamer's Rock*, 120, 168
*The Tent* (*Das Zelt*) (Atwood), 67
*Terrible Times* (*Schlechte Nachrichten*) (Ardagh), 246n7
Tetso, John, 117n6
Thériault, Yves, 112
*Third Solitudes: Tradition and Discontinuity in Jewish-Canadian Literature* (Greenstein), 143, 143n1, 150–51, 160
Thom, Jo-Ann, 119
Thomas, Audrey, 44t2.1, 47n2.2
Thompson, Judith, 165
Thornhill, Jan, 235
Thrasher, Anthony Apakark, 60
*Thrasher: Skid Row Eskimo* (Thrasher), 60
*3 x P und rotes Kanu* ("3 x P and Red Canoe") (Schnell), 225n14
*Thunder through My Veins: Memories of a Métis Childhood* (Scofield), 117n6
Thurman-Hunter, Bernice, 233
Thuswaldner, Anton, 154n20
Tibo, Gilles, 236, 247, 247n12, 248n13
*Titanica* (*Titanica*) (Harrison), 266
"Tito" (Seton), 224n10

*To-Morrow Is with Us* (*Spionagefall Alan Baird*) (Carter), 37, 49
Tomblin, Stephen, 61n11, 78
*The Tomorrow-Tamer* (*Die Stimmen von Adamo: 10 Erzählungen*) (Laurence), 67
*Topography of Love* (*Topographie der Liebe*) (Morgan), 61
*Toronto at Dreamer's Rock* (Glaap), 120
*Toronto at Dreamer's Rock* (Taylor), 120, 168
*Touche pas à mon corps, Tatie Jacotte!* (Lenain), 249n16
*Transitgäste: Erzählungen* (Enzensberger editor), 69
*Traplines* (*Fallen Stellen*) (Robinson), 58–59, 121, 125n11, 141
*Trapping Is My Life* (Tetso), 117n6
*Travelling on into the Light and Other Stories* (*Weiter ins Licht und andere Geschichten*) (Brooks), 62
Tremblay, Larry, 17n14, 264t12.2, 266t12.2
Tremblay, Michel, 184, 259n4, 263t12.2, 267t12.2
*Tristram Shandy* (Sterne), 194
*True Stories* (*Wahre Geschichten*) (Atwood), 82n8
Truhlar, Richard, 76
Truss, Jan, 228
*Truth and Bright Water* (King), 113, 124
"The Turning Point" ("Der Wendepunkt") (Cameron), 41n24, 45, 59
"The Two Fishermen" ("Die beiden Angler") (Callaghan), 63n13
"The Two Fishermen" ("Zwei Männer Angeln") (Callaghan), 63n13
*Two Little Savages: Being the Adventures of Two Boys Who Lived as Indians and What They Learned* (*Zwei kleine Wilde: Ein Buch von Jan und Sam und ihrem Treiben in ihrem Reich und auf der Farm in Sanger*) (Seton), 224, 224n9

"Two Sisters" ("Die beiden Schwestern") (Markoosie), 59–60
"Two Sisters in Geneva" ("Zwei Schwestern in Genf ") (Kreisel), 57, 162
Tyman, James, 117n6
Tymoczko, Maria, 130, 138

**U**

Über Zäune und Mauern (Dispatches from the Front Lines of the Globalization Debate) (Klein), 196, 216
Uhuru Street (Vassanji), 57n8
Uncle Ronald (Doyle), 232
The Unconscious Civilisation (Der Markt frisst seine Kinder) (Saul), 196, 216
"Under Glass" ("Unter Glas") (Atwood), 67
Under the Volcano (Lowry), 24, 34
Under the Volcano (Unter dem Vulkan) (Lowry), 32n11, 34, 50
Une bien curieuse factrice (Demers), 252n24
Unidentified Human Remains and the True Nature of Love (Fraser), 168
Unidentified Human Remains and the True Nature of Love (Unidentifizierte Leichenteile & das wahre Wesen der Liebe) (Fraser), 170t8.1, 179
The Unjust Society (Cardinal), 117
Up in the Tree (Atwood), 238
Up to Low (Doyle), 232
Updike, John, 94
Uppenbrink, Brigitte, 249
Urquhart, Jane, 84, 91
Ursell, Geoffrey, 76
Uthe-Spencker, Angela, 41n24–25, 44, 51, 59, 63n13, 65

**V**

Valgardson, William Dempsey, 44t2.1, 65–66, 68
Van Camp, Richard, 121, 125n11, 136, 141, 226, 235
Van Dyck, Marianne, 156–57

van Herk, Aritha, 36, 62
Vancouver Short Stories (Gerson), 62
Vanderhaeghe, Guy, 44t2.1, 47n2.2, 69
Various Positions: Das Leben Leonard Cohens: Eine Biographie (Nadel), 152, 162
Vassanji, Moyez G., 57n8
Vejen til Schlifa (Marineau), 247n11
Venir au monde (Hébert), 249n19, 254
Le ventriloque (Der Bauchredner) (Tremblay), 266t12.2
Venuti, Lawrence, 2n2, 7, 21, 26, 136, 138
The View from Castle Rock (Himmel und Hölle) (Munro), 72
Vigil (Freudige Erwartung and Meine Tante und ich) (Panych), 172t8.1, 179, 184–85
"Voices from Canada: 25 Canadian Dramas for German Stages" (Stimmen aus Kanada: 25 kanadische Dramen für deutsche Bühnen) (Glaap), 120
Voices from Canada: Focus on Thirty Plays (Glaap), 168, 179, 181
von Flotow, Luise, 270, 282, 283n1
Vonnegut, Kurt, 149

**W**

Wa-Sha-Quon-Asin, 224. See also Belaney, Archibald Stansfeld; Grey Owl
Waddington, Miriam, 44t2.1, 47n2.2, 147, 163
Wagamese, Richard, 132, 136
  Keeper'n Me (Hüter der Trommel), 59, 124, 125n11, 131–32, 139
  A Quality of Light, 124
Wagner, Reinhard
  "A Small Piece of Blue," 145
  Blood and Belonging, 198–99
  In Lower Town, 146n4
  One Way Ticket: I Don't Want to Know Anyone Well (Ein kleines Stückchen Blau), 39, 50, 145

"Schlagfertig, aber atemlos: Michael Ignatieffs Nationalismus-kritik," 198n8
Wagner, Richard, 198, 198n8, 199
*Waiting for Time* (*Am Ende des Meeres*) (Morgan), 61
"Walk Well, My Brother" (Mowat), 63
Walker, George F., 176, 185–86
   *Adult Entertainment* (*Nur für Erwachsene*), 173t8.1, 179
   *Criminal Genius* (*Genie und Verbrechen*), 172t8.1
   *The End of Civilization* (*Das Ende der Zivilisation*), 172t8.1
   *Featuring Loretta* (*Loretta*), 173t8.1, 179
   *Heaven* (*Heaven*), 173t8.1
   *Problem Child* (*Problemkind*), 179
   *Risk Everything*, 174–76, 174n2, 179, 186
   *Suburban Motel*, 166, 174n2, 186
Wallace, Ian, 235–36
Waltner-Toews, David, 44t2.1, 47n2.2
*The Warrior's Honour: Ethnic War and the Modern Conscience* (Ignatieff), 200, 205, 216
*The Warrior's Honour: Ethnic War and the Modern Conscience* (*Zivilisierung des Krieges*) (Ignatieff), 201
*The Wars* (Findley), 36
*Was für ein Besuch!* (Pratt), 246n5
"Wasser auf Mervyn's Mühle" (Richler), 153n17
"Wasser" ("Water") (Grove), 56
*The Watch that Ends the Night* (*Die Nacht der Versöhnung*) (MacLennan), 38, 50
Waterton, Betty, 234
Watt, Melanie, 236
*Way out West!* (Ursell), 76
*The Ways of My Grandmothers* (Hungry Wolf), 124–25
*We So Seldom Look on Love: Stories* (*Seltsam wie die Liebe*) (Gowdy), 73

Weaver, Robert, 41n25, 75, 81, 92
*Weesaquachak and the Lost Ones* (Slipperjack), 124
Wegner, Matthias, 87, 87n22
*The Weight of Oranges* (Michaels), 155
Weiland, Severin, 204n13
Weinzweig, Helen, 147, 163
*Weißt du dass die Bäume reden: Weisheit der Indiane* ("Do You Know that the Trees Talk? Indian Wisdom") (Recheis), 121n9
Weniger, Silke, 247, 247n9
*West of Fiction* (Flater et al.), 62
*Whalesinger* (*Wenn Wale singen*) (Wilton Katz), 237n27
*What Can't Be Changed Shouldn't Be Mourned* (Valgardson), 66
*What's That Noise?* (*Was hört der Bär*) (Lemieux), 251, 251n22
*What's the Most Beautiful Thing You Know about Horses?* (Littlechild), 235
"Whee-skay-chak and Kah-kah-ge / Whee-skaychak und Kah-kah-ge" (Kenny), 123
Wheeler, Jordan, 121
"When It Happens" ("Wenn es passiert") (Atwood), 45, 67
"Where Is the Voice Coming From?" ("Die rätselhafte Stimme") (Wiebe), 64
*Whispering in the Shadows* (Armstrong), 124
Whitaker, Muriel, 62
*The White Bone* (*Der weiße Knochen*) (Gowdy), 74
*The White Leader* (*Der weiße Häuptling*) (Lindsay Skinner), 228
*Who Do You Think You Are?* (*Das Bettlermädchen*) (Munro), 88
*Who Do You Think You Are?* (Munro), 66, 71–72, 77, 88
"Who Do You Think You Are? ("Was glaubst du, wer du bist?") (Munro), 72
*Who Is Francis Rain?* (Buffie), 233

"Who's Political Here? " ("Wer ist hier eigentlich politisch?") (Maracle), 59, 122, 140
Wiebe, Heinrich, 56, 56n5, 77
Wiebe, R., 44t2.1, 62, 64, 64n14, 68, 112
Wieler, Diana, 238
*Wild Animals I Have Known* (*Bingo und andere Tierhelden*) (Seton), 223
*Wild in the City* (Thornhill), 235
"Wild Swans" ("Wilde Schwäne") (Munro), 72
*Wilderness Tips* (*Tips für die Wildnis*) (Atwood), 66
*Will to Win* (*Ich werd' es schaffen!*) (Blakeslee), 237n27
Willis, Jane, 117n6
Wilson, Ethel, 36
Wilton Katz, Welwyn, 237n27
"The Wind Is Our Breath: Harmony with the Earth—Indian Wisdom Texts" (*Der Wind ist unser Atem: Harmonie mit der Erde—Indianische Weisheitstexte*) (Baumann), 121–22n9, 137
*Winners* (*Siksika*) (Collura), 226
*Winsome Winnie and Other New Nonsense Novels* (*Die liebreizende Winnie: Neue Nonsens-Novellen*) (Leacock), 65
*Wisdom of the Wilderness* (*Die Burg im Grase*) (Roberts), 55n4
"With Half a Heart" (*Mit der Hälfte des Herzens*) (Maillet), 284, 284n2, 290
Withrow, Sarah, 233
*Wo alle Straßen enden* ("Where All Streets End") (Helke), 225n14
*Wo die Berge namenlos sind* ("Where the Mountains Have No Names") (Bittner), 239
Wolffsohn, Michael, 204, 204n13
"Words like Traces: Indian Wisdom" (*Worte wie Spuren: Weisheit der Indianer*) (Otto), 121–22n9, 136, 140
"Work on Myth" (*Arbeit am Mythos*) (Blumenberg), 192
*Write It on Your Heart* (Robinson), 124
Wuorio, Eva Lis, 228
Wurzenberger, Gerda, 248n13
Wynne-Jones, T, 233–34, 237–38, 240, 242

**Y**
Yee, Paul, 233, 235
*Yeux noirs* (Tibo), 247n12
Young, Lisa, 61n11, 78
Young-Ing, Greg, 115–16, 119, 139–40
"The Young Priest" ("Der junge Priester") (Callaghan), 63

**Z**
*Zack* (*South on 61*) (Bell), 237n27, 239
Zaü, 248, 248n13
Zauneck, Patrizia, 85n17
"Zeit der Zauberbräute" (Duhm-Heitzmann), 85n15, 86n20
*Zeitschrift für Kanada-Studien*, 19
Zeman, Ludmilla, 55
Zerpner, Annette, 253n26
*Zoom at Sea* (Wynne-Jones), 234
*Zoom Away* (Wynne-Jones), 234
*Zottelohr und andere Geschichten* (Seton), 55
"Zur Behandlung anglo-kanadischer Kurzgeschichten: Tendenzen, Materialien und Hilfsmittel." (Nischik), 147, 160, 162

# SUBJECT INDEX

**A**

AECB. *See* Association for the Export of Canadian Books (AECB)
AELC. *See* Association pour l'exportation du livre canadien (AELC)
AIM. *See* American Indian Movement (AIM)
Alliance française, 3
American Indian Movement (AIM), 118
ANEL. *See* Association nationale des éditeurs de livre (ANEL)
*Anne of Green Gables*, 229–31
Annick Press, 231, 237, 245, 246n5, 249, 249n17
anti-Americanism
    Atwood's *Surfacing*, 32, 45, 82, 100
    Atwood's *Surfacing*, Bock's afterword, 4, 104–5, 105n14
    Atwood's "When It Happens," 41
    Canadian, 20, 34
    German liberal stance, 97
    *Strömung*, para- and metatext for, 32n12
Anvil Performance Series, 173
Anvil Press, 173
Arche éditeur, 261–63
Association for Canadian Studies in German-Speaking Countries, 165
Association for the Export of Canadian Books (AECB), 10n2, 23, 23n21–22
Association nationale des éditeurs de livre (ANEL), 248
Association of Canadian Studies, 185
Association of Drama Writers and Composers, 261
Association of Jewish Theatre of North America, 274
Association pour l'exportation du livre canadien (AELC), 248
Atwood, Margaret. *See also* anti-Americanism; feminist writing
    German reviews, 86–91
    overview, 93–94
    prominence in Germany, 96–98
    scholarly research on, 95
    status in Germany, 94–95
    "*Surfacing*" in Germany, 98–99
    translations, analysis of, 101–8
    translations, cultural factors influencing, 100–101
    translations, production history of, 99
Aufbau-Verlag, 31, 38

**B**

Baum Publications, 128
Beltz und Gelberg, 235, 251
Berlin Children's Festival, 251
Berlin Verlag, 66–67, 71–72, 76, 156
Berliner Schaubühne, 263
Bitterfeld Conference, 30

Bologna Children's Book Fair (Fiera del Libro per Ragazzi), 231
Booker Prize, 24, 71, 90
Brick (publisher), 128n15
British Council, 3, 15
Bronfman Centre for the Arts, 274

C
Canada Council for the Arts / Conseil des arts du Canada
   budget for export of culture, 270
   Canadian identity, promotes, 18n15
   French Canadian literature, 248
   funding agency, 3
   funding for foreign publishers, 10n2
   funding for translation of children's literature, 236–37
   funding for translation of literature, 17, 22, 22n20, 23–24, 24n23, 73, 99, 233, 248–49, 282
   publishing grant, 232
Canadian anthologies, 40–46, 47t2.2, 48
Canadian Children's Book Centre, 253
Canadian Children's Literature/Littérature canadienne pour la jeunesse, 231
Canadian Embassy in Germany, 18n16, 19n18, 36n20, 94, 232, 237, 282
Canadian female writers, 20
Canadian literary and political theory
   Frye, Northrop, 6, 189–95
   Ignatieff, Michael, 196–207
   overview, 187–88
   Taylor, Charles, 207–14
   travelling theory, 188–89
Canadian Native people stories, 220–21
Canadian short story
   authors, popularity of, 66–73
   best, 75
   Canada as modern nation, 62–66
   ethnicity and multiculturalism, 55–60
   exotic otherness of Canada, 54–55
   gender roles and relations, 62–63

Inuit literature, 60
literary qualities, 73–74
Native literature, 58–61
regionalism, 61–62
themes, 41
translating and marketing, 53–54
translation, reasons for, 54, 74–76
Canadian Studies
   academics in, 13n7
   Association of, 185
   Canadian identity, promotes, 18n15, 24
   chair in, establishment of, 10, 10n7
   English Canadian authors, 79
   in German Universities, 10, 18, 147, 220n2, 284
   Graz Centre for, 285, 288
   Indian representative, token, 113
Canadian women writers
   Cosmopolitan, 85n15, 86, 86n20
   feminist writing, 39–40, 83, 84n12, 86–88, 90, 103, 126, 128
   French-Canadian, 79n1
   genre of stereotypes, 85
   German reviews of Atwood, Munro and Shields, 86–91
   "homeland"/"fatherland" theme, 83
   overview, 79–80
   pioneers in, 80–84
   reception of, 84–86
   women reviewers, 84
   as "women who are different," 91
CanLit, 19, 189, 227n17
Carl Hanser (publisher), 153
Carl-Zuckmayer-Medal, 245
Centre d'essai des auteurs dramatiques (CEAD), 11, 166, 173–74, 260
Claassen, 66, 99, 99n11, 145–46
Clarkson, Governor General Adrienne, 9
Cohen, Leonard, 144, 148–52
Commonwealth Prize for the Americas, 155

## Subject Index

Communication Jeunesse, 253
*Cosmopolitan,* 85n15, 86, 86n20
Coteau Books, 116n5, 128n15
Council for Canadian Studies, 7
Cron, Anna, 183–84
cultural diplomacy
    Canadian conundrums in, 22–25
    Canadian Ministry of Heritage, 11–12
    Canadian Studies in Germany, 18–20
    Canadian Studies program, 13
    "Canadian wilderness" myth, 10
    German publishers/reviewers, 21–22
    German-speaking academics, 20
    Governor General of Canada, 9–10
    literature as cultural export, 17
    national branding, 15–16
    overview, 9–10
    public policy or, 11–15, 12n5
    stories, translating, 17–18
    "Trade Routes" program, 11, 15
    university courses in CanLit, 19

### D

De-ba-jih-mu-jig Theatre Group, 120
Department of Canadian Heritage, 15
Department of External Affairs, 231
Department of Foreign Affairs and International Trade (DFAIT)
    Canadian identity and culture, 11, 11n3
    Canadian Studies program, 13n7, 15
    cultural export and funding support, 270, 270n3
    database of Canadian literature, 94n3
    funding for translation, 23
    German Canadian Studies Association, 18, 18n16
    International Cultural Relations Program, 23
Deutsche Jugendbuchpreis, 245
Deutscher Jugendliteraturpreis, 124, 224, 246n7, 285
DFAIT. *See* Department of Foreign Affairs and International Trade (DFAIT)
Diederichs (publisher), 128

### E

Les éditions des 400 coups, 249
Les éditions Québec/Amérique, 250
Elizabeth Mrazik-Cleaver Picture Book Award, 235n24
English Canadian children's literature
    adventure and survival, 226–29
    *Anne of Green Gables,* 229–31
    Canadian Native people stories, 220–21
    Children's Book Centre, 231
    German Youth Literature Prize, 224, 226–27, 235
    "great white North" myth, 5
    images of Canada, traditional, 221–22
    "Indianthusiasm," 226
    Nazi lists of "approved literature," 224
    overview, 219–21
    picture books, 234–36
    promotion and funding, 236–39
    summary, 239–40
    target cultures, changes in, 231–34
    wild animals, real men and natives, 222–26
    writers, early, 220–21
English Canadian plays
    Cron, Anna, 183–84
    German theatre critics, 184–85
    German theatres, staging in, 168–69
    Germany, introduction into, 165–69
    Jandl, Andreas, 180–81
    McLeod, Joan, 182–83
    promoting and marketing, 173–74
    Scharfenberg, Ute, 181–82
    translating contemporary, 174–79
    translations, English titled, 179
    translations, free, 179

translations, literal, 179
translators and translation, 179–84
Entr'Actes agency, 261
Erika Klopp Verlag, 235, 250
Eulenspiegel (publisher), 37

**F**
Federal Republic of Germany (FRG)
   Canada's indigenous people, 38, 38n22
   Canadian anthologies, 40–46, 47t2.2, 48
   Canadian authors, individual, 35–40
   Canadian literature in, 27–35
   Canadian literature study, 27n1
feminist writing
   Atwood's *Surfacing*, 39, 98, 102–3
   Atwood's *The Handmaid's Tale*, 39–40, 87
   Atwood's *The Robber Bride*, 86
   Canadian, 83
   Canadian novels in GDR, 39–40
   GDR, prominent writers of, 39n23
   German, 83, 84n12, 87
   German *vs.* Canadian, 86, 88
   Laurence's *The Stone Angel*, 39
   Munro's *The Moons of Jupiter*, 88
   Native literature, 128
   "new" language of, 83
   Shield's *The Stone Diaries*, 90–91
   "The Wise Women of the Indians," 126
   women writers, prominent Canadian, 4
Festival of Jewish Arts and Culture, 274
Fiera del Libro per Ragazzi (Bologna Children's Book Fair), 231
Fifth House (publisher), 116n5
films, 17
*Financial Post* bestseller list, 156
First Nations. *See* Native Canadian writing
Fondation Beaumarchais, 261–62
Frankfurt Book Fair, 95, 99, 124, 128n15, 153–54, 248, 251

Frauenoffensive (publisher), 128
Frederking & Thaler (publisher), 128
French Canadian children's literature
   Christian moral values, 244
   detours, 246–48
   "early years," 243–44
   international marketing, 248–53
   outlook, 253–54
   Québécité, 244–46
   sex education bestseller, 244
   wilderness absent/ girls abound, 5
French Canadian drama. *See also Sperm Count* (Orlov)
   agencies, 258–59t12.1
   German titles, 263–67t12.2
   Germany, access by France, 258–59
   Germany, no direct contact, 257–58
   performances, 263–67t12.2
   playwrights, 263–67t12.2
   productions, 258–59t12.1
   publishers, 258–59t12.1
   routes into Germany, 258–59t12.1
   theatre festivals, 258–59t12.1
   theatre productions, 258–59t12.1
   theatre publishers, 260–68
   year of translation, 263–67t12.2
FRG. *See* Federal Republic of Germany (FRG)
Frye, Northrop, 6, 189–95

**G**
Gabriel Dumont Institute Press, 116n5
GDR. *See* German Democratic Republic (GDR)
German Canadian Studies Association, 18, 18n16
German Canadian Studies Association (Gesellschaft für Kanada-Studien), 18, 18n16
German Democratic Republic (GDR)
   Anglo-American literature, 27–28, 35
   Canada's indigenous people, 38, 38n22

## SUBJECT INDEX 337

Canadian anthologies, 40–46, 47t2.2
Canadian authors, individual, 35–40
Canadian literature in, 27–35
Canadian women's novels, 39–40
censorship by publishing houses, 31, 31n10, 32–33, 100
feminist writers in, 39n23
"Indianthusiasm," infatuation with, 4–6, 112–13, 138, 226
paratext in books, 33–34, 46
political objectives, 29–30
print-licence, official, 28, 31
prominent feminist writers of, 39n23
German Youth Literature Prize, 224, 226–27, 235
Giller Prize, 24
Gläserner Bär ("Glass Bear"), 251
Goethe-Institute, 3, 15, 251n22, 253
Goldmann Verlag, 157n22
Goncourt Prize. *See* Prix Goncourt
Governor General's Literary Award, 24, 248
*The Beggar Maid* (Munro), 71
for Children's Literature, 231
*Dance of the Happy Shades* (Munro), 70, 88
*The Diviners* (Laurence), 68
*Forms of Devotion: Stories and Pictures (Formen der Zuneigung: Geschichten und Bilder)* (Schoemperlen), 74
*Green Grass, Running Water* (King), 126
*Home Truths* (Gallant), 70
*Man Descending* (Vanderhaeghe), 69
*Miner's Pond* (Michaels), 155
Montgomery, L. M., 231
*Nkwalla (Nikwalla der Indianer-Junge)* (Sharp), 226
*The Progress of Love (Der Mond über der Eisbahn: Liebesgeschichten)* (Munro), 71
*The Roaring Girl* (Hollingshead), 76

*Vigil* (Panych), 184
Weniger, Silke, 247
Grasset & Fasquelle, 283
Graz Centre for Canadian Studies, 285, 288
Groundwood (press), 245, 245n3–4

### H
Hamburg Literaturhaus, 156
Hauptverwaltung Verlage und Buchhandel (HV), 31, 31n10, 32, 34, 38–39, 45
Heritage Canada, 23, 270
Husum-Verlag, 128

### I
Ignatieff, Michael, 196–207
Indian. *See* Native Canadian writing
International Council for Canadian Studies, 7, 9–11
International Translation Program, 11, 237
International Youth Library (IYL), 237–38, 253–54

### J
Jandl, Andreas, 180–81
JewCanLit, 152
Jewish Canadian writing
  Cohen, Leonard, 144, 148–52
  in German, 160–63
  Holocaust survivor, 143, 156–57, 271, 279–80
  Klein, Naomi, 143–44, 157–59
  Levine, Norman, 143, 145–47
  Michaels, Anne, 143, 155–57
  overview, 143–44
  poetry, 144, 148, 150–51, 155, 157
  religious/ethnic affiliations ignored, 5
  Richler, Mordecai, 143, 152–55
  translations, early, 144–45
Jörg Schröder, 148, 148n14

## K

Kegedonce Press, 116n5
Klein, Naomi, 143–44, 157–59
Klett-Cotta and Fischer, 66, 71, 88

## L

Levine, Norman, 143, 145–47
Loughborough International Summer Seminar, 237

## M

Maillet, Antoine
  overview, 283–84
  *Pélagie-la-charrette*, paratexts, 287–88
  *Pélagie-la-charrette*, story line, 286
  *Pélagie-la-charrette*, translation, 286, 288–89
  *Pélagie-la-charrette* in German, 287–88
  publishers, persuading, 284–86
Manesse-Verlag, 40
März Verlag, 148, 148n13
Massey Commission, 13n8, 20, 127
McLeod, Joan, 182–83
Medici Prize, 20, 24, 80
Michaels, Anne, 143, 155–57
Ministry of Canadian Heritage, 23n22
Missio (publisher), 128
Mr. Christie's Book Award, 247–48
multicultural writers, 6, 22, 24, 53, 86

## N

Native Canadian writing
  "Native Canadian" vs. "First Nation," 111n2
  "authentic" Indian authors, first, 116
  autobiography, 116–17, 139
  books for German market, 125–26
  Canadian publishers and, 116
  code-switching, 131–32
  contemporary writing, 115
  drama, 119–21
  feminist, 128
  First Nation writers vs. "Indianthusiasm," 4–5
  German interest in, 4
  German translations of, 114–29
  Indian myths and legends, 122–23n10, 122–24
  "Indianthusiasm," 112–13
  marketing, 127n13
  monographs, various, 141
  Native-run presses, 116, 116n5
  novels, 124–25
  overview, 111–14
  poetry, 118–19, 139–40
  prose fiction, 140–41
  publishers of, 128
  short stories, 121–24, 121n9*
  translating idosyncracies, 129–35
  translations, recent, 136
  Trudeau "White Paper," 115, 117
  white Canadian authors accounts, 112
  wordplay, 133–35
Nobel Prize for Literature, 68, 83, 145

## O

Orange Prize, 90
Osnabrück Bilingual Editions of Minority/Marginalized Authors (OBEMA), 125n11, 126, 130

## P

*Pélagie-la-charrette*
  German version, 287–88
  paratexts, 287–88
  story line, 286
  translation, 286, 288–89
Pemmican Publications, 116n5
Peter Hammer (publisher), 128
Playwrights Canada Press, 173–74
Playwrights Guild of Canada (PGC), 173–74, 271, 278
Playwrights' Union, 11
Press Gang, 116n5

Prix Goncourt, 20, 24, 283, 287, 290
Prix Médici, 20, 24, 80
Pulitzer Prize, 90

**Q**
Quebec immigrant writers, 20
Quebec Ministry of Culture and Communication, 253
Quebec plays. *See* French Canadian drama; Sperm Count (Orlov)

**R**
Raincoast Books, 247, 247n10
Ravensburger (publisher), 128
Reclam Leipzig, 27n2, 31, 33, 39, 73, 99, 147
Richler, Mordecai, 143, 152–55
Riemann Verlag, 157
Rowohlt Taschenbuch Verlag, 34, 114n4, 128, 149–50, 259t12.1, 262
Rowohlt Theaterverlag, 264–65t12.2, 267t12.2

**S**
SACD. *See* Société des auteurs et compositeurs dramatiques (SACD)
Saskatoon Native Theatre, 120
Scharfenberg, Ute, 181–82
Scholastic Canada, 237
Scirocco Drama, 173
Seven Seas, 28n4, 38
Seventh Generation Books, 116n5
Sister Vision (publisher), 116n5
Société de développement des entreprises culturelles (SODEC), 248–49, 249n18
Société des auteurs et compositeurs dramatiques (SACD), 258t12.1, 261–62, 262n5
SODEC. *See* Société de développement des entreprises culturelles (SODEC)

*Sperm Count* (Orlov)
about the play, 270–74
contract discusssions, 276–78
development and reception, 274–76
misunderstandings, 276–78
overview, 269–70
translation of, 278–82
Spirit Song Native Indian Theatre Company, 120
St. Benno-Verlag, 41, 63
State of Bavaria Quebec Office, 253

**T**
Talonbooks, 116n5, 173
Taylor, Charles, 207–14
Theytus Books, 116n5
"Trade Routes" program, 11, 15
translation
American *vs.* British English, 3
Canada, images and perceptions of, 2
Canadian text, reasons for, 4, 54
as cultural transfer, 1–3, 6, 18, 101, 111, 129, 131
definition, 2
as vital connector, 1
translation in FRG and GDR
Canadian anthologies, 40–46, 47t2.2, 48
Canadian authors, individual, 35–40
Canadian literature in FRG/GDR, 27–35
Trudeau, Pierre, 115, 117
Tundra Books, 128n15, 231, 234n23, 237, 239

**V**
Volk und Welt (publisher), 29, 31, 34, 40, 146n4

**W**
Whalesong Verlag, 276–82
"White Paper" proposal, 115, 117

Women's Press, 116n5
Write-on-Publishers, 116n5

**Z**
Zweitausendeins, 36, 148–49

LIBRARY AND ARCHIVES CANADA CATALOGUING IN PUBLICATION

Translating Canada: charting the institutions and influences of cultural transfer: Canada in German/y / edited by Luise von Flotow and Reingard M. Nischik.

(Perspectives on translation, ISSN 1487-6396)
Includes bibliographical references and index.
ISBN 978-0-7766-0661-3 (pbk.)

1. Canadian literature--Appreciation--Germany. 2. Canadian literature—Translations into German—History and criticism. I. Nischik, Reingard M. II. Von Flotow, Luise, 1951- III. Series.

PS8097.G4T73 2007    C810.9    C2007-905433-1

Copy-editing: Dallas Harrison
Cover design: Johanna Pedersen
Interior design and typesetting: Richard Thompson
Proofreading: Sally Gray
Indexing: Clive Pyne

The display type was set in Duty.
The text was set in Dante.

Printed in Canada by Imprimerie Gauvin
2007